MACRO-NATIONALISMS

GLOBAL PERSPECTIVES IN HISTORY AND POLITICS, *edited by George Schwab,* is a subseries to CONTRIBUTIONS IN POLITICAL SCIENCE. Recent titles include:

Nationalism: Essays
Edited by Michael Palumbo and William O. Shanahan

Global Mini-Nationalisms: Autonomy or Independence
Louis L. Snyder

Socialism of a Different Kind: Reshaping the Left in France
Bernard E. Brown

From Dictatorship to Democracy: Coping with the Legacies of Authoritarianism and Totalitarianism
Edited by John H. Herz

Neighbors Across the Pacific: The Development of Economic and Political Relations Between Canada and Japan
Klaus H. Pringsheim

United States Foreign Policy at the Crossroads
Edited by George Schwab

The Press and the Rebirth of Iberian Democracy
Edited by Kenneth Maxwell

MACRO-NATIONALISMS
A History of
the Pan-Movements

LOUIS L. SNYDER

CONTRIBUTIONS IN POLITICAL SCIENCE, NUMBER 112
GLOBAL PERSPECTIVES IN HISTORY AND POLITICS

Greenwood Press
Westport, Connecticut • London, England

Library of Congress Cataloging in Publication Data

Snyder, Louis Leo, 1907-
  Macro-nationalisms.

  (Contributions in political science, ISSN 0147-1066 ;
no. 112. Global perspectives in history and politics)
  Companion to: Global mini-nationalisms : autonomy or
independence / Louis L. Snyder.
  Bibliography: p.
  Includes index.
  1. Nationalism.   2. Internationalism.   3. Regionalism.
I. Snyder, Louis Leo, 1907-   . Global mini-nationalisms.   II. Title.   III. Series: Contributions in
political science ; no. 112.   IV. Series: Contributions
in political science. Global perspectives in history
and politics.
JC311.S5493   1984   320.5'4   83-18600
ISBN 0-313-23191-5 (lib. bdg.)

Library of Congress Catalog Card Number: 83-18600
ISBN: 0-313-23191-5
ISSN: 0147-1066

First published in 1984

Greenwood Press
A division of Congressional Information Service, Inc.
88 Post Road West
Westport, Connecticut 06881

Printed in the United States of America

10   9   8   7   6   5   4   3   2   1

To

BARBARA TUCHMAN

Brilliance plus gentilesse

CONTENTS _____

PREFACE _____

While working as resident scholar at the magnificent Villa Serbelloni, high in the Italian Alps overlooking Lake Como, I came to the reluctant conclusion that the original concept of this study was impractical. I had hoped, with the assistance of the Rockefeller Foundation and the Alexander von Humboldt Foundation, to produce a comparative study in one volume of worldwide mini-nationalisms and macro-nationalisms, the most important peripheral movements of nationalism. Faced, however, with an enormous amount of material, I decided that it was best to divide the work into two studies. The first volume, *Global Mini-Nationalisms: Autonomy or Independence,* was published in 1982 by Greenwood Press. The present book is designed as a companion volume to that earlier study.

It is with pleasure that I express my thanks to John J. McKelvey, Jr., of the Rockefeller Foundation, and to Dr. Heinrich Pfeiffer, Director of the Alexander von Humboldt Foundation, and his assistant, Dr. Dietrich Pappenfuss, of the Federal Republic of West Germany. While serving as Fulbright Visiting Professor of History at the University of Cologne in 1979, my work was facilitated considerably by Dr. Erich Angermann, Director of the Anglo-American Division of the Historical Seminar at the University of Cologne; his colleagues Drs. Marie-Luise Frings Wellenreuther and Hermann Wellenreuther; and Dr. Ulrich Littmann, Director of the Fulbright Kommission in Bonn-Bad Godesberg.

I should like to express my thanks to the staffs of the Princeton Public Library, the New York Public Library, the British Museum, the libraries at the universities of Cologne and Bonn, and especially to that gem of a research center—the Wiener Library in London.

Until recently the author-editor relationship has been a positive feature of

American publishing. That happy state of affairs has changed considerably in the era of conglomerates, in which many old established houses were absorbed by great corporations. Some of these conglomerates, specializing in frozen foods, typewriters, and bankrupt shoe factories, regard their acquired publishing houses as mere tax shelters, important only for their bottom line. Much of the hitherto valuable author-editor mutual reciprocity was lost in this process. In this respect I have been fortunate again to work with Dr. James T. Sabin, chief editor of Greenwood Press, and with George Schwab, editor of the fine series, Global Perspectives in History and Politics. The sense of direction and the suggestions of these two able editors have been invaluable in the production of both studies.

Again, as always, I wish to note my appreciation of the work of Ida Mae Brown Snyder, my lifelong companion, who gave up her own career as author-editor to assist me in all phases of our work from research to published product. More collaborator than assistant, she has rescued me again and again from the pitfalls awaiting any writer.

Princeton, New Jersey   LOUIS L. SNYDER

About the Author

LOUIS L. SNYDER is Emeritus Professor of History at the City College and the City University of New York and the author of 58 books including *Global Mini-Nationalisms* and *Louis L. Snyder's Historical Guide to World War II*, both published by Greenwood Press in 1982. The recipient of Rockefeller, Ford, and von Humboldt fellowships, Snyder is also the general editor of a 128-volume Anvil series of original paperbacks on history.

MACRO-NATIONALISMS

CHAPTER 1

NATIONALISM WRIT LARGE ____

O my fatherland! . . . I am French. I am one of thy
representatives. . . . O sublime people! Accept the sacrifice of my entire being. Happy is the man born in thy
midst; happier is he who could die for thy happiness.
—Maximilien de Robespierre, *"Rapport sur les fêtes
nationales,"* 18 floréal an II (Paris, 1794), p. 6.

Peripheries of Nationalism

Nationalism, as was pointed out by Carlton J. H. Hayes, late great scholar
of the historical phenomenon, may be either blessing or curse. In its
quiescent form it is a positive sentiment devoted to the recognition and
maintenance of cultural differences. In its integral form, however, it is a
mania, a kind of exaggerated egoism reflecting an intolerant attitude toward
other peoples, an intense belief in the imperial mission of one's own
nationality, and a narrow spirit of exclusiveness.[1] From the late 18th century
to the present day, nationalism in varying types has remained one of the
most powerful historical forces. Far from disappearing in the solvent of
internationalism, it has retained its resiliency in the contemporary world
and gives no evidence of disappearing by the end of the 20th century.

Scholars have been entranced by the complexities of this truly formidable
historical ism, by its inconsistencies, contradictions, and paradoxes. A huge
literature is devoted to the meaning, characteristics, and development of
nationalism.[2] Not only historians, but also political scientists, sociologists,
social psychologists, psychiatrists, and psychoanalysts have sought to
throw light on a subject of major importance for existence on this planet.

Running concurrently with established nationalisms are two lesser-
known but important satellite movements, one on a small scale, the other a
larger manifestation. The many mini-nationalisms inside the established
nation-states seek to break away from the larger units.[3] Among these are
Scottish and Welsh devolution, the confrontation between Flemings and
Walloons in Belgium, the Breton freedom movement, Basque separatism,
the Croatian drive for independence, Ukrainian and Armenian calls for
nationhood, and Francophones versus Anglophones in Canada. The desire

for autonomy or independence is not restricted to any one continent—it is global in extent and it exists everywhere. Once a mini-nationalism wins its way to independence, it is no longer a mini-nationalism, but takes its place in the community of nations as an established state (Israel).

At another level, when the nationalism of an established nation-state is expanded to a supranational form, there emerges a larger macro-nationalism. We shall examine the meaning, characteristics, and classification of these pan-movements in the next three sections, but at this point they may be described as politico-cultural movements promoting the solidarity of peoples united by common or kindred languages, group identification, traditions, or some other characteristic such as geographical proximity. These traits may exist separately or in common. They may be either spontaneous or planned. On occasion, they may arise in small states seeking to extend their prestige by linking themselves with a larger and more powerful state. In most cases, however, they reveal an aggressive impulse seeking to extend control over contiguous or non-contiguous territory in the name of territorial imperative. Macro-nationalisms differ in infrastructures, but almost always there is an element of domination—the mother nationalism demands control of her children everywhere.

Another common attribute of the macro-nationalisms, in addition to the power syndrome, is common linguistic identity, more significant in some cases than in others. Added to language affinities is usually another outstanding element: messianic zeal (Pan-Slavism); territorial expansionism (Pan-Germanism); religious zeal (Pan-Islāmism); racial unity (Pan-Africanism); or anti-colonialism (Pan-Asianism). There is no set pattern in the macro-nationalisms—the movements may be vague and sometimes defiant of logical analysis. The key fact is that they exist and by their very existence lend themselves to scrutiny.

A Matter of Definition

Macro-nationalisms—or a synonym, the pan-movements—may be regarded as extended nationalisms on the political scene. They paint nationalism on a much broader canvas to include all (*pan*) those who by reason of geography, race, religion, or language, or by a combination of any or all of them, are included in the same group category. It is the outcome of an aggressive nationalism, by which the we-group enlarges its unity to include all those who "should belong" to the fatherland or motherland.

Meaning centers around the Greek word *pan* (all). Originally, Pan was a Greek divinity, son of Hermes and guardian of flocks and herds. Legend has it that Pan, distinguished by his horns, snub-nose, and goat's legs, wandered through the mountains and valleys of Arcadia leading a dance of nymphs to the tune of pipes ("pipes of Pan"), his own invention. His sudden appearance was dreaded by the people ("panic fear"). Eventually, he came to be regarded as the personification of Nature, including everything in the existing order of things.

This idea of all-inclusiveness, gathering together all those of like background and sentiment into one whole, carried over into the Age of Nationalism. If one people managed to carve out a viable nation-state in competition with others, then that same people would have the benefit of including all kindred people of similar background in an enlarged nation-state. It was simply a question of more power exerted in the competition among nations. The pan-movements—the macro-nationalisms—grouped together those of similar sentiment who believed that they belonged together, with a common history, traditions, national heroes, and goals.

As a concession to the Socratic urge for basic and simple definitions, let us attempt a workable summary of meaning: the pan-movements are politico-cultural movements seeking to enhance and promote the solidarity of peoples bound together by common or kindred language, cultural similarities, the same historical traditions, and/or geographical proximity. They postulate the nation writ large in the world's community of nations.

Characteristics

Because of the variety of disparate elements making up the macro-nationalisms, perhaps it is best to seek clues to meaning in terms of characteristics instead of a precise definition. There are, indeed, certain common denominators for most, if not all, the pan-movements. There may be differences, small or large, in environment, organization, methods, and goals, but there are also common characteristics which merit our attention.

1. Implicit in each pan-movement is the idea of uniqueness. Just as most religious sects consider their dogma as preferable to all others, each pan-movement tends to regard itself as an expression of a favored branch of the human family. This element of uniqueness, or at least a firm belief in it, distinguishes all the larger nationalisms.

2. Added to the concept of uniqueness is a conscious or unconscious sense of superiority. In this respect the pan-movements reveal a similar face to that of established nationalisms. They see themselves as chosen by destiny to play a great role and to assume a high place in the global family of nations.

3. There is a decided preference for militancy. Though coated with a veneer of intellectualism and presented in the form of a favored ideology, most pan-movements are characterized by a choice for action over words. There is some variation here as to the extent of militancy: Pan-Islāmism, with its advocacy of *jihād*, or holy war, in the interest of faith, is more militant than the Pan-Americanism based on economic and cultural ties.

4. Militancy is geared to a mood for expansion. Though the ideologists of pan-movements usually stress linguistic, "ethnic," and cultural ties, their aim of gathering all people of common background and interests into one centralized union brings them into conflict with others motivated by similar ideas. In a crowded world of many nations, the extension of one territorial unit can take place only at the expense of another or others. Pan-Germanism, Pan-Slavism, and Pan-Turkism all were associated closely with what amounts to imperial aggression. Each saw its goal as an extension of existing boundaries beyond those already set up by war or conquest. This element of expansionism was obviously scarcely conducive to international peace.

5. *Most pan-movements have been unsuccessful in achieving their aims.* Pan-Germanism and Pan-Slavism were drained to impotence after two world wars. Pan-Arabism was weakened by the inability of Arab states to work together. Pan-Africanism was shaken by tribal jealousies. Pan-Americanism preached lofty ideals of unanimity, but it was never able to rise above a bitter hate-the-Yankee complex.

Behind this lack of success of the pan-movements was the familiar historical process of Hegelian thrust-and-counter-thrust. When any one nationalism sought status as a larger macro-nationalism, it generally found a counter-movement of equal or greater strength. A classic example was the confrontation of Pan-Germanism and Pan-Slavism in World War I—two expansionist imperialisms in deadly conflict. Both emerged as considerably weakened ideologies.

6. *Despite this record of failure, the macro-nationalistic idea has not disappeared.* The urge to union on a larger scale has not vanished completely. The idea persists in one form or another. The goal of including all peoples of one kind in a common society still retains its attractiveness. Its appeal seems to be much greater than the call for one world. Despite the flow of words at the United Nations, there is little interest in the brother-hood of man, in the problems of humanity scattered over a single overcrowded planet. Instead, there is much more of a belief in the brother-hood of Slavs, Arabs, Africans, Nordics, Celts, or Muslims.

As the 20th century moves to its end, the historical phenomenon we know as nationalism maintains its vigor and strength as the dominating ism of our times. Above and below it, the macro-nationalisms and mini-nationalisms, remain as corollary or peripheral movements, both unable to dislodge the existing system of nation-states.

Classification

It may be convenient to classify the macro-nationalisms, or pan-movements, into major groups: national, "racial," cultural, religious, and continental. Each possesses its own characteristics, although as in anything connected with nationalism, there is overlapping.

National. Emerging in the 19th century, national pan-movements were simply extensions of the existing nationalisms. Behind them was a powerful political motivation as, for example, in the unification of Germany. Pan-Germans regarded the national unity won by Iron-and-Blood Chancellor Otto von Bismarck as a preliminary step to German expansion. Similarly, political factors were equally as significant in Pan-Arabism, an offshoot of religious Pan-Islāmism.

"Racial." Several pan-movements assumed falsely that they possess a common "ethnic" identity. There is no such thing as a Slavic race, but this did not prevent Pan-Slavs from calling for "racial emancipation." Pan-Germans, too, infected with the unscientific notions of the Englishman Houston Stewart Chamberlain and the Frenchman Count Arthur de Gobineau, saw themselves as an incontestably superior Indo-European-Aryan-Nordic Teutonic "race," a totally false conception.

The racial factor had considerably more meaning in the case of Pan-Africanism, dedicated as it was to a conflict between black and white men. Here the racial element was biologically clear-cut—black African natives versus white colonial exploiters. Other differences took second place to color confrontation

Cultural. Most pan-movements stressed the idea of a traditional culture rooted in the past. Historians, poets, and novelists sought common elements in records of the past, costumes, stories, sagas, poems, songs, dances, and folklore. What ancestors favored was to be passed on to posterity. To maintain and extend such traditions became the trade mark of pan-ideologists.

In some cases cultural affinity was considered sufficient as a binding element and was not extended into the political sphere. This kind of cultural unity was expressed in such movements as Pan-Nordicism in the Scandinavian countries, or in Pan-Hispanism and its close relatives, Pan-Lusitanism and Pan-Iberianism.

Religious. Here the emphasis shifted to ecclesiastical forms. Whereas other pan-movements were dominantly political in ideology, these pan-movements saw primacy in the need to combine peoples of one religious faith into a supranational state. Lines of combination generally were vague and more theoretical than real. There was the same drive for unity of like-minded peoples, but it was grounded on religious faith and pursued with fanatical zeal.

There were differences in intensity of the religious approach. Pan-Christianity (ideal of the Middle Ages) and Pan-Anglicanism (starting with Henry VIII) lost their momentum in modern times. Most active of the religious movements was Pan-Islāmism, which called for the union of all Muslims on a basis of a common religion, a common religious book (Koran), and a common language (Arabic). All Muslims were expected to unite in a religious community under God's law as revealed to Muḥammad.

Followers of Islām in the Middle East and North Africa urged union of the faithful all over the world, including Asia and their "subjugated brethren" in Europe who had failed to win that continent for Muḥammad.

Pan-Islāmism, like most pan-movements, wanted more than it possibly could achieve. The movement, as we shall see, never was able to overcome the political rivalries of its component parts. The ambitions of individual Muslim rulers proved to be far stronger than religious fundamentalism. Added to these political differences were deep sectarian rivalries such as hostility between Sunnītes Shī ʿites.

Continental. Another type of pan-movement was geographically oriented and continental in scope.[4] Here the tendency was to supersede the nation-state and organize in its stead a supranational order based on common continental territory. Although the goal was always continental unity, in the process there was much linguistic and cultural confusion. Pan-Europeanism accented economic unity in a Common Market, with lesser attention to the political unity of a European Parliament. Pan-Americanism stressed an economic community with two major languages—Spanish and English. Pan-Africanism lacking the bond of linguistic unity, sought to combine the black peoples of the continent in a common front against white exploiters, and based its appeal on the common racial stock of a host of unrelated tribes. Pan-Asianism saw continental unity as anti-colonialism directed against those who would expropriate the riches of Asia.

Behind the continental pan-movements was the idea of a super-territorial-imperative. The difficulty was that geographical boundaries in the continents already were frozen in the formation of nation-states. Changes could be made only by war and conquest. It made no difference that there were elements of artificiality in the process. In Africa, territories were carved out by 19th-century imperialists without regard for tribal affinities. This procedure was repeated in the mid-20th century with the retreat of European colonialism and the liberation of African peoples. Once again, antagonistic tribes were forced into unions of convenience.

Continental pan-movements, as other macro-nationalisms, have had little success. Nationalism writ either large or small has not won its way to dominance in the contemporary world of nation-states.

Historical Roots: Precedents and Prototypes

The macro concept (Gr. *makros*, long), a combining form meaning long in extent or duration, specifically an enlargement, has deep historical roots. The urge of peoples to extend their existing frontiers has existed since the early recording of history. Although the macro-nationalisms with which we are concerned are strictly speaking a relatively recent historical phenomenon emerging in the 19th century as a corollary of developing nationalisms, there are clues to origins to be found in past human behavior.

Again and again, there were trends to larger unions, an extension of the family tribal unit to a larger scale to include those of similar background. It was in effect a means of assuring security—a basic drive in human behavior.

The continuing impulse already was strong in the two cradlelands of Western civilization, in both dynastic Egypt and the Fertile Crescent of the Tigris-Euphrates Valley. In both fluvial, or river-made-civilizations, there was a transition from a food-gathering to a food-producing economy. As population grew and social organization was advanced in Egypt, two distinct kingdoms came into existence: Lower Egypt, including Memphis and the Nile delta, and Upper Egypt, extending along the river-valley as far as Aswan. The desire for unity was always present. Eventually, a territorial state was created from a multitude of rival kinship groups—a significant advance in government and one that was to be developed elsewhere along similar lines. About 3200 B.C. the two kingdoms of Egypt were united by Menes, and a single capital city was established. The idea of extension, of largeness, of macro-organization, had come into existence.

This urge to combine kinship groups into a larger unity existed also in ancient Mesopotamia and the Fertile Crescent area. The development here, with its succeeding dominant civilizations, was different from that of Egypt, but the same trend to extension and largeness was present. Here the story was concerned with achievements of the early Sumerians, succeeded by Hammurabi's Babylonian civilization. The Hittites later conquered Syria and Babylon. Small nearby nations, such as Phoenicia and the Hebrew kingdom, enjoyed a brief period of independence. Political diversity was ended by the rise of the Assyrian Empire (900-600 B.C.), which gave way to the Chaldeans under Nebuchadnezzar. The Persians then went on to set up a great empire. In each of these early civilizations the drive for extension, for largeness, was always present.

A similar development took place in the Far East. The ancient civilizations of India and China reveal this same process of expansion, assimilation, and synthesis, a capacity to include varying and even contradictory beliefs in the drive for a larger unity. From 2200 to 1300 B.C. the Indian counterpart of the Nile and Tigris-Euphrates cultures existed in the Indus Valley. In 1500 B.C., invading Indo-Aryan nomads came to India and brought with them a new culture, including the joint-family, the autonomous village, and the caste system. This same process of amalgamation took place on the Chinese mainland: the Shang civilization, beginning about 1500 B.C. in the Hwang Ho Valley, was replaced by the long-lasting Chou dynasty.

The ancient Greeks were responsible for dazzling achievements in almost everything they attempted—except in the crucial sphere of politics. Here their famous sense of proportion failed them. Instead of settling their differences and combining into a single union, the individualistic city-states quarreled interminably—democratic Athens against militant Sparta. Ironically, domestic Athenian democracy was accompanied by imperial policies abroad—here, too, the impulse to largeness was present. The victory over Persia was made possible by the temporary combination of Hellenic arms, but once victory was assured, the unity promptly dissolved. After the disastrous Peloponnesian War, the quarreling Greek city-states were subjugated by Philip of Macedonia, himself ambitious for expansion. His son, Alexander the Great, conquered the Near East and laid the boundaries for three large empires in his conquered lands.

Rome, the great intermediary, passed on the contributions of Egypt, the Tigris-Euphrates region, and Greece to form the basis of Western civilization. Replacing Hellenistic anarchy with their own version of law and order, the Romans, fascinated by the macro-process, fashioned a huge state extending to the Rhine and the Euphrates. Originating in a small, muddy village along the banks of the Tiber, they became masters of the Mediterranean and eventually of the entire known Western world. It was a classic story of conquest, of drive toward the larger unity. After crushing all resistance in the Italian peninsula, the Romans smashed Carthage, and then turned to the east to defeat the successors of Alexander the Great. The expansion process slowed down under the triple burdens of domestic degeneration, Germanic barbarians, and the new Christianity. This long and complex story culminated in 476 A.D., when the line of emperors inaugurated by Augustus ended, and Italy came under control of Germanic leaders.

Memory of the enlarged Roman Empire persisted after its fall. Charlemagne was motivated by an urge for unity, but his temporary success was followed by disruption of his empire after his death. The whole European continent seemed to fall into confusion. Invasions by Northmen took place with accompanying devastation and slaughter, while Avars and Magyars marauded lands in the east. The conquering tide of Islām, pushing westward across North Africa, nearly succeeded in impressing its religion and culture upon the whole Western world. Helpless against the fury of invaders, Europeans were forced to delegate governmental functions to powerful local officials. The outcome was feudalism, based on a reciprocal relationship between suzerain and vassal—the substitute for central government. Order was maintained by the fighting class, while the soil was worked by peasants under the parallel manorial system.

Yet, in the midst of feudal particularism, the old idea of the larger unit persisted. Implicit in the medieval reorganization of Europe was the concept of a revived Roman pan-movement under ecclesiastical auspices. Throughout the thousand years of the Middle Ages, this idea of a macro-unity held on. The goal was a combination of *sacerdotium* and *imperium*, of ecclesiastical and imperial power, of Church and State, of Pope and Emperor.[5] This was, in reality, the constitution of medieval society. The vast governmental structure called the Holy Roman Empire, proclaimed by Otto I in 962 A.D., gave ample evidence of this tenacious human desire for the larger entity.

The idea of a Christian commonwealth or a European federation survived medieval society, and continued on in the Age of Nationalism. In his unhappy final days at St. Helena, Napoleon protested that all he wanted to do was to achieve a union of European nations in a United States of Europe, under his own leadership, of course. The 19th century saw the appearance of the powerful British Empire, an enlarged state "on which the sun never sets." It also witnessed the emergence not only of national states in Europe but also such early macro-nationalisms as Pan-Slavism and Pan-Germanism. The concept of extension carried over into the 20th century. For a brief period before and during World War II, Adolf Hitler wore not only his German uniform but assumed the mantle of Pan-German leader. The Nazi dictator brought virtually all of Western Europe under his domination as a preliminary step in his drive for a thousand-year Reich. It took a world alliance and millions of lives to convince Hitler that his plans for expansion could not work.

Through all these dramatic centuries, the pattern of drive for unity through military conquest has recurred constantly as an enduring phenomenon. The pressure of combination for peoples of similar character-istics has never ceased. On one level it was expressed in the explosive nationalism which appeared with the outbreak of the French Revolution and which took color and content from early 19th-century romanticism. This nationalism, responsible for forging modern nation-states, left a map of many colors. Superimposed on it was the call for nationalism writ large. The story of this enlarged nationalism becomes the theme of this study of global pan-movements.

Transnationalism: Conglomerates Transcending Nations?

The cascading development of transnational corporations has led some observers to conclude that we now have a new kind of pan-movement which gradually is turning national boundaries into mere administrative nuisances. This view holds that the 300-year-old convention of attributing to distinct territorial units the role of authority in the global area is now over. The nation-state concept of world politics, it is asserted, is an outdated paradigm.[6] Transnational boundaries, it is claimed, operate below and above visible nation-state controls, and expose deep contradictions between the world's official political system and socio-economic reality.

It is a radical picture: contemporary governments are losing their influence over important transnational flows of peoples, materials, money, and ideas. Multinational corporations, as well as professional and trade organizations, have surged forward to allocate resources, privileges, and penalties without regard to national boundaries. Multinational corporations not only sell in more than one country, but also obtain their raw materials and capital, and produce their goods in several or many countries. As autonomous economic oligarchies, they operate without attention to governmental controls. Most important are the multinational business enterprises, of which 85 each have assets larger than 50 members of the United Nations.[7] Such conglomerates as GM, Unilever, and IBM can move large amounts of resources over international boundaries in a way that is at variance with the existing governments of countries in which the giant corporations have subsidiaries. By using high-speed communication and transportation services, these multinationals can make rapid transcontinental moves, such as the instantaneous transfer of capital.[8]

Some economists see the transnational relationship as taking on a post-colonial form of private economic imperialism. This kind of neocolonialism, they say, affects even affluent countries, as, for example, the relationship of sectors of the Canadian economy to United States industries. In the developing countries the multinationals are accused of everything from exploiting labor to stealing national resources. L. K. Jha, chairman of the United Nations Group of Eminent Persons, charged: "Multinational corporations are not *per se* agents of development. The technology they employ, the products they market, may not always be the right ones for a developing country."[9]

In a study published in 1972, Hugh Stephenson, a British economist, predicted a coming clash between the idea of the nation-state and the new giant industrial leviathans.[10] He opposed what he called a concentration on the need for better *national* control of transnational corporations. The central point, he argued, is that these modern corporations contradict our traditional ideas about nation-states and national sovereignty. It is more than a question, he asserted, of whether international companies can circumvent particular laws and regulations. The 300 or 400 large-scale industrial corporations have a range of activity far overriding the national frame. Lawyers and politicians, all conservative in outlook, would continue jealously to guard forms of national sovereignty. But in substance rather than in form the existing political system is adjusting already to the effective loss of sovereignty involved. Stephenson pointed to the process in the last decade, without parallel in history, in which pressures have continued to exist for industry to break out of the national framework. These corporations have an emphatic international loyalty. They have shifted the historic balance between governments (as guardians of the public interest), organized labor, and industrial management in favor of the latter. In sum, Stephenson claimed that when the history of the late 20th century comes to be written, it surely will be said that multinationals did more than anything else to undermine the overwhelming dominance that the nation-state has had over the condition of man for the past three centuries.

Exception must be taken to these views. First of all, it is unnecessary to examine the multinationals here in detail as a new form of pan-movement. True, the concept of largeness, of extension beyond national frontiers, is present. But the key fact remains that macro-nationalisms are dominantly political and cultural movements, while the multinationals are almost completely economic in nature. One cannot extract a whole apple from the apple sauce; there is, indeed, such a thing as economic nationalism which affects all other forms of nationalism. The transnationals, however, remain economic in nature, and have not yet penetrated into the political and cultural fields. To predict the imminent disappearance of the nation-state because of interlocking international economic relationships goes far beyond the boundaries of reality.

The problem is complicated because there is little agreement about the future relationship of multinational enterprises with the nation-state. Some observers, as we have seen, regard them as a threat to the existing system of nation-states, as a few hundred corporations assume responsibility for world production. Others see them as bringing an end to middle-class society. Still others regard as open the question of whether the nation-state is the more durable of the two institutions.[11]

J. S. Nye, professor of government and program director of the Center of International Affairs at Harvard University, sees multinational corporations as *potentially* important forces for regional integration. At the same time, he warns that extra-regional enterprises may weaken some integrative forces and worsen conditions for integration. He argues that if multinational enterprises are promoting global political integration, the process is far from a universal one.[12]

Despite combined economic activities, multinationals encounter fundamental obstacles in existing nationalisms as well as in the maintained structure of the nation-state. Nationalistic resistance to outsiders is aroused by multinationals which penetrate into nations to extract profits. These giant corporations may well be a potentially important machine of integration, but they are far from advancing political integration either on a regional or global scale. Especially the less developed countries are wary of multinationals, and tend to view them as instruments through which they can be subjugated to the West. According to Robert S. Walters, of the University of Pittsburgh: "It is doubtful that we will soon see the emergence of a new global organization to focus states' attempts to oversee the behavior of these enterprises as they affect international relations."[13] Other observers are equally skeptical.[14]

There is little historical evidence for the projected change. When the interests of a powerful nation clash with international or private transnational concerns, the national government almost invariably wins. No amount of hedging can divert us from this basic assumption. Certainly, the new transnationalism is creating among nations a new interdependence, but this has not affected the boundaries of national sovereignty. The classic case is that of the European Economic Community (EEC), the Common Market in Western Europe. Agreements on production, markets, and sales are made and carried out, but the sense of unity stops at the line of political sovereignty. This is indicated additionally by the European Assembly at Strasbourg, where representatives of every country draw a fine line between politics and economics. Flag and anthem are more important than transnational economic agreements. It is wishful thinking to announce the end of the 20th-century nation-state.

Nationalism itself remains the most powerful of political forces in the contemporary world. Before his death British historian Arnold Toynbee expressed this view, but with sad resignation. He welcomed the movement toward European unity, but saw nationalism as the continuing dominant force in human affairs. West Europeans, he warned, just did not like the troubling and complicated movement toward federation.[15] Transnationals, it should be added, have not altered Toynbee's accurate estimate of the situation.

Pan-Orthodoxism and Pan-Communism

Identification of the pan-movements with the macro-nationalisms is made here in a limited sense only. In each case treated in this study, from Pan-Slavism to Pan-Asianism, the pan-movements are analyzed as enlargements of established modern nationalisms that include peoples of similar language, culture, or traditions in what might be called extended nationalisms. There are also other still greater pan-movements which do not fit into this category and which will not be considered here. These come closer to what we understand as international movements. They differ from macro-nationalisms in that they are concerned with the whole of mankind and not one people set aside by similar characteristics. Among them are Pan-Orthodoxism and Pan-Communism.

Here, too, there is the idea of including "all"—the essence of the pan-idea. But the "all" in this sense applies to global conquest; it does not limit itself to the umbrella for one closely related people.

Pan-Orthodoxism sees faith in true Christianity as the only way to salvation for the people of this planet. It projects a continuation of medieval polity before the rise of modern nationalism. In its behalf, Christian missionaries moved to all corners of the earth, from the jungles of Africa to the hinterlands of Brazil, to bring the "one true faith" to those who know nothing of orthodox Christianity. This type of a broader pan-movement still exists today, but it has lost its earlier impetus and is no longer a historical force of major importance.

The second major effort seeks to promote a perfect social order. Originating in the mind of Karl Marx, it was given its practical test by

Lenin. Pan-Communism promotes faith in "the true social doctrine" as the only source of salvation here on earth. The goal shifts from the mysteries of religion to what is claimed to be the reality of materialism, from religious utopianism to economic determinism. Marx called for a dictatorship of the proletariat as the necessary preliminary step in winning a society of perfect justice which would fulfill and terminate the historical process. The idea received its first test in the Russian October Revolution of 1917. The subsequent deadly feud between Trotsky (international Communism) and Stalin (national Communism) ended with an ice pick in the head of Trotsky and with Stalin's triumph. Stalin's successors saw Russian leadership as indispensable for the extension of Pan-Communism. The notion of priority for the Kremlin has persisted despite Yugoslavic and Chinese heresies.

In both cases, Pan-Orthodoxism and Pan-Communism, there has been a failure to overcome the power of established nationalisms. In the world of political reality, these two global movements have remained unfulfilled dreams.

Collective Parataxis (perceived together)

The critical element in nationalism and its peripheries is the fact that they are psychological sentiments consciously or unconsciously adopted to assure the life force of security. Social psychologists, psychiatrists, and psychoanalysts have hoped that their disciplines might be able to help avert disasters associated with nationalism, war, racism, and political and religious persecution. It is a sad commentary on the status of current civilization to note that it is questionable whether such psychological explorations can do much to change mass behavior.

Harry Stack Sullivan, the late psychoanalyst, defined collective parataxis as group distortion.[16] He saw parataxic distortions as projections into others. "There is not a shared definition of the situation. Parataxis can only be shared as all parties concur, resulting in a kind of syntaxis of the social order. The parataxis of one then becomes the shared parataxis of many."[17]

Sullivan regarded nationalism as a historical phenomenon based on idolatry, on immature excessive love or veneration for an image or myth. Idolatry appeals to the immature because it allows for the fixing of blame and the shunning of responsibility, such as blind worship of nation, race, language, or religion. This identification of individual with group sentiment results in a kind of collective neurosis or even collective insanity, which does not lend itself to treatment on a massive scale. In Sullivan's view, the interdependence of human beings is an inescapable fact: that it is necessary for humans to reject all their precious records of genealogy to eliminate the strictures of nationalism and to hasten progress toward the goal of universal assimilation.

Sullivan's estimate of nationalism, similar to that of historian Arnold

Toynbee, held that the myth of national identity is suffused with delusions of grandeur. The only way to approach such a mystical entity, Sullivan recommended, is to say: "Leave *me* out of *we!*" In this way, the individual citizen could refuse to conform to what was or easily could be collective insanity.

Unfortunately, the advice of Sullivan and Toynbee has what amounts in our society to a defect—it is sane and logical. Human beings are not noted for "sane and logical" behavior. Nationalism and its corollaries have been responsible to a large extent for man's inhumanity to man, for confrontation, for conflict, for the barbarism of war. To paraphrase a well-known railroad aphorism, in its integral, expansionist form, nationalism remains a bizarre way to run a world society.

CHAPTER 2

PAN-SLAVISM: THE URGE FOR UNION _____

Most Pan-Slavs shared the Slavophil faith of Russian Messianism, according to which the Russian people were chosen by God to lead mankind to salvation.
> —Hans Kohn, *Nationalism: Its Meaning and History*
> (Princeton, N.J., 1955, 1965), p. 72.

The Dream of Slavic Unity

Like most pan-movements, Pan-Slavism, eldest of the macro-nationalisms, was never a coherent, stable ideology with clear-cut characteristics, but rather a conglomeration of ideas calling for unity. It never developed a viable organization nor was it successful in winning a mass following. Again like other movements of its kind, it called originally for cultural unity, but later took on an extremist coloration. In the long run, it was a political failure.

In its early romantic phase, Pan-Slavism proposed the awakening of Slavs in the Austrian and Ottoman Empires. It projected the ideas that all Slavs possess a common distant past and that their survival depends upon their political unification. Czechs, Slovenes, Serbs, Croats, or Bulgars—all Slavs—believed themselves to have common moral and spiritual qualities distinguishing them from other peoples, especially Teutons, the dangerous hereditary enemy. To the Slavic mind, all the world could see that Germanic as well as Latin peoples were in decline, their day long past, while Slavs in their incorruptible youthfulness were heroes of the historical process. The Slavic mission would be fulfilled one day after unity was achieved when all Slavs would see that divergent interests should be cast aside and merged in a larger nationalism. These concepts of Slavic superiority and the Slavic mission were presented by intellectuals in philosophical, theological, and literary terms.

Lurking in the background, however, was a dangerous enemy—the Russian bear. In the Age of Nationalism, Imperial Russia saw herself as the proper agency for controlling the Slavs. From the time of Catherine II, Russians had looked beyond the shores of the Bosporus. They gave to Constantinople the name of Tsarigrad, the Imperial City, which Russian

Orthodoxy should liberate from the infidel. Thus, Imperial Russia would expand by incorporating all Slavic-speaking peoples, whether or not they were willing, into a Greater Russia. Cultural Slavophilism was acceptable, but "true Pan-Slavism" was seen as Russia's historic mission and consisted of liberating all Slavs in the neighboring Balkans from the Hapsburg and Ottoman Empires, and maintaining the subsequent union under firm Russian control.

In this way early Slavophilism merged into Russian-controlled Pan-Slavism. Inside Russia the new macro-nationalism attracted the support of Army officers, Orthodox clergy, publicists, pamphleteers, and propagandists. However, it never became a mass movement nor did it have a central organization. Under Tsars Alexander III and Nicholas II Slavophilism became a reactionary ideology devoted to Russian expansion.

The clash of Pan-Slavism and Pan-Germanism was one of the contributory factors leading to the outbreak of World War I. The Great War brought freedom to virtually all Slavic peoples, with the exception of Ukrainians and Byelorussians, who were forcibly retained inside the new Soviet state. The pattern was established; nationalism was shown to be more powerful than any projected larger nationalism. Moreover, Slavic peoples were influenced strongly by their own national aspirations: Czechs, Yugoslavs, and Poles were unimpressed by calls for a larger unity of Slavs. All they wanted was freedom for themselves, and not an unrealistic combination with "foreign" Slavs.

Angered when Hitler turned on the Soviet Union in June 1941, Stalin sought desperately for every possible means of resistance to the German *Fuehrer*. He added a new rallying cry—"Slavic union against the Nazi invader." Early Pan-Slavism had been non-governmental, even anti-governmental, but now Stalin saw it as a necessary ally. He ordered his efficient propaganda machine to mobilize Slavic public opinion against the Nazi menace.

Stalin's turn to Pan-Slavism was only partly effective. The movement was already in its terminal stage. After the war Marshal Tito, always a rigid Yugoslav nationalist, challenged Kremlin power and survived. This was a telling blow in the battle of ideologies—Tito's defection meant the end of a workable Pan-Slavism under Russian auspices. From then on, Pan-Slavism exerted little appeal either inside or outside the Soviet Union.

Thus, the earliest and largest macro-nationalism succumbed to pressures of local nationalisms. "Pan-Slavic aspirations," wrote Hans Kohn, "foundered on the rock of the national diversities of the various Slavic peoples, of their different traditions and interests. The ill-defined movement aroused hopes in some, fears in others; it rarely was an effective force politically, economically, or culturally."[1]

Slavs, like Germans, were enthusiastic about scholarly research on their antiquity. They happily supported linguistic, archaeological, and folkloric studies. But when it came to impingement on traditional borders, Poles, Croats, and Serbs rejected the call of supranationalism. Pan-Slavism remained a dream of a small group of intellectuals. Its failure set a precedent for other pan-movements.

The Herder Impulse

Pan-Slavism has owed much to the teaching of Johann Gottfried von Herder (1744-1803), German critic and poet. A gigantic figure in the history of romanticism, Herder set a standard for linguistic Pan-Germanism in his *Stimmen der Völker in Liedern,* a collection of folk songs (1778-1779).[2] Along with Ernst Moritz Arndt and Johann Gottlieb Fichte, Herder proclaimed the national language as a most powerful factor in the formation of a sense of national loyalty. From then on, language became an element of prime importance in the structure of nationalism.

Herder's influence in the development of German national consciousness was vital, but it was even more significant in the growth of Pan-Slavism. In his masterpiece, *Ideas for the Philosophy of the History of Mankind* (1784), he devoted a brief section of three pages in Chapter 4 of Book 16 to "The Slavic People."[3] Highly favorable to Slavs and Slavdom, Herder's words had an electrifying effect on the Slavic world and the Slavic image.

As a disciple of Jean-Jacques Rousseau, Herder was impressed by the rural life of the Slavs, as opposed to the city life introduced by Romance and Germanic peoples. He told how Slavs had settled in the Don area and later the Danube region, but never became, as did the Germans, aggressive warriors. The Germans, motivated by aristocratic fighting traditions dating from the era of Charlemagne, conquered and oppressed the Slavs. Dedicated to peace, Slavs turned to literature and music rather than to war. "They loved agriculture, herds and grain, also many household arts, and opened with the products of their land and their industry a useful trade. . . . In Germany they became miners, understood the melting and purification of metals, produced salt, manufactured linens, brewed mead, planted fruit trees, and led in their manner a happy, musical life." Herder praised the Slavs' sense of freedom, their modesty and sense of obedience, their contempt for robbery and plunder. "They never wanted conquest of the world, and had no war-happy hereditary princes. Therefore, many nations, mostly those of German stock, sinned harshly against them." Whereas Western Europeans looked down on Slavs as backward in civilization and culture, Herder extolled them as a fine branch of humanity.

The devastating wars by Germans against Slavs were openly economic in origin, but they were waged in the name of religion. Aggressive Franks regarded Slavs as menials and vassals. What the Franks began, the Saxons continued. The Germans rooted Slavs out of entire provinces and distributed their lands to bishops and nobles in much the same way that Spaniards had treated Peruvians. "Is it any wonder," Herder asked, "that after centuries of oppression, this nation reacted with deep bitterness against its Christian rulers?"

Herder was certain that the 19th century would vindicate the Slavs. He urged Slavic intellectuals to study their native language instead of abandoning it for French or German. Slavs should retain their heroic past, he said, by collecting their folklore and folk songs. He looked forward to a turn of the wheel of history to a new "garden of humanity": "It is to be hoped that there will be a halt to the increasing disappearance of their customs, songs, and legends, and that finally a complete history of this people will appear which will benefit the canvas of humanity."[4]

This understanding passage by the great German thinker had a soothing effect on the pride of the often hurt Slavs. His favorable attitude undoubtedly was due more to his own philosophical convictions than to historical reality, but it had an enormous effect on Slavic intellectuals. Slavic historians, impressed by Herder's words, began to search their past for corroboration of his metaphysical views, and to justify their position in the world.

Hans Kohn, pioneer student of nationalism, saw a slight exaggeration in this appeal to history: "To the undisputed affinity of language from which was deduced a doubtful common descent, there was added the nebulous affinity of a Slavic *Volksgeist*. Just as German political and social thought of the War of Liberation against Napoleon was influenced by the West and showed little originality in spite of its claim to profound originality, to a mythical German *Eigenart*, so the corresponding Slav thought, in spite of its anti-German attitude and its insistence on Slav originality or *samobytnost*, was deeply indebted to the Germans."[5] Kohn's analysis is correct: here, as elsewhere, the myth-making of nationalism combined linguistic and biological factors in a vague, hazy union.

Still, Herder's lofty estimate of the Slavs helped give direction to the Pan-Slavic movement. Polish, Czech, Russian, and Croatian intellectuals began to revise their defensive thinking about themselves and their status in the world. Despite national differences, they turned their eyes to an overall Slavic unit which, in fact, did not exist. It was a trend typical of other pan-movements in the 19th and 20th centuries, at a time when patriots were immersed in a fog of wishful thinking. Slavs of the world were to unite—they had nothing to lose but their local, national chains.

Czech Apostle: František Palacký

František Palacký (1798-1876), historian, politician, and nationalist leader, was the first important apostle of early Pan-Slavism. Born on June 14, 1798, at Hodslavice (Hotzendorf) in Moravia to a Protestant family, he engaged for some years in private teaching. In 1823 he settled in Prague, where by noble patronage and an advantageous marriage he was able to devote himself exclusively to his scholarly and patriotic interests. In 1827 he became the first editor of the *Journal of the Bohemian Museum* (*Casopia ceského Musea*) published in both Czech and German. In this publication he opposed any far-reaching changes in the Czech language. During his career he produced many works devoted to the Czech nationalist ideal.[6]

Influenced by Herder's attention to Slavic folklore, by Rousseau's eulogy of Slavic agricultural life, and by Kant's philosophical speculations, Palacký visualized a free, independent nation as the respected bearer of the democratic ideal. He called for a federation of free and equal Czech nations inside the Austrian empire as the best counterpart to Germanic and Russian pressure. He urged his fellow Czechs to win national liberation through enlightenment and education rather than by the cumbersome machinery of revolution.

In April 1848 the *Fünfziger Ausschuss*, Committee of Fifty, of the German Preliminary Parliament of the German National Assembly sitting at Frankfurt-am-Main, invited Palacký to attend its sessions. In a reply dated April 11, 1848, addressed to Alexander von Soiren, chairman of the *Vorparlament*, Palacký declined to attend on the ground that as a Czech he had no interest in German affairs. At that time he favored a strong Austrian Empire, which, he believed, would consist of a federation of southern German and Slavic states all retaining their individual rights.

The Frankfurt invitation gave Palacký the opportunity to express, in what became a famous letter, the essence of his liberal Pan-Slavism:

I am a Czech of Slav descent and with all the little I own and possess I have devoted myself wholly and forever to the service of my nation. That nation is small, it is true, but from time immemorial it has been an independent nation with its own character; its rulers have participated since old times in the federation of German princes, but the nation never regarded itself nor was it regarded by others throughout all the centuries, as part of the German nation. The whole union of the Czech lands first with the Holy Roman Empire and then with the German Confederation was always a purely dynastic one of which the Czech nation, the Czech Estates, hardly wished to know and which they hardly noticed.[7]

Palacký went on to deny that he was an enemy of the Russians. He proclaimed "loudly and publicly" that, on the contrary, he observed with joyful sympathy every step "by which this great nation within its natural borders progresses along the road to civilization." At the same time, he stated that the bare possibility of a Russian universal monarchy had no more determined opponent than himself, "not because that monarchy would be Russian but because it would be universal."

In conclusion, Palacký expressed his conviction that those who asked that Austria (and with it Bohemia) should unite on national lines with the German Empire, demanded its suicide, which was morally and politically meaningless. On the contrary, he ventured, it would be more meaningful to demand that Germany should unite with the Austrian Empire. As that, however, did not accord with German national sentiment and opinion, nothing remained for the two Powers, the Austrian and German Empires, but to organize themselves on a footing of equality. He expressed himself at every moment as glad to give a helping hand in all activities that would not endanger the independence, integrity, and growth in power of the Austrian Empire.

Palacký saw three dangers—an expansive Germany then epitomized in the Frankfurt Assembly of 1848, a domineering Magyar nationalism, and a Russian universal state. He would strengthen Austria by transforming it into a federation of equal nationalities. He urged a leadership role for Austrian Slavs in consonance with the peaceful, democratic inclinations advocated by Herder. For these reasons he declined the invitation extended by the *Vorparlament* at Frankfurt.

Palacký's advocacy of a federation within the Austrian Empire received some sympathetic consideration in Vienna, but by 1852 the idea of such a federalism collapsed. Palacký retired from politics. After liberal concessions were made in 1860 and 1861, he became a life member of the Austrian Senate. Discouraged by a lack of support, he made it a practice to avoid appearing in the Senate.

Palacký retained his seat in the Bohemian *Landtag*, in which he became the leader of the Nationalist-Federal Party. He called for the establishment of a Czech kingdom to include Bohemia, Moravia, and Silesia, and urged extreme Catholics and the conservative nobility to support him. He took part also in both Pan-Slavic Congresses at Prague (1848) and Moscow (1867). He died at Prague on May 26, 1876, acclaimed as the respected father of Czech Pan-Slavism.

The Prague Congress of 1848

The initial major event in the emergence of Pan-Slavism was the Congress of Prague beginning on June 2, 1848. Summoned by Slav leaders under the presidency of František Palacký, the gathering of 341 delegates devoted itself to fostering mutual understanding and cooperation among all Slavs. The meeting took place in the 1848 atmosphere of national and liberal sentiment then prevalent in central Europe. The goal was to unify western Slavs (Czechs, Moravians, Silesians, and Slovaks), eastern Slavs (Poles and Ukrainians), and southern Slavs (Croatians, Slovenes, Serbians, and Dalmatians).

The Congress was expected to include all Slavs, but it did not attain that goal. Non-Austrian Slavs, such as Russians, Bulgarians, and Lusatian Serbs, were invited, but declined to participate. The absence of Russians was a major problem; two unofficial Russian delegates were hardly representative, for example, Mikhail Bakunin, (1814-1876), who later became the famous anarchist and revolutionary.[8] In fact, the Congress took on a distinct anti-Russian bias.

Behind the meeting was a sentiment then current among Austrian Slavs that they must strengthen their position against Germans, Magyars, and Russians. In fact, delegates were concerned about three dangers: German expansionism, Magyar domination, and Russian universalism. The delegates were moderate men, loyal to the monarchy, who simply wanted to express Slavic cohesion.

There was unrestrained joy in the streets of Prague as the Congress met. For the first time an overlooked minority had gathered to discuss its mutual interests. The new Slav tricolor—blue, white, and red—was displayed conspicuously. Slavs were dressed in colorful traditional costumes, addressed one another with the catchword "Slava!" instead of the customary "Heil!," and sang the old Slovak song, "Hej Slovane."[9]

The proceedings began with an outburst of eloquent and emotional oratory. In his welcoming address, Palacký called for a synthesis of the Slav character hailed by Herder with the new spirit of liberty coming from the West: "The freedom which we are now seeking is not a newly arrived stranger among us; it is not a scion brought to us from abroad; it is a tree which has grown of its own on our domestic soil, it is the native and first-born heritage of our ancestors."[10] Other speakers glorified the Slav spirit and hailed the Slavs as the important third branch of mankind side by side with Latins and Germans. They identified Slavs with humanitarianism, democracy, and peace, as examples of great humanity and pure Christianity. Slavs, they said, had a unique character and mission in this world.

After the oratory, the delegates turned to a discussion of such concrete problems as the status of Slavs in Austria and their mutual needs, relations with non-Slavic Austrians, connections with non-Austrian Slavs, and finally relations with non-Slavs throughout Europe. The Congress quickly became politicized: some delegates called for help against Polish oppression; southern Slavs denounced the Magyars; and Polish exiles demanded a strong stand against the Tsar, "enemy of all the Slavs."

Three declarations were drawn up, none of which was officially accepted—a petition to the Austrian Emperor, a manifesto addressed to the Slavic world, and an appeal to the nations of Europe. The delegates could not agree on whether to ask the Austrian Emperor for a federation of the varied kingdoms or one based on linguistic affinities in the population. A proclamation to the Slav people proposed that the Slav Congress be perpetuated by meeting continuously in the month of May each time in a different Slav city. Jan Kollár (1793-1892), whose *"Daughter of Slava,"* glorifying the dream of Slavic unity, had fired the imagination of Czechs, called for publication of a Slav periodical, a Slav Academy, a Slav library, and both central and national committees for political and cultural affairs.

The third declaration addressed to the nations of Europe spoke of Slavic hearts beating in unison in an identity of spiritual interest: "The Latin and Germanic nations, formerly famous in Europe as powerful conquerors, have for centuries established their independence by the strength of the sword. . . . Only today, owing to the strength of public opinion which like the spirit of God has suddenly spread throughout all lands, the people have succeeded in breaking the fetters of feudalism and in returning to the individuals the inalienable rights of mankind. Now, the Slav, long rejected, again raises his head. . . . Strong in numbers and even stronger in his will and in his newly acquired brotherly union, he remains, nevertheless, faithful to his natural character and to the principles of his ancestors; he demands neither domination nor conquest, he claims liberty for himself for all, he asks that it be generally recognized without exception as the most sacred right of man. Therefore, we Slavs reject and abhor all domination by mere force . . . *liberty, equality* and *fraternity* for all who live in the state is our watchword today, as it was a thousand years ago."[11]

Despite the high-sounding oratory, the Congress produced few positive results. It proclaimed the principle of "Mutuality," but there were irreconcilable differences among the various Slav groups attending the meeting. The radical group, led by Bakunin in the interests of revolutionary Pan-Slavism, was small, but it was annoying to the vast majority of moderates loyal to the monarchy. Then, on June 12, just two days before the scheduled close of the Congress, there was an uprising of radical students and workers in Prague. Although quickly suppressed by the Austrian army, the event was enough to bring a prompt end to the Congress before the proceedings could be brought to a formal conclusion.

The Prague Congress, although seemingly a failure, did have a positive effect. For the first time, a people who considered themselves to be downtrodden, had shown evidence of a will to exist as a separate unity. Their representatives had spoken to the nations of Europe of the Slav will to exist. It was a tremendous psychological lift for all Slavs. The Slavic peoples had suffered in subjugation, but henceforth they would cast off their chains and take their rightful place in world society.

Moreover, the Congress marked the transition of Pan-Slavism from romantic idealism to politicization. With the Prague Congress, Pan-Slavism became political. The earlier romanticism clothed with idealism had given way to an urge for political solidarity to end the second-class status of Slavic peoples, and to allow them to play their "destined role" in service to all humanity.

Toward a Russian Monopoly

Russians looked at the Prague Congress of 1848 with undisguised hostility. Palacký had confined its membership to representatives of Slavs inside the Austrian monarchy; he had hoped to form an Austro-Slav alliance against the Germans. But there were others who believed that Pan-Slavism should extend beyond a call for cultural union and should be politically unified under Russian leadership. From this point of view, the movement needed the support of a state power and the natural choice, geographically and power-wise, was Tsarist Russia.[12] It was an attitude thoroughly understood and favored in Moscow.

Behind Russian Pan-Slavism was the earlier ideology of Moscovite Slavophilism, with which it is often confused. During the early 19th century, Russian intelligentsia turned to a romantic Slavophilism, which stressed the Slavic nature of Russian society and which called for a revival of great past traditions. The movement advocated a return to the good old days before the Western innovations of Peter the Great—to Tsar, Church, and People. There were various contributory elements—cultural, religious, and political.

Culturally, the Slavophile philosophy was similar to that of Slavs in the Austrian monarchy. Interwoven with Western European thought, it was influenced by Herder, Rousseau, Fichte, and Hegel, and the Romanticism stressing the greatness of Slavic culture. At the same time, despite Western influence, there was a tendency to separate Russian cultural values from those of the West, and to seek a return to the old Russian traditions.

Slavophiles based their anti-Western sentiment on the argument that the West had overemphasized the role of reason in human affairs and had ignored the power of emotion and feeling. Western empiricism, they charged, had withered the great traditions of the past and had erred in substituting experience for faith. Burdened by a combination of Roman, Teutonic, and Christian elements, the West had unsolvable class and racial differences. With its violence and debilitating competition, said the Slavophiles, Western society was in cultural decline, a barren wasteland.

Anti-Western Slavophilism had a strong religious motivation. For centuries, Moscow had considered itself to be the true home of Orthodoxy. Its prestige became even greater after the invasion of Byzantium in 1453. Moscovite monks claimed that Byzantium had been punished by God for the sin of the Union of Florence in 1439, which had brought about a coalition of the Roman and Eastern Orthodox Churches.[13] This led eventually to the "Third Rome" doctrine: "Two Romes have fallen but the Third shall remain." The Third Rome was Moscow.

This religious impulse was responsible in part for the new Eastern Messianism promoted by the Tsars. Russian monarchs began to see themselves as leaders not only of the Russian Orthodox Church but also of the entire Orthodox world, even of global Christianity. As Byzantine Caesaro-Papist theocrats, they would take in hand disparate peoples and shape them to their own Messianic needs.

Added to cultural and religious impulses for Slavophilism were important political motives. Much of the Slavophile contempt for the West had its origin in a hatred for Napoleon. Not satisfied with French expansion in Western Europe, the conqueror had sought to add the mighty Russian realm to the list of his victims. For the Russian masses, Napoleon was the anti-Christ, the satanic leader of the Roman Catholic West against Moscow. Fortunately for civilization, said the Slavophiles, Russians had freed themselves from Napoleonic domination.

Slavophilism was stimulated further by the rising sense of national consciousness in successful Russian wars against Persia (1826-1828) and Turkey (1827-1829), as well as by suppression of a Polish uprising (1830-1831). Apparently, the Russians were making their way in a hostile world.

Slavophiles saw Russians as God's chosen people, unlike the immoral Western barbarians corrupted by materialism. Holy Russia, "the first state in the world," and Moscow, "citadel of the true faith," would lead the peoples of the earth to the paradise of true Christianity. Russians, like the early Greeks, were the true guardians of the living tradition of truth. Prince Odoevsky criticized the strange spectacle of Western Europe, where opinion struggled against opinion, power against power, throne against throne. The young and fresh Russians had taken no part in the crimes of Europe. They had a great mission to fulfill—their names were already inscribed on the tablets of victory—in science, art, and faith, in glaring contrast to the tottering ruins of Europe. Thus ran the Slavophile argument.

Slavophilism attracted wide support throughout Russian society, among nobility, the rising middle class, and peasantry. University students geared Hegelianism to their structured society and set it off on a different historical course. The vast illiterate peasantry, oppressed by taxation, military service, and poverty, would take part in this coming regeneration. The lowly Russian serf, the preferred servant of God, would take the lead in spreading the gospel of social justice to all the peoples of the world.

The Prague Congress of 1848 took place at a time when these ideas were being generated inside Russia. After Russia's defeat in the Crimean War (1853-1856), a vague Slavophilism was transformed into a militant and nationalistic Pan-Slavism. What has started out as a cultural movement led by a Czech historian inside the Austrian Empire and subsequently politicized at Prague, was now appropriated by the Russians as an ideology dedicated to their mission. Pan-Slavism would be run from Moscow, not from Prague or the minor Slavic states. There would be a great Slavic federation, not under Austrian but under Russian leadership, that would comprise all of Central Europe—a unified land mass from the Baltic Sea down to Constantinople. What originally had been a shadowy dream was thus transformed into a new aggressive, expansionist Pan-Slavism.

Danilevsky and Dostoevsky

The Russian version of Pan-Slavism was promoted assiduously by Nikolai Yakovlvich Danilevsky (1822-1865), scientist and anti-Darwinist, whose philosophy of history as a series of distinct civilizations preceded Spengler, Toynbee,[14] and Alfred Weber. The major work of this influential drumbeater for Pan-Slavism was titled *Russia and Europe*, first published in 1869.[15] According to Danilevsky, the Slavs played a determining role in the history of civilization. In the beginning, there were two streams of world history starting on the banks of the Nile. One, the heavenly and godly, proceeded through Jerusalem and reached Kiev and Moscow "in serene purity." The other, earthly and human, split into two main parts and flowed over Athens, Alexandria, and Rome into Western Europe. All the streams on the wide surface of Slavdom joined together on the soil of Russia to form a mighty torrent.

Danilevsky saw a major incompatibility between Slavic and Western civilizations. In his view, the Slavic type was superior, the first to embody four characteristics—religious, political, esthetic-scientific, and socio-economic. Western Europe, on the other hand, had degenerated into religious anarchy, epitomized in the despotism of Catholicism and the "foolish Protestant ethic" of basing religious truth on personal authority. Contrast this, he said, with the "religious truth of Slavic Orthodoxy."

Danilevsky's glorification of the Slav heritage was eloquent and highly emotional. He saw his fellow Slavs as the most politically gifted family of the human race. Unlike the English, the Russians, leaders of the Slavic world did not send out colonists to build new political societies. Instead, they expanded gradually and irresistibly on all sides, assimilating foreign peoples. In the socio-economic sphere, Russia was the only great state with "a powerful stability provided by peasant ownership of the land."

Under Russian leadership, said Danilevsky, the Slavs would combine in an unassailable union to eradicate the kind of imitativeness and servility such as existed in the West. They would liberate their brothers by instilling in them a spirit of independence and Pan-Slavic consciousness. Then would come the conquest of Constantinople and the Near East. Whatever the future brought, the Slavs were entitled, on the evidence of the past alone, to consider themselves among the most gifted families of the human race. There would be a long conflict between Russia and Europe followed by a union of Slavic states with Greeks, Magyars, and Rumanians. But the real *sine qua non* was strong and powerful Russian leadership in the liberation of Slavdom and in Pan-Slavic consciousness.

Along with Danilevsky the most fervent Pan-Slavic apostle was the famed Russian novelist Feodor Mikhailovich Dostoevsky (1821-1881).[16] In *The Possessed* (1873), Dostoevsky described a discussion between the student, Shatov, a former serf, and Nikolai Stavrogin, a brilliant aristocrat.[17] The words by the revolutionary Shatov presented the author's own views. Russians, said the student, were the only truly God-fearing people on earth. They were destined "to regenerate and save the world in the name of a new God and to whom are given the keys of life and of the new world."[18] And further: "If a great people did not believe that the truth is only to be found in itself alone, if it did not believe that it alone is destined to save all the rest by its truth it would at once sink into an ethnographical material. But there is only one truth, and therefore only a single one out of the nations can have the true God. That is the Russian people."[19]

Shatov, speaking for Dostoevsky, was lyrical in his praise: "I believe in Russia. . . . I believe in her Orthodoxy. . . . I believe in the body of Christ. . . . I believe that a new advent will take place in Russia. . . . I believe. . . ."[20]

In his *Diary*, Dostoevsky called attention to the Russian genius as the only hope of an unhappy world:

Our great Russia, as the head of the united Slavs, will utter to the world, to the whole of European mankind and to civilization, her new, sane and as yet unheard-of word. That word will be uttered in a new brotherly, universal union, which starts from the Slav genius, above all from the spirit of the Russian people who have suffered so long, who during so many centuries have been doomed to silence, but who have always possessed great powers for clarifying and settling many bitter and fatal misunderstandings of Western European civilization.[21]

It is clear that Dostoevsky was possessed by the theme of a Pan-Slavic mission. He denounced Westernizers because Europe was unalterably opposed to Russia and unable to understand her true intentions. In sarcastic tones he criticized Western plutocracy, worship of money, the stock exchange, Catholics, and Jews. Against Western corruption he placed the hope of salvation in the faith of the Russian people, and their national messianic vocation as expressed in Pan-Slavism. The Russian national genius he was certain, was the hope of the world. Russian wars were never devoted to conquest, only dedicated to the liberation of the oppressed. The Russo-Turkish conflict, then being waged, was an altruistic war waged to liberate the Near East; eventually, it would be converted into an all-European war ending with victory for the East. Western Europe would be regenerated through Russian victory.

Dostoevsky returned to this theme in his famous address on Pushkin, delivered on June 8, 1880, at a Moscow meeting of the Lovers of Russian Literature.[22] Passionately eulogizing Pushkin as a great national treasure, Dostoevsky spoke of the poet's special gift of universal comprehension. He said that Pushkin represented Russia, which was the only nation qualified to understand, reconcile, and inspire the rest of Europe. In the process of making herself more essentially European, Russia would become more completely European. Pushkin was the first to recognize the magnificent Russian spirit:

[Pushkin] was the first—precisely the first, and there was no one prior to him—to discern and give us the artistic type of Russian beauty directly emerging from the Russian spirit, beauty which resides in the people's truth, in our soil. . . . I merely say that among all the nations the Russian soul, the genius of the Russian people, is perhaps more apt to embrace the idea of a universal fellowship of man, of brotherly love—that sober point of view which forgives all that is hostile, while distinguishes and excuses that which is disparate, which removes contradiction.[23]

Dostoevsky saw the Russian leadership of the Slavic world as a necessity for the progress of civilization. Constantinople would be taken in due time by an expanding Pan-Slavism. Russians would then dominate all Asia ("Asia will be our salvation.") As "civilizers," they would bring an advanced culture to the great continent. Asia would become "Russia's America," where innovative Russians would produce great wealth by exploiting the rich natural resources there and by building mighty industries. With her new power a regenerated Russia would be strong enough to fulfil her world mission. While this process was going on, Western Europe would dissolve in quarrels and undergo a stupendous crash. Russia, leader of the Pan-Slavic world, would then step into the vacuum and assume world control. This, in Dostoevsky's view, was the inevitable destiny of Slavdom.

The Second Pan-Slav Congress, 1867

In the late 1850s and early 1860s, leadership of the Pan-Slav movement drifted toward Moscow. The initiative at first was private and not governmental. In 1857 a Slav Committee was organized in Moscow to support the southern Slavs. In 1867 the Society of Friends of Natural Science at Moscow University arranged a Slav ethnographic exhibition. It invited Slavs outside Russia to attend. Eighty-four non-Russian Slavs, including František Palacký, attended. Poles, the second most important Slavic people after the Ukrainians, remained ostentatiously absent.[24]

Tsar Alexander II received the "Slav pilgrims" graciously, but he was careful to devote himself to generalities; he avoided any political implications. Speakers at the Congress, however, were less inhibited. They hailed the "Tsar-Liberator" in adulatory speeches and stressed the political brotherhood which united other Slavs with their kinsmen in Russia. "Russia is no longer Russia," said one delegate, "it is Slavonia, nay Pan-Slavonia."[25] The heart of Pan-Slavism was being transferred from Prague to Moscow.

Despite emotional claims for Slav brotherhood, differences soon emerged between the Russians and their guests. The meeting had been called in conjunction with an ethnographic exhibition dedicated to all Slavic peoples, but its Russian promoters demanded that Russian become the official language of all Slavs. Russians present greeted the call with thunderous applause, while visiting Slavs remained silent. It began to dawn on the Slavic guests that there were conflicting views about the meaning of Pan-Slavism. To them, Pan-Slavism meant the equality of all Slavs. Their Russian hosts, on the other hand, saw the movement as dedicated to supremacy of the Russian language, the Orthodox faith, and the Russification of all Slavs even in the Balkans.

Most embarrassing of all was the Polish question, which threw a shadow over the whole Congress. Russian speakers made it plain that the Polish "nation" had been created by Russia in 1815, but that Poles had remained unaccountably ungrateful for this "generosity," and by their inexplicable uprising "had lost irretrievably the liberty granted to them." Poles were reminded that they were no longer a nation, because "the sword had decided against them." When delegates arose to declare that no Slavic nation should control another, they were greeted with a storm of indignant responses by Russians present.

Other speakers tried to soothe resentment by pronouncing all Slavs as one nation welded together by ties of blood and mind. They urged the unity of Slavs, as other peoples had been unified, "and the name of the great nation would be 'Giant!'" Every Slav idiom should develop in its own way, but there was to be a common treasure of a Pan-Slav language covering all Slav lands from the Adriatic Sea and Prague to Archangel and the Pacific Ocean.

It was beautiful, enthusiastic oratory, in an atmosphere of artificial and strained unity. There were the usual proposals—a Pan-Slav University, publications devoted to encouraging the movement, calls for a biennial meeting—all the "Mutuality" suggested at the Prague Congress of 1848. The Congress ended in a display of enthusiasm with fiery speeches and thunderous applause. Delegates agreed that they would see each other in two years in the month of August in Belgrade.

The European press was impressed by this "grave event" in European history. In Moscow, Prague, and Belgrade, centers of Slavic sentiment, there were emotional reactions to what was believed to be great progress on the road to Pan-Slavic union. The Slavs were showing a skeptical world what could be done by its policy of "love" as the key to Slavic unification.

Despite the euphoria, practical results of the Congress were miniscule. The proposed meeting in Belgrade in two years never took place, and four decades were to pass before additional congresses in Prague (1908) and Sophia (1910). Efforts to achieve political union failed. There was continued resentment against Russian domination of the movement: Slav leaders in the Balkans looked on Moscow as a citadel of violence and reaction. Pan-Slavic ideals remained hopelessly confused, a mélange of mystical idealism, conservative fantasies, and political unrealism. As elsewhere, this macro-nationalist movement could not overcome the varied, even contradictory, elements in its composition.

Pan-Slavism from 1867 to 1914

For the next three decades Pan-Slavism was seriously impeded by internal differences. On the one side was the Russian version dictated by the Big Slav Brother from Moscow. Russian Pan-Slavism became more and more dedicated to the national policy of Russification. In external affairs it was used as a political weapon in diplomatic struggles with other Grear Powers. Pan-Slavic ideals were promoted zealously by Count Ignatyev, Russian Ambassador to the Porte from 1864 to 1877, and acted as a compelling factor in the outbreak of the Russo-Turkish War of 1876-1878. Russian Pan-Slavism prospered in the 1880s under Alexander III, who came to the throne in 1881, and who was even more autocratic and reactionary than his father. Alexander III was convinced of the essential correctness of the Pan-Slavic belief that all Slavs had special spiritual and moral qualities distinguishing them from Germans, and that Russia had a divinely appointed mission to lead all other Slavs.

At this time, Pan-Slavic opinion in the Balkans was divided. On one hand, the Little Slav Brothers resented the fact that under Moscow's auspices Pan-Slavism had become synonymous with Russian imperialism. On the other hand, there were many, not entirely averse to Russian leadership, who were angered by the *Ausgleich* of 1867, the "compromise" which recognized the equality of Austrians and Hungarians in the Austrian Empire, but ignored the Slavs. Holding that they had little to gain from Vienna, these Slavs looked eastward for guidance and support.

Pan-Slavism in the Balkans was weakened further by a growing hostility between Slavic peoples there. In Poland the movement was threatened by a rival macro-nationalism, a Pan-Polish ideal, which called for a *Polonia magna*, a large territory reaching from the Black Sea to the Baltic and including even the Ukraine. Nevertheless, despite these weakening tendencies, Pan-Slavism in the Balkans was kept alive by the efforts of Czechs, who saw in it the proper response to a rising Pan-Germanism. In 1898 they celebrated the centenary of Palacký's birth with a great Pan-Slavic demonstration. The movement was strengthened by gatherings of Slav students, formation of a union of Slavic journalists, and founding of many Slavic gymnastic clubs (*Sokols*).

The regeneration of Czech Pan-Slavism carried over into the 20th century. The Czech statesman, Karel Kramar, promoted a liberal Pan-Slavic movement which he called Neo-Slavism. A Pan-Slav Congress was held at Prague in 1908 and another at Sofia in 1910. Again the movement was hampered by dissension—Serbs against Croats, Czechs against Slovaks, Poles against Ukrainians. These persistent antagonisms worked against any effective Slavic collaboration. Delegates discussed the possibility of war between Russia and the Western Powers, some urged assistance to the Russians while others demanded a hands-off policy.

Meanwhile, the Russians held their own Pan-Slav Congress in 1909 at St. Petersburg. At this time the entire Pan-Slavic movement was cast into the shadow of the Balkan Wars of 1912-1913, in which Serbia, Montenegro, Bulgaria, and Greece jointly made war on the Ottoman Empire, and then went to war with one another over the spoils. Austrians and Serbians, Teutons and Slavs, became deadly enemies in the Balkans, thus preparing the way for a gigantic clash between Pan-Slavism and its rival, Pan-Germanism, and for the ultimate supremacy of eastern Europe.

Pan-Slavism and the World Wars

World War I marked a watershed for the Pan-Slavic movement. On the surface it would seem that Palacký's demands of 1848 had been won. Four great dynasties, the Hapsburg, Hohenzollern, Romanov, and Ottoman, which had controlled the destiny of Central Europe, were gone. New nation-states had won their liberation: three western Slav states—Poland, Czechoslovakia, and Yugoslavia (Kingdom of the Serbs, Croats, and Slovenes)—emerged from the holocaust. The spirit of the Prague Congress of 1848 was in the air: the three new Western Slav states boasted of liberal, democratic constitutions, and for the moment both German and Russian interference in Balkan affairs was terminated.

However, the seeming triumph of Slavic aspirations, built on weak foundations, was to be of short duration. Pan-Slavic dreams had been fulfilled partially, but actually Pan-Slavism was in a state of decline. Differences between the three new Western Slav states had intensified rather than diminished. Rivalries between Poles and Ukrainians, between Serbs and Bulgars, were accentuated, while the new federated Yugoslavia was wracked by long-lasting hostility between the dominant Serbs and angry Croats.

Immediately after the Russian October Revolution of 1917, the new Soviet Government renounced Pan-Slavism. In the flush of victory the Bolsheviks damned Pan-Slavism as a cloak for the expansionism of the Tsarist empire. Had not Karl Marx, the founding father, excoriated Pan-Slavism as a "ludicrous anti-historical movement behind which stood the terrible reality of the Russian Empire? "Central Europe is well acquainted with the intrigues through which Russian policy supports the new-fangled system of Pan-Slavism; no better system could be invented to suit [Russia's] purpose."[26] Friedrich Engels, too, denounced Pan-Slavism in the work of

Slavic dilettantes "as an absurd anti-historical current the aim of which is to subordinate the civilized West to the barbarian East, the city to the village, trade, industry and education to the primitive agriculture of Slavic serfs." Engels stated that the intrigues by which Russian diplomacy supported the recently invented Pan-Slavism were well-known in Central Europe—a doctrine which could not have corresponded better to its aims.[27]

For euphoric Bolshevik revolutionaries, Pan-Slavism was clearly a reactionary, imperialist movement which had no place in a Communist society. Once again, however, the historical process gave evidence of political reality succeeding persisting ideology. According to Marxism, a society based on class solidarity and internationalism had no room for a Pan-Slavic union grounded on linguistic or "racial" affinity. That was the theory, but in practice the society turned out differently. Soviet enthusiasts did not dream that Pan-Slavism would be revived several decades later and that most of its goals would be achieved in a new interpretation of Pan-Slavic philosophy.

When Hitler turned on the Soviet Union on June 22, 1941, a fearful but angry Stalin called for a mighty struggle of Russians and their "Slavic Brothers against the beastly Nazi invaders." That summer, as German troops surged across Russian soil, a Pan-Slavic Committee was founded in Moscow. Resolutions were passed proclaiming the "racial" and cultural community of all Slavs as opposed to the barbaric Teutonic Nazis, and summoning all Slavs to rise in wrath against the despoilers of Slavic soil. Suddenly, the idea of "racial brotherhood" emerged as a new adjunct to Soviet philosophy. Poles, Czechs, Serbs, Croats, and Slovenes were urged to unite against the common enemy of all Slavic peoples. The entire Slavic world was required to unite and devote its combined strength to the utter destruction of Fascism.

The call for unity against Nazism was successful. Even non-Communist Slavs were convinced of the need to destroy the Hitler menace. Several additional Pan-Slav conferences were held in Moscow during the war: a second on April 7, 1942, followed by a third May 10-16, 1942. The theme was always the same—Moscow's leadership in the burning desire of the Slavic peoples to free themselves of Nazi barbarism. Soviet Russia was the Big Brother of all Slavs, and its triumphant Red Army would seal the fate of Hitler. As the war progressed, Pan-Slavism was used increasingly to work for a peace which would ensure the integration of all Slavs under the Kremlin's leadership.

Meanwhile, all-Slav Congresses were called for people of Slavic descent living in the United States, Canada, and Latin America to support the struggle of Slav brothers in Europe against Nazism. Leaders of American Slavic organizations met in Pittsburgh in early October 1941 to build the unity of Americans of Slav descent. Branches were organized in New York, Chicago, Milwaukee, St. Louis, Akron, Cleveland, and Detroit. The

Second American Slav Congress was held in Pittsburgh from September 23 to 24, 1944. Immediately after the war, when the nature of the new Pan-Slavism abroad was understood, American support evaporated.

What was happening in Europe was clear: the Kremlin had decided to mold World War II Pan-Slavism to mesh with its own thinking and to bring it in line with Soviet ideology. It called for a meeting of all Pan-Slav committees in Belgrade in July 1946. A Pan-Slav Congress opened there on December 8, 1946, with an address by Marshal Tito, Communist dictator of Yugoslavia, and apparently an enthusiastic supporter of the Kremlin's Pan-Slavism. But the situation changed drastically in June 1948 with the open break between Tito and Stalin and the defection of Tito from the Cominform.

The Kremlin then announced the formal disbanding of the Comintern, the Communist world organization for promoting revolution, and replaced it with a limited coalition of Communist nations. Thus, the Soviet Union retreated in effect to leadership of a Slavic entente, maintaining on its western borders a *cordon sanitaire* of Slavic states as a buffer against Western capitalism. Soviet tanks in Prague symbolized that intention.

The old Pan-Slavism retreated into the background, to be succeeded by a version closely associated with Soviet imperialism. The Kremlin would dominate not only Slavs but also non-Slavic peoples in its sphere of influence in Eastern Europe. Thus, Pan-Slavism had become an arm of the new Soviet imperialism.

Failure of the Pan-Slavic Mission

The oldest and best-known of the macro-nationalisms, Pan-Slavism was the first to embody supra-nationalist trends. For the first time an attempt was made to mold nationalism on a larger scale, and to unite peoples of supposedly like backgrounds and historical traditions into a powerful unified whole. Pan-Slavism became the progenitor of other pan-movements with a fate similar to that of other macro-nationalisms.

In its early form, Pan-Slavism, promoted by enthusiastic intellectuals, took on a cultural and moral complexion. Its program to unify all Slavs was designed to shape the cultural destinies of mankind. In the early 1800s, the Slavic peoples were minorities in the Austrian, Russian, Prussian, and Turkish empires. Although the roots of their languages were similar, there was in fact no integrated Pan-Slavic literature or culture. With the awakening of national consciousness during and after the French Revolution and the Napoleonic era, Slavs, as well as Germans and Italians, began to seek union for themselves. Slavic intellectuals asserted that the varied Slavic languages were merely dialects of one great linguistic form and that varied Slavs living in subjugation in four great empires were merely tribes of a single nation.

Slavic ideologists called for liberation of the great human family. Linking romanticism with the newly rising nationalism, they began to call also for leadership in a Europe where the old Latin-Germanic culture was in decline.

Despite some gains by the mid-20th-century, Pan-Slavism was weakened from its beginnings by national diversities and differing traditions and interests. Its theory was always vague, inconsistent, on occasion even incoherent. Slavic unity was more myth than fact.

Geographical Fragmentation. Although Western Slavs claimed land cohesion in the Balkans, actually the Slavic world had been broken up by the early movement of Magyar peoples into the Danubian basin. The partitions of Poland contributed to further geographical separation into segments.

Diversity of Peoples. There never was a closely related Slav people with the same identity that Germans, Italians, or French recognize. Various Slavs in the Balkans and in the Russian Empire evolved under quite different circumstances, and there was no united Slavic people to confront the Teutonic-Magyar order. Indeed, Slavic unity existed only in the pamphlets of publicists.

Religious Differences. Western Slavs—Poles, Croatians, and Czechs—were firm Roman Catholics and had little use for "schismatic" Slavs in the Russian Empire. That hostility was shared by Russian Slavs who preferred their own Orthodox version of Christianity. This deep-rooted religious rivalry could not be overcome in the drive for a greater Slav unity.

Psychological. Psychologically, Pan-Slavism was unprepared for rapid changes in historical trends. It soon outlived its usefulness in a revolutionary world. Pan-Slavic enthusiasts worked within the existing order and called only for liberation. Pan-Slavism was never really revolutionary minded, a decided handicap in an era of war and revolution. Out of step with increasingly powerful forces, it ceased eventually to be of practical value.

Political Bonds. With its built-in incoherence, Western Slavism eventually succumbed to Russian authoritarianism. The movement was taken over by Moscow as an official ideology of a powerful government. Pan-Slavism became merely another term for the political goals of Russia, first under the Tsarist regime and then under Soviet Bolshevism. The Kremlin utilized ill-formed theories about the supposed affinity of all Slavs merely as an argument to support the aims of a rigid autocracy.

Cultural Pan-Slavism disappeared in the solvent of Russian nationalism. After World War II the Kremlin called for a compulsory deference of the Western Slavic "younger brothers" in a broader Pan-Slavic frame. Had not the great Soviet Union "liberated" the Slavs of the Balkans? Good Western Slavs were expected to be obedient to the demands of the elder brothers in the Kremlin; the "bad Slavs" of Czechoslovakia were punished by intervention in August 1968. No polycentric tendencies of disloyal Slavs were to be tolerated.

To accent its own version, the Kremlin rejected the term Pan-Slavism and referred instead to "People's Slavism," in effect a combination of Russian nationalism and Communist internationalism. All peoples, both in the USSR and its satellite states, were included in a broadened national frame, whether they were Christians or Muslims. In this way Pan-Slavism was absorbed into a centralized, totalitarian state.

The failure of the Russian Pan-Slavic movement was revealed in recent years by the continuing disaffection of Poland. The Solidarity movement, opposed by Soviet puppets in Warsaw, was an expression of Polish discontent with Russian dominance. With a Polish Pope in Rome there was an upsurge of Catholicism among Poles opposed to Communist atheism. The Polish economy, geared to Moscow, was in shambles. Under such circumstances, a little Slav Brother was more than unhappy with the Big Slav Brother in the Kremlin.

CHAPTER 3

PAN-GERMANISM: THE TEUTONIC MISSION _____

Where is the German's Fatherland!
Name me at length that mighty land!
Where'er resounds the German tongue,
Where'er its hymns to God are sung.
Be this the land,
Brave German, this thy Fatherland!
—Ernst Moritz Arndt, "The German's Fatherland,"
in Alfred Baskerville, *The Poetry of Germany* (Baden
Baden and Hamburg, 1876), p. 151.

Macro-Nationalism as Power Syndrome

The history of Pan-Germanism is somewhat briefer than that of Pan-Slavism, its rival. Unlike Pan-Slavism, which sought to combine supposedly related peoples of many nations, Pan-Germanism was confined to one people—the Germans. Organized with efficiency, its *Gründlichkeit* gave it influence far beyond the number of its adherents.

The term Pan-Germanism (*Alldeutschtum*) is derived from its leading organization, the Pan-German League (*Alldeutscher Verband*). Grounded in early 19th-century romantic nationalism, it was a revolutionary movement which took advantage of the national temper. It was developed during the foundation years of the Second Reich under Chancellor Otto von Bismarck.

Like Pan-Slavism, Pan-Germanism as an ideology was never clearly defined. Some Pan-Germanists called for unity of the German-speaking population of Central Europe (Germany, Austria, the Baltic Provinces of Russia, Switzerland, and the Low Countries). Other Pan-Germanists included the Germans of Eastern Europe because they belonged to the old medieval empire. Still others claimed Germans in the Scandinavian countries. By the 20th century, some Pan-Germanists called for global involvement, believing that Germans throughout the world should be included in a single hegemony. Varied interpretations of Pan-Germanism ranged from the modest cultivation of German patriotism with emphasis on cultural attributes to a global community based on outright territorial expansion. All interpretations, however, were designed to strengthen German national consciousness.

Behind the expansionist form of Pan-Germanism was the desire to present a united front against Britain, France, and Russia, all potential enemies. For

Pan-Germanists the great industrial progress of Germany at the turn of the century called for a more important place in the sun. No longer were they satisfied with mere national unity achieved after centuries of particularism. By that time the old vague program was extended into an explosive mixture of imperialism, Anglophobia, rivalry with France, anti-Slavism, anti-socialism, and anti-Semitism. Other powerful nations had barred the way for legitimate German expansion. Those doors would be battered down by application of the *Macht* principle—power to the strongest.

This goal was far beyond the earlier call for the cultural homogeneity of German peoples. To Pan-Germanists, a new colonialism, supported by a Big Navy, was the *sine qua non* for German existence. To the concerned British Foreign Office, Pan-Germanism meant literally "world domination as a rightful goal."

It was Hegelian thrust and counter-thrust once again. Expansionist Pan-German ideology aroused fears elsewhere, not only among Pan-Slavs but also among the British, French, and Americans, all of whom resented policies detrimental to their own territorial imperatives. Pan-German doctrine was a contributory factor to the outbreak of both World Wars I and II, in each of which rival Great Powers subjugated their own differences in the deadly challenge of an expanding Germany. It is a kind of Parkinson's law of nationalism—when one macro-nationalism sets a goal which impinges violently on other established nationalisms, it generally finds itself in combat with a coalition too powerful for its continued existence. Neither Wilhelm II nor Adolf Hitler understood this historical truism.

Despite its painstaking organization and its grandiose claims, Pan-Germanism never succeeded in winning the wholehearted support of the German majority. Although the majority was sympathetic toward many Pan-German views, it did not participate actively in the movement and felt a sense of unease about its cold concept of power. Only a modest few thousand Germans became zealous supporters and contributed financially. The vital factor was the Pan-German trend in foreign policy because governmental circles concurred willingly with the Pan-German program of colonialism, militarism, navalism, and Anglophobia. In the Wilhelminian era this attitude eventually brought Germany to the edge of the abyss and the tragedy of World War I.

This kind of aggressive macro-nationalism was revived by Hitler after the defeat in World War I and the humiliating Treaty of Versailles. The *Fuehrer* adopted the political theories of Pan-Germanism in his blueprint, *Mein Kampf.* He would unite the Germans of the world from Berlin to Rio de Janeiro in a triumphant Third Reich, a goal which the eccentric Wilhelm II had failed to reach. Again came the counterthrust of another global coalition to smash the Nazi version of Pan-Germanism. It was more evidence of the fact that world society does not tolerate the pretensions of any macro-nationalism for extended power.

Ideological Roots

The ideological roots of Pan-Germanism may be found in the German romanticism of the early 19th century, which gave direction to the later concept of a European, or world, mission of the Germans.[1] Early German nationalism was born and nurtured in the era of Napoleonic despotism. The Corsican adventurer bestrode the European mainland, shedding the blood of Frenchmen and non-Frenchmen alike in a grand design to bring glory first to himself, second to his family, and third to France. It is one of the mysteries of history how the intelligent French public, the people of liberty, equality, and fraternity, could contribute their lives and fortunes to such dangerous goals.

Napoleon saw fertile ground to the east where the disunited Germanies consisted of some 1,789 states and principalities, a veritable geographical expression. In 1806 he put an end to the shadowy Holy Roman Empire, and set up in Paris a kind of glorified real-estate office to do away with German disunity. In 1807 he formed the Confederation of the Rhine for that purpose. Such interference in the affairs of the German people, far from reacting to Napoleon's advantage, turned out to be a giant step in spreading the seeds of German nationalism. German eyes were directed to the path of national unity, to be achieved later by Bismarck's iron-and-blood policy.

The ideology of Pan-Germanism, the Teutonic counterpart of Pan-Slavism, was generated by a series of advocates who saw it as a logical extension of German nationalism. The philosopher Johann Gottlieb Fichte (1762-1814) prophesied a great destiny for Germans because, in contrast to Latins, they possessed a unique spirit of regeneration.[2] Angered by Napoleon's interference in German affairs, he delivered fourteen addresses to the German people (*Reden an die deutsche Nation*, 1807-1808) to enthusiastic audiences in Berlin. He reminded his listeners that their German forefathers had refused to remain under foreign control. He called upon them to establish German freedom on the highest moral basis, to refuse submission to Napoleon, and to be aware of their great historical mission.[3]

Like other German romantics, Fichte placed great stress upon the excellence of the German language. He ridiculed the English tongue because there was no "true culture" in England. It was important, he said, to give the whole world the benefit of the German language.

Among other apostles of romantic nationalism who contributed to nascent Pan-Germanism was Friedrich Ludwig Jahn (1772-1852), pedagogical reformer, father of gymnastics, and an unconventional patriarch who combined physical exercise with patriotism.[4] In his *Das deutsche Volkstum* (1810), Turnvater Jahn called for a renewal of the ancient Teutonic civilization and the glorification of the German *Volk*. He regretted that the feeling of nationalism, or "German-ness," was disappearing more and more. "We must return to the lost past and re-create Nation, German-ness, Fatherland. A nation is not made up by the outer band of the state which encloses it. Much more important is what exists inside—the quiet, trustful community of interests and mutual love. Only by a study of the general inner life and characteristics of a people can we answer the questions and solve the puzzles which have remained too difficult for the mere state history. *Volkstum* is the true measuring rod of peoples, the right scale to weigh their values."[5]

Even more effective in stimulating early German nationalism was Ernst Moritz Arndt (1769-1860), poet of the War of Liberation. In stirring pamphlets, poems, and songs, Arndt called for a crusade against the French conqueror. He condemned German princes for "selling their people into bondage" and called upon Germans to rise in wrath against Napoleon. "It is possible," he said, "to defeat Napoleon only with his own weapons. His soldiers are ordinary mortals and as soldiers, are less brave than Hungarians, Austrians, and Swedes. . . . German generals. Trust and believe in your men. They are firm, stout-hearted, loyal, and courageous. When the final reckoning comes, . . . they must be inspired by justice and Fatherland!"[6]

Thus was the theme of German expansionism, the heart of Pan-Germanism, expressed. In answering the crucial question: "Where is the German's Fatherland?" Arndt replied: "Where'er resounds the German tongue, Where'er its hymns to God are sung." This was standard operating procedure for German Romantics, all of whom turned their eyes backward to a great legendary past, when the old Imperial Germany had been the cockpit of Europe. All sought to draw strength from German antiquity, German landscape, German language, customs, and art. These three Romantics—Fichte, Jahn, and Arndt—were by no means alone in this quest: similar views were expressed by the Schlegel brothers, Tieck, Novalis, Herder, Schelling, Schleiermacher, and the Grimm brothers. All linked the idea of German liberty with national aspirations. These early nationalists saw no clearly defined ideal Germany: they included in it sweeping claims to territories of the old Empire, in which Germans had settled among non-Germanic peoples. The vague demands were to be continued later when Pan-Germanism developed into an organized movement.

In addition to the early German Romantics, another group of German nationalists began to call for the formation of a powerful European confederation in central Europe under German leadership. Control of *Mitteleuropa*, they claimed, was a necessity for peace on the entire continent.

Foremost among advocates of *Mitteleuropa* was the political economist Friedrich List (1789-1846). A battered and bruised soul during his lifetime, the target of German industrialists and the prey of Austrian secret police,

List was denounced as "revolutionary," "Jacobin," and "demagogue." To Metternich he was "an heroic swindler," "the tool of German manufacturers." Yet, this man was the moving spirit in the formation of the *Zollverein*, the customs union that led eventually to German national unification.[7] He promoted the German railway system, merchant marine, navy, and colonialism, while his theories of political economy—protective tariffs, Greater Germany, and *Mitteleuropa*—paved the way for Germany's industrial progress. Only after his death was List placed on a pedestal as a great German patriot-hero, and hailed as "a great German without Germany," as "Germany's Colbert," an economic genius who embodied the best thinking of Cromwell, Canning, Quesnay, Robert Peel, and even Aristotle.

In his early career List presented his views on German nationalism in liberal terms. Desiring to move away from an antiquated and partly feudal economy, he called for "an independent, free, enterprising, industrially diligent, and prosperous nation." He saw a united Germany much like that of Britain. But somwhere along the line, List's vague liberalism was transformed into a different attitude. Hans Kohn recognized this change when he described List as not only the father of German economic nationalism, but at the same time "one of the most extreme of Pan-German imperialists."[8] In the confrontation between an intensifying nationalism in the Bismarckian power-mold and a weakening German liberalism, List chose the side of the former.

List, like Napoleon before him, urged the formation of a strong Continental System, which, he believed, should be under German control. Here he expressed what was to become the essence of Pan-Germanism. Germany, he said, needed *Ergänzungsgebiete* (supplementary territories), "as much as breath." Even more, he supported an ambitious oceanic policy that would extend German power throughout the world. This idea of "vital living space" later emerged in the Pan-German ideas of such expansionists as Wilhelm II ("Germany needs a place in the sun!") and Adolf Hitler ("We want *Lebensraum* [living space]").

Another champion of the "Central European" idea was the political theorist Constantin Frantz (1817-1891), who became a strong critic of Prussian federalism. He held that both Prussia and Austria must yield to a "higher unity" of a *Mitteleuropa*, a Central European federal union. He recommended that Austro-Prussian rivalry be neutralized only by *Pangermanismus*, an alliance of all Germantic states, including the Netherlands, Scandinavia, and England. Reiterating the old *Drang nach Osten* program, which had been initiated as early as the 9th century, he called for an expanded Germany, not under Hohenzollern but under Hapsburg rule, which would act as a counterbalance between the powerful Americans and flanking Russians. This was a curious blend of Pan-German expansionism and traditional universalism. Later, Frantz called for expansion of his proposed Germanic Bund into a Western European confederation, which would include Belgium, Switzerland, Italy, and Spain.[9]

Such views were held, too, by Orientalist Paul Anton de Lagarde (1827-1891), professor at Göttingen University from 1869 to his death. Lagarde held that the German nation could be united only on the basis of what he called a "national Christianity." He, too, wanted the formation of a powerful *Mitteleuropa* under German leadership, a confederation running from Flanders to the Black Sea, and from Burgundy to the Vistula. Only in this way, he insisted, could European peace be maintained. Like Frantz, Lagarde had a strong anti-Semitic strain in his political thought. He excoriated Jews as a hindrance to a viable federalism, and as "parasitical tapeworms" undermining the organism of the Christian people.[10]

These early apostles of German nationalism set the tone for the Pan-Germanic movement emerging at the end of the 19th century. All considered Germany in desperate need of national unity. In their estimation, German *Kultur* and German *Weltanschauung* (world-view) were far superior to the cultural attributes of other peoples, especially the decadent French, shopkeeper Britons, and barbaric Russians. German expansion, they contended, was logical and necessary. In their minds, the historical continuum was clear-cut—expressed in logical drives toward national unity, German confederation, *Mitteleuropa*, and global Pan-Germanism.

Characteristics of Pan-Germanism

For Pan-Germans it was all very simple. Theirs was a revolutionary movement designed to elevate German-ness to the top of world society. Opposed to both rationalism and traditional religion, they called for a biological racialism based on Indo-European-Aryan-Nordic-Teutonic supremacy.[11] They would bring into perfect union all those who spoke German or a related tongue. The "civilizing mission" was to extend the sort of colonization practiced in the medieval German Empire. First, Pan-Germans would extend their influence to cover *Mitteleuropa* and then continue their mission on a global scale.

How was this goal to be achieved? Starting on the domestic scene, all Germans were expected to be subservient to the centralized authority—in this case the Hohenzollern monarchy. Let others preach the foolish virtues of humanitarianism—the world was composed of tigers and sheep, and it would be best to be tigers. All necessary means should be used to advance the cause—exploitation of irrational emotions, violence, even war as a biological necessity. To Pan-Germans, fanaticism was equated with heroic valor. The true German should sacrifice everything for the cause.

These characteristics, however, explain only a part of the Pan-German movement. Its ideology was never clearly or authoritatively defined. It was a conglomeration of vague, intangible ideals, a mixture which makes analysis difficult. It borrowed its ideas indiscriminately from Machiavellian power principles, biological racialism, hidebound conservatism, populist democracy, Christian Socialism, and Marxian Socialism. It adopted concepts from both Right and Left: from rightist conservatives the idea of subjection to authority, from leftist radicals the unity of state and people. It supported the power principle of a centralized authority, while at the same time calling for a democratically mobilized national consensus.

From conservatives the Pan-Germans drew ideas of the traditional value of hierarchy, biological superiority, territorial imperative, veneration of the national above the international, the placing of caste before class, and veneration of the *Obrigkeit*, the magisterial authority. They rejected the rationalism of the Enlightenment, dismissing it as an invention of the Jews. More important in their eyes were intuition, mysticism, rightist radicalism, and revolutionary fanaticism. They dismissed moderate conservatism as unrealistic, and ridiculed its advocacy of law and order and stability. For Pan-Germans, only an extremist adaptation of conservatism made sense.

In much the same way, Pan-Germans borrowed from democrats and socialists, accepting what coincided with their own goals, and rejecting anything else. Their views were much closer to the later version of Soviet "democratic centralism" ("People's Republics") than to the traditional French, British, Swiss, or American versions of democracy. For Pan-Germans, democracy meant a powerful mass movement of people dedicated to leadership, discipline, and militarism. Democratic criticism of the establishment was permissible whenever the government departed from Pan-German ideals. Here, too, Pan-Germans extracted from democratic forms only those ideas which equipped a *Herrenvolk* (master people) with the "right" kind of nationalism and racialism.

Similarly, Pan-Germans accepted Socialist or Communist revolutionary fervor, while at the same time rejecting the theory of class conflict. They praised the anti-Semitism of Adolf Stoecker (1835-1909),[12] Wilhelm II's court-chaplain, advocate of the anti-Semitic movement in Germany, and founder of the Christian Social Party, as well as the anti-Semitism of Karl Lueger (1844-1910),[13] Viennese politician and co-founder of the Austrian Christian Social Party. At the same time, Pan-Germans criticized both Stoecker and Lueger as being "too sensitive to the old order"—to Church, Army, police, and bureaucracy, instead of relying on mass support by a nationalistically inspired German people.

For Communism and the Internationale, Pan-Germans had only contempt, extracting from them only the efficacy of extremism. Pan-German theorists saw value in Marx, Lenin, and Stalin only in their contempt for moderation, negotiation, compromise, and human rights. Anything for the cause was their position—enemies should be eliminated without pity, and conciliation would be political suicide. Human antagonisms, in their view, were irreconcilable—the winner should take all, the loser should be destroyed. Therefore, victory should be total, enemy surrender unconditional, and the vanquished given no right to salvation. Pan-Germans equated compromise with surrender: they should triumph or disappear.

A dangerous transformation occurred in the nature of Pan-Germanism. In its original form it was merely a general desire to promote the cultural unity of all Germans, no matter where they lived. Later in the century, Pan-Germanism took on an extremist coloration. Preached zealously in the cafés of Vienna, it strongly influenced the young Hitler, who, absorbing the legacy of Pan-Germanism, utilized it to bring on the tragedy of World War II.

The Pan-German League

"My map of Africa lies in Berlin." And again: "A colonial policy for us would be just like the silken sables of Polish noble families who have no shirts."[14] Such were Bismarck's early acidulous reactions to pleas for German colonial expansion. Colonies, he said, were only a means of providing sinecures for officials, too costly for Germany. He saw as obstacles to German colonialism his confrontation with the Catholic Church in the *Kulturkampf*, the irritableness of Britain, the jealousy of France, and Germany's own insecure position in international affairs.

Yet, the great man, always the pragmatist, began to see possibilities in the Dark Continent. By the early 1880s he reversed his stand. That critical conversion marked the change of German nationalism into aggressive expansionism.[15] Bismarck's new attitude captured the imagination of the German people, especially after black African natives were marched through the streets of Berlin. With the new German colonialism came a spurt in Pan-Germanic sentiment.

Behind the new militant nationalism was Dr. Karl Peters (1856-1918), colonial explorer and propagandist, who had won a wide reputation for his travels through Africa. On February 27, 1885, King Wilhelm I issued an imperial rescript, countersigned by Bismarck, giving governmental support and official safe conduct to Peters for territorial acquisitions in East Africa:

We, Wilhelm, by the grace of God, German Emperor and King of Prussia, declare and ordain the following:

According to the then chairman of the Society for German Colonization, Dr. Karl Peters, and our Chamberlain, Felix, Count Behr-Bandeln, have petitioned us for protection for the territorial acquisitions of the society in East Africa, west of the territory of the Sultan of Zanzibar, outside the authority of other powers; and according as the said Dr. Karl Peters in November and December of last year concluded treaties with the rulers of Usagara, Mguru, Useguba, and Ukani, by which these territories were taken over by the Society for German colonization with the right of sovereignty, and has petitioned me to place these territories under our authority; so do we confirm that we have taken over this authority and we have placed these territories under our imperial protection. . . .[16]

In 1886 Peters convened a General German Congress (*Allgemeiner Deutscher Verband*) in Berlin, to which he invited representatives of all national associations, including religious, industrial, and colonial organizations. He was anxious to forge a liaison between Germans at home and abroad, sponsor emigration to German territories abroad, and maintain the spirit of German nationalism in an organization to be called the German League. He soon found difficult and annoying problems. Delegates began to quarrel over procedures. When Peters went off to Africa again, his neophyte organization was left without a guiding hand and in disarray. It was dissolved.

Peters returned from Africa in 1890 still convinced of the necessity for an organization devoted to Pan-German ideals. The enforced resignation of the mighty Bismarck and public disappointment with the Zanzibar Treaty of 1890[17] convinced the general public, and especially members of the older nationalistic organizations, that something must be done to influence the government in the right direction.[18] Accordingly, the Old German League was reconstituted as the General German League.

At first, the new organization proved to be as weak as its predecessor. Membership was open to anyone on the payment of an annual fee of one mark. There was friction as Saxons and Bavarians lined up against Prussians. Moreover, some members were alienated by rising anti-Semitism in their ranks. Membership soon sank from 21,000 to 5,000. Once again the organization seemed to be on the verge of dissolution.

Then entered the gladiator who became the father of Pan-Germanism. Dr. Ernst Hasse (1848-1908), Professor of Colonial Politics at the University of Leipzig and *Reichstag* deputy for Leipzig, conservative, monarchist, and energetic nationalist, took over the management of the society. He attempted to produce a semblance of order. Elected president in 1894 of what was then the Pan-German (*Alldeutscher Verband*), he gave vigorous leadership to the movement until his death. That same year he issued the first edition of *Pan-German Leaves* (*Alldeutsche Blätter*), under the editorship of Dr. Lehr, a publication that became the bible of the movement. The motto of the new organization was that of the Great Elector: "Remember, you are a German."

To solicit members, the newly formed Pan-German League sent out tens of thousands of circulars informing the public that something should be done to counter the apathy that had followed the great events of 1870-1871. National feeling, it was charged, has been nearly destroyed by economic interests and social problems. While other peoples successfully defended the holy traditions of their "race," Germans were consuming their energy in inter-party quarrels. The German public was urged not to place national tasks behind socio-economic ones, and to remember that Germany's development did not end with the year 1871.

The call for action associated Kaiser Wilhelm II directly with the Pan-Germanic idea:

We ought not to forget that beyond the boundary lines compassed by the black, white, and red flag thousands of Germans reside; that the German nation is justified and in duty bound, no less than other nations, to take its share as a dominant power in the history of the whole world; and that, in our progress towards the position of a world power, we only took the first step when the German Empire was founded.

That our demands are not unrealizable was demonstrated by the speech of our Emperor, January 18, 1896, at the banquet in celebration of the foundation of the German Empire, when the Emperor pointed out that Germany had become a world power, whose subjects dwelt in far-off lands, whose interests in the world were estimated at 'milliards' of marks, whose duty it had therefore become to protect the many thousands of Germans in foreign parts, and to link this greater German Empire closer to the home country.[19]

Aims, Policies, and Membership

The aims of the Pan-German League were presented in clear-cut form in the introductory section of its constitution:

1. The Pan-German League seeks to quicken the national sentiment of Germans and especially to awaken and promote racial and cultural homogeneity (*Zusammengehörigkeit*) of all sections of the German people.
2. These aims show that the Pan-German League seeks:
   A. Preservation of German *Volkstum* in Europe and overseas and support of it wherever it is threatened;
   B. Settlement of all cultural, educational, and school problems in ways favorable to German *Volkstum;*
   C. Opposition of all forces that hinder national development;
   D. Furtherance of German interests in the entire world, especially continuance of the German colonial movement.
3. The League pursues its aims through:
   A. Club activities as provided for in its constitution. In countries outside of Germany, members may function under different plans and for special goals, but only with approval of the League's secretary.
   B. Publication of the periodical, *Alldeutsche Blätter.*[20]

In its 1898 Convention, the Pan-German League adopted a list of policies, condensed here:

The Pan-German League is primarily concerned with the following problems: the Polish question; formation of a Big Navy; Anglo-German relations; reform of the citizenship law; conditions in Alsace-Lorraine and North Schleswig; and the foreign policy of the Empire, especially in relation to Austria-Hungary. More specifically, a list indicating the scope of the organization was appended:

1. Adoption of a bill for reorganization of the Navy.

2. Laying of a cable from Kiao-chau to Port Arthur.

3. Strengthening of the German foothold on Kiao-chau.

4. German coaling and cable stations in the Red Sea, the West Indies, and alongside Singapore.

5. German possession of Samoa.

6. Subsidized German steamship lines to Kiao-chau and Korea.

7. Understandings with France, Spain, Portugal, and the Netherlands about the laying of an independent cable from the Congo to German East Africa, Madagascar, Batavia, and Tongkin to Kiao-chou.

8. Development of harbor of Swakapmund in German Southwest Africa.

9. Concessions for business and industry in Asia minor.

10. Raising of funds for German schools in foreign countries.

11. Additional endowment of the Colonization Commission with 100 million marks.

12. Transfer to the west of all local officials and military men of Polish extraction.

13. Guarantee of pay increases to German officials in Polish parts of the East Province.

14. Extension of imperial holdings in Alsace-Lorraine and the Danish border in Schleswig.

15. Use of only German labor in all imperial and state domains.

16. Prohibition of the immigration of "less worthy elements" into the German Empire.

17. Requiring all Germans residing in foreign countries to hold German citizenship.

18. Taxation of foreign-language firms.

19. Prohibition of foreign languages in clubs and meetings.

20. Germanization of all foreign place names in the German Empire.

21. Establishment of a German consulate-general in a German town in Bohemia.

22. Increase in number of German commercial consuls in the Levant, Far East, South Africa, Central and South America.

23. Increase in German public libraries in Eastern provinces, Schleswig, and Alsace-Lorraine.

24. Funds in the colonial office treasury to be used for supporting the education in German schools in the Fatherland of sons of Germans living abroad.

25. Germanization of foreign words in official language, such as *Kommandant* to *Befehlshaber*.[21]

These aims and policies, based as they were upon a strong national sentiment, attracted many people—businessmen, writers, industrialists, farmers, hand workers, retired army officers, landed proprietors, librarians, accountants, clerks, orchestra leaders, and chimney sweeps. Such goals were favored especially by university professors and teachers at lower levels, all of whom actively spread Pan-Germanic doctrines among their students. Membership grew along with the League's prosperity. In 1894 there were 5,742 members, by 1900 there were 21,361.[22] Several factors contributed to an increased membership at the turn of the century: the Anglophobia current in Germany during the Boer War (1899-1902), Wilhelm II's decision to promote a Big Navy, and the demands in Austria for the relief of "distressed Germans" there.

By the end of 1903, there were 41 delegates of the *Reichstag* who also held membership in the Pan-German League. These included Ernst Bassermann and Gustav Stresemann, leaders of the National Party; Wilhelm von Kardorff, leader of the Conservative Party; Liebermann von Sinnenberg, Agrarian and anti-Semite; and Count zu Stolberg-Wernigerode, Vice-President of the *Reichstag*. Other prominent members included Emil Kirdorf, head of Germany's largest cartel; the academician Dietrich Schäfer; Dr. Liman, prominent journalist and author of a work on Bismarck; Herr Lucas, director of the East African Company; and Herr Zeiss, the celebrated optical instrument maker.[23]

Additional support for the Pan-Germanic idea and further membership came from some 50 ancillary organizations, all of which pursued practically identical aims and supported the League.[24] All these associations were actively engaged in promoting *Deutschtum* by various means. Enthusiastic Germans joined several of these societies and associations "in support of the national idea." The Navy League was considered a natural complement of the Colonial Society, both of which were dedicated to the preservation of *Deutschtum*. The Pan-German League was considered "the father of them all," watching over, stimulating, advising, and publicizing them. Leaders of the Pan-German League hoped to merge all ancillary organizations into one central Pan-German association "without detriment to their respective spheres of activity, without even necessitating much alteration in their respective programs, without horrifying any of their respective members, and probably greatly to the advantage of their several and joint efforts, and of their prestige and influence upon 'the General.'"[25]

Activities: Domestic and Foreign

The Pan-German League took an active role in both domestic and foreign affairs. There was scarcely any phase of German political, economic, social, and even religious life on the domestic scene that did not attract its interest. It opposed all movements working "against national development." It devoted itself to fiscal reforms in the Reich, citizenship problems, foreigners living in Germany, emigration, and industrial politics. It worked to placate the Guelphs in Hanover, which had been annexed forcibly to Prussia in 1866. Above all, it inaugurated an intensive propaganda campaign for naval supremacy.

League leadership called loudly for maintaining the borders of the Second German Empire fashioned by Bismarck in 1871. It also demanded ruthless suppression of any enemies inside the Reich, which meant the Germanization of Alsace-Lorraine (*Westmark*), Schleswig-Holstein (*Nordmark*), and Posen and West Prussia (*Ostmark*).[26]

For a thousand years the Germans and French had conflicted over the *Zwischenland*, the "in-between land" of Alsace and Lorraine. By the Peace of Frankfurt, signed on January 28, 1871, Germany received all of Alsace except Belfort and the eastern part of Lorraine. Alsace-Lorraine, an important industrial region, formed Bismarck's "imperial land" (*Reichsland*), held in common by the German states forming the empire. Bismarck immediately began a policy of Germanization, which forced many Alsatians to emigrate to France. The Pan-German League gave its unqualified support to the Iron Chancellor's stratagem.

Special attention was devoted to Alsace-Lorraine in a series of Pan-German Congresses. At the 1899 meeting held in Frankfurt-am-Main, a resolution was passed urging that young men in the *Reichsland* attend German universities throughout the Reich in greater numbers and calling for reforms in the teaching system so that all students would have the advantage of a national German training.[27] At the 1907 Congress held in Wiesbaden, League authorities, after hearing the report of an Alsatian pastor, resolved that too much French was spoken in Alsace, a situation they denounced as dangerous to the national interest.[28] At the Congress of 1909, held in Schandau, a report concerning headway made in abolishing two-language schools in Alsace was received with acclaim.

The League's attitude toward the *Nordmark* was precisely the same. The 1898 Congress held at Mainz denounced the efforts of Danes in Schleswig-Holstein to become subjects of the king of Denmark. "It is high time," according to one resolution, "that we show finally through energetic acts that we are masters in our own house and intend to remain so."[29] It was recommended that the authorities deal with the situation "from the national viewpoint." At the 1907 Congress held at Wiesbaden, a resolution criticized the weak policy of the government in dealing with Danes. It called for suppression of Danish agitation, support for Germans against their Danish neighbors, and assistance for German industry in the area.[30] The 1908 Congress held in Berlin charged that Danes were forcing Germans to sell their land, that Danish political societies were growing in alarming fashion, and that a far-sighted conspiracy against *Deutschtum* was under way. The League warned the German Government to abandon its policy of conciliation supported by liberals: "The German work of a generation is there, in spite of opposition and heavy losses. Let us hope that a change will occur not too late, that a system of political strength and justice, which has been the backbone of *Deutschtum*, shall break the enthusiasm of the foreign nationality." The Congress adopted the slogan: "*Markgraf, werde hart!*" ("*Margrave become hard!*")[31] There were similar reports and resolutions at the 1909 Schandau Congress. *Deutschtum* was urged on its way with "shining shield and clean weapons" to fight for Germanization.[32]

Pan-Germans regarded Germanization of the *Ostmark* as necessary because of threatening Pan-Slavism. They warned the press to raise its voice against the ever-growing Polish danger.[33] The Pan-German League worked together with the H.K.T. Verein (East Mark Association) in agitating for the Germanization of Posen and West Prussia.[34] Both societies called for an increase in the number of German farmers and workers in "this nationally endangered land," expropriation of Polish property, prohibition of immigration of Slavic workers where they would be "nationally dangerous," limitation of other languages than German, and liberal credit facilities for German industrialists and businessmen.

In addition to domestic affairs, the League displayed intense interest in the world position of the German Empire. Close to home were Germans in the Austro-Hungarian Empire, Switzerland, and Belgium. To Pan-Germans, these citizens belonged to the Fatherland, and should not be subjected to the domination of Magyars, Slavs, and Czechs. Again and again at annual Congresses, special attention was devoted to the matter of German rights and privileges in bordering states. In Pan-German eyes, these citizens were distinctly German, devoted to *Deutschtum*, and belonged to the Pan-German entity.

In foreign affairs the Pan-German League took a firm anti-British stand. Germany was supposed to be neutral in the confrontation between Britain and South Africa, but the League paid little attention to neutrality. As early as 1895 the Jameson raid against the Transvaal gave League propagandists an opportunity to excite the nation against British imperialism. During the Boer War from 1899 to 1902, the League set up a special war fund to help Germans leave the fighting area. It sent telegrams of support to Paul Kruger, champion of Boer independence, and others, protested vehemently to London about "British atrocities," and collected money for "blood brothers" in South Africa. When British Colonial Minister Joseph Chamberlain made deprecating remarks about the German Army, he was burned in effigy.[35] When former President Kruger arrived in Europe in 1900, the League exchanged flattering letters with him and sought without success to arrange an official reception in Berlin.

Wherever German interests were concerned anywhere in the world, the League took a stand in defense of national interests. When Germany and the United States clashed over the Samoan Islands in the south central Pacific, the League presented German claims with special zeal.[36] Throughout the Moroccan crises of 1905 and 1911, when the interests of the Triple Alliance and Triple Entente clashed in North Africa, the Pan-German League maintained a heated propaganda campaign in defense of the German Empire. Although Germans had stated earlier that they had no interest in Morocco, Wilhelm II was determined to demonstrate to France that Morocco was independent. On March 31, 1905, he landed at Tangier and in a speech declared Germany's support for the Moroccans. Meanwhile, the League denounced Britain's recognition of French influence in Morocco in return for French recognition of Egypt as a British protectorate. The League called for a protest by the entire German nation.[37] Again, in 1911, the League hailed with delight the dispatch of a German cruiser to Agadir to protect German concerns. After Germany won sections of French Equatorial Africa in exchange for an abandonment of her interests in Morocco, the League, though still unsatisfied, considered its agitation to have been effective.

Officials of the Pan-German League regarded the emigration of Germans to the United States as a matter of grave concern. They called for the "reawakening" of Germans there for *Deutschtum*. They were anxious to build a reservoir of good will among German-Americans in the event that naval rivalry might lead to a clash between Germany and the United States. Germans in the United States, they said, must be educated to a sense of German national pride. American authorities were angered by what they regarded as an unacceptable attitude toward United States citizenship. Moreover, the League's support of Spain during the Spanish-American War caused much indignation in Washington.

The League was more successful in Brazil, where thousands of Germans had emigrated at the end of the 19th century. The League was instrumental in repealing a German law providing that emigrants who failed to register and pay a fee for the privilege during ten years after their emigration, would forfeit their right to German citizenship. When insurrections broke out in Brazil in 1891 against governmental corruption, the League petitioned Chancellor Georg Leo Graf von Caprivi to send a warship to Brazil to protect German interests there.[38] At the same time, the League protested against the von der Heydt proscript, which had prohibited emigration of Germans to Brazil. The proscript was repealed at the insistence of the League. In the eyes of Pan-German leaders, Germans remained Germans no matter where they went.

The Austrian Connection

From its beginning, Pan-Germanism exerted a strong appeal in Austria. Inside Germany, historian Theodor Mommsen, unimpressed by their propaganda, likened Pan-Germans to schoolboys and idiots. In Austria the appeal of Pan-Germanism had a considerably more favorable response. This was due in large part to the efforts of one man, Georg von Schoenerer, who became a crusader for Pan-Germanism.

Georg Ritter von Schoenerer was born in Vienna on July 12, 1842.[39] His name did not match his personality—*schoen* in German means beautiful, handsome, fine, fair, or lovely. Critics saw little that could be termed fine or lovely about a man they described as an arrogant, obnoxious, and vicious petty politician. Although some Austrians revered him as a democrat-at-heart, others reviled him as a barbarian who preferred destruction to creation, vendetta to forgiveness, ideology to human sympathy, crudeness to courtesy, brutal subjection to the brotherhood of man.[40]

Turning his attention to politics, von Schoenerer became a member of the Austrian House of Delegates in 1873. He served there on and off until 1907. Always a controversial figure, he bestrode the political scene like a colossus, reveling in strife, displaying a fiery temper, and denouncing his enemies in fierce tirades. He slandered others; in turn, his enemies reviled him and threatened him with physical violence. Operating in an atmosphere of hatred, he bullied his followers and excoriated his opponents. He accused others of dishonesty and guile, while proclaiming himself as an honest and independent man.

Dissatisfied with the Hapsburg monarchy, Austrian clericalism, and liberalism, Schoenerer in 1879 turned to German nationalism as his legitimate home. In 1882 he took part in fashioning the Linz program dedicated to the supremacy of German over Austrian nationalism. Meanwhile, attributing all the ills of German and Austrian societies to Jews, he became known as Austria's foremost anti-Semite.[41] In 1888 he was imprisoned as a common felon. Restlessly seeking action, he added Roman Catholicism to the list of his *bêtes noires*, was converted to Protestantism, and led the Free from Rome (*Los vom Rome*) movement. From 1897 to 1907 he again served in the Austrian House of Delegates, continuing his career of strife and conflict. He died at Gut Tosenau-bei-Zewttl, Niederoesterreich, on December 12, 1921. At his grave site a simple granite slab bears these words:

Georg Ritter von Schoenerer
Kämpfer für Alldeutschland [Fighter for Pan-Germany]

This was the bizarre character who permanently impressed on the Austrian Pan-German movement an obedience to his own ideas, personality, and standards of behavior.[42] A master of agitational techniques, he was a zealous advocate of the movement. Let others provide the intellectual haze; he was the man of action who would realize the aims and policies of Pan-Germanism. In his view, the Austro-Hungarian Empire was a fraud, and everything about it was to be destroyed in favor of a glorious Pan-Germanism, the capstone of modern morality. Anyone standing in the way should be obliterated.

Schoenerer equated Pan-Germanism with his own personality and character. He gave it direction, made it obedient to his own whims, and insisted that all his followers submit without questions to his orders. The Austrian version of Pan-Germanism came to reflect the life and political ideology of a flamboyant activist.

Typical of Schoenerer's approach was a speech delivered before the Austrian House of Delegates on December 18, 1878, when he spoke of Pan-Germanism as a moral absolute. The audience had other ideas:

More and more I hear in these lands the call: if only we belonged to the German nation. (*Cries of "Hoho! Oho! Oho! not true!" Lively contradiction.*)

As someone said at another time that something was rotten in Denmark, so I will slightly paraphrase the statement and say: "Today in the state of Austria almost everything is rotten." (*Cries of Hoho!*)[43]

Neither in Germany nor in Austria did most people favor a union between the two countries. This kind of constricted expansion, favored by von Schoenerer, clashed uncomfortably with the aims of German *Weltpolitik*, which preferred an overseas goal for Pan-Germanism and was not interested especially in a narrow German-Austrian union. Even Heinrich Class, head of the Pan-German League, rejected the idea of a political union with Austria.[44]

Nevertheless, Pan-Germans inside Germany regarded the fate of Germans living in the Austro-Hungarian Empire as a legitimate concern for their movement. Including German-speaking Austrians was important, as well as Germans elsewhere. Pan-German propagandists tried to attract the attention of Germans living in Austria, Switzerland, and Belgium "without actually interfering in the affairs of those countries." Germans in the conglomerate empire were urged to maintain their language and traditions in the face of Magyars, Slavs, and Czechs.[45] At annual meetings of the Pan-German League, resolutions were introduced invariably proposing that the fight for German rights and privileges in the Austro-Hungarian Empire should never be lessened.[46] The matter was regarded as urgent at the turn of the century, when there began an agitation for universal suffrage in the Dual Empire, which threatened the status of Germans there.

For Schoenerer, Pan-Germanism meant not only the inclusion of Austrian Germans, but those of the entire Austro-Hungarian Empire. He would settle for nothing less than *Anschluss* (union) with Berlin as the base for a powerful global Pan-Germanism.

Pan-Germanism and World War I

The confrontation between Pan-Slavism and Pan-Germanism was one of the remote causes of World War I.[47] The outbreak of the war called for a dramatic expression of the Pan-German program, especially after an initial series of rapid German victories. The German people and, indeed, all the world, expected an overwhelming drive on Paris by powerful German armies, and, perhaps, a quick end to the conflict.

Unfortunately for the Germans, month after month went by without the predicted annihilating advance. In early March 1915 a rumor spread through Europe that the German Government was about to conclude a compromise peace with the Allies. Pan-Germans became alarmed at the prospect. They felt it necessary to warn the German public of what they were fighting for, and what they must do before the war was ended. Junker landowners and wealthy manufacturers, organized in a number of associations,[48] and saw danger in the possibility of Chancellor Theobald von Bethmann-Hollweg being unable to resist the pressure for peace brought on him. Accordingly, five of the six associations drew up a memorandum to be presented to the Chancellor. Afterward joined by a sixth association, they presented the memorandum to the Chancellor on May 20, 1915.

The memorandum presented a straight Pan-German program, including an annexationist policy.[49] The petitioners claimed that they represented the whole German people in their determination to endure to the end, notwithstanding every sacrifice, "in this struggle for life and death which has been forced upon Germany." Because the whole German people recognized this aim as their own, the rumors recently circulating about peace were bound to be most disquieting. "No competent judge would dream of sacrificing Germany's favorable military position in order to conclude a premature peace with any of her enemies."

Germany's aims, said the petitioners, could only be achieved by a peace which would bring her better security for frontiers on both East and West, an extension of the foundations of German sea power, and political, economic, naval, and miltary strength "which will guarantee to us a stronger position in the world." "Any peace which does not bring us these results will make a speedy renewal of the struggle inevitable under circumstances less favorable to Germany. Therefore, no premature peace! For from a premature peace we could not hope for a sufficient prize of victory."

Concessions, continued the petitioners, would be fraught "with the most dangerous consequences for the domestic peace of our Fatherland."

Hundreds of thousands have given their lives: the prize of victory must correspond to the sacrifice.

The petition went on to present the Pan-German program. "We must demand a colonial Empire adequate to satisfy Germany's manifold economic interests, we must safeguard our future policy in matters of customs and commerce, and we must secure a war indemnity to be paid in a form suitable to our requirements." To secure Germany's position against England, Belgium must be subjected to German Imperial legislation, both in military and tariff matters. Walloon and Flemish territory must be separated. "All economic and industrial undertakings and real estate, which are so vital for the government of the country, must be transferred into German hands."

Similarly, French territory must be regarded from the same point of view. French coastal districts from the Belgian frontier approximately as far as the Somme, must be taken by Germany to obtain access to the Atlantic Ocean. The French iron-ore district of Briey must be annexed, as well as the coal country in the *departement* of the Nord and the Pas-de-Calais area.

The petitioners also called for an equivalent annexation of agricultural territory in the East to counterbalance the great additions of manufacturing resources anticipated in the West. Parts of the Baltic Provinces were to be annexed. The war indemnity to be paid by Russia would consist in large measure of cession of land.

"To recapitulate: The realization of the war aims . . . will also guarantee our military strength, and consequently our political independence and power; moreover, we shall thus secure an extended field for our economic activity, which will afford and guarantee increased opportunities for work, and thus benefit our working classes as a whole."

The Six Associations did not limit themselves to presenting their petition to the government, but also printed it in the form of a confidential pamphlet for their members in all parts of Germany. The Wilhelmstrasse, embarrassed by the openly expressed annexation policy of the associations, refused to allow the petition to be reproduced in German newspapers. French and Swiss newspapers, however, obtained copies and printed them within a short time.[50]

Even more expressive of Pan-German sentiment in World War I was the petition of German professors, diplomats, and government officials at a meeting held on June 20, 1915, in the *Kunstlerhaus* (Artists' Hall) to be presented to the German Chancellor. Among the signatories were Dietrich Schäfer, Professor of History at the University of Berlin; Reinhard Seeburg, Professor of Theology at the University of Berlin; and Dr. E. Kirdorf, General Director of the Gelsenheimer Mining Company.[51]

The manifesto was not published in the press, but was circulated privately. Yet it became widely known. Like the program of the Six

Associations, it was attacked by Radicals and Socialists, who objected to it as a Pan-German program falsely said to be a matter of life-or-death for the country.

The manifesto of the intellectuals began on a defensive note by denying that Germany, despite her position of power on the international scene "never thought of transgressing the narrow bounds of her possessions on the European continent with a view to conquest":

To our enemies, however, even these narrow limits and a share of the world's trade necessary to our existence seemed too much, and they formed plans which aimed at the very annihilation of the German Empire. Then we Germans rose as one man, from the highest to the meanest, realizing that we must defend not only our physical existence but also our inner, spiritual, and moral life—in short, defend European civilization (*Kultur*) against barbarian hordes from the east, and lust for vengeance and domination from the west. With God's help, hand in hand with our trusted allies, we have been able to maintain ourselves victoriously against half a world of enemies. . . .

Let us make no mistake. We do not wish to dominate the world, but to have a standing in it fully corresponding to our great position as a civilized Power and to our economic and military strength. It may be that, owing to the numerical superiority of our enemies, we cannot obtain at a single stroke all that is required in order thus to insure our national position; but the military results of this war, obtained by such great sacrifices, must be utilized to the utmost possible extent. This, we repeat, is the firm determination of the German people.

To give clear expression to this resolute popular determination, so that it may be at the service of the Government and may afford it strong support in its difficult task of enforcing Germany's necessary claims against a few faint-hearted individuals at home as well as against stubborn enemies abroad, is the right and duty of those whose education and position raise them to the level of intellectual leaders and protagonists of public opinion. We appeal to them to fulfill this duty.[52]

After denying any intention of aggression, the manifesto of the intellectuals went on to outline an expansionist Pan-German program. Germany must lead the way to *Mitteleuropa*, a concept basic in the Pan-German ideology. The manifesto called for a great belt of German power from the North Sea to the Persian Gulf, to include control of the Turkish Empire. Whereas the Six Associations called for a colonial empire "adequate to satisfy Germany's economic interests," the intellectuals demanded, in addition to German dominance in *Mitteleuropa*, control of *Mittelafrika* as well. Specific expansionist demands included:

1. *France:* Because of the irrepressible demand of the French for *revanche*, the intellectuals called for "rectification of our whole Western frontier from Belfort to the coast." "We must acquire part of the North

French Channel, if possible, in order to be safe strategically as regards England and to secure better access to the ocean. . . . We must have no mercy on France. . . . We must impose on her a heavy indemnity. . . . England will take France's disproportionately large colonial possessions if we do not help ourselves to them."

2. *Belgium.* The intellectuals insisted that the German people considered a firm hold on Belgium an absolutely unquestionable necessity. This would require a prodigious increase of German power, as well as a considerable addition of population. Belgium was to be emancipated from its "artificial grip of French culture" and to recognize the Teutonic affiliation of many of its people.

3. *Russia.* The manifesto urged Germans also to set up a strong boundary wall against Russification. "This demands land which Russian must cede to us." This territory was needed for the increase in German population (an idea later to be called *"Lebensraum"*—living space). The intellectuals argued that Russia, excessively rich in land, would not miss the expropriated territory. "To conclude peace with Russia without the diminution of Russian preponderance, and without acquiring those territorial acquisitions which Germany needs, would be to lose a great opportunity for promoting Germany's political, economic, and social regeneration, and to impose upon future generations the burden of the final settlement with Russia—in other words, Germany and European civilization would be confronted with the certainty of a renewal of their life-and-death struggle."

4. *England.* The ultimate origin of the war, charged the intellectuals, was England's assault on German trade, naval power, and world prestige. "We must wrest a free field for our foreign trade, we must enforce the recognition of our naval power, and our world prestige in spite of England." England's chain of naval bases, which encircled the globe, must be broken by a corresponding number of German bases.

5. *Indemnity.* Indemnities must cover the costs of the war to make restoration possible in East Prussia and Alsace, to guarantee pension funds for cripples, widows, and orphans, for losses "inflicted contrary to international law," and to provide for the renewal and further development of German armaments. "England has set the whole world against us, and chiefly for money. The purse is the sensitive spot in this nation of shopkeepers."

6. Kultur *and Power.* "The German mind is beyond all doubt our one supremely valuable asset. It is the one precious possession among all our possessions. It alone justifies our people's existence and their impulse to maintain and assert themselves in the world; and to it they owe their superiority over all other people. . . . We shall create the necessary healthy body for the German mind. The expansion of the German body which we have demanded will do the German mind no injury."

The manifesto closed with a sentence of Bismarck's: "It is palpably true in politics, if it is true anywhere, that 'faith moves mountains,' that courage and victory are not cause and effect but identical words with one another."[53]

Such was the highly emotional appeal of German intellectuals operating in a war milieu. Under the impact of the war spirit, the offense became a matter of defense. After absolving themselves of expansionist ideas, the petitioners went on to present a Pan-German program that could not possibly have been implemented without aggression, conquest, and annexation. In this sense, Pan-Germanism was similar to other macro-nationalisms—winning the goal of a larger nationalism meant a brusque rejection of the rights of others occupying the same territory. Pan-German intellectuals gauged the issue correctly: it was, indeed, a matter of power.

Pan-Germanism and Allied War Propaganda

Pan-Germanism provided the Allies with a valuable ideological weapon in World War I. In the battle of propaganda which began with the outbreak of the war in August 1914, both Allies and Central Powers sought to build public morale by denigrating the enemy in every possible way. In London, Paris, and later in New York, one book after another was published to denounce Pan-Germanism for its aggressive drive for world control.[54]

The classic attack on Pan-Germanism came even before the beginning of the war. In February 1913, Roland G. Usher, then Associate Professor of History at Washington University in St. Louis, published his *Pan-Germanism*.[55] After the outbreak of the war, he issued a new edition with additional material.[56]

Usher's thesis was simple and direct: aggressive Pan-Germanism was dedicated to the destruction of the British Empire, the disruption of the French Republic, and the domination of the world. "The Germans aim at nothing less than the domination of Europe and the world by the Germanic race."[57] It was an error, Usher claimed, for idealists and advocates of peace to treat Pan-German aggressiveness as unreal. He saw it as a stupendous enterprise, which had fired the spirit of the whole nation. He blamed the situation on Bismarck: "It is literally true that Germany has become Bismarckian. His heavy spirit has settled upon it. It wears his scowl. It has adopted his brutality, as it has his greatness. It has taken his criterion of truth, which is Germanic; his indifference to justice, which is savage; his conception of a state, which is sublime."[58]

Usher cited the vital factor in the international situation to be the aggressive instinct of Pan-Germans. He insisted that the most significant question then before the Anglo-Saxon race [*sic!*] was the truth or falsity of notions of strategic geography, of military and naval organization, of finance and commerce upon which vast schemes were based. If the factors, on which the Germans relied, were what they thought they were, the domination by Germany and her allies could be only a question of time.[59]

Usher's assault on Pan-Germanism was only the forerunner of a series of similar books denouncing Pan-Germanism as having contributed to the outbreak of the war. Allied propagandists presented the movement as a blustering drive for world hegemony which had to be stopped. The propaganda was effective—it was believed widely in the Allied world that an aggressive Pan-Germanism was responsible for the catastrophic blood bath.

Germans protested bitterly against such accusations. They denounced "the lies and calumnies with which our enemies are endeavoring to stain the honor of Germany in her hard struggle for existence—in a struggle that was forced on her." Allied propagandists, they charged, were using the poisonous weapon of the lie against Germans who were never guilty of causing the war. They would carry on to the end as a civilized nation, "to whom the legacy of a Goethe, a Beethoven, a Kant, is just as sacred as its own hearth and home."[60] Allied propagandists used a tone of sarcasm and irony in presenting such denials of aggressive Pan-Germanism.

Pan-Germanism was dealt a devastating blow by the outcome of World War I and the resultant Treaty of Versailles. Among those chiefly responsible for its decline was Thomas Woodrow Wilson, 28th President of the United States, and Allied war leader in the struggle against the Central Powers. In September 1919, during his trip to the West in support of the treaty and the projected League of Nations, Wilson hailed the end of Pan-Germanism. He asked the question, "What was the old formula of Pan-Germanism?" And gave his own answer:

Look at the map. What lies between Bremen and Bagdad? After you get past the German territory, there is Poland. There is Bohemia which we have made into Czechoslovakia. There is Hungary, which is divided from Austria and does not share Austria's strength. There is Rumania. There is Jugo-Slavia. There is broken Turkey; and then Persia and Bagdad.[61]

Wilson was pleased by the part he had played in what he regarded as a battle for decency against Pan-German aggression. But the dragon was not yet dead.

Pan-Germanism in the Nazi Mold

During the Long Armistice from 1919 to 1939, the Pan-German League went into decline, but not Pan-Germanism as an ideology. For a time the League worked in harmony with the parties of the right, notably the *Deutsch-Nationale Volks Partei* and the early National Socialists. Heinrich Class, leader of the Pan-German League, at first welcomed the rise of Hitler, and protested when the Nazi *Fuehrer* was on the verge of being expelled from Germany after the failure of the Munich Beer-Hall *Putsch* in 1923. At that time he saw Hitler as a German patriot who should not be thrown out of the country when Eastern European Jews were being admitted from Poland. But gradually Class began to have doubts about Hitler and finally broke all ties with him. By 1932 the leader of the Pan-German League was publicly comdemning Hitler as an upstart.[62] Hitler, in turn, disbanded the Pan-German League as unnecessary.

Varied Volkish groups continued to propagate the Pan-German faith among the masses, but it was Hitler's National Socialist German Workers' Party which became the strongest champion of the movement. Where Pan-Germans before World War I had regarded the British Empire as the main obstacle to their own goals, Hitler projected his own version of Pan-Germanism and directed it primarily to the east. For him the Soviet Union became the prime enemy.

In Hitler's hands, Pan-Germanism took on a new and extremist form, a blending of absolute faith in Indo-European-Aryan-Nordic supremacy and a cult of violence to achieve its objectives. From his early days he became the driving force behind the new Pan-Germanism.

Most historians recognize this development. Konrad Heiden spoke of the Hitler regime as "a child of the Pan-Germans."[63] Hannah Arendt wrote that "Nazism . . . owes more to Pan-Germanism . . . than to any other ideology or political movement."[64] Hitler, himself, showed his deep interest in Pan-Germanic ideals. As a young man he claimed that he refused to report for military service because his Pan-Germanic outlook would not allow him to mingle with a motley collection of nationalities, including even Jews.[65] At his trial for treason in Munich (February 26-March 24, 1924), he described himself as "Pan-German in my convictions."[66] However, he preferred his own version of Pan-Germanism. In *Mein Kampf*, he wrote about the strength and weakness of the movement: "The Pan-German movement was quite right in its main views about the aims of a German regeneration, but it was unfortunate in its choice of means. It was, indeed, nationalistic but unfortunately not social enough in order to win support of the masses. Its anti-Semitism, however, was based on the correct understanding of the racial problem and not on religious ideas."[67] Hitler would take the unsatisfactory Pan-Germanism of the past and endow it with a social tinge in his blending of nationalism and socialism.

It was the grievous misfortune of the German people to fall under the sway of an Austrian who, in the view of most historians, takes rank with Attila the Hun and Joseph Stalin as one of the most vicious human beings in recorded history. For more than 12 years, from 1933 to 1945, Hitler controlled the destiny of the Germans in what was supposed to be a Thousand-Year Reich. Millions of German lives were sacrificed and billions in property destroyed in the Nazi campaign to implement the goals of Hitler's special form of aggressive Pan-Germanism. Trapped in an iron dictatorship, unsuspecting Germans paid dearly for their confidence in Adolf Hitler. The great German poet Johann Wolfgang von Goethe is said to have made a prescient observation: "May God help the German people if ever a Napoleon appears among them." Unfortunately, Germans got their Napoleon.

According to *Mein Kampf*, German nationalism appealed to Hitler even in his early years. As a young pupil, he listened enthusiastically to his teacher, Dr. Leopold Pötsch, at the Realschule at Linz. "We sat at the feet of our old professor, often enthusiastic to the bursting point, sometimes even breaking into tears. . . . Our little version of national fanaticism was a means by which he could educate us; he only had to appeal to our national honor in order to bring us around to his viewpoint more quickly than he could in any other way."[68] Like his teacher, the young Hitler rejected the Hapsburg house as a misfortune for Germany, and called for the absorption of Austria in a Greater Germany. "When I look back after so many years, I see one thing of importance in my childhood. First, I became a nationalist. Second, I learned to understand and grasp the real meaning of history. . . . When I was but fifteen years old, I knew the difference between dynastic 'patriotism' and racial 'nationalism,' and at the time I knew only the latter."[69] Even though he was an Austrian, as a child he sang, "*Deutschland über Alles!*" with fervor. He preferred it to the "*Kaiserlied*" in spite of warnings at school. "In a short time I developed into a fanatical German nationalist."[70]

In Vienna, where he failed to pass the entrance examination for the Painting Academy, the young Hitler learned about the views of the Pan-German von Schoenerer, and was duly impressed. In 1912, when he went to Munich, the capital of Bavaria ("A German city! What a difference from Vienna!"), he became even more aware of Pan-Germanic doctrine and the anti-Semitism which went along with it.

After his experience in the war and his entrance into politics, Hitler began to have grandiose ideas about his future. He would work to unify all those of German "race," starting with *Anschluss* (union) with his native Austria. Then would come the day when millions of Germans living abroad, such as those in the Sudetenland in Czechoslovakia, would be brought home. It was absolutely necessary, he believed, to revive German power by extending Otto I's medieval First Reich (962) and Bismarck's Second Reich (1871) into a new and vigorous Third Reich. It was Germany's mission, he was sure, to erase the boundaries set up in central and eastern Europe by the iniquitous treaties of Versailles, Saint-Germain, and Trianon. Germany must control *Mitteleuropa* as the starting point for a revived Pan-Germanism.

After the unsuccessful Beer-Hall *Putsch* in 1923, Hitler was sentenced to prison at Landsberg-am-Lech. Here, from one of his fellow prisoners, Rudolf Hess, he learned about a new political theory, geopolitics, which was to become the core of his expansionist Pan-Germanism. Behind the concept was political theorist Karl Haushofer.[71] Born on June 27, 1867, in Munich, Haushofer was commissioned in the Bavarian army in 1880. He served for two years in Japan (1908-1910), during which time he studied Japan's expansionist policies in Asia. He was promoted to major general in 1910 and held that post through World War I. In 1921 he became Professor of Geography at the University of Munich, where he had obtained his doctorate.

To justify Germany's role as a great power, Haushofer came to the conclusion that Pan-Germanism was the logical historical expression of the country's need for living space (*Lebensraum*). In 1924 he founded the journal, *Zeitschrift für Geopolitik*, of which he became editor and principal contributor. At Munich he created a new Institute of Geopolitics.

The geopolitical theory promoted by Haushofer was a mixture of both sound and hazy scientific principles, a blend of geography, political science, and contemporary topical politics. Much of it was based on the work of German geographer Friedrich Ratzel, who saw the state as a biological organism; and the Swedish political scientist, Rudolf Kjellen, who conceived of the state as an organism with a natural right to growth. An additional forerunner was Sir Halford John Mackinder, British political geographer, who conceived of the globe as divided into two "heartlands," the dominant Eurasian heartland and the subordinate maritime lands, including all the other continents.

Haushofer became an enthusiastic champion of Mackinder's heartland theory. After the defeat of his Fatherland in World War I, he began to call for its regeneration by "growing into its largest living space." Of the several ideal heartlands in the world, he saw a critically important one in a combination of Germany (industry) and Russian Ukraine (wheat). He, therefore, called for Russo-German collaboration. It was the right of every country, Haushofer said, to hold territory sufficient to support its population. This did not necessarily mean a policy of conquest, but a reversion to a normal state of affairs.

Budding young politician Hitler was fascinated by Haushofer's thinking. He accepted its basic tenets, but rejected the notion that Germany's *Lebensraum* could be won without conquest. Germany must stand up for her rights, destroy the iniquitous Treaty of Versailles, and smash her own way to living space. For the *Fuehrer*, the only way Germany could again become a world power was through military force, not through the good grace of her enemies.

Haushofer was destined for a tragic end. During the early years of World War II, he passionately defended Germany's right to expansion. He opposed the invasion of the Soviet Union because it meant war on two fronts. He soon became suspect because he was married to a woman of Jewish descent, the ultimate crime in the *Fuehrer's* lexicon of criminal behavior. His eldest son, Albrecht, Professor of Geopolitics at Berlin, and who had won a name for himself as a distinguished poet, joined the underground conspiracy against Hitler. He was arrested by the *Gestapo*, and executed as a traitor. Haushofer, himself, was imprisoned after the July 20, 1944, attentat on Hitler's life. After the war he faced the prospect of trial for alleged war crimes. On March 13, 1946, he and his wife committed suicide.

While Haushofer was the dominating influence in molding Hitler's special brand of Pan-Germanism, there were others who contributed to his understanding of the movement. For his blend of racialism and Pan-Germanism, Hitler turned to the French diplomat and social thinker, Count Joseph-Arthur de Gobineau (1816-1882), whose idea of racial determinism had an enormous influence, especially in Germany, upon the subsequent development of racial theories.[72] Similarly, Hitler was well acquainted with the work of Houston Stewart Chamberlain (1855-1927), Germanophile English political philosopher, whose advocacy of Aryan racial and cultural superiority had an enormous influence upon Pan-German and German nationalist thought.[73]

Added to Gobineau and Chamberlain were such writers as Hans Grimm (1875-1959), whose popular expression of Pan-Germanism in *Volk ohne Raum* ("People Without Space") [1926] helped create a favorable climate in Germany for the spread of extreme expansionism. Grimm contrasted the wide-open spaces of South Africa with Germany's "cramped position" in Europe, a point of view which Hitler supported throughout his career. Hitler paid special attention to the work of Ewald Banse, geographer and author of *Raum und Volk im Weltkriege* ("Space and People in the World War") [1933]. Banse combined Pan-German ideals with the cult of militarism: "The sword will come into its own again, and the pen, after fourteen years of exaggerated prestige, will be put in its place. Certainly the pen is good but the sword is good too and often far better, and we want both to be equally honored among the German people."[74] Immediately after Hitler came to power, Banse was appointed Professor of Military Science at Brunswick Technical College.

It is unnecessary here to present the overwhelming evidence of Hitler's guilt as an aggressor in World War II. Virtually all competent historians on the World War II era agree that documents and actions reveal his expansionist goals and his determination to achieve them through military action. In England, where eccentricity is condoned and even encouraged, an Oxford don, Fellow at Magdalen College, once described as "a professional thrower of banana skins," emerged to present a revisionist view of the origins of World War II. The English public greeted his hyperbole with much amusement.

The accepted view of Hitler's war guilt is clear-cut and obvious. Prime Minister Neville Chamberlain's policy of appeasement at Munich had failed to satisfy the *Fuehrer's* growing demands and his increasingly aggressive actions in central Europe, all of which culminated in the unprovoked move on Poland on September 1, 1939. Hitler's attack on June 22, 1941, on Soviet Russia, with which he had concluded a non-aggression pact almost two years before, added emphasis to his will to war. His words in *Mein Kampf* and his *Table Talk* suggested a premeditated plan for world conquest. There is solid evidence in the "Hossbach Memorandum" of November 5, 1937, in which Hitler stated his intentions to deal with Czechoslovakia. There is additional proof in his confidential remarks to his generals on August 22, 1939, one day before signing the Non-Aggression Pact with Soviet Russia and one week before the invasion of Poland. No sophistry, no doublespeak, no extenuating circumstances can argue away Hitler's plans for aggression and his actions in seeking to implement them.

The Oxford don was A.J.P. Taylor, a prolific writer, who had published works on German colonial policy, the Hapsburg monarchy, European diplomacy, World War I, and recent English history. His *The Course of German History* (1946) is considered to be one of the most brilliant works on recent German history ever published. He was much admired for his superb writing style.

Then in 1961 Taylor published his *The Origins of the Second World War*, a book which astonished and bewildered historians everywhere. He implied that Hitler was not guilty of being the prime instigator of the war, as charged in the Nuremberg Trials. The main responsibility, according to Taylor, should be placed on Chamberlain and others, who by their own errors pushed Hitler into action. British mistakes helped bring on the war. Hitler himself, said Taylor, was a blunderer who was pressed into aggression by outsiders under circumstances beyond his control. He was not a maniac bent upon world conquest, but instead, a traditional German statesman in the category of Frederick the Great, Bismarck, and Gustav Stresemann. Like the statesmen of Weimar, he wanted a peaceful revision of the Treaty of Versailles. He did not plan war with Britain and France in 1939, or at any other time. The only war Hitler wanted, argued Taylor, was the one in which he excelled—the war of nerves. He had no way of knowing that Britain and France would fight for Danzig.

Mein Kampf, said Taylor, was simply a grandiose day dream. Hitler's *Table Talk* was merely the conversation of a conqueror, corrupted by success, who "dreamt of some fantastic Empire which would rationalize his career of conquest." The documents produced at Nuremberg were part of a loaded "lawyer's brief," to be approached with caution. Taylor deprecated the famous Hossbach Memorandum as not a discussion of foreign policy or plans for conquest, but rather an argument purely for domestic consumption. The British author merely ignored the conference of August 22, 1939.

Taylor's book caused a storm of controversy. Critics denounced it as a whitewash of Hitler and as an apology for appeasement. The most devastating criticism came from Taylor's colleague, Hugh R. Trevor-Roper, Regius Professor of Modern History at Oxford (apparently, Trevor-Roper and Taylor were rivals for the post).[75] Trevor-Roper charged Taylor with wilfully misusing documents ("perversion of evidence"); with being an apologist for Hitler, Stalin, and appeasement; and with strengthening the forces of neo-fascism. Taylor's book was "demonstrably false" and "utterly erroneous," even if it was written with the author's "old resources of learning, paradox, and *gaminerie*." "Is it, as some have suggested, a gesture of posthumous defiance to his former master, Sir Lewis Namier, in revenge for some imagined slight?"

Taylor refused to retreat. He merely thanked his critics for "the free publicity they have given my book."[76] In the United States the book was condemned almost unanimously: according to Taylor "because American professors dislike revising their lecture notes."[77] Only Harry Elmer Barnes, World War I revisionist historian, gave it a favorable American review.

There is little point in entering the vitriolic debate here. Defenders of Taylor explain that he wrote in irony. If so, this was a serious flaw in historical writing, where ambiguity makes little sense. Hitler's Pan-Germanism cannot be dismissed by smartalecky history—even from the pen of the gifted A.J.P. Taylor.

The End of Pan-Germanism

Hitler's version of Pan-Germanism died with him in the cloud-cuckoo-land of his Berlin bunker on April 30, 1945. Its intellectual base was suffocated by Haushofer's suicide a year later. Haushofer was falsely identified as a Nazi. He had the somewhat naive notion that Germany could win her living space by intelligent argument, arbitration, and treaty, an unrealistic assumption in a world of power politics governed by brute force. Germany's catastrophic defeat in World War II brought an end not only to the Third Reich and its European hegemony but to any possibility of the union of Germany and the Ukraine as Haushofer's favorite heartland. In the Federal Republic of West Germany, Haushofer's and Hitler's versions of Pan-Germanism were removed from the category of a realizable dream to the status of a terrible nightmare.

CHAPTER 4

PAN-EUROPA: DISTANT AND FRAGILE DREAM

> The peoples of Europe have only to wake up one morning and resolve to be happy and free by becoming one family of nations, banded together from the Atlantic to the Black Sea for mutual aid and protection. One spasm of resolve! One single gesture!
> —Winston Churchill, Zürich, 1946

> The creeping vine of national egoism grows and threatens the future of the continent.
> —Hans Apel, West German State Secretary
> for European Affairs, 1974

The Fissiparous Tribes of Europe

Throughout its history the continent of Europe has been beset by two opposing forces—unity and fragmentation. The urge for unity appeared as early as the 4th century B.C., when the independent city-states of Greece, highly civilized but militarily weak, found their liberty threatened by such powerful neighbors as Macedonia and Rome. As a countermeasure they decided to seek the benefits of unity. In the process they made the mistake of forming two combinations instead of one, the Aetolian League in northern Greece and the Achaean League in the south. Nevertheless, both unions were pioneers in solving the problem of how democratic peoples could build supranational institutions without severely damaging their own identities.[1]

Militant Romans were able to achieve an even greater unity. They saw all western Europe as their natural domain, and for some centuries were able to maintain a comparatively stable state. But even the mighty Roman Empire was destined for dissolution. There developed a conflict between three distinct powers contending for dominance—the old Roman superstructure, the new Christianity, and the German barbarians. Caught between these powerful contending forces, Rome finally collapsed in 476 A.D. Charlemagne (Charles the Great—*Der grosse Karl* to the Germans) fashioned a Christianized Roman Empire later to be called the Holy Roman Empire (Voltaire is credited with describing it as "neither holy, Roman, nor an empire"). There was, indeed, a new unity, but it was not a firm one. Maintained shakily by Charlemagne's successors, the Carolingian Empire was grounded on religion, in which a supranational organization controlled multitudinous states, a combination of Church and State, of Pope and Emperor.

The Middle Ages saw increasing fragmentation. The characteristic medieval institutions were feudalism, a system of polity based upon the relationship of lord to vassal (homage, service of the tenants, wardship, marriage, reliefs, aids, escheat, and forfeiture), and manorialism, which governed the means of landholding. Catholicism was the binding factor—everyone was a member of a universal church governed from Rome. Citizenship was not French, German, or English, but Roman Catholic. There were no "French" people as such, but peoples of Brittany, Languedoc, Burgundy, and Picardy. At this time, the word "nation" from the Latin *nasci* (to be born) referred to what was essentially a tribal community, to those who happened to live in one particular region.

Medieval Catholicism seemed on the surface to be a unifying force, but there were increasing signs of dissolution. Toward the end of the Middle Ages, successive Popes began to abandon their role as spiritual leaders of Christendom and started to function as temporal princes. Prestige of the papacy began to sink to a level where it was unable to maintain the spiritual unity of the West. There were disruptions, challenges first by Huss and Wycliffe and later by Luther and Calvin.[2] The Protestant Reformation in the early 16th century resulted in the formation of many diverse Christian sects, each certain of its own interpretation of the Christian message. The old continental-wide loyalty to a single Catholic Church (the Latin term *catholicus* means universal or general) gave way to national churches. Europe turned to a fissiparous modern tribalism called nationalism.

The key development in this new tribalism came with the French Revolution in ten years that shook the world. What had been achieved under Christian auspices was rejected by French Jacobins. The new skepticism stressed in the Enlightenment led to doubts about the sovereignty of a single supranational God. Church and State were separated permanently. Christianity was relegated to the role of a passive clericalism.

Despite the emotional drama of the French Revolution, the old urge for continental unity did not disappear as the 18th century merged into the 19th. At this point a Corsican-Frenchman was propelled into power in a France close to anarchy, and set out to use his military strength to mold Europe into one mighty state. After some years of conquest, his career was dashed on the wintry plains of Russia and on the rock of British determination. In exile at St. Helena, a chastened Napoleon made the familiar excuse that he only wanted to form a workable United States of Europe. Instead of winning continental union, he actually stimulated the fires of nationalism in nations to which he brought his conquering armies. "Who counsels peace," asked poet Robert Southey, "when innocent blood from the four corners of the world cries out for justice upon one accursed head."[3]

From the Napoleonic era on, the struggle of nations became the theme of modern European history, with accumulated hatreds between peoples, international boundary disputes, wars, and revolutions. The alternate ideology to medieval ecclesiastical union was split into liberalism and nationalism. Liberalism took on the tint of Voltaire's call for tolerance and Adam Smith's *laissez-faire* philosophy. The 19th century was to be burdened by increasing economic discontent, which led to the explosions of 1830 and 1848. Liberalism gave way to the powerful force of nationalism. This extension of primitive tribalism was said to be rooted in the elemental instincts of man.[4] The policy of fragmentation continued as Europe broke down into a multiplicity of separate states, each with its own structure which, although they did not always act in total isolation from one another, came together only in temporary *ad hoc* groupings.[5]

What kind of nationalism was it to be—the humanitarian nationalism of Herder or a more integral form?[6] A Prussian Junker presented the key to the century when he made a famous declaration of policy in which he stated that the great questions of the day would be settled not by speeches and parliamentary majorities but by iron and blood.[7] Throughout his career Otto von Bismarck, always acting on the power principle, worked to maintain the *status quo*, to assure Prusso-Germany's political supremacy, economic health, and military efficiency. He had little use for William Ewart Gladstone's Concert of the Powers, "the highest and most authentic of modern Christian civilization," nor for Gladstone's public law of Europe. In his stiff form of traditional conservative nationalism, Bismarck represented accurately the thinking of other European statesmen. To them Europe was a combination of multitudinous but separate nation-states, each with its own problems. They saw the idea of an integrated Europe as nothing more than political evangelism, outside the proper range of any *Realpolitiker*. Twentieth-century successors to these statesmen were imbued equally with this narrow nationalistic ideology.

Urge for European Integration

This drift toward fragmentation in the neo-tribalism that is nationalism did not mean necessarily the obliteration of calls for European integration.[8] There were sporadic efforts at unity by eminent Europeans. The idea had been presented as early as the 14th century by Dante and the 16th century by Machiavelli. In 1849, in the midst of concurrent outbursts of nationalism throughout the continent, novelist Victor Hugo presented the concept of a "United States of Europe." The idea persisted for the next century. Adolf Hitler, too, looked forward to a United States of Europe, but under Nazi control. His proclaimed "Thousand-Year Reich" was intended to include all Europe. In his case, the dream turned into a nightmare, fulfilling the forecast of Austrian poet Franz Grillparzer that "the road leads from humanity through nationalism to bestiality."

The call for Pan-Europa intensified after World War II. Whereas Pan-Slavism and Pan-Germanism had been dominantly linguistic and cultural,

Pan-Europeanism turned out to be primarily geographical and economical, and secondarily political. Those who called for European unity were disgusted with the plethora of passports, currencies, and tariffs on the continent. Faced with the new rivalry between the United States and the Soviet Union, Pan-Europeans aimed to project Europe as a third major world power. They would seek to remove the strictures of the old nationalisms.

First things first. Pan-Europeans deemed it a necessity to move slowly. They would first pool their economic resources, especially in agriculture, in a common market, whose economic measures would be designed to benefit all members of the union. Production and consumption of foodstuffs and goods would be planned carefully for European needs with every member contributing to the common goal.

All this, in the view of Pan-Europeans, would be but preliminary to the political unification of continental nation-states. Countries taking part in the new venture would elect delegates to a European parliament situated in Strasbourg. Eventually, this democratically elected body would present the world with a united European front, and take its place as representative of the third politico-economic power on earth.

So much for the dream. For a mystical reverie it was, despite exaggerated claims of its proponents. We shall see that, after a somewhat uncertain start, the European Economic Community (EEC) actually was translated into some kind of reality. Members adhered, at first reluctantly, to quotas for the production of eggs, hams, and fruit. The idea was attractive: to work for common economic goals, for everyone's benefit.

We shall also see, however, that there was little support for the long-awaited transfer from economic to political unity. Each European state duly elected members to the European Parliament. Delegates at Strasbourg delivered eloquent sermons on the desirability of European union. But at home the government of each nation-state had not the slightest intention of cutting its sovereignty in favor of continental political union. Economic agreement—yes, as long as the national interest was not weakened; political union—emphatically, no.

In considering the Pan-European dream, we can see once more an illustration of the themes of this study: (1) we are firmly embedded still in the era of the nation-state; (2) established nationalisms take precedence over the larger macro-nationalisms and the smaller mini-nationalisms; and (3) far from diminishing in strength, a sense of national consciousness, the neo-tribalism of the contemporary era, seems to be growing ever stronger throughout the world.

Democratic Federalists versus Functionalists

Behind the call for Pan-Europeanism were several perplexing questions. Would there be a new unitary European state? Would there be a league of national states, each maintaining its independence and bound together only by an economic customs union? Would Europe be a federal state, a federation of states, or a confederation? Would it be a community of some kind?[9] Stated in summary, would the new United States of Europe be a state, community, or federation, acting as a balance between the United States and the Soviet Union? Would it be a political "*Europe des états,*" a Europe of states, or merely, as Charles de Gaulle envisioned, a loose political union with economic ties?

Such were the questions posed after the tragedy of World War II when Pan-Europeans recommended a new extended nation-state covering the entire continent, much like the conventional nations of the past, only much larger, as a means of preventing a possible third World War. The old European structure, they said, had made the two global conflicts inevitable, with a terrible loss of life and great destruction of property. In their view, a continental union would be effective in preventing those dangerous politico-economic clashes in the old nation-state system that had led directly to confrontation and war. In their minds the form of unity was less important than the absolute necessity for union of some kind.

A dichotomy in federalist ideology was in the making. On the one side were democratic federalists, on the other, functionalists. Democratic federalists saw the root cause of Europe's troubles in the system of self-interested federal states. They viewed Europe as a collection of more than thirty fragmented nations, each acting unilaterally in a balance-of-power system. Separated by trade barriers, large and small nations during the Long Armistice between World Wars, 1919 to 1939, went straight ahead to impending economic collapse. The situation was made-to-order for such exploitative dictators as Mussolini and Hitler. The only hope for avoiding such a catastrophe in the future, according to the democratic federalists, was a total merger of European strength. Nationalism, they argued, had reached its peak, and was on the verge of being succeeded by international communism. Only a new unified Europe would be able to maintain the peace.

Functionalists, on the other hand, presented a less drastic view. They supported the general idea of federalism, but they recommended a functional approach to integration—a step-by-step advance toward unity. The nation-state, in their view, would retain independence in the new polity, but would agree to pool its sovereignty and allow limited functions but real power over a portion of their economies. There would be a long pause after each step in the process to assess the realistic functioning of proposals before uniting in action in another sector.[10]

The democratic federalists of the United European Movement looked to Winston Churchill for inspiration. The old war horse had spoken eloquently of the need for a Europe purged of ancient slavery, a continent on which men would be proud to say: "I am a European." Millions were influenced by Churchill's words, as they had been during the trying days of the war. But when federalists on the Continent called for a European federal parliament, France at first supported the proposal but Britain rejected it. To the dismay of democratic federalists, when Churchill was returned to power he explained that his vision of a federated Europe, which he had proclaimed while he was in the Opposition, was limited to a union of nations on the Continent, not one including Britain. France and Germany, he said, must work together for continental unity, while Britain would approve the reconciliation from the sidelines. For democratic federalists, Churchill's change of heart was a bitter blow.[11]

Functionalists saw themselves as less concerned with democratic institutions than with inter-governmental contacts. They would become the bureaucrats, technocrats, the elites who would supervise the steps of European integration.[12] They regarded themselves as *Realpolitiker* in the Bismarckian sense, the governors of the step-by-step process, far advanced beyond the vague do-goodist ideology of democratic federalists.

The debate between democratic federalists and functionalists came to a head when the Soviet Union acquired a nuclear capability and when Washington demanded that the Federal Republic of West Germany be brought into the Western alliance. Democratic federalists, unable to win support for the projected political Council of Europe, at long last agreed that the functionalists' step-by-step approach was the only practical procedure under the circumstances. Both sides agreed that a Franco-German reconciliation, recommended by Churchill, was in order. But it was also felt that Pan-Europa must go far beyond Churchill's golden words and be given a cast-iron mold. Jean Monnet, then head of France's national planning board, seized the initiative and proposed the creation of the European Coal and Steel Community (ECSC) to Robert Schuman, then Foreign Minister of France. The entire French and German steel, iron, and coal resources on each side of the frontier would be placed under a common authority.

This was the initial step in postwar European economic integration. Democratic federalists and functionalists agreed to a truce. To win the support of functionalists, the system was to be called a community.

Enter Coudenhove-Kalergi

The human animal is a persistent creature. Again and again a loner appears who is so convinced of the sacred truth of his cause that he transforms advocacy into a crusade. Such a man was the Austrian Count Richard N. Coudenhove-Kalergi, who during the Long Armistice between the two World Wars, projected his federalist Pan-Europa. Small in stature but a giant in resolution, he received little popular support for his movement, but that made no difference to a fiery zealot.

Of mixed parentage, Coudenhove-Kalergi was born in Tokyo on November 16, 1894, the son of the *chargé-d'affaires* in the Austro-Hungarian embassy and Mitsui Aoyama, an upper-class Japanese girl fifteen years younger than her husband. The boy grew up in Bohemia in a household that included nine nationalities. Early in life he became convinced that nationalism was a dangerous historical phenomenon, and that cooperation should be the goal of all civilized human beings. In his view, nationalism was "a terrifying force," and it might continue to exist for centuries to come.

While studying in Vienna for his doctorate, Coudenhove-Kalergi was appalled by the Pan-Germanism advocated by his fellow students, and especially by the rampant anti-Semitism in Viennese circles. Exempt from military service in World War I because of a lung condition, he became a passionate Wilsonian after the entry of the United States into the war. After the war he became an ardent advocate of the League of Nations, and regarded himself as a citizen of the world. He decided to work "not for one country but for the brotherhood of man." He was saddened by the inability of the League to rise above "the law of the jungle" in relations between twenty-six nations of Europe. What was needed desperately, in his view, was a federated Europe on the model of the United States and Switzerland. To implement that goal became his lifelong pursuit.

Coudenhove-Kalergi was convinced that the League of Nations could not possibly work without U.S. participation. He urged the reorganization of the League into six autonomous regional units—the British Commonwealth, the Soviet Union, Pan-Europa, Pan-America, China, and Japan. There could be no united world, he warned, with a disunited Europe. League officials were not impressed. They saw the suggestion as contrary to the spirit of a world organization.

Undiscouraged, Coudenhove-Kalergi went ahead with his one-man crusade. In 1922 he presented the first draft of his program for Pan-Europa in the *Neue Freie Press* (Vienna) and the *Vossische Zeitung* (Berlin). He then began to search for the support of important sponsors. Walther Rathenau, Thomas Masaryk, and Joseph Caillaux, all distinguished statesmen, gave him encouragement, but did not or could not head his movement. He appealed to Mussolini to help promote a European federation, but was met by uncharacteristic silence. He decided to go on alone.

Coudenhove-Kalergi began publishing a long series of books on the Pan-Europa idea.[13] He traveled throughout Europe delivering lectures for his cause. He enlisted the support of Winston Churchill, Aristide Briand, José Ortega y Gasset, and others. Coming to the United States in 1925, he reorganized the American Cooperative Committee for the Pan-European Union under the chairmanship of the educator Dr. Stephen Pierce Duggan, head of the Institute of International Education.[14]

Convinced that he was making headway, Coudenhove-Kalergi in

October 1926 called the Pan-European Congress in Vienna, the first of a series of such meetings. Twenty-four hundred supporters from many European nations attended the gathering, and unanimously elected Coudenhove-Kalergi as President of the Pan-European Union.

The Second Pan-European Congress was convened in Berlin in May 1930. This time there was considerably less enthusiasm. The British, still obsessed with the old traditional balance of power, blocked Briand's efforts for union.[15] The Germans, with Stresemann dead, seemed to have lost sympathy for the European idea.

The third Pan-European Congress, held at Basel in 1932, was overshadowed by the menacing rise of Nazism. Coudenhove-Kalergi denounced Hitler and National Socialism, for he deplored the revival of Pan-Germanism with a Nazi tinge. As soon as he came to power in 1933, Hitler struck back by banning the German Pan-European Union.

The Fourth Pan-European Congress convened in Vienna in May 1935, the Fifth Congress in November 1937.[16] Coudenhove-Kalergi called for the introduction of Pan-European schools, as well as for the elimination of duties on agricultural goods. This was the first projection of the Common Market idea.

In March 1939, after ordering an invasion of Czechoslovakia in flat defiance of his Munich pledge, Hitler proclaimed annexation of the country. Coudenhove-Kalergi opted for French citizenship. He called for an international meeting for European union, while at the same time working for Pan-Europeanism among delegates of the French Chamber of Deputies. In April 1940 he called on the French Pan-European Committee to achieve Franco-British unity. After the fall of France, he left for the United States.

As research associate in history at New York University, Coudenhove-Kalergi headed a Seminar for Postwar European Federation. In March 1943, shortly after Churchill had made a speech favoring a United States of Europe, Coudenhove-Kalergi called the Sixth Pan-European Congress. The next year he drew up a constitution for a United States of Europe, and submitted it to all the heads and foreign ministers of nations represented in the United Nations. He included provisions for a central European bank; unification of the European transportation system; European free trade; a Continental customs union; a federal army; a "House of States" with one delegate for each small nation and two for each large one; a House of Representatives with one to ten delegates per state; an Executive Council elected by both houses and consisting of one delegate per state; a President elected for a one-year term; and Supreme Court judges appointed by the Executive Council.

In 1947, at a meeting held at Gstaad, Switzerland, the European Parliamentary Union was founded with Coudenhove-Kalergi as Secretary-General. The passionate crusader seemed to be making progress.

There was, however, an underlying weakness. Coudenhove-Kalergi's idea of Pan-Europa attracted the attention and support of like-minded intellectuals, but, unfortunately, it lacked a mass base. This did not deter the energetic Austrian, nor was he discouraged when European statesmen returned to the dangerous traditions of prewar diplomacy. But the impulse for Pan-Europa began to pass to other hands.

Eventually, Coudenhove-Kalergi's draft constitution for a United States of Europe was to be realized in the formation of the European Parliament. However, this institution, as we shall see, was to become an ineffective extension of economic union. Neither Coudenhove-Kalergi nor the European Parliament succeeded in winning mass support for Pan-Europa.

Schuman and Monnet

Macro-nationalisms are usually generated in the minds of idealists who propose the idea, give it nourishment, and seek to translate it into reality. Linguistic and cultural Pan-Slavism had its champions in Danilevsky and Dostoevsky, who proclaimed the superiority of the Slavic mind. Imperialistic Pan-Germanism had its Hasse and Class to depict the glory of a great Teutonic empire. Similarly, a unified Europe was called for by two French statesmen who worked for economic and political unity in an eventual United States of Europe.

Robert Schuman was born in Luxembourg on June 29, 1886. Brought up in Lorraine, at that time a German province, he was a brilliant scholar who attended universities at Strasbourg, Bonn, Berlin, and Munich. Qualified in jurisprudence, he began the practice of law at Metz. Refusing to serve in the German armed forces in World War I, he spent the war years in a German prison. In 1919 he was elected to the French Chamber of Deputies as a representative from Moselle. In World War II he was again arrested and imprisoned by the Germans. In September 1940, after the fall of France, he was taken by the *Gestapo* and sent to prison. Escaping in 1942, he worked with the Resistance until the liberation of France in 1944. Then began a scintillating political career—Minister of Finance (1946, 1947); Premier (1947-1948); Foreign Minister (1948-1952); and Minister of Justice (1955-1956).

During this active political career, Schuman became known for his scrupulous sense of economy. The story is told that he berated an underling who carelessly used scissors to cut the twine around a package instead of saving it whole for future use. He was known also as advocate of a working blend of Christianity and socialism. A founder of the Roman Catholic *Mouvement Républicain Populaire* (MRP), he regarded Christianity as providing the guiding light not only for his own country but for all Europe. His religious faith enhanced an idea growing slowly in his consciousness— the salvation of Europe could be found in its original Christian roots, a Europe whose lineaments could be traced back to Charlemagne and the

Carolingian Empire. A native of an area which had been both French and German, he had been imprisoned ignominiously in both world wars. Why this unnecessary rivalry? Schuman would devote himself to the creation of a new moral and spiritual climate in which a united Europe would flourish with no enmity between Frenchmen and Germans. He would support "a community based on the equality of rights of each confederated state under a common authority and discipline."[17] He was convinced that the formation of a European community would open hitherto undreamed of perspectives. Europe has a "noble primacy," which should not be yielded to others. It was a goal decreed by Providence. It was not only a continental but a global necessity. "Europe must strengthen herself inwardly, not in her own interest, but for the sake of humanity."[18] In these pious words Schuman linked his view of a European macro-nationalism with the good of mankind.

In 1950 while Foreign Minister, Schuman, in cooperation with Jean Monnet, introduced the Schuman Plan, which proposed to place national coal and steel resources under a supranational authority.[19] The project called for European economic and military unity, and especially for Franco-German rapprochement to prevent another war between the two countries. The economic level of the plan was realized in 1952 with the formation of the European Coal and Steel Community (ECSC), forerunner of the Common Market.

Linked closely with the name of Schuman was that of Jean Monnet, the second leading apostle of European unity. Political economist and diplomat, Monnet was born at Cognac, France, on November 9, 1888. He left high school to join the brandy business of his father, and in this capacity went to Canada, where he noted a special enthusiasm for teamwork and pooling of resources, ideas which were to influence him for the rest of his life. Returning to France at the outbreak of World War I, he was appalled to find a chaotic allocation of scarce materials in both France and England. He worked in London as liaison officer for the French Ministry of Commerce, the agency devoted to coordinating supplies and shipping. After the war he was made a French representative on the Inter-Allied Maritime Commission. From 1919 to 1923 he held the post of Deputy Secretary-General of the League of Nations.

In June 1940, at the time of Hitler's invasion of and subsequent humiliation of his country, Monnet suggested to Churchill an immediate Franco-British union. He served with the British Supply Council until 1943, and later went to Algiers, where he worked for the Free French Government as Commissioner of Arms, Supplies, and Reconstruction. After the war, from 1947 to 1952, he was responsible for drafting plans for rebuilding French industry.

Monnet, like Schuman, was becoming more and more convinced that there could be no real peace in Europe until quarreling nation-states were reconstituted on the basis of continental unity. He began to speak in terms of Pan-Europa and "a European entity": "The countries of Europe are too cramped to ensure for their people a prosperity which modern conditions make possible and consequently necessary. They must have larger markets. . . . Their prosperity and indispensable social developments are impossible, unless the states of Europe form themselves into a federation or a 'European entity,' which will make of it a common economic unit."[20]

Much of Monnet's career had been devoted to the task of gaining harmony among conflicting groups, an experience he began to call on in promoting the cause of European unity. In 1952, working together with Foreign Minister Robert Schuman, he became president of the European Coal and Steel Community, by which six nations (France, the Federal Republic of West Germany, The Netherlands, Belgium, Luxembourg, and Italy) pooled their resources under a supranational authority. He also gave the impulse for enlarging the idea into the European Economic Community (EEC). In 1955 he organized the Action Committee for a United States of Europe and became its chairman the next year.

Both Schuman and Monnet were gradualists who advocated a step-by-step process to continental unity. In their estimation, economic unity was the *sine qua non* for political consolidation. They held a fragmented Europe as responsible for the loss of millions of lives and untold damages to property. They believed the day of the sovereign European nation-state was ended, and held that national sovereignty must be transferred eventually to a consolidated, harmonious United States of Europe. In their view, this was not merely a desirable situation but an absolute necessity.

Despite the enthusiasm of these two apostles for unity, despite the glowing and optimistic speechmaking, any fair conclusion must recognize that Pan-Europa remains a distant and fragile dream. The report of the death of nationalism on the European continent is highly exaggerated.

Toward the Common Market

Schuman and Monnet were operating in a milieu they regarded as favorable to their cause. After the trauma of World War II, there was, indeed, a rising sentiment for European unity. The movement was given strong impetus when on September 19, 1946, as mentioned previously, in a speech at the University of Zürich, Winston Churchill, obviously elated by the outcome of the war, proposed what he called a "sovereign remedy" for European ills. "We must," he said, "recreate the European family or as much of it as we can, and provide it with a structure under which it can dwell in peace, in safety and in freedom. We must build a kind of United States of Europe." If Europe was to be saved from misery and final doom, Churchill went on, there must be an act of faith in the European family and an act of oblivion against the crimes and foibles of the past. The time might be short, but there was a breathing space; the fighting had stopped, but the dangers had not stopped. If there were to be a United States of Europe, a beginning must be made at once. The first step ("I am now going to say something that will astonish you") must be a partnership between France and Germany.[21]

Nine months later came an important step in the development of an integrated economy in Europe. On June 7, 1947, in a speech at Harvard University, George C. Marshall, U.S. Secretary of State, announced that the United States would do whatever it could to assure the return of economic health to the world. He added that, before the United States could help start Europe on the way to recovery, some agreement had to be shown among European countries by the drafting of a "European program," agreed upon by a number, if not all, European nations. Sixteen countries replied affirmatively.[22] Thus began the famous Marshall Plan. In response to Marshall's request for cooperation, the Organization for European Economic Cooperation (OEEC) was set up in 1948. Later, in 1961, it became the Organization for Economic Cooperation and Development (OECD), with American and Canadian participation. Although it broadened its scope to give extensive aid to developing countries, OECD remained much involved with European affairs.

Meanwhile, on May 9, 1950, Schuman made a historic declaration:

Europe will not be built at once or through a single comprehensive plan. It will be built through concrete achievements, which will first create a *de facto* solidarity. The comity of European nations requires that the rivalry of France and Germany should be eliminated. . . . The pooling of the production of coal and steel will immediately establish a common basis for economic development.

Thus will be realized, simply and rapidly, the fusion of interests which will be indispensable for establishing an economic community between countries long opposed by bloody conflict. This will establish the basis for a European confederation indispensable for the safeguarding of peace.[23]

The treaty establishing the European Coal and Steel Community (ECSC) was signed on April 18, 1951, and entered into force on July 25, 1952.[24] Called the Paris Treaty, it had a number of attached protocols and conventions dealing with such fields as energy. This functional, or sectional, approach meant that one sector of the European economy would be placed under the control of a supranational authority as merely a first step. The idea was to demonstrate to all participants the advantages to be won from economic integration. The movement of goods, labor, and capital within the coal and steel industries would set an example for similar developments elsewhere.

The ECSC immediately showed results in increasing trade among its members. Production and distribution rose rapidly. But there were problems: oil was beginning to replace coal as the basic fuel of Western Europe. In response to this development, the High Authority of ECSC began to phase out uneconomical coal mines, especially in Belgium and West Germany.

It soon became apparent that a sectorial approach to integration was not enough to assure European union. Eurocrats began to insist that the Continent's problems could be solved only by a greater union involving all sectors of the economy, not merely coal and steel.

In 1955 an intergovernmental group of experts was formed under the chairmanship of the Belgian Paul Henri Spaak to consider how economic integration could be expanded. The Spaak Report, issued on April 20, 1956, called upon the six ECSC members to form an economic union or Common Market. Its goal was the abolition of all obstacles to internal trade for a period of 12 years. Labor and capital would circulate freely among the members. There would be a special program for agriculture.

The Spaak Report led to the Treaty of Rome, signed on March 25, 1957, and quickly ratified. The European Economic Community (EEC) was founded.[25] The treaty contained not only the basis for the Common Market but outlined, in general, additional policies intended to lead to full economic union. Goals were stated in the preamble:

HIS MAJESTY THE KING OF THE BELGIANS, THE PRESIDENT OF THE FEDERAL REPUBLIC OF WEST GERMANY, THE PRESIDENT OF THE FRENCH REPUBLIC, THE PRESIDENT OF THE ITALIAN REPUBLIC, HER ROYAL HIGHNESS THE GRAND DUCHESS OF LUXEMBOURG, HER MAJESTY THE QUEEN OF THE BELGIANS.

DETERMINED to establish the foundations of an ever closer union among European peoples,

RESOLVED to ensure by common action the economic and social progress of their countries by eliminating the barriers which divide Europe,

AFFIRMING as the essential objective of their efforts the constant improvement of the living and working conditions of their peoples,

RECOGNISING that the removal of existing obstacles calls for constant action in order to guarantee steady expansion, balanced trade and fair competition,

ANXIOUS to strengthen the unity of their economies and to ensure their harmonious development by reducing the differences existing between the various regions and the backwardness of the less favored regions,

DESIRING to contribute, by means of a common commercial policy, to the progressive abolition of restrictions on international trade,

INTENDING to confirm the solidarity which binds Europe and overseas countries and desiring to ensure the development of their prosperity, in accordance with the principles of the Charter of the United Nations,

RESOLVED to strengthen the cause of peace and liberty by thus pooling resources and calling upon the other peoples of Europe who share their ideal to join in their efforts,

HAVE DECIDED to create a European Economic Community.[26]

These ringing terms reflected the European vision of Schuman, Monnet, and Spaak, who looked ahead to a united Europe as the only hope for European strength and security, and the only way of preventing another major holocaust. The Rome Treaty was more moderately worded than that of ECSC: it was careful not to use the word "supranationalism." The main decision body was not the High Authority (comprising Eurocrats), but a Council of Ministers representing national governments, thus diminishing the emphasis on federal power. The idea of political union was only hinted at—the Preamble referred to "an ever closer union among European peoples."

Why this dilution of the goal of supranationalism as desired by proponents of Pan-Europa? The spirit was there, but there were insurmountable obstacles. The Marshall Plan had been successful in bringing about European economic recovery. War hatreds were vanishing gradually in a new era of good will. But along with these positive developments came an upsurge of national consciousness throughout Europe, in the original Six of the Common Market as well.

Very important was the early negative attitude of the British, who at first refused to join the Common Market. In 1955 Whitehall even attempted to persuade the West Germans to break away from the EEC, a move that angered Spaak who spoke of "deliberate sabotage." West Germany, as a member of the Common market, Spaak argued, would find it easier to control her extreme nationalists. Monnet, too, appealed to the British: "You British always find it difficult to accept principles and prefer to make your decisions on the basis of facts. We on the Continent first set out the principles believing that the facts will emerge later. They will emerge in our Communities and, when they do, you British will join us."[27] Monnet was quite right. In 1963 and again in 1967, President Charles de Gaulle vetoed British applications to join EEC. In January 1973, Britain, Denmark, and Ireland joined the Common Market.[28]

The EEC policy of tariff reductions was so successful in stimulating trade that the program was accelerated, and by 1968 all customs duties and quotas on industrial goods were abolished for members of the Common Market. Measures were taken also in matters of labor, public housing, social security benefits, and union membership inside the Common Market. Efforts were made also to resolve differences between national banking systems. European companies with a Community rather than a national legal status were formed. All this took place at a time when Western Europe was enjoying satisfying increases in production.

There was, however, much difficulty in organizing a common market in agriculture. The French tried to use the Common Market for their own benefit by demanding additional outlets in the Community for their cereals and beef. President Charles de Gaulle threatened on more than one occasion to hold up progress in other spheres unless he had his way in matters of agriculture. In 1965-1966 he even took France out of the Common Market for a period of seven months.

One of the more aggravating problems in agriculture was that there were unexpected surpluses in cereals and dairy products, which were dumped from one member country to another. The cost of subsidizing imports and maintaining price levels proved to be a heavy financial burden for EEC. Farmers who felt themselves to be victims of discrimination often turned to violent demonstrations There were repeated clashes, unresolved rivalries, and mutual recriminations, especially among wine producers. In mid-August 1981, an Italian armada of five small wine tankers moved to the French Mediterranean port of Sète. Carrying more than two million bottles of inferior Italian wines, the tankers unloaded the wine and sold it to French marketers, who would take the "plonk" and mix it with rougher French wines to be sold at inflated prices on supermarket shelves. A commando force of French wine growers stormed aboard one of the Italian ships and poured fuel into large tanks of Sicilian wines. This kind of dumping and commercial exploitation, they said, would force them out of business.

The problem was not restricted to the south of France. The English complained bitterly about the dumping of French wines and eggs. French sheep farmers were furious about the competition of cheap British lamb. Dutch potatoes were added to the list of "competitive" agricultural products.[29]

Despite these clashing interests, Eurocrats called the Common Market a milestone on the road to Pan-Europa. The fact remained, however, that even modest steps toward economic union did not succeed in overcoming the strong sense of national consciousness in all the Common Market countries. Members of the Community were unwilling to drop their distinctive national coinage in favor of a European coinage system. Nowhere was there a willingness to sublimate national sovereignty to the administration of a United States of Europe. The spirit was there, but it was still hesitant and weak. In 1969 at a meeting held at The Hague, German Chancellor Willy Brandt spoke optimistically: "Our Community must not be a new power bloc, but an exemplary system which can serve as an element in the forging of a well-balanced Pan-European peace settlement."[30]

The then West German Chancellor saw Europe as something more than a collection of market organizations. The young, he said, must realize that Europe is something other than the memory of a past of somber glory."[31]

The idea persisted. Eurocrats saw the Common Market as the vital economic step to political union, an irreversible development certain to lead to a continental union capable of assuming common responsibilities, and able to make contributions commensurate with past traditions. These were fine words, but despite the optimism of the Eurocrats, theirs proved to be an evanescent goal.

"The New York Times" Survey

The argument presented above was substantiated in March 1982 when *The New York Times*, on the twenty-fifth anniversary of the formation of the Common Market under the Treaty of Rome, assigned Paul Lewis, an able foreign correspondent, to investigate the progress of the Community. His report, which began on the front page, was titled "Nationalism Is Straining Europe's Economic Unity." The conclusion was that free trade and closer economic integration brought by the Common Market to Western Europe was being threatened by a new spirit of nationalism "spawned partly by the passage of time and the dimming of earlier ideals, but also by the worldwide recession, against which the Rome treaty has proved no protection."[32]

Lewis judged that the Rome Treaty and the Common Market it created changed Europe's economic situation in many ways:

1. The ten member nations became the most important force in world trade, the largest single market on the globe, with roughly 270 million consumers, buying a quarter of the world's imported goods and selling a fifth of its exports.

2. Prosperity increased faster in Europe since 1957 than in the United States. During the Common Market's existence, its citizens increased their private spending seven times against a fourfold rise for Americans.

3. Trade between the six founder members grew consistently faster than world trade until the first oil shock in the mid-1970s. The expansion of trade probably contributed to the emergence of France as a major industrial power and to the development of the industrial north of Italy.

4. The Common Market made world trade freer, prompting successive American administrations to launch major international tariff-cutting negotiations.

5. Economic integration encouraged the Community's members to harmonize foreign policies in the hope of wielding more political influence in the world.

Despite these important achievements, Lewis saw the Common Market in deep trouble. "Those who hoped free trade would eventually produce a political confederation, a 'United States of Europe,' have been disappointed. Instead of responding to the world economic crisis by drawing closer together, the community's members seem to be splitting apart, resisting further attempts at integration."[33] According to the survey, historians and political scientists had agreed generally, when the Common Market was set up in 1957, that it was based on an implicit compromise that eventually broke down. There was stiffening national resistance to any further steps toward free trade or toward increased competition between members.

Lewis quoted Baron Jean Charles Snoy et d'Oppuers, who as Belgium's Foreign Minister was one of the Rome Treaty's original signers: "A sense of danger has come back, Government's are trying again to solve their problems at the expense of others."[34] The signers of the Rome Treaty had hoped for an eventual transition from European economic integration to political union, but already economic divergencies within Europe were aggravated.

De Gaulle Says "Non!"

Among the more important obstacles not only to the Common Market but especially to the idea of European political union was a tall Frenchman with piercing eyes and an extraordinary amount of Gallic arrogance. An impatient Churchill in World War II regarded him as an insufferable bore, while Roosevelt dismissed him as an *ersatz* Joan of Arc. Yet, this Frenchman was a military genius, whose early conception of armored warfare was appropriated by the Germans in their own *Blitzkrieg* version which brought chaos and misery to a weakened France. After the fall of his country in 1940, he assumed leadership of Free France. He kept the cross of Lorraine in action against Hitler's armies.

Charles de Gaulle thought of himself not merely as a leader of France, he was France itself. His mind was like the Louvre, filled with pictures of battles in which the French were always victors. France could not be France without greatness:

Our country, with her tinted sky, her varied contours, her fertile soil, her fields full of fine corn and vines and livestock, our industry, our gifts of initiative, adaptation, and self-respect, make us, above all others, a race created for brilliant deeds(1934).

The emotional side of me tends to imagine France, like the princess in the stories or the Madonnas in the frescoes, as dedicated to an exalted and exceptional destiny. But the positive side of my mind also assures me that France is not really herself unless in the front rank; that only vast enterprises are capable of counterbalancing the divisive ferments which are inherent in her people. In short, in my mind, France cannot be France without greatness (1955).[35]

In his *War Memoirs,* in which he spoke of himself both in the first and third persons, de Gaulle identified the nation with himself: "And today I was at the head of a ruined, decimated, lacerated nation, surrounded by ill-will. Hearing my voice France had been able to unite and march to her liberation."[36] It was more than the French Government, it was "Charles de Gaulle's Government": "The immediate dismemberment of Charles de Gaulle's Government did not, of course, escape the notice of the various foreign offices."[37] For him, France was not merely a *patrie*—it was a mystique.

De Gaulle's attitude was important for both the European Economic Community and the European Parliament. Holding no office when EEC was formed in 1958, he had no influence on shaping the organization in his early days. He supported the Community during his early years of power. On December 28, 1958, shortly after his recall to power, he made the abrupt decision to allow France to participate in the Common Market on an equal basis with other members.[38] He made it clear, however, that economic unity, in his estimation, did not imply a step toward European political integration. He felt that the lack of federative aspects in EEC was sufficient to bring France into the Common Market without sacrificing his principle of national grandeur. He would adapt the European Community to his own view by opposing openly or surreptitiously its still embryonic supranational features. He accepted Chancellor Konrad Adenauer of the Federal Republic of West Germany as a partner, because de Gaulle believed that he, himself, could easily dominate the new Germany.

Slowly but surely, de Gaulle's attitude toward the Common Market hardened when he became convinced that its Eurocrat leadership was working toward a common European government. He began to place barriers in the way of Common Market expansion. In January 1963 he opposed British entry into the Community. He was concerned lest British participation in the Continental bloc might serve to dilute French leadership on the Continent, and, furthermore, might further American influence in Europe. On several occasions he forced Common Market decisions on unwilling partners. In July 1965 he boycotted an EEC meeting in Brussels. Shortly afterward he attacked architects of the Common Market as "a technocratic, stateless, and irresponsible clique," and their plans as "a project removed from reality."[39] He would not allow decisions affecting the superior interests of France to be imposed by a "stateless bureaucracy" with "its supranational pretensions." Above all, he would not allow France to lose her veto on Common Market decisions.

Eurocrats were appalled by de Gaulle's increasingly hard line on the Common Market. His countryman, Jean Monnet, was concerned: "The most striking thing about General de Gaulle is his nationalistic view of world affairs."[40] German, Italian, and Dutch members of EEC expressed their disappointment. None of this had the slightest effect on the stiff-necked Frenchman.

At the root of de Gaulle's thinking was the fear that Eurocrats supporting the Common Market had more than economics in mind when they set up the Community. He was concerned lest economic integration would lead to political unity. His fears were justified by the increasing calls for a European Parliament. For de Gaulle, this was impossible—unless a European political union was organized, led, and controlled from Paris. He would support a Grand Design, a confederated *"L'Europe des patries,"* a "Europe of the Nations," which would defend national independence by avoiding any decisions imposed from beyond national boundaries. He never explained how this happy state of affairs could be realized while at the same time Europe was being controlled from Paris. He was certain that Paris was not only the center of Europe, but also the fulcrum of the entire world.

De Gaulle had no intention of relinquishing a tiniest element of French sovereignty to a political parliament representing Pan-Europa. In his estimation, no matter how important the studies and advice of the Brussels Commission, the powers and duties of the French executive belonged only to his government. He believed that neither the Common Market nor the European Parliament should be allowed to challenge the status of France as a sovereign state. He poured scorn on what he called "the European hybrid." The federator, he warned, would not be Europe but the United States. This became a theme of his objection: European integration meant "vassalage and subordination to the United States."

In placing his faith in the permanence of national states, de Gaulle delivered a powerful blow to the idea of European unity. Most other European statesmen, though not gifted with his sense of grandeur, felt the same way.

From Council of Europe to European Parliament

For Eurocrats, the Common Market was merely the first step on the road to implementation of political integration. Thursday, June 7, 1979, was for them a joyous date of fulfillment. On that day and on three succeeding days, 175 million people of the European Community from northern Scotland to Calabria in southern Italy, from the Bay of Biscay to the Elbe River, voted in a single election for delegates to the first European Parliament. Although the mode of election differed from country to country according to national tradition and preference, these were European elections. At long last, after decades of debate, the critical move was made from economic to political unity.[41]

The groundwork had been prepared for more than three decades. In May 1948, approximately 750 European delegates convened at The Hague to set up a European Assembly. They agreed to collaborate in forming a federation. Called at first the "Congress of Europe," it met under the presidency of Winston Churchill. A year later, in May 1949, came the formation of the Council of Europe, consisting of ten countries: Belgium,

Britain, Denmark, France, Ireland, Italy, Luxembourg, the Netherlands, Norway, and Sweden.[42]

The goal of the Council of Europe was high sounding: "To protect human rights, bring European countries closer together, and voice the views of the European public on the main political and economic problems of the day." There would be a Consultative Assembly, a quasi-legislative body, a staff of representatives recruited from national bureaucracies, and an independent judiciary to arbitrate legal problems between member states. The Consultative Assembly would consist of 144 members chosen by their governments with Communists excluded. There would also be a Committee of Ministers with one representative from each national government. Headquarters were set up in an elegant new House of Europe in Strasbourg.

There were problems from the beginning. For the English the name "Consultative Assembly" meant only an instrument for consultation at governmental and parliamentary levels. The French, supported by their own bloc of friendly nations, called for an assembly with real legislative powers in restricted fields.

There were dramatic and emotional debates in the Consultative Assembly. Yet, its members were never able to convince the Committee of Ministers to grant it any real power. Recommendation followed recommendation, with most of them turned down. After two years of frustrating debate, Paul Henri Spaak, President of the Consultative Assembly, resigned in disgust, after denouncing the English, Swedes, Norwegians, and Danes for restricting the body to mere debate instead of fostering joint political action.

There were some minor successes, mostly cultural. The Consultative Assembly drew up a European Convention for the Protection of Human Rights and Freedoms (1950), and a European Court of Human Rights consisting of 15 judges from member states (1955). Complaints by states or individuals concerning violations of human rights or fundamental freedoms would be submitted to a special body connected with the Council of Europe. In 1962 a Council for Cultural Cooperation was established by work for mutual recognition of university degrees, wider student exchange, and elimination of national chauvinism in history textbooks published in the member nations. This body also defined minimum standards for old age pensions and social security benefits.

Critics geared to the old nationalism, and there were many, denounced the Council of Europe as merely another impractical vehicle for do-gooders. No statesman, they argued, could take it upon himself to diminish the sovereignty of his homeland—that would be close to treason. They admitted that nationalism had its evil aspects, but they did not see the day at hand for transmittal of national sovereignty to a Pan-European legislative body at Strasbourg.

Eurocrats were disappointed, but not dismayed, by this continuing criticism. National economies, they insisted, were "melting" already in the

Common Market, which had turned out to be a giant step to political integration. Pan-Europa, they said, the new European super-state, was well on its way. The process was continuous, and must be promoted at a cautious pace. The framework of a United States of Europe might be a loose one for the time being; each member nation would be able to preserve its special qualities while functioning in an overall structure. This was a new type of unity, they argued, a conquest of provincialism that would set a standard for the entire world. Each year in May the European flag of gold stars on an azure field would fly over palaces and public buildings in the member states. For Eurocrats this was a signal of fulfillment of their dreams.

On March 30, 1962, what was then known as the European Parliamentary Assembly changed its name to European Parliament. A new system of direct universal suffrage was set up with a common system of election for all member nations.[43] Annual sessions were to be held in March in addition to eleven part-sessions each year. The Parliament appointed its own president and officers, and adopted its own rules of procedure. Decisions were to be made by an absolute majority of votes cast. Public discussions were to be held on the annual general report submitted to it by a special Commission. If a motion of censure for the Commission was tabled, a vote would be taken not less than three days later. If the motion of censure was supported by a two-thirds majority of votes cast and by a majority of members of the Parliament, the Commission members collectively would resign their offices. Parliamentary control over the executive was considerable but not complete.

From its beginning, the European Parliament was faced with the difficult problem of its relations with national parliaments. Even though direct elections were held, the balance between national and supranational elements in the Community's constitutional structure was uncertain. There remained an aggravating question: Would the future European Union be no more than another intergovernmental organization, or was the Community indeed developing into a new form of politico-economic association on a transnational scale?[44] The issue remained excruciatingly unsolved.

The European Parliament never attained the status wished for it by enthusiastic Eurocrats. The body has remained deficient in real legislative power *vis-à-vis* national parliaments. Worst of all in prognosis for the future was the lack of any mass movement in member states calling for the transfer of sovereignty from the national to the European level. The French (and all other nationals) continued to think of themselves primarily as citizens of a nation and only secondarily as Europeans.

Auxiliaries for Integration

Unlike other macro-nationalisms, Pan-Europa was fragmented into a number of separate organizations. For Eurocrats, this meant merely a gradualist approach to a desired end. For critics, it meant the bankruptcy of the very idea of integration.

Added to the European Coal and Steel Community and the European Economic Community was a third institution, the European Atomic Energy Community (Euratom), legally separate but sharing the common European Parliament and the Court of Justice. Formed in 1958, Euratom consisted of the same original six states of EEC, namely Belgium, France, the Federal Republic of West Germany, Italy, Luxembourg, and the Netherlands.[45] Its aim was "to contribute in the raising of the standard of living in member states and to the development of commercial exchanges with other countries by the creation of conditions necessary for the speedy establishment and growth of nuclear industries."

Euratom set up research centers in member countries, exchanged scientific and technical advice, and sponsored common projects by universities and private companies. It drew up health codes for nuclear workers, as well as a method for controlling the sale of fissionable material. It worked closely with the European Committee for Nuclear Research (CERN).[46]

From its beginning, Euratom ran into difficulties. There were serious doubts about the efficacy of the program. The rush to atomic energy had been precipitated by the increasingly high cost of conventional energy, especially of oil resources. The Euratom program was producing energy but at high cost, and there was always the possibility of dangerous accidents. Moreover, Community research efforts collided with growing national programs, at a time when the commercial potential of nuclear investigation had increased.

In 1960, two years after the formation of Euratom, three additional programs were formed in dedication to the idea of European integration. The Benelux Economic Union, consisting of Belgium, Luxembourg, and the Netherlands, was formed to achieve the complete economic union of its members as a subdivision of the European Economic Community. The European Free Trade Association (EFTA) was set up with headquarters in Geneva to promote the elimination of internal tariffs among its members. Called the Outer Seven (Austria, Denmark, Great Britain, Norway, Portugal, Sweden, and Switzerland), it was designed to complement the Inner Six of EEC. The Organization for Economic Cooperation and Development (OECD) was founded to promote stable economic growth in member countries, as well as in the world at large. As successor to the Organization for European Economic Cooperation (OEEC), set up in 1948 to oversee Marshall Plan reconstruction, OECD had a somewhat broadened scope designed to extend aid to developing countries. OECD also warned of dangers facing the European monetary system by outbursts of currency speculation throughout the Continent.

Other impulses to European integration were militarily oriented. The

Cold War with the Soviet Union began soon after the end of World War II, when it became obvious that Stalin had no intention of holding to agreements with the Western Allies. In April 1949 the North Atlantic Treaty Organization (NATO) was formed as a mutual defense bloc for Western Europe and North America. Conventional forces in Western Europe were increased to add to the power of American deterrent weapons, submarine-based atomic warheads, and ballistic missiles in both Europe and the United States.

For optimistic Eurocrats, all these organizations indicated a steady move to the desired goal of a macro-nationalistic Europa. But there were serious strains in all the programs. Loose agreements had been reached only after difficult and prolonged negotiations, in which national rivalries persisted. There were aggravating difficulties in economic cooperation. For example, EFTA was shocked when Britain, shifting from splendid isolation to close economic ties with the Continent, applied for EEC membership and was vetoed twice by France. In 1973, together with Norway, Britain withdrew from the Outer Seven to join the Common Market.

There were even greater problems in military matters. The European Defense Community moved hesitantly on a rocky road. In West Germany the NATO Treaty was ratified only after a fierce struggle. The Italian Parliament at first refused to vote on it. NATO was also rejected originally by the French, who objected to the disbanding of the national French Army and the rearming of Germany. The French sent no military representatives to NATO but maintained a loose liaison. In response to NATO, the Eastern European Mutual Assistance Treaty (Warsaw Pact) was formed in 1955. Consisting of Bulgaria, Czechoslovakia, East Germany, Poland, Rumania, and the Soviet Union, this bloc, like NATO, was composed of military elements from member countries. Western Europe and Eastern Europe were split permanently into opposing military unions. An extended Continental Pan-Europa thus became impossible.

The NATO alliance was further endangered in late 1983 by the deepening missile crisis. The proposed deployment of new American missiles in Western Europe was greeted not only by angry Soviet protests but also by large antimissile demonstrations in West Germany, Britain, France, Holland, and elsewhere. Whatever unity existed, was endangered by a unity of protest. The situation worsened when the United States joined with six small Caribbean countries to invade Grenada and throw out the Cubans and Soviet agents gathered there.

By Disunity Possessed

With this impressive array of organizations for integration, it would seem that Pan-Europa was no longer a distant goal, but one visible through a darkened tunnel. Supranational and intergovernmental organs seemed to provide a sturdy framework for eventual unity. A collective nationalism, a successful macro-nationalism providing a new stage in European history, seemed to be well on the way.

Unfortunately for Eurocrats, political unity, and the desired pooling of sovereignty, remained an unfulfilled dream. A certain amount of economic unity had been won, but the idea of political union was lost in technicalities. Pan-Europa succumbed to the traditional power of the nation-state. The European Parliament remained a mere debating society, not a legislative body.

What was responsible for this gloomy state of affairs? As always the causes were complex and inter-related:

The ambivalence of Europe. From its beginning, the European Community was burdened by a strange duality implicit in the idea itself and, in various mixtures, in all supporters.[47] On the one side, founders Schuman and Monnet saw the necessity of reconciling former enemies as a prerequisite for Continental unity and world peace. This liberal approach, reformist in tone, was applied to a continent that had frustrated such conquerors as Napoleon and Hitler.

On the other hand, from the moment of its inception there was a struggle for power inside the movement itself. Even the founding fathers regarded European integration as a power-vehicle for confronting the two super-powers, the United States and the Soviet Union. This urge for a third Pan-European power was in direct contrast to the liberal stance of the Eurocrats.

The result of these clashing ideas was an ambiguity in the ultimate purpose of Western European integration. What Schuman and Monnet wanted remained in contradiction to political realities and the traditional idea of balance of power. There could be no effective dual hegemony—of national states inside a European super-state.

Lack of mass basis and consensus. Pan-Europa was never able to win the mass support needed for a European super-power. Mass interest and advocacy were lacking. English, French, Spanish, or Danish citizens still regarded themselves as patriots of their own countries, and continued to accept anthem and flag as symbols of their nationalism. There was little sense of loyalty to Europa. When an Italian soccer team lost its match with a World Cup rival, it was unable to return to a Rome airport, where hundreds of angered fans awaited the melancholy "traitors" to the Italian cause.

Pan-Europeanism remained the pet child of a handful of statesmen and a weak minority of Eurocrats. There were emotional speeches in meetings and congresses; there were magazines and books to promote the cause, but efforts were successful in altering the European mood of loyalty to the nation-state.

Erosion of governmental support. Added to the lack of a mass base was weakened governmental support, and whatever governmental advocacy existed for the European idea was almost always conditioned by national needs. Both national policy and national traits tend to resist change. In Britain, where tradition is respected, succeeding governments still saw relations with the Continent in terms of splendid isolation and a balance of power. Reluctance to join the Common Market was overcome eventually, but British membership remained shaky. In France, the nation of patriots, there was little governmental support for Pan-Europa, despite the efforts of Schuman and Monnet. For many Frenchmen, EEC was merely a huge market for their beef and cereals, while for most Frenchmen the idea of a joint military defense was an anathema. Italians, despite the efforts of federalists Alcide De Gasperi and Altiero Spinelli, remained indifferent to Pan-Europa.[48]

There was also waning support for Pan-Europa among West Germans. At first there was enthusiasm for unity by a people who had undergone the shock and trauma of two World Wars. Apparently, they had experienced enough of the nationalism and militarism that had robbed them of their precious youth, so that they were willing to subordinate their nationalism to a larger allegiance. Thousands of Germans began to use the EU (for Europe) emblem on their cars. The Bonn Government contributed a large share of operating expenses for the European Community. Political leaders agreed on the necessity for the European idea as salvation for their country. Franz Josef Strauss, leader of the government's opposition, put it bluntly: "Whoever wishes to be German must see to it that he becomes a European while there is still time. We must have patriotism in an entirely new understanding of the word."[49]

In the early 1980s, however, West German support for the European Community began to waver, a change of heart reflecting a worsening economic situation. The German economic miracle (*Wirtschaftswunder*) was beginning to lose its momentum with a decline in gross national product, rising unemployment, and a beginning of inflational trends. Germans who remembered the catastrophic 1923 inflation began to worry.

Simultaneously, Germans who had once championed European unity now began to see flaws in the movement. They were alienated by the constant petty bickering among members of the Common Market, by priorities given to national producers, and by a lack of unity in the face of Soviet intransigence. The waning of German support was a severe blow to Eurocrats and to the idea of Pan-Europa.[50]

Competition between European and national Parliaments. Added to the lack of a mass base and erosion of governmental support was a continuing struggle for the control of legislative power.[51] The key issue was the proper exercise of sovereignty.[52] Nationalists felt that any acquisition of legislative competence by the European Parliament would be at the expense of their own national legislative bodies. In their minds, the European Parliament would try to exercise powers which it was not supposed to possess. They wanted no enforced conformity to legislation from Strasbourg. They saw the European Parliament as founded on intergovernmental, not federal or supranational, auspices. They pointed to the Treaty of Rome, which specified that in a clash between national and Community laws, the latter would take precedence. No, argued the nationalists, the very idea of enforced integration at the parliamentary level was dangerous precisely because it meant that established nation-states would be divested of their precious autonomy and sovereignty.

Eurocrats countered that such fears were unreasonable. This attitude, they argued, misunderstood the scope, authority, and limited competence of the Economic Community as indicated in the Rome Treaty. Moreover, they said, political power ultimately lay with member governments.

East-West dichotomy. A continental-wide unity became impossible after World War II with the creation of the Communist bloc in Eastern Europe. Though Western and Eastern Europe had worked together in the critical task of smashing Hitlerism, the unity was at best a precarious one in view of suspicions on both sides. Stalin was almost paranoiac in his mistrust of Western motives. Churchill, too, mistrusting the Russians, aimed to keep them as far east as possible. There was little possibility that such suspicions would ease after the war.

Moves toward integration in Western Europe were followed by similar efforts to fashion multilateral ties among the Communist nations of Eastern Europe. A Communist bloc was fashioned, consisting of satellite states which, with the exception of Yugoslavia and Albania, looked to Moscow for guidance.

In January 1949, following the formation of the Organization for European Economic Organization in the West, the Soviet Union, Bulgaria, Czechoslovakia, Hungary, Poland, and Rumania joined the new Council for Mutual Economic Assistance (COMECON).[53] The Council convened only a few times before the death of Stalin. Nikita Khrushchev, Stalin's successor, made some limited efforts to transform COMECON into a more effective supranational body, but he was unsuccessful. Although the idea was supported in Czechoslovakia and East Germany, it was opposed vigorously by Rumania, which was expected to limit its industrialization in favor of agriculture and oil production. Economic integration in the COMECON states was limited when compared with that in Western Europe.

There was a basic difference between movements for integration in Western Europe and Eastern Europe. Western nations tended to regard integration as a movement between equals, though some statesmen, notably French, saw themselves as more equal than others. In Eastern Europe, on the other hand, the Kremlin regarded itself as the fulcrum of Communism, and its geographical buffer states as satellites subject to Moscow's control. Under such circumstances any possibility of a continental-wide United States of Europe was exceedingly remote. Not even the fear of the Soviet Union and its missles was enough to force Western Europe into a meaningful integration.

In summary, Western European countries looked increasingly inward despite the survival and even progress of the Common Market, and despite the increasing conformity in many aspects of European life. Most observers of the European scene regard the vision of Europe, a community which would replace the rivalries of the past, as a fading phenomenon. They see statesmen preaching internationalism, but failing to practice what they preach. They see people feeding and clothing themselves with products from all over the world, but at the same time expressing indifference to a workable world order. The idea of international cooperation has remained a seemingly unattainable ideal.

What exists in contemporary Europe is the maintainence of parochialism, the persistence of nationalism, and not the emergence of a supranationalism. The expectation of political unity has receded from the realm of the concrete. What once seemed to be a possible goal has moved into the realm of unfulfilled hopes.

CHAPTER 5

THE TRIBES OF EUROPE: FROM ANGLO-SAXONISM TO PAN-SCANDINAVIANISM _____

The English, ah! the English—they are quite a race apart.
                                                    —"Puzzler"

True, ye come of The Blood.
                                —"England's Answer"

Divisive Trends in Europe

The dream of Pan-Europa was handicapped by a persistent sense of national self-consciousness. Additionally responsible for its weakness were several smaller pan-movements throughout the Continent, each of which in its own way sought to unify peoples of supposed affinity. Among them were Anglo-Saxonism in the northwest, Pan-Latinism in the south, Pan-Lusitanism and Pan-Hispanism in the Iberian peninsula, and Great Netherlands and Pan-Scandinavianism in the north and northeast.

In contrast to Pan-Slavism and Pan-Germanism, both of which attempted political organization, these pan-movements remained even more vaguely defined and evanescent in nature. All had some elements in common. Enthusiastic scholars for the cause of pan-union looked to the past and found signs of what they deemed to be "racial" and cultural unity. Seeing bonds in early tribal affiliations, they insisted that peoples of like background—Anglo-Saxons, Celts, Iberians, or Nordics, belonged together in a higher combination even if they lived in different nation-states. National boundaries, they claimed, were inconsequential.

European advocates of tribalism, like Eurocrats who called for continental-wide unity, failed to win real recognition for their cause. Scholars who investigated every aspect of Celtic culture, from stone monuments to folk songs, found it impossible to link all the Celts distributed among established states. Scandinavian intellectuals, who saw a common Nordic heritage in Sweden, Norway, and Denmark, found the existence of national sovereignty much too strong for them. Transnational unity was possible in mutual economic unity and in folk music, but the idea of political integration was rejected as impractical and undesirable. General rapprochement based on tradition and sentiment was acceptable, but not political reorganization that would challenge established sovereignty. Here again we see the strength of nationalism in contemporary society.

Imperialism and the Pan-Movements

Closely associated with fissiparous tribalism on the European scene was the urge for territorial expansion expressed in modern imperialism. In the drive to build empires, adventurers living inside set boundaries sought to extend their control to contiguous or non-contiguous territory. Motivated by gold, glory, and God—in that order—they acquired colonies and built up great empires. It became the *mission civilisatrice* of the mother country to bring the benefits of a superior "race" to unfortunate inferior peoples scattered throughout the world.

During this process, nationalist historians, novelists, poets, publicists, statesmen, and politicians went about the business of constructing a myth of imperial majesty centered in the mother country. Historians found lodestones of common characteristics, such as a unity of blood lines; cultural homogeneity expressed in language, literature, and art; and a distinct national character. The imperial idea was then transformed into a pan-movement designed to spread its octopus arms in all directions.

The familiar process of expansion from a small area into a macro-state existed in both ancient and modern times. Rome, originally a small trading post on the heights of a favorable crossing on the lower Tiber, expanded into a great empire in one of the most important drives in the history of the world. In modern times the phenomenon was repeated from London and the small British Isles, from which seamen, explorers, and adventurers moved across the oceans and created an empire extending to the far corners of the globe. To justify this expansion, British ideologists fashioned an Anglo-Saxon myth designed to proclaim the superiority of the island people, and to bring British administration, laws, traditions, and customs to backward peoples. That enormous profits went to London in the process was considered, of course, quite satisfactory and desirable.

Other European peoples reacted in much the same way. Portuguese expansion stimulated the ideology of Pan-Lusitanism. The conquests of Spanish *conquistadores*, who went to areas in North and South America in the 16th century, provided arguments for Pan-Hispanism. Such pan-movements represented an effort to extend national consciousness into a larger nationalism. Almost invariably they remained the province of a small group of super-patriots. In the Age of Nationalism, with its fixed boundaries, these European pan-movements remained decidedly anachronistic.

Anglo-Saxonism: Myth and Fallacy

In contrast to those macro-nationalisms which took on political and social characteristics, Anglo-Saxonism was a hazily defined movement enshrouded in myth. The idea of British consanguinity, a false identification with race, took the form of a mystical Anglo-Saxon legend.

Anglo-Saxonism as a pan-movement was a concomitant of a rapidly expanding imperialism. During the First Industrial Revolution in the late 18th and early 19th centuries, England moved to first place as the most industrialized nation on earth. Her factories were kept busy supplying the wants of her own people and those on the Continent. In the mid-19th century, at a time when Britain was ready for global expansion, empire-conscious historians and publicists began to fashion the Anglo-Saxon myth. In their view, there was adequate reason for Britain's mission to bring civilization to backward regions. Obviously, Anglo-Saxons were a superior "race" qualified to bring their customs, laws, and manners to less fortunate peoples. Anglo-Saxons belonged together and should stay together to maintain their superiority.

From its beginnings, Anglo-Saxonism took on a spurious racial image. Its advocates felt an ethnic affinity with early Teutons. Fourteenth-century Angles and Saxons had fused with Franco-Normans to form a new and vital "British race." Historians attributed great British institutions to the dominant Teutonic strain in their background. They accepted Cromwell's Puritan concept that the British race was chosen by God and that it alone expressed the divine will. Not the old Israelites, but English Protestants instead, were the favored people of God destined to bring enlightenment to a dark world.

The Anglo-Saxon myth was promoted by four eminent British historians, all of whom added to the confusion of race and nation. The trend was started in 1849 by J. M. Kemble, who in his *Saxons in England* linked Anglo-Saxons and Teutons by race. Thomas Babington Macaulay, in his *History of the Glorious Revolution of 1688* (1848-1855), praised "the great noble race" descending from vigorous Teutons, and in his *History of England* (5 vols., 1849-1861) assumed that English bourgeois standards of culture and progress were forever to be the norm for less favored peoples.[1] James Anthony Froude, in his *History of England from the Fall of Wolsey to the Defeat of the Spanish Armada* (1856-1870), glorified the heroic past of a superior people. His contemporaries criticized Froude for inaccuracies but failed to condemn his fallacious racial theory.[2] Edward Augustus Freeman, Fellow of Trinity College, Oxford, in his *History of the Norman Conquest of England, Its Causes and Results* (1867-1876), praised Teutonic elements of "the masterful English folk." Dubbed the "Prince of Teutonists," he was criticized by modern scholars who suggested that he placed too much stress on the Teutonic origins of English institutions.[3]

Though these historians won popular acclaim, even more effective in promoting the mysticism of Anglo-Saxonism was Thomas Carlyle, who spent a lifetime linking British and Teutonic institutions. He disregarded scientific facts about race. In his historical treatises, essays, and biographies, Carlyle did much to spread the fallacies of racialism. Praising German idealism, moral intuition, and political institutions, he stressed the mission of the Anglo-Saxon "race" to control backward regions of the earth, "Our little Isle is grown too narrow for us," he wrote, "but the world is wide enough yet for another Six Thousand Years."[4] Thus were Britons spreading the seeds of Anglo-Saxon greatness in a vigorous extension of the methods of early Teutons, blood ancestors of British traders. "Just as Mycale was the Pan-Ionian rendezvous of all the tribes of Ion for all Greece so must London long continue as the Anglo-Saxon home, rendezvous of all the 'Children of the Harz Rock!' "[5] There was a glorious future for descendants of the great Teutons. Carlyle quoted from Goethe's *Wilhelm Meister:*

> In what land, the sun does visit
> Brisk are we, whate'er betide;
> To give space, for wandering is it
> That the world was made so wide.

Novelists joined in building the Anglo-Saxon myth. In *Westward Ho!* (1855), Charles Kingsley re-created the glorious days of Queen Elizabeth, when her subjects sailed the seas searching for gold and Spaniards. An Anglican clergyman, Kingsley supported Darwin's theory of natural selection. He was noted for his aggressive sense of patriotism. His blend of jingoism and anti-popery coincided nicely with the tastes of Queen Victoria, who invited him to preach at Buckingham Palace.[6] He contrasted the Romans of the dying Empire with "young and virile Teutonic forest children," intimating that Germans had given Britain her most powerful racial strain. "Hold fast to English fortitude," he advised his fellow countrymen.[7]

Publicists and poets contributed their share in furthering the manifest destiny of imperial Britain. While the work of historians reached only a limited audience, that of popular writers had an enormous influence in winning public support for the glories of imperialism. Charles Wentworth Dilke, after study at Cambridge, at the age of twenty-three circumnavigated the globe, and recorded his impressions in a book entitled *Greater Britain* (1868, 1876). Dilke saw the great Anglo-Saxon race as destined to conquer the world. His travels, he said, left him with a conception of the grandeur of the British race, which already girdled the world. "The British remain the only extirpating race. . . . The true moral of America is the vigor of the British race. . . . There are men who say that Britain in her age will claim the glory of having planted great England across the seas. They fail to see that she had done more than found plantations of her own—that she has imposed her institutions upon the offshoots of Germany, of Ireland, of Scandinavia, and of Spain. Through America, England is speaking to the world."[8]

Dilke's concept of British racial supremacy was carried on by John Robert Seeley in his *Expansion of England* (1882). In highly emotional prose, Seeley showed how Great Britain had won India and her colonies. Exalting the positive character of the great Empire, he advised his fellow countrymen to maintain its glory. The British Empire, he said, was the embodiment of Anglo-Saxon racial supremacy. The English race should work at maintaining its heritage.

Both Dilke and Seeley were effective propagandists for empire, but Rudyard Kipling was more successful in reaching the masses. Fanning the flames of patriotism he urged all Britons to be aware of their special role in civilized society. He praised the continuity of British history, and predicted a brilliant future for England. He warned that inherited racial instincts must not be disregarded in artificial times—the virility of the race must be maintained. There must be no sheltered life of "Little England," and British influence must be extended to the far corners of the world. "What should they know of England who only England know?"

To Kipling, Darwinsim meant a contest for the survival of the great Anglo-Saxon race, whose duty it was to bring civilization to backward races. Only the fittest could survive and the British must be among them. There was a special responsibility:

Take up the White Man's Burden,
Send forth the best ye breed,
Go bind your sons to exile,
To serve your captive's need.[9]

The British public was delighted by Kipling's siren song of Anglo-Saxonism. Most Britons, from fox-hunting aristocrats to workers in the pubs, became aware through Kipling of the civilizing mission of the Anglo-Saxon race. "He [Kipling] strikes chords within us, to which we are capable of vibrating sympathetically, though but for his touch our country would have remained unknown to us."[10] Devotion to Kipling took on the characteristics of a cult: "Let us softly repeat to ourselves Mr. Kipling's alliterative lines, until a holy calm steals over us, and acts as a kind of natural sedative after our noble but nerve-setting mission of land-grabbing and money-spinning."[11]

Ideologists of Anglo-Saxonism were assisted by a long line of politicians and statesmen, each of whom added his bit to perpetuating the myth. Disraeli praised the British race: "For my part I believe that England is safe in the race of men who inhabit her."[12] He predicted a glorious future for the British race. Lord Archibald Rosebery was not sure of the scientific validity of race, but he sensed something of value in Britain: "I do not plead for the word Anglo-Saxon. I would welcome any other term which in a more conciliatory, a more scientific, and more adequate manner could describe the thing I want to describe. But whether you call it British or Anglo-Saxon, or whatever you call it, the fact is that the race is there and the sympathy of the race is there."[13]

This kind of muddleheaded thinking was not rare, Joseph Chamberlain often spoke of the destiny of the British race. Lord George Curzon used the term loosely: "It is because I believe in the future of our country and the capacity of our own race to guide it to goals that it has never hitherto attained, that I keep courage and press forward."[14] Arthur James Balfour, though of Scottish heritage, saw a "unity of the stream": "Although different strains have met together to make our kingdom and our empire, none of them need feel that difference destroys the unity of the stream that has resulted from their coalescence."[15] Cecil Rhodes, the empire-builder, saw it as his mission to acquire South Africa for the British "race."

This fallacious identification of race with nation received even more impetus from the golden tongue of Winston Churchill. Again and again in his speeches and prolific writings, Churchill used the term "British race" as if it represented scientific validity. Unfortunately, the great statesman added to semantic confusion by using the term in an improper sense as a cultural community. The "British race" never existed beyond his fertile imagination. His last book, an abridgment of his *History of the English-speaking People* (1956-1958), appeared some months before his death (1965) under the title of *The Island Race*. Churchill was using the word in its Victorian meaning (Englishmen at that time generally criticized the cultural values of other communities). Churchill was a magnificent war leader, but he must be given poor marks as a lexical specialist or a logical linguist.

The confusion of race and nation was not only the fallacy of British historians, publicists, and poets, but also of their American peers. Herbert Baxter Adams praised the Germanic origin of New England towns as well as the continuity of English institutions in America. John W. Burgess traced the history of all civilized peoples and came to the conclusion that of all those who had learned the Darwinian lesson of survival of the fittest, the Teutonic was the only race of superior stock. There was a vast difference, he said, in political capacity of races, and it was "the white man's mission, his duty, and his right, to hold the reins of political power in his hands for the civilization of the world and the welfare of mankind."[16] John Fiske held that the day would come when four-fifths of the human race would trace its pedigree to English forefathers. He claimed that the Anglo-Saxon race originated the political institution of federalism, the fittest of all political institutions, which some day would be accepted throughout the world.[17]

American clergymen and publicists joined in the chorus of approval for the Anglo-Saxon race. In 1885, Josiah Strong, a Congregationalist minister, published a book titled *Our Country: Its Possible Future and Its Present Crisis,* in which he held that the Anglo-Saxon race was the most vital force on earth. This was the race he wrote, which had brought to modern civilization the ideals of civil liberty and spiritual Christianity. He was optimistic about its great future: "If I read not amiss, this powerful race will move down upon Mexico, down upon Central and South America out upon the islands of the sea, over upon Africa and beyond. And can anyone doubt that the result of this competition of races will be the 'survival of the fittest'?"[18] Strong's book won high popular acclaim.

In the early 20th century the term Anglo-Saxon was supplanted by "Nordic" as a new school of racialists emerged in the United States. The Nordic school aimed to rescue civilization from inferior races, Leaders of the new movement were Madison Grant and Lothrop Stoddard, amateur anthropologists, and Henry Fairfield Osborn, professional paleontologist.

In *The Passing of a Great Race, or the Racial Basis of European History* (1916), Madison Grant presented the doctrine of the superiority of the Nordic race. Repeating the stock doctrine of British Anglo-Saxonists, he insisted that only race counted. The most vigorous have been in control and will remain in control in one form or another until such time as democracy and its illegitimate offspring, socialism, would establish "cacocracy," which he defined as the rule by the worst. Race mixture, he warned, would result in degeneration, and the mixture of two races in the long run would mean a reversion to an ancient, generalized, and lower type. Christ was Nordic: "In depicting the crucifixion no artist hesitates to make the two thieves brunet in contrast to the blond Saviour. This is something more than a convention, as such quasi-authentic traditions as we have of our Lord strongly suggest his Nordic, possibly Greek, physical and moral attributes."[19]

Henry Fairfield Osborn, elder doyen of American racialism, had a more scholarly background than Grant. Osborn, too, feared the arrest and decay of human progress if the Nordic race should continue to lose its fertility and become absorbed in other races. He saw the force and stability of heredity as more enduring and potent than environment.[20] In World War I, the Anglo-Saxon branch of the Nordic race, as compared with other races, again showed itself to be that race "upon which the nation must depend for leadership, for courage, for unity and harmony of action, for self-sacrifice and devotion to an ideal."[21] For Osborn, the conservation of the Nordic race was necessary for "the true spirit of Americanism."

Even more ardent as an advocate of Nordicism was lawyer and publicist Lothrop Stoddard. In a series of popular books,[22] he viewed with alarm what he called denoridicization in the United States. For Stoddard, the "Law of Inequality" of races was as universal and inflexible as the Law of Gravitation. He attacked Locke, Hume, Rousseau, John Stuart Mill, and Lamarck as deluded environmentalists, who misunderstood the transcendent importance of heredity by advocating the equality of human beings. In his *Revolt Against Civilization: The Menace of the Under-Man* (1922), Stoddard described how racial impoverishment had wrecked the great civilizations of the past and threatened to destroy American society. The influx of inferior races was an unmitigated disaster: bestial "under-men" were a grim peril to civilization. In his *Rising Tide of Color Against White World Supremacy* (1920), Stoddard started out to revise his earlier views on Nordicism, only to end up by re-stating his theories. The United States, he wrote, which originally had been settled by Nordics, had allowed the immigration of Alpines, Mediterraneans, Levantines, and Jews, all of whom were beginning to crowd out native Nordic Americans. The result was a mongrelized off-spring, "a walking chaos, so consumed by the jarring heredities that he is quite worthless."

It is hardly necessary to point out the fallacies of Anglo-Saxonism.[23] There is no more an Anglo-Saxon race or a British race than an American race. Race is a biological or anthropological term referring to species of human beings, based on such characteristics as skin color, hair texture, stature, and other physical or inherited characteristics. It denotes common biological descent, not common cultural characteristics. There is no such thing as a *pure* race as advocated by Anglo-Saxonists. For centuries the races have intermingled, and the process of mixing continues. Hitler's concept of a "pure Aryan race" was a simple fraud—Aryan or Indo-European are linguistic, not racial, terms.

The illogical claim of Anglo-Saxonists and Pan-Nordicists for the purity of the Anglo-Saxon race was demolished by Karl Pearson, a British eugenist, who gave a devastating analysis of the so-called "pure-blooded Englishman":

We are accustomed to speak of a typical Englishman. For example, Charles Darwin; we think of his mind as a typical English mind, working in the typical English manner, yet when we come to study his pedigree we seek in vain for "purity of race."

He is descended in four different lines from Irish kinglets; he is descended in as many lines from Scottish and Pictish kings. He has Manx blood. He claims descent in as many lines from Alfred the Great, and so links up with Anglo-Saxon blood, but he links up also in several lines with Charlemagne and his Carlovingians. He sprang also from the Saxon emperor of Germany as well as Barbarossa and the Hohenstaufens. He has Norwegian blood and much Norman blood. He has descent from the Dukes of Bavaria, of Saxony, of Flanders, the Prince of Savoy, and Kings of Italy. He has the blood in his veins of Franks, Alemans, Merovingians, Burgundians, and Langobards. He sprang in direct descent from the Hun rulers of Hungary and Greek Emperors of Constantinople. If I recollect rightly, Ivan the Terrible provides a Russian link. There is probably not one of the races of Europe concerned in folk-wanderings which has not had a share in the ancestry of Charles Darwin.[24]

Contrary to the claim of racialists, there is no such thing as a "superior" race. Every civilized group of which we have a record has been a hybrid combination. There is no evidence to support the theory that cross-bred peoples are inferior to the so-called pure-bred ones. The idea that any one race—white, black, or red—is superior in meeting the challenges of its environment is merely wishful thinking. The growth of civilization has proceeded with serene indifference to racial lines. The assertion that only the white race is capable of founding and sustaining culture cannot be demonstrated historically. The white race came into civilization rather late at a time when Chinese culture was already in a high stage of development. No one race can claim the exclusive right to represent the final stage of human evolution.

Anglo-Saxonists went off the rational beam when they confused race with nation or nationality. Loose usage of the terms "race" and "nation" as synonymous is responsible for much of the confusion surrounding both words. In popular thinking, race and nation are often identified as meaning one and the same thing. Most people find it difficult to conceive of a close social unity without a physical bond, and cannot think of a common mentality without common blood. The idea of solidarity between members of a nation takes on the implication of a real relationship between members of a family. This was the delusive idea of those who spoke carelessly of a British "race."

The term "nation" belongs properly in the sphere of the social sciences, while "race" should be reserved for the natural sciences. Nation designates historical and social characteristics that can be altered by society, while race refers to hereditary, biological traits not easily changed by education or assimilation. There never has been a French, Spanish, or Italian race, but there are French, Spanish, and Italian nations.

A nation is not the physical fact of one blood, but the mental fact of one tradition. Race refers to a common physical type, nation to a common mental content. Race is a natural fact, nation is an artificial structure constructed by the thoughts, feelings, and wills of the human mind.

Anglo-Saxonists also made the mistake of confusing race with culture. Race is essentially a matter of heredity, while culture is one of tradition. Race is concerned with the inheritance of bodily characteristics, while culture is transmitted through social organization. Culture refers to a whole structure of beliefs, knowledge, and literature, of concepts, sentiments, and institutions carried from one generation to another through the vehicle of language. Anglo-Saxonists failed to see this distinction.

In summary, Anglo-Saxonism as a pan-movement was based on false reasoning and misleading argument. In presenting a theory based on race, it opened a can of semantic worms. As a macro-nationalism, it remained a loose and ephemeral ideology which never took on the characteristics of an organized movement. In both British and American versions, it called for white Anglo-Saxon superiority in what it deemed to be a conflict between races. It took this idea of superiority for granted and found it unnecessary to prove it. It remained a misty ideology, suffused with mysticism. Where Pan-Slavism and Pan-Germanism were institutionalized and promoted, holding congresses to perpetuate the movement, and where champions of Pan-Europa worked diligently to establish a United States of Europe, champions of Anglo-Saxonism found it unnecessary to set up any kind of viable organization. For them it was superfluous to transform ideology into movement.

Phoenix in Haze: Pan-Latinism

Where Anglo-Saxonism originated on the periphery of the Continent, there were additional pan-movements on the mainland inspired by the idea of imperial destiny. Pan-Latinism found its motivation in the desire to re-create the imperial majesty of Rome.

In 476 A.D., Odoacer, a barbarian who had entered the Roman imperial service, drove Romulus Augustus, young puppet emperor, from the throne at Rome, and was proclaimed emperor by his fellow warriors. That date—August 23, 476 A.D.—marked the political end of the great empire that had dominated the Western world. Yet, in the strict sense of the word, Rome never "fell." Rather it disintegrated over a long period of time due to a combination of causes—declining agriculture, trade, and industry; a rigid caste system of priviledged and unprivileged social groups; graft, corruption, inefficiency, favoritism, and waste in administration; mental and moral dry rot; and the rise of Christianity. The political organism disappeared, but there was an important residue of contributions—Roman bridges, roads, and aqueducts; Roman legal codes and literature; and the Latin language.

There was political decline, but the ideal of a Roman Empire was revived. After infiltration and invasions by Germanic barbarians, the Franks brought about a temporary consolidation in the 8th and 9th centuries. With support from the Bishop of Rome, the Carolingians revived the empire under papal auspices. But the failure of Charlemagne to establish any firm unity in his empire, added to invasions by Northmen, led to the disruption of the empire after his death.

The idea of Roman unity died hard. Nevertheless, a small group of intellectuals saw unity, and proposed a tenuous movement called Pan-Latinism. On the European scene it was the southern counterpart of the Nordic movement in the Scandinavian countries. Three nations—Spain, France, and Italy—were involved.

The supposed unity hinged on a common linguistic base. The Latin language was an Indo-European tongue belonging to the Italic group, the ancestral language of modern Romance languages. Spoken originally by tribes on the lower Tiber, it spread along with the Roman Republic through the Italian peninsula, and with the Roman Empire through most of western and southern Europe and the central and western Mediterranean coastal regions of North Africa. Modern Romance languages developed from spoken Latin. During the Middle Ages and until today, Latin remained the language of the Roman Catholic Church. Through the medieval era it was used in scholarly and literary circles.

Pan-Latinists, confusing the concept of language, called for a union of those people whose basic tongue was Latin. Once again a pan-movement came into being. Remaining an evanescent dream, it was never transformed into institutionalized reality. The cause was simple: Spaniards, French, and Italians became divided permanently by historical traditions, political ambitions, and imperial goals. They wanted no unifying *Pax Romana* to disturb their national sovereignty, and threaten the borders they had fashioned for themselves. They had emerged as nation-states in what was an Age of Nationalism, and they had no intention of dissolving their hard-won unity in favor of an unsteady macro-nationalism.

Behind Pan-Latinism, like Anglo-Saxonism, Pan-Lusitanism, and Pan-Hispanism, was the familiar urge to attain a nationalism writ large, and to extend the nation-state into imperial majesty on a common linguistic base. Those who spoke Romance languages, derived from Latin, were supposed to belong together in a super-state. The desire for union was present, but the means for implementation were lacking. Pan-Latinism, like other pan-movements, was the victim of a powerful historical trend—the persistence of national consciousness in the established nation-states. It remained only an obscure, loosely knit idea pursued by a few intellectuals, who never were able to win wide popular support.

Portuguese Pan-Lusitanism

Like Anglo-Saxonism, Pan-Lusitanism called for the unity of an empire-minded people on the assumption that they had a community of interests. It aimed at the solidarity of Portuguese-speaking peoples in a special relationship of cultural reciprocity and mutual history and traditions. It sought for a sympathetic relationship rather than the kind of political organization called for by Pan-Germanism or Pan-Slavism.

Again like Anglo-Saxonism, Pan-Lusitanism originated in a small country. Portugal, with an area of 35,340 square miles, occupies the southwestern part of the Iberian peninsula, and is bordered by Spain and the Atlantic. The small country, however, played a major role in the discovery of the world's highway in early modern times.[25]

Pan-movement ideologists generally delve deeply into their history for evidence of mutual interests. Champions of Pan-Lusitanism are no exception. Portuguese have long thought themselves to be descendants of Lusitanians, who had their stronghold in the Serra da Estrêla. This early tribe swept down in raids on the rich plains. A Celtic people, Lusitanians under the brilliant leadership of Viriathus in the 2nd century B.C., and under Certorius in the 1st century B.C., resisted Roman inroads. Julius Caesar and Augustus finally managed to subdue the Lusitanians, who adopted Roman ways and a Romance tongue which ultimately became Portuguese. The whole Iberian Peninsula was overrun by Germanic Visigoths. After the defeat of the Visigoths in 711, most of the peninsula fell to the Moors.

During the early medieval era, Portugal remained an obscure region of Spain and shared its history. A kingdom was established between 1279 and 1415, despite opposition from the nobility, Church, and Castile. The nation was unified by 1500. Meanwhile, Portugal emerged as a prosperous maritime state, the first colonial empire of modern times, reaching from Brazil to the East Indies. This development was due in large part to the planning of Prince Henry the Navigator (1394-1460).[26] After taking part in crusades against the Moors, he led expeditions along the African coastline, during which he tried to establish contact with Prester John, a legendary ruler who was said to have set up a Christian kingdom in the East. In 1419, Prince Henry founded a school at Sagres on the southwest tip of Portugal, a research institute with shipyards, an observatory, and classrooms. Here he trained captains, pilots, navigators, astronomers, and cartographers, who sailed southward and westward to the Madeiras, Cape Verde Islands, and the Azores.

After the death of Prince Henry in 1460, Portuguese captains attempted the circumnavigation of Africa, a venture completed in 1497, when Vasco da Gama rounded the Cape of Good Hope and sailed boldly across the Indian Ocean.[27] Portuguese explorers moved into the Sahara hinterland, the interior of Africa, the Far East, and the New World. King Manuel of Portugal (1495-1521) assumed the title of "Lord of the Conquest, Navigation, and Commerce of India, Ethiopia, Arabia, and Persia," a designation confirmed by the papacy.

The Portuguese were successful in constructing a huge commercial empire at a time when Italian cities were decaying and Mediterranean trade was declining. Lisbon became a center of trade in bullion, ivory, and slaves. Portuguese merchants set up a string of settlements between homeland and the Orient. Their fleets of merchant ships came home laden with gold and slaves, the latter regarded as unfortunates whose souls were to be saved.

For a brief century, the Portuguese in the Far East and the Spanish in America shared the fruits of what amounted to a trade monopoly. In 1580, however, Portugal's decline began when Spain invaded the country, and held her in captivity for sixty years. The thinly spread Portuguese commercial fleet then could not serve the needs of expanding trade, and Portuguese entrepreneurs, short of funds, found themselves in the grip of

German and Italian financiers. At the same time, the Portuguese colonial administration was weakened by inefficiency and corruption. The dynasty restored in 1640 found itself in competition with Dutch, French, and English entrepreneurs, who had unlimited supplies of capital and manpower.

Early in the 19th century, Portugal lost her American possessions, notably Brazil, but later managed to hold an extensive colonial empire elsewhere—the Cape Verde Islands off West Africa; Angola, Portuguese Guinea, and Mozambique in Africa; Goa in India; and Macoa in China. Resources of the small country were strained by the cost of administering this far-flung empire.

The story of Portugal in the 19th century was one filled with dynastic quarrels and civil strife. Many thousands of Portuguese, angered by misrule, excessive taxation, and delay in needed reforms, emigrated. The country entered the 20th century with a government burdened by inefficiency, incompetence, and corruption.

Portugal and Spain were the first to come to Africa, and the last to leave it. In the mid-20th century, at a time of receding colonialism, both countries continued to designate their African possessions as "overseas provinces," in theory holding the same rights as metropolitan provinces, but actually remaining under colonial control. Portugal was the last European nation to hold an extensive empire in Africa. In 1961 India annexed the Portuguese conclave of Goa. In April 1974 the Portuguese government reached agreements providing independence for Guinea-Bissau, Mozambique, Cape Verde Islands, Angola, and Saõ Thomé and Principe.

Despite the dissolution of a once-prosperous empire, the usual group of scholars and publicists emerged to sponsor a pan-movement. For such dedicated nationalists, the loss of an empire was merely an aberration in Portuguese history. Tradition and sentiment, they insisted, called for a general rapprochement of all Portuguese. They went far back into history to find the original Lusitanian tribes as typically Portuguese, with fine disregard for the fact that modern Portuguese were a mixture of Celts, Phoenicians, Greeks, Roman, Visigoths, and Arabs. Champions of macro-nationalism are not distinguished by respect for logic or fact.

Pan-Lusitanians pointed to Portuguese as the mother tongue of some 135 million people living on two continents. They saw it as a distinctive language even though it contained many Arab, Teutonic, and Asian words. For them Portugal was wherever Portuguese was spoken.

Pan-Lusitanians presented their own Portuguese literary heroes. Fernão Lopes (c. 1378-1460), leading medieval historian, appointed Chronicler of the Realm, wrote vivid accounts of the founding of the nation, its territorial conquests, and its tenacious defense of independence. The favorite of the Pan-Lusitanians was Luís Camões (1524-1580), the great national poet. In Os Lusiadas (1572; The Lusiads, 1952), Camoes composed a literary masterpiece of ten cantos devoted to the praise of Portugal, Prince Henry the Navigator, Vasco da Gama, and other heroes of the Golden Age of Discovery. Motivated by the Roman poet Virgil, Camões poured into his epic his own Portuguese passion and patriotism. His poem about the Portuguese political pride and national character had an extraordinary impact on both Portuguese and Brazilian literature.

Like other macro-nationalists, Pan-Lusitanians were attracted by the work of Romanticists after 1830. This was in keeping with the general movement of European romanticism, which among its many strands included an emotional return to indigenous and traditional themes. This literary development indicated a close nexus between romanticism and nationalism. Almeida Garrett heaped praise on the Lusitanian genius and brought literature back to Portuguese soil, especially in his *Viagens na Minha Terra (Travels Through My Land)* (1846). His historical epic poems and plays gave him rank as the greatest of Portuguese Romantics and an outstanding figure in Portuguese literature. Alexandre Herculano, the father of modern Portuguese historiography, used critical methods in examining the Portuguese past, and also introduced the historical novel in his country. António Feliciano de Castilho, the third great Romantic, was noted for the purity of his vernacular style.

The work of Romantics in stressing the heroic national past was continued through the 19th and 20th centuries. When the Republic was established in 1910, writers broke into two opposing groups, those who favored the new regime and reform and those who emphasized traditional values. The former, calling themselves the *Renasença Portuguesa*, included the poet Teixeira de Pascoais and the philosopher Leonardo Coimbra. The latter, known as the *Integalismo Lusitano*, hewed to the Romantic line of traditional nationalism (António Sardinha, poet and essayist, was its leader). There were differences, but both groups praised the mournfully contemplative Lusitanian temperament.

Despite the optimistic claims of its adherents, Pan-Lusitanism remained an unattained goal of emotional patriots. It shared the weaknesses of other pan-movements dedicated to reviving the glory of a once-prosperous empire. As an extension of the national idea, Pan-Lusitanism sought to promote exclusiveness, superiority, and xenophobia. Like other pan-movements, it remained only a historical oddity, still another unfulfilled dream.

Pan-Hispanism

The idea of imperial glory also permeated Pan-Hispanism, the twin of Pan-Lusitanism. Spanish nationalism, like nationalisms elsewhere in Europe, was stimulated by the 18th-century Enlightenment, by dissatisfaction with the reactionary monarchy, and by the general unhappy pattern of Spanish social and economic life. Its immediate origin, however, was in the French invasion of 1808. In Spain, as elsewhere, there was an outburst of hatred against the conqueror Napoleon and the foreign rule he had imposed. There were loud outcries against French perfidy. In 1809, a journalist predicted that "we will recover our former customs, sing our own songs, dance our own dances, and dress in ancient style [because the] nation is formed, not by the number of individuals, but by the union of wills, the conformity of the laws, customs, and language, which maintain and keep them together from generation to generation."[28] With the aid of the British, the Spanish managed to drive out Napoleon's invaders by 1813. By this time Spanish nationalism had come of age.[29]

Like Pan-Lusitanians, Pan-Hispanics went beyond the early stages of Spanish nationalism to a movement designed to include all Spaniards in a revived Greater Spain. Behind this goal was the story of Spanish colonial enterprise, which matched and even went beyond that of the Portuguese. While Portugal painstakingly planned her way to empire, Spain's rewards fell to her accidentally and unexpectedly. By the end of the 15th century, her long crusade against Muslim power had come to an end. The country was also unified in 1469 with the marriage of Ferdinand of Aragon and Isabella of Castile, which joined the central pastoral kingdom with the eastern agricultural and commercial areas.

With the accidental discovery of the New World in 1492, the Spanish began to construct a colonial empire. In the process, they emerged for a time as the most powerful European nation. The story of Spanish enterprise during the half century after the voyages of Christopher Columbus is a familiar one and need not be repeated in detail here.[30] Spanish navigators and *conquistadores* set out on expeditions to the New World to stake their claim. Like the Portuguese, they were attracted by gold, glory, and God. Originally, they were interested in prized commodities in the Far East, but they shifted their field of vision after hearing reports of fabulous wealth in the New World.

It was a movement of discovery, conquest, and colonization. Ponce de León landed in Florida in 1513 in search of the legendary fountain of perpetual youth. In the same year, Vasco Nuñez de Balboa crossed Central America and became the first European to behold the waters of the Pacific. Intoxicated by reports of gold, Hernando Cortés led an army into Mexico (1519-1521), conquering the Aztec government. Between 1531 and 1535 Francisco Pizarro subjugated the rich Inca empire centering in Peru. In 1540 Francisco Vasquez de Coronado set out to explore the western area of North America. The next year Fernando de Soto discovered the Mississippi River.

Following these explorations, there came the construction of a Spanish empire in the grand manner, colored by avarice and bigotry. Soldiers and settlers, anxious for gold and glory, were accompanied by missionaries pledged to convert the natives to Christianity. *Conquistadores* became rich beyond their wildest dreams, striking down the prosperous Aztecs and Incas until they lay prostrate. They insisted on *encomiendas*, the right to extract tribute and services, in return for which they would civilize backward tribes. In her Golden Century, Spain acquired a colonial empire which included Central and South America (excluding Portuguese Brazil), the West Indies, Florida, California, and Mexico—one of the most extensive empires the world had ever known.

The great Spanish Empire was destined to be shattered by paralyzing absolutism and economic deficits. A combination of unfavorable political and economic factors worked for its disintegration. Politically, the Spanish colonial system turned out to be merely an appendage of royal absolutism. The Spanish dynasty could not cope with this huge construction. It dissipated its energies in attempting to retain its power on the European Continent, rule the Netherlands, extirpate Protestantism, and fight the Turks, while at the same time building a huge empire in the New World. The centralized bureaucracy in Madrid attempted unsuccessfully to direct colonial administration. Distances were too great; there were problems of transportation and communication, and there was dogged resistance in the colonies.

Gold turned out to be the danger in the process. From the beginning, the *conquistadores* were obsessed with lust for the precious metal. Spanish merchants and capitalists, neglecting to emphasize their industry and commerce, sent their gold to other countries to buy luxury products, instead of using it at home to bolster the national economy. The Spanish masses were oppressed by taxation and inflation. With business initiative stifled, tax evasion rampant, bribery in official circles, and general economic discontent, the economy went into decline. Moreover, there was strong competition from the Netherlands, France, and England.

The final blow came in 1588 when Spain's proud Invincible Armada was annihilated by a combination of British seamanship and unfriendly Nature. The empire went into decline after this decisive defeat, though the Spanish cultural heritage remained durable in the New World.

For champions of Pan-Hispanism, the melancholy outcome of this experiment in empire was unimportant. More significant, in their view, were the days of glory of a vast empire. They saw Hispania as a division of the ancestral Roman Empire, housing a people of undoubted superiority, who were destined to control a huge empire. The Spanish people, they said, belonged together not only by tradition and sentiment, but also by the compulsion of common interests. They were bound together by a common language as well as by a relationship of cultural reciprocity. The Spanish tongue and Spanish art and literature meant Spanish solidarity.

This was the essence not only of Spanish nationalism, but also of its extension into the realm of a pan-movement. Spanish Hispanics even called for the restoration of the old colonial empire on a democratic basis. The world should be given the benefits of the Spanish national character, with its courage, enterprise, and sense of dignity which distinguished Spaniards from all other peoples (*dignidad*).

For evidence of *Hispanidad*, pride in being Spanish, both nationalists and Pan-Hispanics presented their special cultural attributes. For those who limited their patriotic fervor to the Iberian Peninsula, as well as those who saw *Hispanidad* as extending wherever Spanish was spoken, pride and dignity were to be found in a wide variety of pursuits, from music to flamenco dancing. If one wants to observe Spanish national character, let him walk through the Prado and gaze at the distinctive art of Velasquez, Murillo, and Goya. Let him sit in the shade at the Madrid bull ring to observe Spanish calm and nobility in the face of death.

Like their peers elsewhere, Spanish nationalists pointed to their literature as the expression of a gifted, superior people. There was, indeed, much to justify this sense of self-esteem. In its long and rich tradition, Spanish literature combined such opposing elements as idealism and realism, religion and materialism, noble and low behavior—all in lofty and rich language. Spanish literature is noted for its dignity, stoicism, and use of the honor theme. Nationalists praised the medieval Castilian *Poema el Cid*. This anonymous epic, written about 1140, extols the deeds of Spain's national hero, Ruy Díaz de Bivar. Remarkable for its historical and geographical realism, it is set apart from other epic poems of European literature. Filled with exaggerated fantasies and strange improbabilities, it presents those sentiments of pride, honor, and pity long associated with the Spanish mind and soul.

Spanish nationalists also pointed to their brilliant Golden Age of literature, including the Renaissance of the 16th century and the Baroque of the 17th century. Among the masterpieces of this era was *Don Quixote of the Mancha* (1605, 1615), by Miguel de Cervantes, the most important figure in Spanish literature. The first modern novel and one of the greatest in world literature, *Don Quixote* was begun as a satire of romances of chivalry. It grew slowly into a vast panorama of Spanish life. It offered not only a magnificent view of 17th-century Spain, but also of many enduring characteristics of the Spanish people. Known everywhere as the story of an idealistic lunatic, Don Quixote, who regarded himself as a medieval knight, and his faithful paladin, Sancho Panza, the story is much more than a series of comical adventures arising from the knight's efforts to conform to the noble code of chivalry which he sought to revive. It depicts the conflict of noble dreams in the truculent world of fact. Spanish nationalists were rightly proud of this great literary achievement.

Spanish nationalists, again like other European nationalists, saw the literature of their Romantic era as giving special support for their cause. Among the important characteristics of Spanish Romanticism, especially during the period from 1830 to 1850, was a return to forms and themes considered implicit in the Spanish soul. Spanish writers revived interest in medieval poetry and in the Golden Age. They rediscovered the country's myths and heroes, exalted the sentiments of the individual, and emphasized the importance of nature in Spanish national life. The literary work of this and succeeding eras always drew attention to special Spanish traits. As elsewhere, literature became the cement of a structured nationalism. But it was unable to further the cause of a larger Pan-Hispanism.

Pan-Iberianism

Because Spain and Portugal shared a common peninsula and even a common history for a time, there were those who conceived of a pan-movement to include both peoples. Behind that view was the fact that the Romans, taking most of the peninsula, had combined the early Iberian tribes with Celts under Roman control. Except for Basques in the north, the Iberian peoples became thoroughly Romanized. Only later was there a breakdown into Portuguese and Spanish segments.

The broad category of Iberian culture is applied usually to the civilization that emerged in the south and east during the five or six centuries before Christ. Pan-Iberian enthusiasts believed that the entire peninsula by historical tradition should be united in its original form. Pan-Iberians noted an intermixture of peoples, but they called attention instead to the national character shared by both peoples. These traits included love of pageantry, lack of prejudice, and flexibility as a behavior pattern.

Pan-Iberians were overly optimistic about the community of Portuguese and Spanish life styles. Their common history was brief, and both nations developed along different lines. Portuguese professed themselves amused by Spanish sensitivity and the tendency to suffer at the merest hint of an insult. They saw themselves as more easygoing, as more tolerant of differing customs, perhaps a bit more melancholy.

For Pan-Iberians this evidence of national character and concomitant stereotypes made no difference. All the peoples of the peninsula, they argued, represented merely an extension of an indigenous culture. Hence, by history and tradition they belonged together in a greater nationalism. It was the classic cry of macro-nationalists everywhere. Like other pan-movements, however, it never reached a state of organization, but instead remained the dream of a small band of dedicated nationalists.

Great Netherlands

Dutch nationalists had no intention of being left out of the pan-sweepstakes. They, too, had visions of a great empire with a community of Dutch traditions and interests. Dutch nationalism joined the stream of European nationalisms. From Scandinavia to Spain, from the Atlantic to the Volga, the peoples of Europe were fashioning their own national states even before the French Revolution. As early as the 17th century, Dutchmen began to assert their own sense of national consciousness.[31] The

Netherlands was a small country, but here, too, a little group of dedicated patriots called for nationalism writ large.

One of the Low Countries, the Netherlands had no unified history until the 16th century.[32] During the days of the Roman Empire, it formed the Roman province of Lower Germany inhabited by Batavi Frisians. German infiltration into the area continued for centuries. From the 5th to the 8th centuries, the territory was taken by the Franks. There was no "pure blood" in the Netherlands—the Dutch were a mixture of Frisians, Franks, and Saxons.

Dutch nationalists looked to the past, and found it highly attractive. With a favorable geographical position but limited soil, the people turned to maritime enterprise. In the late 16th and early 17th centuries, Dutch merchants, breaking into Oriental trade at the expense of Portugal, acquired Ceylon, Sumatra, the Spice Islands, and Java. Explorers and merchant adventurers ventured into South Africa, Brazil, and the West Indies. They established a settlement at New Amsterdam, the site of New York City. By the 17th century, Dutch merchants supplanted their Portuguese and Spanish competitors and became the commercial masters of Europe. Their interests were wide: Norway was their forest, the banks of the Rhine and the Garonne their vineyards, the Germanies, Spain, and Ireland their grain fields, and India and Arabia their spice gardens. For a time, Amsterdam became the financial center of Europe and the world.

However, the glorious Dutch colonial entity did not survive the 17th century. Slowly, it succumbed to the aggressive competition of France and Britain. This did not deter Dutch nationalists, anymore than it did Portuguese and Spanish nationalists, all of whom were reluctant to drop their vision of a past brilliant empire. Dutch nationalists began to call for a Greater Netherlands, a revival of past imperial majesty.

It was an unheard cry in the dark. Dutchmen had enough on their hands in the continuing battle to preserve the homeland from the ravages of the North Sea. With extraordinary skill and hard work, they managed to keep their land above dangerous waters. The days of imperial glory were long past for the small country. As with other similar pan-movements, the Great Netherlands movement remained a tiny, insubstantial one supported only by a handful of Dutch patriots.

The Nordic Movement: Pan-Scandinavianism

The most successful of all European pan-movements has been the Nordic combination of Denmark, Norway, Sweden, Iceland, and Finland. Holding the belief that one vigorous voice would be more effective than five weak ones, these Nordic nations have shared what they called their "transnational character." Linked by similar parliamentary systems, laws, education, Lutheran background, and a passion for social reform, the five nations have come closer to relinquishing national sovereignty than any other European pan-movement. There has even been a trend toward common citizenship. The goal is to have all citizens of the Nordic bloc live, work, and draw welfare benefits almost anywhere in Scandinavia.

Behind this development was a common historical pattern.[33] In 1815, after the downfall of Napoleon, the statesmen of Vienna, intent upon remaking the map of Europe on the basis of "legitimacy and compensations," recognized Sweden's annexation of Norway. Norway was taken from Denmark, which had sided with France in the Napoleonic Wars. The union of Norway, inhabited by fishermen, merchants, and peasants, and Sweden, a country of large estates and tenant farmers, was not a happy one, but it lasted for nearly a century. On June 7, 1905, the *Storting*, the Norwegian Parliament, declared the union with Sweden dissolved, a decision ratified by popular vote. The Swedish *Riksdag* acquiesced, whereupon the Norwegian Parliament invited a Danish prince to the Norwegian throne as King Haakon VII. A treaty provided that all disputes were to be settled by arbitration and that no fortifications be erected on the common frontier.

This peaceful separation, a rare event in European history, indicated a desire for close relationship between Nordic peoples. Separated by physical barriers and historic rivalries, Scandinavian peoples have developed distinctive national characteristics, sometimes extended into national stereotypes. The Swedes are said to be stiff, thorough, and neurotic; the Norwegians simple, rough, and courageous; the Danes jolly, friendly, and sophisticated; the Finns introverted, dour, and melancholy. There is probably a measure of truth in these generalizations.

Nevertheless, these diverse Nordic peoples have had much in common. All have produced egalitarian states, unhampered by poverty, unemployment, and illiteracy. In many respects, Scandinavians have presented an object lesson to peoples divided by national rivalries. Dedicated to peace, they regard war as cannibalism, as the sure way to despair and hopelessness. Scandinavian intelligence also has produced great achievements in social reform, setting a standard for all the world.

The urge for Scandinavian union had deep roots. In 1850 Karl XV, King of Norway-Sweden, pointing to history, tradition, and preference, declared that Norwegians, Swedes, and Danes belonged together as a Nordic people. At this time, the Schleswig-Holstein question in Denmark was heating to the boiling point. The Germans, with their national revival gathering momentum, were turning their attention to the two Danish provinces, which they claimed as their own. German orators spoke of "gallant Schleswig-Holsteiners," who were resisting Danish "aggression and tyrannical rule." Emboldened by growing support from Germany, Holsteiners rejected the Danish plan for a common constitution, and called for a return to the pre-1848 institution of four distinct assemblies, two Danish and two German. Danes turned the proposal down.

In Denmark a movement, named Eider-Danish, called for the union of Denmark and Schleswig. Pan-Scandinavianism, sponsored in Norway, supported the Eider-Danish. In the succeeding involved negotiations, Bismarck seized the initiative to strengthen his own drive for national unity. However, when war came in 1864, the Danes received no help from Norway, Sweden, or the Pan-Scandinavian movement, and only a few Norwegian and Swedish volunteers fought alongside the Danes in their hopeless struggle against combined Prussian and Austrian military power.

Despite that blow to Scandinavian unity, the idea of Nordic communion persisted. In 1952, the five countries formed the Nordic Council to arrange cooperation among members in legal, social, and economic matters. No official headquarters existed, but meetings were held at various capitals, and legal and social integration became well advanced with the establishment of a common passport area, and the extension of working rights and social benefits to citizens of member countries. In 1959 the Nordic Council voted to function within the European Free Trade Association (EFTA). Suggestions were made for working together in a customs union which would be presumably of wider scope than that encompassed by EFTA.[34]

In the United Nations, the five Nordic nations, working together as a bloc, have exerted collective influence on such issues as human rights and world peace. More and more, the Scandinavians have acted as if they belonged to one family, as if they were seeking to enjoy much more leverage by common action. The working arrangement was informal, but carefully structured with five ambassadors holding weekly meetings. Common positions were set by a designated speaker from among the five nations. As in close relationships, there have been differences of opinion, but these have been kept within the family. The image conveyed, however, has been one of fraternal unity of the Nordic nations.

In a world characterized by more rifts than rapport, the five Nordic nations, with a combined population of 22 million, have presented a rare unity of peoples. Pooling their information, they have formed the only Western European bloc acting as an entity at the United Nations. There has been close cooperation there, but certainly no mitigation of national sovereignty. Despite the community of interests, Pan-Scandinavianism has remained an insubstantial movement. There have been many common positions, but national identity has not submerged. This has been the usual attribute of virtually all macro-nationalisms.

CHAPTER **6**

TURKISH DILEMMA: PAN-OTTOMANISM, PAN-TURKISM, AND PAN-TURANISM

The country of the Turks is not Turkey, nor yet Turkestan,
That country is a broad and everlasting land—Turan.
> —Ziyā Gökalp, 1911, quoted in
> Elie Kedouri, *Nationalism in Asia and Africa*
> (New York, 1970), p. 51.

Pan-Movements in Multiplicity

Whereas pan-movements like Pan-Slavism and Pan-Germanism developed along unitary lines, macro-nationalism in Turkey broke down into four different factions. Each faction attracted its own following and all retreated eventually into obscurity. Typical of rivalries in the Islāmic world, each pan-movement saw itself as the bearer of a wider Turkish nationalism.

All four of these pan-movements were offshoots of Young Turk ideology. Each had its own road to power. Pan-Ottomanism sought to unite all peoples of the Ottoman Empire—Turks, Arabs, Greeks, Albanians, and Jews—into one super-Ottoman nationality. Pan-Islāmism called for the union of all Muslims, including those in Turkey, into one ecclesiastical nation. Pan-Turkism insisted that all those who lived in the Empire should become Turks, including those non-Turks who spoke the Turkish language. Finally, Pan-Turanism advocated a close alliance with Turkish-speaking peoples residing in Turan (Central Asia), ancestral home of the Turks, in the Caucasus, the lower Volga, and the Crimea.

All four Turkish pan-movements were closely related, though they differed in primary goals. There was a sense of rivalry between Pan-Islāmism and Pan-Turanism. The latter attempted not only to glorify its pre-Islāmic past but also to divest the "pure" Turkish tongue of all Arabic and Persian elements. It would go beyond Islām to seek its origin in an independent tradition as a prerequisite for a great future.

The Turks in History

When the Seljuk Turks were unable to maintain the integrity of their empire against Christian Crusaders, they were supplanted by the more aggressive Ottoman Turks.[1] Taking their name from Osman, Ottoman Turks overran the Asian provinces that at one time had been under Roman control. They seized Constantinople in 1453, a seminal event in European history, by which the door was closed for Western Europeans to the Far East, and by which the discovery of the world's highway was stimulated. With Constantinople as their capital, the Ottoman Turks combined Turkish, Byzantine, and Islāmic traditions in a despotic regime, which reached heights of real splendor under Suleiman the Magnificent (r.1520-1566). Thereafter, the story is one of continuous decline.

Not a common nationality but a common religion formed the basis of Ottoman rule. The dominant hierarchy of Ottoman Turks had little in common with Arab-speaking peoples in their empire other than the religion of Islām. Ottoman Turks regarded Arabs as provincial vassals living in religious communities called millets, and forming states within the Ottoman state. Ottoman Turks had little use or understanding for the Western concept of the national state. Instead they were subjects in a religious state, whose sultan was restricted in his despotism only by the laws of Islām.

Turkish autocracy culminated in the rule of Sultan Abdül Hamid II from 1876 to 1909, a reign for which he was given the European title of "Red Sultan" and William Gladstone's designation as the "Great Assassin." He used Pan-Islāmism as a means of bolstering his dictatorship. He called for international Muslim subscriptions to build the Hedjaz Railway to Damascus and Medina. He went to war with Serbia (1876), Russia (1877-1878), and Greece (1897). His government also condoned atrocities against Armenians (1894-1896), which aroused worldwide condemnation. Even today, Turkish diplomats are being assassinated by revengeful Armenian nationalists.

Abdül Hamid II was angered by the growing sentiment of dissatisfaction, which he felt was undermining the foundations of his empire. To counter any disintegrative tendencies, he presented himself as a champion of Islām, because he was certain that his people, strongly religious, would support him against the rising tide of minority nationalisms in his conglomerate empire.

It was a hopeless task, for the Ottoman Empire was in the process of dissolution. Disintegrative factors included: misrule, corruption in administration, lawlessness, and a clamor for autonomy or independence by dissenting minorities. So great were pressures on the state that it became known elsewhere as "the sick man of Europe." Moscow, the traditional enemy, looked forward with anticipation to the collapse of the Ottoman state. For a time it was rescued by the intervention of the British and French, who had no intention of allowing Russians to penetrate into the warm waters of the Mediterranean. The final collapse, however, could be delayed only temporarily.

Inside the shaky Ottoman Empire there began a call for reform, at first muted and then resounding. Islām was great, but its medieval tenets had left

Turkey far behind the rest of Europe. What was needed, in the view of increasingly vocal reformers, was a liberal constitution, parliamentarianism, and the Western educational process. Only then could Turkey take her place as a modern, prosperous state. Turkish students, who had been exposed to liberal European ideas, were humiliated in a comparison with Western European standards.

The most fervent opponents of Abdül Hamid II were the Young Turks, Europeanized intellectuals who from their exile in London and Paris waged a campaign against despotism at home.[2] They were convinced that the only salvation for their homeland lay in its transformation into a wholly European nation. With the battle cry *"Khalga doghru"* ("To the People"),[3] they called for a blend of diverse nationalities in the Empire in a modernized nation. They would remove Arabic and Persian words from the Turkish language. Above all, they demanded an end to the supremacy of Islām and its hierarchy of law-theologians, and called for equality of all religions. In effect, they opted for political instead of religious nationalism.

In 1906, the Young Turks transferred their headquarters from Paris to Salonika. They then took the name of the Committee of Union and Progress (*Ittihad ve Terakki*), and continued a steady drumfire for reform. When they gained support among army officers, the alarmed sultan responded with arrests, exile, and executions, but it was too late. Army officers moved from Salonika to Istanbul in 1908. Abdül Hamid then granted a constitutional government, but in April 1908 he was deposed. His brother, Mehmed V, was installed as a constitutional monarch.

In the capitals of Europe as well as in the Balkans, the Young Turk Revolution was regarded with favor. It soon became obvious, however, that despite their claims for liberalism, constitutionalism and modernization, Young Turks had no intention of allowing too much reform. They began to show themselves as despotic as the regime they displaced. The period of their rule (1908-1918) marked a growing estrangement between Turks and Arabs and a series of wars took place which drained the empire of its strength.

The business of government was more difficult than the Young Turks had supposed. They were unable to resolve the contradiction between the multinational empire, which they wanted to preserve, and the modern nation-state, which they hoped to create.[4] Intellectually, they suffered from serious inside differences. They regarded Pan-Islāmism as a divisive religious movement, but they could not agree on anything to take its place. Internecine rivalries emerged in four differing, but sometimes overlapping, movements—Pan-Ottomanism, Pan-Islāmism, Pan-Turkism, and Pan-Turanism, each with its own supporters.

Nationalist Apostle Ziyā Gökalp

Most Turks saw their nationalist hero in Ziyā Gökalp (1875-1924), pseudonym of Mehmad Ziyā, journalist, sociologist, and philosopher. For both nationalists and pan-nationalists, he was the voice of Turkish aspirations, the nationalist *par excellence* expressing the will of the Turkish people.

Gökalp saw three currents of thought in the development of Turkish nationalism.[5] First, came the period of need for modernization originating in the reign of Selim III (1789-1807). The strong movement toward Islāmization followed. The third era, Turkism, emerged in the mid-20th century.

According to Gökalp, Turkish nationalism, once awakened, led to a revival in political and economic life, language, literature, and even morality. It reinforced feelings of solidarity, sacrifice, and struggle. The idea of nationalism appeared in the Ottoman Empire originally among non-Muslims, then among Albanians and Arabs, and finally among Turks. Its appearance last among Turks was not accidental. The state was a nation already established, whereas the ideal of nationality meant the nucleus of a sentiment based on will (*nation de volonté*). Turks, with intuitive cautiousness, were reluctant at first to endanger a reality for the sake of an idea. Therefore, they came to believe not in Turkism but in Ottomanism.

The movement for Turkish modernization, in Gökalp's view, started with the *Kamzimat* policy initiated by the Reform Charter of 1839. Those who supported this movement believed that it was possible to create a nation based on the will of the existing nationalities and religions. They sought to give a new meaning devoid of any color of nationality to the older term "Ottoman," which had a certain historical meaning, but painful experience proved that this new meaning of "Ottoman" was welcomed by no one except the originators of the term. Inventing this new conception, Gökalp said, was not only useless but also detrimental, because it led to harmful consequences for both the state and the nationalities, especially for the Turks themselves.

At first, Gökalp was motivated primarily by the Islāmic faith. He saw the Balkan Wars preceding World War I as a *jihād*, a holy war of Muslims against Christians. At this stage, his heart's desire, he said, were two—religion and Fatherland; God must be called upon to make Islām flourish. By 1914, however, he began to have doubts about the primacy of religion. He criticized the Ottoman government for failing to declare a *jihād* on the Allies. He was angered by the participation of troops from India and other Muslim countries on the side of the enemy. He was annoyed also by the growing Arab revolt against the Sultan. By 1918 he was convinced that the unity of Islām was an impossible messianic hope. Theocratic Pan-Islāmism was, perhaps, an acceptable goal, but at the time it stood directly in the way of Turkish revival. In his view, if religion were to be used at all, it must serve the now truncated state. Islām in Turkey, he warned, must retain a unique Turkish character. National confidence had been shaken by the decline of Ottoman power, requiring a revival of ancient Turkish folklore, customs, and popular traditions.

According to Gökalp, there was, in fact, a homeland which was beloved by all Turks. It was called Turan: "The Ottoman territories are the portion of Islām which have remained independent. A portion of them is both the home of the Turks and a part of Turan. Another portion of them is the homeland of the Arabs which is again a part of the great Arab Fatherland."[6] Although he conceded the greatness of Islām, Gökalp, retreating from Pan-Islāmism, called for emphasis on Turkish nationalism, which he proclaimed in emotional poetry:

A land in which the call to prayer resounds from the mosque in the Turkish tongue,
Where the peasant understands the meaning of his prayers.
A land where the schoolboy reads the Koran in his mother tongue,
O son of the Turks, that is thy Fatherland.

Gökalp remained ambivalent about the relation of religion to state. As a Turkish nationalist, he supported the primacy of the state, but he was uncomfortable in the knowledge that he might be accused of failing to promote orthodox Islām. By twisted reasoning, he combined both nationalism and religion:

The state is not a power existing by itself. The state derives its power from the nation and from the *ümmet sharaf al-makān bil-makin* ["the glory of the residence is with the residents"]: Thus there are only two things which are sacred; the nation and the *ümmet* [the totality of those people who profess the same religion: the state consists of those who are administered by the same government; the nation is composed of all those who speak the same language]. As the objects of reverence are two, their symbols are the homeland of the *ümmet* and the homeland of the nation.[7]

Gökalp tried to reconcile the varied forms of nationalism in his homeland. Turkish nationalism, he said, was not contrary to the interests of the Ottoman state: "In fact it is its most important support. As in all young movements, there are some extremists among those who uphold Turkish nationalism, mainly among a portion of the youth who have caused certain misunderstandings to arise. In fact, Turkish is the real support of Islām and of the Ottoman state, and it is against cosmopolitanism."[8]

In seeking to reconcile the varied strands of nationalism in Turkey, Gökalp used a kind of tortuous reasoning typical of nationalists everywhere. He revered Islām but would not concede that it should dominate the state. He was never quite clear in his definitions. On the one hand, he regarded the state and religion as one, while on the other he saw an incompatibility between Turkish nationalism and Islām.

Among the basic themes presented by Gökalp were nationality and a concept he called "internationality." In his view, when Turkish thinkers entertained the idea of Ottoman nationality composed of different religious communities, they did not feel the necessity of Islāmization, but as soon as the idea of Turkism arose, "the need for Islāmization made itself felt." This was hazy thinking, but it made little difference to his supporters.

Pan-Ottomanism, Pan-Islāmism, Pan-Turkism, and Pan-Turanism simply used those portions of Gökalp's views which harmonized with their special goals. In common with pan-movements everywhere, each saw its cause as historically justified.

Pan-Ottomanism

Pan-Ottomanism was dedicated to the revival of the major Muslim power that had dominated southeastern Europe, the Middle East, and North Africa for centuries. Osman I, Muslim prince of northwestern Anatolia, and his Ottoman successors, annexed the Byzantine territories of western Anatolia, took Christian Balkan states into vassalage, and conquered Constantinople. By the end of the 16th century, the Ottoman Empire included nearly all of the Balkans, as well as most of the Muslin East and North Africa.

Reviving the glory and prosperity of this once great empire became the goal of mid-19th century intellectuals known as Young Ottomans. In 1865 they formed a secret society, named "Patriotic Alliance," and called for one common Ottoman nationality for all the varied peoples living in the empire. Meeting in Paris and London, they did not form an active political party, probably due to the diversity of views ranging from secularism to Islāmic traditionalism, from conservatism to revolution, and from nationalism to cosmopolitanism. However, they were united in their belief in the superiority of the Ottoman tradition. They envisioned a Pan-Ottoman Empire that would include different religions and cultures, and that would face the world as a modernized state. All its peoples would be controlled by the dominant Ottomans. They used the word "Turk" almost as a term of derision, connoting something like "yokel."

The attitude of the Young Ottomans to Islām was ambivalent. Most, however, adhered to early Islāmic concepts, and also looked with favor upon Pan-Islāmism as a unifying factor in the Ottoman state. Political Pan-Islāmism had begun as early as 1774 in a treaty with Russia, at a time when the Ottoman sultan claimed religious control over Muslims, even those outside his jurisdiction. As hitherto independent Muslim states were absorbed by European powers, Pan-Ottomans began to present the idea that the caliphate had been transferred to the Ottoman sultan.

Pan-Ottomans also differed among themselves about the value of adopting Western traditions. Some believed that they had much to learn from the West, while others maintained that the best that the West had to offer was already present in Islām. For example, Westerners boasted of their democratic institutions, but Pan-Ottomans pointed out that the idea of representative assemblies already existed in early Islāmic precepts and practices. Fatherland *and* Islām became dominating ideas in Ottoman ideology.

The most important figure among the Young Ottomans was Namik Kemal (1840-1888), who presented Ottomanist views in lucid prose. He opposed indiscriminate adoption of Western ways as unnecessary, because most of them were already present in Islām. He called for loyalty to the Ottoman Fatherland of all the varied peoples living in the empire. He also helped to popularize the call for a constitution. Many of his ideas were presented in such Young Ottoman newspapers as *Tercüman-i Ahval* (1860) and *Tasvir-i Efkâr* (1862).

In the early days of the Young Turk movement, Pan-Ottomans dominated the councils of the Young Turks. In the long run, however, Pan-Ottomanism failed to solve the problem of union of the various national movements in the sultan's domains. Pan-Ottomanism lost its thrust, because it sought to dominate rather than to conciliate. It was not able to combine varied strains of thought on the proper formation of state and nation.

Appeal of Pan-Turkism

At the beginning of the 20th century, the basic ideology of the state remained Ottomanism and Islām. Small groups of intellectuals espoused Pan-Ottomanism and Pan-Islāmism. But at this time there emerged a new sense of Turkish identity. Pan-Turkism called for the political union of all Turkish peoples, including those in the Middle East and Asia, the Tatars of the Crimea, and residents of the Volga region. All would be combined in one state, which would include both Ottoman and Russian Turks. The idea found increasing favor among Young Turks.

Pan-Turkism took on an increasing secular complexion. It turned from Islām, which it began to regard as an outmoded clerical ideology, and from a close collaboration with other Muslim peoples. Instead, Pan-Turkism placed emphasis on Turkish nationalism. Although it veered away from Pan-Islāmism, it did repeat Pan-Islāmic reactions against the encroachment of other nationalisms, especially Russian. For Young Turks, Turkish nationalism was preferable to Abdül Hamid's preemption of the status of caliphs as the focus of a unified Islāmic movement.

Russian intellectuals prevailed upon Young Turks to demand the union of all Turks, no matter where they lived. The concept of Pan-Turkism began in the Crimea and the Volga region. It found its most eloquent spokesman in Ismail Bey Gasprinski (Gaspirali) (1815-1914), a Crimean Tatar. Directing his appeal to the vast Russian masses, and influenced by the language unifying aspects of Pan-Slavism, he attempted to create a common

Turkish language to meet the needs of his fellow Tatars. At the same time, he accepted some elements of Pan-Islāmism as applicable to his cause.

Many Pan-Turks, especially after the Revolution of 1905, emigrated to Ottoman lands. Among them was the Russian Tatar Yasuf Akçuraǧoglu (1876-1935), who, influenced in his student days in Paris by Hegel, Renan, Count de Gobineau, and Houston Stewart Chamberlain, called for the political union of all Russians and Ottoman Turks. In his *Üç tarzi-i syaset* ("Three Kinds of Policy") (1903), he argued that the Turkish language provided a better basis for the Ottoman Empire than either Ottomanism or Islāmism. He was inclined to reject the idea of Pan-Islāmism on the ground that it had passed its prime.

In the first decade of the 20th century, Pan-Turkism was promoted in an energetic propaganda campaign. In several Muslim congresses, advocates of Pan-Turkism took a stand opposed to Islām and the Ottoman past. Pan-Turks who were forced to leave Russia came to Constantinople, where they exerted strong influence on the views of reformist Young Turks. While Pan-Turks won attention from Young Turks, they never managed to attain exclusive leadership of the Young Turk movement. It was too much to expect that Tatars, Turkomans, Kazaks, Uzbeks, Azerbaijani, and others, all differing in historical traditions and aspirations, would combine successfully in a Turkish-Russian Pan-Turkism.

Pan-Turkish ideas found little approval within the Ottoman government. Ottoman leaders suspected that Young Turks were following a deliberate policy of Turkification within the empire as a means of alienating non-Turks and assisting in the rise of Arab as well as Albanian nationalism.

Pan-Turkish agitation reached its height in 1914 with the outbreak of World War I. Pan-Turkism received a powerful blow when Turkey lined up with the Central Powers, while Russia turned to the Western Allies, thus effectively splitting the Turks of Turkey and Russia. Muslims in central Asia—Kazaks, Kirghiz, and Uzbeks, who saw themselves as exempt from military service, rebelled angrily against the military draft.

The Russian Revolutions of 1917 and the Turkish collapse in 1918 meant the end of Pan-Turkish dreams. Inside defeated Turkey, the movement lost its impetus: in Russia it was smothered by the New Soviet administration. Thereafter, Turkish patriots turned to Turkey's nationalism and retreated from Pan-Turkish ideology.

The Mechanics of Pan-Turanism

Still another macro-nationalism on the Turkish scene was Pan-Turanism. More linguistic-minded than either Pan-Ottomanism or Pan-Turkism (and in this respect close to the ideology of Pan-Slavism), Pan-Turanism developed out of the much disputed common origin of Turkish, Mongol

Finnish, Hungarian, and other languages, all of which were said to have originated not in Turkey or Turkestan but in the "broad and everlasting land of Turan" northeast of Persia. In political terms, according to Pan-Turanians, the peoples who spoke these languages, extending from Hungary to the Pacific, belonged together in a greater pan-movement.

The idea of Pan-Turanism grew out of the teachings of Ziyā Gökalp, who believed that the Turkish "race" originated in legendary Turan, a mythical land described in Persian epic poetry. He was certain of his facts: "There is, in fact, a homeland of Islām which is the beloved land of all Muslims. The other one is the national home which, for Turks, is what we call *Turan*. The Ottoman territories are that portion of Islāmdom which have remained independent. One portion is the home of the Turks, and is at the same time a portion of *Turan*. Another portion is the homeland of the Arabs, which is again a part of the great Arab Fatherland."[9] According to Gökalp, modern Turks belong to the Ural-Altaic group, to the Islamic *ümmet* and to Western internationality.

Turan, in Gökalp's view, had produced many poets, philosophers, and scientists, but, unfortunately, their works were printed in many languages, including Arabic, Persian, Russian, and Chinese. The glory of all these peoples, from Arabs to Chinese, had been the result of the Turkish sword. The Turk, who was the man of Turan was the product not of one but of many histories. Pan-Turanism would revive the prestige of Attila, Genghis Khan, and Tamerlane. A new Pan-Turanian Attila one day would unite Ottomans, Crimean Turks, Azerbaijan Turks, Uzbeks, Kirghiz, and all other diverse fragments of Turkism into one great Turanian nation, advocates believed.

From the political point of view, Pan-Turanians saw the old Ottoman Empire as a top-heavy multilinguistic and religious state which needed to be purged of non-Turanian elements. It was necessary to divest the Turkish language of all its Persian and Arabic words and allow it to revert to its pure pristine Turanian status. Islām, too, in the view of Pan-Turanians, was far too wide a concept, which tended to hurt Turanian national aspirations. Pan-Turanians sought to cut through the layers of Pan-Islāmism and to unite the Turanian elite by emphasizing national pride rather than the internationalism of religion. Place religion in its place as the spiritual food of the people, they argued, but let it not impinge on the political aspirations of a people united by a common language.

Pan-Turanians believed that people who once called themselves Turks should also identify themselves as Turanians, long united by language, even by flesh and blood, and with a history and destiny of their own. Their ancestors, their *Urfolk*, were the people of Turan, and it was their destiny to remedy the damage that had been done by fragmentation of a people who belonged together. They were Turks by "race" and by religion; they were exalted by Allah, and they would unite all their people in a surging Pan-

Turanian movement. Thus Ottoman Turks, Seljuk Turks, Mongols, and Azerbaijani, all belonged together in one great pan-movement.

Although the Pan-Turanian movement was significant mainly for its cultural aspects, it had some political repercussions. The vision tended to clash with political realities. Because some Turks were subject to Russian domination, Pan-Turanism gave Turkish authorities a weapon against Moscow, similarly, Pan-Slavism had been used by Russians in Moscow's confrontations with Turks and Austrians. After the Bolshevik Revolution of October 1917, Soviet leaders considered their Turkish subjects on the same plane with other nationalists in the Soviet Union, a shrewd move in that it took much of the impulse out of the Russian version of Pan-Turanism.

Pan-Turanism became impractical after World War I when the idea slid into obscurity, as postwar Turkish leaders concentrated their attention on the regeneration of Turkey proper. More attention was paid then to the cultural aspects of Pan-Turkism than to the linguistic niceties of Pan-Turanism. Originally a movement for national regeneration, Pan-Turanism broadened its objectives and attempted to cut through several layers of culture—Islāmic, Persian, and Arabic—to combine all Turkish-speaking peoples into one vast supranationalism. However, Pan-Turanism failed in that objective, although it did serve as a stimulus to nationalism in Turkey proper before it began to recede. Complex linguistic gymnastics could not unite a multilinguistic empire. Pan-Turanism and other macro-nationalisms could not combine the uncombinable.

Role of Mustafa Kemal

After World War I the Pan-Turanian movement was replaced by a strong revival of Pan-Turkism. This development was the work of Mustafa Kemal (1881-1938), whom the Turks regard as the founder of their modern country.[10] Subsequently, he assumed the name of Kemal Atatürk. Emerging from obscure origins, he became active as a Young Turk conspirator, and worked to break the sultan's despotism and set up a modern constitutional government.

Even before the war broke out in 1914, Kemal had pledged to relieve his country from the blight of Western imperialism. "Turkey for the Turks!" he proclaimed, a slogan which became the guideline for his political life. He emerged from the war with a reputation as a great military leader. Turning to politics, he organized his followers into the Republican People's Party.

Kemal had only contempt for the old Ottoman Empire, which he regarded as an outmoded structure not worthy of preservation. To replace it, he announced a six-point program: (1) republicanism, (2) secularism, (3) populism, (4) nationalism, (5) statism, and (6) continuous reform. He would concentrate on the regeneration of Turkey proper.

Kemal rejected Pan-Ottomanism, Pan-Turanism, and Pan-Islāmism in favor of a powerful Pan-Turkism. He denounced the "chimera" of Pan-Ottomanism, the attempt to melt down the various elements of the empire in the Ottoman crucible and to create out of heterogeneous elements a single unified nation.[11] In his view, it was wise to heed the words of Namil Kemal, the great patriotic poet: *"Cihangâranc bir deviet cirkardik bir aşirrettan"* ("We have transformed a tribe into a global empire"). It was incorrect, he said, to assume that the Turkish people's history had begun with an Asian tribe numbering four hundred tents. It was wrong to associate the Turkish name with tents, tribes, horses, armies, wars, and massacres. It was high time to make the whole world, as well as the Turks themselves, understand that Turkish history did not begin with Osman's tribe, but in fact some twelve thousand years before Christ. The exploits of the Osmanli Turks constituted merely one episode in the history of the Turkish nation, which had founded several other empires each with its own special era of brilliant splendor and greatness. Turks should only follow the example of their prehistoric ancestors, who were the first cultured people of the world. In Kemal's view, it was time for the world, including the Turks themselves, to understand that for thousands of years the Turks had been agents of culture and progress, except when subjugated by foreign culture and moral force.

Kemal was equally opposed to Pan-Turanism. He denounced Ziyā Gökalp for "timidly" replacing "Mongol" by "Turanian" or "Ural-Altaic." What was an "ethnic" term had been replaced by a geographical one, and this did not prove that the Turks belonged to the great Indo-European family. The Turks were beautiful specimens of the white race and were wrongly designated as Turanians or Ural-Altaic. They were "pure Aryans," as indicated by the beauty of their physique, the nobility of their soul, and the pre-eminence of their achievements. According to Kemal, the age-old prejudice concerning the Mongoloid origin of the Turkish people was obsolete. The Turks, he said, occupied a prominent position among Indo-European peoples. Had not the Persian poet Firdusi described legendary Turkish heroes, whose morphological characteristics had absolutely nothing in common with those of the Mongols? One needs only to consult Persian works written seven to eight centuries ago to have a true picture of the Turkish Seljukid heroes, describing almost all of them as having gigantic stature, elongated Aryan faces, broad chests, and long and wavy hair. Arab authors of ten centuries ago had also described the early Turkish princes with a white complexion and tall stature, with broad foreheads and large and beautiful eyes. Clearly, in Kemal's view, a retroactive renascence of the true Turkish "race" was in order.

Kemal favored retention of Islām, but he opposed Pan-Islāmism as unsuited to the Turkish national state. He believed it was necessary to secularize Islām and to replace Muslim religious law with a legal code borrowed from the Swiss. He would abolish religious schools in favor of civil education. He would close shrines, mausoleums, and dervish houses. He would forbid polygamy and outlaw wearing the fez. He would decree that Sunday, rather than Friday, should be the day of rest.

All these secular reforms were instituted once Kemal came to power. The Kemalist revolution had two goals: to create a new Turkish nationalism, and to prepare for thoroughgoing Westernization. At the same time, he was careful not to abandon the cultural side of Pan-Turanism. He supported glorification of the pre-Islāmic past. He tried to create a "pure" Turkish language purged of Arabic elements, abolishing the diffuse Arabic script and replacing it with a Latin-type alphabet. Urging his fellow citizens to use Turkish family names, he, himself, took the title Atatürk (Father of the Turks).

For his country, Kemal proposed a rapid Westernization. It was absolutely necessary, he insisted, that Turkey throw off her medieval raiment and take advantage of Western culture and mores. There must be a continuing social reform, which he called *Devrim* ("overturning" or "revolution"). As examples, he adopted the Western Gregorian calendar, and emancipated women, allowing them to mix freely in public with men for the first time in Turkish history.

Elected President in 1923, Kemal thereafter ruled Turkey as a benevolent dicator until his death. His regime was devoted to what he called the "restoration of Turkish history." He sponsored the Ankara Institute of Historical Research, whose historians, archaeologists, and anthropologists worked on the historical geneology of the Turkish nation. He created special chairs for Turkish history and civilization in the universities. Every Turkish child was to learn that true Turks were not those enslaved by the foreigner, by their own tyrannical rulers, by religious obscurantism, or by foreign social and cultural institutions, but that Turks were rather those who had laid the foundations of civilization in Central Asia for thousands of years before the Christian era and thereafter had spread it in different parts of the world. Turks were "pure Aryans" and not to be confused with Mongols.

The Turkish "Race"

As elsewhere, Kemal's scholars, in their anxiety to promote the cause of Pan-Turkism, fell into the quicksands of racial fallacy. They would dig beneath the layers of Islāmic, Ottoman, Turanian, and Arabic clutures, and discover the true origins of a "pure Aryan race." They would clarify the history of the Grand Turk, the last of the "Great Turkish Race". The word "Aryan" itself, they said, was of Turkish origin. They pointed out that "*Ari*," a term much used in Turkish, meant "pure" or "clean." At a time when the "Great Turkish Race" had reached a high level of culture, the peoples of Europe were still in a savage state living in complete ignorance.

Who are the Turks? There is no historical or scientific evidence to set the Turks apart as a distinct, pure race. There is no more a pure-blooded Turk than a pure-blooded Englishman. The Turks are an amalgam of a wide variety of peoples. Like most people on earth, they are an anthropological amalgam, a mixture of many diverse strains.

The history of the Turks reveals a blending of a variety of peoples. They appear to be of Asian origin, but it is impossible to trace with any degree of accuracy the region from which they migrated to Europe. They probably were Ural-Altaic in origin, comprising peoples from northern Asia to the Pacific Ocean, Finland, the Balkans, and Asia Minor. They may well have been a branch of the Aschin (Asona) Huns, who formed a kingdom in Mongolia about 1200 B.C., and who for centuries took part in wars against the Chinese. The early Tukui were leaders of Central Asian nomads. In 560 A.D. they entered into diplomatic relations with Constantinople and occupied East Turkestan. The Tukui combined with other peoples in Asia Minor, Finland, and the Balkan peninsula. Like most people, they were a biological hodgepodge.

In the late 11th century, Seljuk Turks migrated across northern Persia and settled permanently in Asia Minor. In the 14th century, Osmanli Turks invaded the Balkan peninsula. The process of intermixture continued as Seljuk Turks blended with Afghans, Kurds, Turkoman nomads, Arabs, and Persians. Osmanli Turks intermingled with the Turkomans of Persia, Russia, and Afghanistan, as well as with Azerbaijani Iranians of the Caucasus. There is no evidence for the existence of any "pure" Turkish blood in this conglomeration of diverse tribes.

Historical evidence clearly refutes the claim for the existence of a pure Turkish race. Scientific proof is equally lacking. Advocates of Pan-Turkism spoke confidently, if mistakenly, of the existence of a pure Turkish race. Tekin Alp quoted with favor "the categorical verdict of Dr. Adrien-Marie Legendre, a French scientist: "The Turk is one of the most beautiful specimens of the white race, big in stature with an elongated and oval face, a fine nose either straight or aquiline, sensitive lips, eyes opening widely, quite often grey or blue, and with horizontal palpebral slits."[12] At the first Historical Congress held in Ankara in July, 1932, speaker after speaker paid tribute to the Turkish "race." A Miss Affet, Professor of History, announced that the Turks were "pure Aryans": "The natives of Central Asia are Turks. It is nonsensical to try to create there an Indo-European race distinct from that of the Turks. . . . The Turkish children today are not the descendants of a tribe of four hundred tents, but of the pure race of the Ers or Ari, as the Europeans say, a race which is superior and cultured, and many thousands of years old."[13] Dr. Rechit Galip, former Minister of Education, argued in a public lecture on Turkish race and civilization, that the Turkish race belonged to the brachycephalic and Alpine group, and that it is the Turkish tribes who have spread the seeds of culture throughout the world: "We are the worthy descendants of a prodigious race which carries in its veins treasures of strength and ability and we must do our utmost to make the truth triumph in the eyes of all humanity, and to disperse the dark clouds which, during long centuries, have been heaped by fanaticism over Turkish history."[14]

Pan-Turkish claims of Aryan racial purity are unmitigated nonsense, to be included among similar fallacies promoted by Count Arthur de Gobineau, Houston Stewart Chamberlain, Madison Grant, Lothrop Stoddard, and Alfred Rosenberg. The Swiss anthropologist Eugene Pittard testified to Turkish racial mixture: "If we are to deduce the ethnic quality of the Turks from the events which led to the Osmanli invasion, it will appear beyond question that the people could not have been other than an anthropological amalgam."[15] When Pan-Turks speak of "the pure Turkish race," they refer to a complex people whose blood is tempered by Mongolian Kalmucks, by Galchas and Tadjiks of the Himalayas, by Anatolian Gypsies, by Syrians and East Bulgarians, by the conglomerate peoples living in Istanbul. The "pure-blooded Turk" might have light blue eyes and fair hair, a long head, a tall and well-proportioned body, or he might be dark and broad-headed, short and stumpy. Anthropologists differ on the stature, pigmentation, and nasal and cephalic indices of the "typical" Turk. In his vein flows the blood of the Sultan Togrulbeg, the Arabian philosopher Ibn Sina, the dictator Abdül Hamid II, even Attila and Genghis Khan. Biological hybridization has dispelled the notion of a pure-blooded Turkish people, an idea promoted enthusiastically by Pan-Turkish ideologists.

State, Nation, and Religion

Advocates of various pan-movements in Turkey fell into semantic confusion when trying to differentiate between state, nation, and religion. The British scholar, Elie Kedourie, shows how Gökalp tried to reconcile vision with reality by practicing intellectual acrobatics in search of definitions of words like "nation," "state," and "religion." It is an impossible task to reconcile the irreconcilable.[16]

Gökalp made this attempt in his "The Ideal of Nationalism: Three Currents of Thought."[17] It was, indeed, a tortuous task, what Kedourie called "painful gymnastics." A précis of Gökalp's venture indicates the complexity:

When we look at social realities, we cannot fail to see that an Islāmic *ümmet*, an Ottoman state (*devlet*), and a Turkish or an Arab nation (*millet*) do exist. The term *ümmet* denotes the totality of those people who profess the same religion, the "state" comprises all those who are administered under the government, and the "nation" includes all those who speak the same language. Those who do not accept these definitions deny them, not because the meaning does not correspond to reality, but because these words are believed unsuitable to denote the respective meanings.

On the one hand, Islāmists, according to Gökalp, say that the word "nation" [*millet*, Arabic "*milla*"] denotes what is covered generally by the word "*ümmet*." The term "*milla*," in the Islāmic view, means "sect" in Arabic. The Ottomanists, on the other hand, believe that the "state" and the "nation" are synonymous. To them, the sum total of the citizens of a state constitutes a nation. To have a state composed of peoples who speak the same language, or to make only those peoples who speak the same language an independent state, seems more natural and most desirable.

The Turks, criticizing both Islāmics and Ottomanists, come to the conclusions that the *ümmet* and the nation are different things and that the nation and the state are also not the same.

In Gökalp's view, the external realities of the concept of *ümmet*, nation, and state are not altogether independent of each other. The relation between the *ümmet* and the nation is a relation between the general and the particular, the *ümmet* is a whole which comprises several nations belonging to the same religion. Individuals actually constituting a nation are not the only members of a nation. All those who speak the same language will also be members of that nation. "Thus, for example, the Pomaks [Bulgarian Muslims] now speaking Bulgarian and the Cretan Muslims now speaking Greek may learn Turkish in the future and cease to be Bulgarian or Greek-speaking peoples. This means that nationality is not determined by language alone but also by religion."

Gökalp saw a more or less similar relationship between the terms "nation" and "state." As an example, the Ottoman state was a Muslim state—that is, it was formed of Muslim nations. Two great nations, Turks and Arabs, by numbers as well as by culture and learning, served as the basis of the Ottoman state in such a way that the Ottoman state might even be called a Turkish-Arab state. "It should also be remembered that the Turkish and Arab nations are not confined only to those who live within the Ottoman territories. Those who speak the same language but live under foreign rule also belong to those nations."[18]

Gökalp employed such frantic expedients and painful logic to justify the doctrine of Pan-Turanism. It was a desperate attempt to justify his vision of Turkish greatness. This kind of intellectual gymnastics was typical of nationalists everywhere, who were not averse to using flawed reasoning in defending the glories of the Fatherland.

Today Pan-Turanism, despite the efforts of Gökalp to establish an effective tradition, remains muted. The "broad and everlasting land of Turan" remains only a dream for a few persistent ideologists.

CHAPTER **7**

PAN-ISLĀMISM: SEARCH FOR RELIGIOUS UNITY_____

Every nation clings resolutely to its religion, the constituents of its
nationality, and its inherited group instincts.
                            —Shakib Arslan (1869–1946)

Religion and the Pan-Movements: Christianity

Every macro-nationalism has its own special combination of historical
motivations, among which one element generally is more important than
others. Thus, politically oriented Pan-Slavism was based primarily on linguistic affinity, while Pan-Germanism, though it took into account a common language, was even more politico-economic in tone. In Pan-Islāmism,
however, the religious impulse took on greater significance than either linguistic, cultural, political, or economic drives.

Throughout the better part of the Middle Ages, elaborate attempts were
made to create what was, in effect, a Pan-Christianity, an effort to unite
"all" the Western Christian world into a successor state of the Roman
Empire. The Holy Roman Empire was regarded as a revival of the Roman
Empire under Christian auspices. Despite the medieval fragmentation of
society, there was one supranational institution to which almost all peoples
of Western Europe belonged—the Roman Catholic Church. The medieval
polity was a combination of Church and state. Its government combined
the religious and the secular.

This kind of Pan-Christianity favored by the Church began to lose its
impetus in the later Middle Ages. The "universal" Church, the "international" institution, was destined to collide head-on with national ambitions. By
the middle of the 13th century, the papacy was losing its power. Medieval
Rome reached its peak in the pontificate of Innocent III (1198–1216), who
was successful in extending the program for the Holy See set up by Pope
Gregory VII a century earlier. The papacy claimed divine guidance: "We
are established by God above peoples and realms." It used weapons of
excommunication and interdict to maintain its authority.

This was Pan-Christianity in power. But as the Middle Ages moved on, there emerged a strong *los vom Rom*, "Away from Rome," movement, resulting eventually in the breakup of the medieval polity and the rise of a conglomeration of separate national states. The national monarchies of England, France, Spain, and Portugal were in the process of formation. With the Renaissance of the 15th and 16th centuries, followed by the Enlightenment of the 17th and 18th centuries, the Pan-Christian ideal gave way to the rising nationalism.

The French Revolution signaled the end of medievalism, which was given its ultimate blow in 1806, when Napoleon, then at the pinnacle of his power, announced the end of the Holy Roman Empire. From its European habitat, the ideas of nationalism and the primacy of the nation-state spread throughout the world, to North and South America, to Africa and Asia.

Pan-Christianity, weakened by its own ecclesiastical divisions, gave way to nationalism as the most vital historical phenomenon of society. It became more powerful than class—despite the exhortations of Karl Marx and his followers. In modern society, both religion and class played a secondary role to national consciousness.

Emergence of Islām

In the East, as early as the 7th century, Christianity found a rival in the appearance of Islām.[1] Beginning in 622 A.D. with the flight (*hijra*) of Muḥammad from Mecca to Yathrib (Medina, the City of the Prophet), Islām was a proselytizing religion. Its expansion was enormously successful. Muḥammad's successors, the caliphs, first turned Islāmic zeal against the Byzantine Empire, and managed to destroy the old unity of culture and religion in the Mediterranean world. Muslims drove westward across North Africa, moved to Gibraltar, and thrust at the heart of Christian civilization in Spain. The great drive for universal power was halted only by the intercession of Charles Martel, Charles the Hammer, who contained Islāmic power at the critical Battle of Tours in 732 A.D. This was Islām's high water mark. It then receded and left Western Europe to Christianity. The clash of the Crusades between the two religions (1095–1291) was inconclusive.

Islām preached a universalist ideal. It recognized Moses and Jesus as great prophets, but saw Muḥammad as the last and greatest of the three. Its religious goals were associated closely with the pan-ideal—*all* people were to be brought to the Islāmic fold. For the orthodox Muslim, the holy Koran contained the word of God as revealed by the angel Gabriel to Muḥammad. For him the Koran was explicit on the nature of the holy war (*jihād*) to be waged against unbelievers:

And fight for the cause of God against those who fight against you: but commit not the injustice of attacking them first: God loveth not such injustice;

And kill them wherever ye shall find them . . . for civil discord is worse than carnage. . . . Such is the reward of infidels.

Fight therefore against them until there be no more civil discord, and the only worship be that of God. . . . (*Sūrah II.*)

And repute not those slain on God's path to be dead. Nay, alive with their Lord, are they richly sustained.

Filled with joy at the favor of God, and at his bounty, and that God suffereth not the reward or the faithful to perish. (*Sūrah III.*)[2]

The faith preached by Muḥammad gathered millions of adherents throughout the Middle East and elsewhere in the world. Islāmic universalism tried to hold aloof from political entanglements, even though it accepted local political and military authority as a part of Islāmic organization. Islāmic theory recognized the unity of Church and state under the rule of the caliphate, but at the same time the caliph was never allowed to forget that he was at once the instrument and representative of the sacred law of Islām.

This was, indeed, the essence of Pan-Islāmism. Christian universalism was dissolved with the Reformation, but Islāmic universalism carried through to the 20th century. Nationalism shattered Pan-Christianity; it also began to challenge the Pan-Islāmic idea. Nation-states which had embraced the religion of Muḥammad soon found themselves enmeshed in differences and quarrels at the national level. Islāmic intellectuals, entranced with remembrance of things past, pointed to the glories of medieval Islāmic culture, and insisted upon its revival. But they, like their Christian peers, were caught in the confrontation of nationalism and religion.

What was happening was the familiar working of national consciousness. The political systems of the Middle East began to diverge from the Islāmic ideal. Both the nation-state and Islām called for absolute loyalty. The followers of Allah were confused.

Islāmic scholars did their best to bridge the gap and to match vision with reality. They turned to the Koran for support. "Ye are the best people (*"ümma"*) that hath been raised up into mankind."[3] The term *"ümma"* in their view obviously meant "nation." And again: "Verily, ye are the people of one 'nation,' and I, your Lord; therefore, worship me."[4] Arab scholars, too, recognized the affinity of Islām and modern Arabic nationalism: "To Islām is due the birth of a nation, the birth of a state, the birth of a national history, and the birth of a civilization."[5]

Foundations of Pan-Islāmism

Pan-Islāmic theory rested upon five pillars:

1. There must be a strong central authority. After the four patriarchal caliphs, the office of the caliph became monarchical. Under Umayyads,

Abbāsids, and Ottomans, the caliph remained the rallying point of the Sunnī Muslim community.

2. The entire Muslim world was expected to rally to the cause of the caliph.

3. All Muslims must remain obedient to the caliph.

4. The *hijra* called for migration of Muslims from lands conquered by non-Muslims back to Islāmic lands.

5. The *jihād*, or holy war in its modern content, could be either violent or non-violent.[6]

These goals of Pan-Islāmism may be divided into two parts—internal and external. Internally, there was one overriding compulsion—a desire to overcome religious splits in the Islāmic world, especially the enmity between Sunnītes and Shīʿites. There was too much rivalry in Islāmic lands from Turkey to Morocco. The Islāmic religion would provide the binding cement. Religious unity was primary, above that of all political or cultural ties. In Islāmic faith, all believers were equal; human inequalities were unimportant in the presence of God.

Added to these internal goals was an important external factor. Pan-Islāmism would exalt Islāmic values as opposed to harmful Western influences. It was suspicious of both nationalism and democracy, which it saw as Western ideologies stemming from the French Revolution. Such ideas were secular and material and opposed to precepts of the Koran. Pan-Islāmic theorists wanted no Western limitations or Western ideas of geographical boundaries. In their view such concepts ran counter to the most cherished traditions of Islām, with its ideas of religious universality, political theocracy, and exclusive sovereignty.[7]

Because Muslims everywhere were angered by the ongoing collapse of their society, Pan-Islāmic theorists sought to use their traditions as a counterthrust against the Great Powers of Western Europe and against Western civilization and culture in general. They saw Western imperialists as "infidels" who had unfairly taken control of Muslim brothers. Pan-Islāmism would bolster the failing fortunes of those Muslim states that had been unable to resist Western encroachments. If there was to be imperialism, then let it be the religious imperialism of Pan-Islāmism. Only in this way could the threads of a great religion be united as intended by the Koran.

Pan-Islāmism, then, originated in the precepts of the Koran, and received its impetus from the collision of Oriental and Occidental nationalisms and imperialisms. It was in a very real sense an expanding imperialist religious movement. It was dominantly a reactionary movement calling for a return to past values. The Islāmic religion differed from Christianity, which combined a creed and culture. Islām provided, in addition, a common law, a central authority in the caliphate, and a special social system.

Above all, Pan-Islāmism was a utopian idea existing in a climate scarcely conducive to its success. It called for a religious supranationalism at the precise moment when Western nationalism was beginning to stir up the peoples of the Middle East. It aimed to bring together many sects which could not unite without abandoning their faith. Sunnītes and Shīʿites remained implacable enemies. At a time when Turks, Arabs, and Persians were inflamed by the fires of nationalism, Pan-Islāmism urged them to subjugate their national sentiment to a broader religious imperialism. It was too much to expect in the Age of Nationalism. Pan-Islāmism was destined to remain a religious formula, never an organized movement.

Development

Pan-Islāmic ideology began to emerge after the opening of the Suez Canal in 1869, which eased the transportation of pilgrims to Mecca. In 1895, the Great Pilgrimage Year, some 11,000 devout Muslims journeyed to Mecca to spend a month near the Holy Kaʿbah. Those who stayed on longer became conversant with Pan-Islāmic ideas.[8] By this time, Pan-Slavic advocates were operating even in Asia. Dutch authorities in Java, already annoyed by Muslim resistance, were concerned by the appearance of Pan-Islāmic centers on their territory.[9]

In 1903 Abdullah Suhrawardy founded the Pan-Islāmic Society in London, together with a journal Pan-Islām, which stressed opposition to Western society and used humanitarian, as well as socialist phrases, to contrast European "vice" with "Asian virtue." The new organization dedicated itself also to the union of Sunnīte and Shīʿite sects, a formidable task.

Meanwhile, Pan-Islāmic ideas penetrated into India. The movement there was led by Abu'l Kalām Azād (1888–1958), who had traveled to Turkey in 1908, and who had come into contact with Young Turks. Islām, he said, was a cohesive, monolithic religion, the antithesis of chaos and confusion. In true Pan-Islāmic style, he called for a universal caliph as well as a jihād to throw off British control. Similar ideas were expressed in the area of Indo-Pakistan by Sayyod Ahmad Khān (who died in 1898).

The Young Turk Revolution dealt Pan-Islāmism a blow from which it never recovered; thereafter, Pan-Islāmism became a kind of intellectual curiosity. It was projected formally at the Salonika Congress of the Committee of Union and Progress in 1911, but this was half-hearted recognition. By this time, Turkish nationalism far outweighed Islāmic internationalism.

An attempt to revive Pan-Islāmism was made at the start of World War I, when in November 1914 the caliph proclaimed a Holy War against the Allies. Turkish nationalism had combined with German militarism. Both in Berlin and Vienna, Pan-Islāmic propaganda was used to support the war effort of the Central Powers, but there was little enthusiasm for it in Egypt, Arabia, and India.

The collapse of the Turkish Empire at the close of World War I meant the end of the first Pan-Islāmic movement. The second wave of Pan-Islāmism rising in India was even less enduring than the first. Several Pan-Islāmic Congresses held between 1820 and 1931 were unsuccessful. On July 8, 1937, a pact was signed at Teheran by representatives of Turkey, Persia, Iraq, and Afghanistan. The signatories undertook to preserve their common frontiers. Some commentators interpreted Turkey's adherence to this pact as a return to Pan-Islāmism, but this was incorrect, for Mustafa Kemal had already cut his country off from its Oriental and Islāmic past.

After World War II, there was a modest revival of Pan-Islāmic sentiment, especially after the founding of Pakistan and Indonesia, when Pakistan became a new center for Pan-Islāmism. No longer did the ideology concentrate on Pan-Islāmic authority, however, but rather on a common attitude of Islāmic states in meeting their economic, social, and cultural problems. The emphasis was on political rather than religious demands, urging a common foreign policy of Muslim states still under Western control. Pan-Islāmic congresses were held at Karachi (1951), Jerusalem (1953), Mecca (1954), and Lahore (1957–1958). At all these meetings differences prevented a common policy. In 1969 Muḥammad Rezā Shāh Pahlavi of Iran and King Faisal of Saudi Arabia called a conference of Islāmic states to unify Arabs and non-Arab Muslims in a common front against Israel. In all these meetings, the religious unity, which Pan-Islāmism advocated, was subordinated to political and national goals.

Apostles

The outstanding ideologist of Pan-Islāmism, its intellectual philosopher and prophet, was Jamāl ad-Dīn al-Afghānī (1838–1897). Until this fiery champion came on the scene, Pan-Islāmism had been only a vague idea. This intellectual was able, however, to solidify agitation in favor of a revived Islāmic civilization opposed to European domination.

Born in Asābād, Persia, Jamāl ad-Dīn belonged to the Shīʿite sect, one of the two major divisions of Islām. A man of great personal magnetism, with an eloquent tongue, a facile pen, and an enthusiastic manner, he devoted his life work to propaganda for Pan-Islāmism. Much of his activity took place in areas where the rival Sunnītes were dominant. Although he was not of Afghan background, he adopted the name Afghānī probably to hide his Persian origin. As a young man he studied theology and philosophy at Shīʿite centers in southern Mesopotamia and India. Apparently, he became a religious skeptic at an early age.

In 1866 Jamāl ad-Dīn began to take part in local politics in Afghanistan. For two years he served as confidential adviser to the throne, but was expelled from the country. In 1870 he appeared in Istanbul as a lecturer, but was denounced as a heretic when he spoke of the importance of human skills in the prophetic office. The next year he moved to Cairo.

In Egypt, Jamāl ad-Dīn attracted a number of young followers, including Muḥammad Abduh, later to become the leader of the modernist movement in Islām, and Saᶜd Pasha Zaglui, founder of Wafd, the Egyptian nationalist party. In Cairo, Jamāl ad-Dīn won a reputation as heretic and unbeliever. In fiery speeches he denounced Khedive Ismā-ᶜil, Egypt's ruler as a spendthrift who mismanaged the country's economy. The Khedive's activities led not only to widespread public discontent but also to threats by European creditors. British and French pressure finally led Ismā-ᶜil's suzerain, the Ottoman sultan, to depose him. Jamāl ad-Dīn then tried to win favor with Ismā-ᶜil's son and successor, Tawfiq Ismā-ᶜil, but the latter, fearing a republican revolution, deported Jamāl ad-Dīn in 1879.

Jamāl ad-Dīn then moved to Hyderābād and Calcutta, always preaching the necessity of Muslim unity. In June 1883 he arrived in Paris, where he was known as an exiled Islāmic reformer. In 1884, together with his disciple, Muḥammad Abduh, he published an anti-British Arabic newspaper, called *The Indissoluble Link*, in which he called for the unity of all Muslim peoples and states against Western aggression and domination. While in Paris, he engaged in a famous polemic directed against Ernest Renan, the historian-philosopher, who in a lecture at the Sorbonne had spoken of Islām's opposition to science.[10] He also tried unsuccessfully to have the British government use him as an intermediary in negotiations with Abdül Hamid II, the Ottoman sultan. He made several visits to Russia from 1887 to 1889. While in St. Petersburg, he induced the Tsar to allow his Muslim subjects to print the Koran and other Islāmic religious books. Russian authorities employed him for anti-British propaganda directed to the peoples of India.

Jamāl ad-Dīn next appeared in Persia, where again he was suspected of heretical views. He denounced the Persian Shāh Nāṣer od-Dīn as a traitor to Islām for having given a tobacco monopoly to British interests. London was his next stop. Here again he edited a newspaper which attacked the Shāh's absolutism and corruption in high administrative circles.

In 1892, Turkish Arabs in London, attracted by Jamāl ad-Dīn's Pan-Islāmic agitation, invited him to settle in Istanbul on a life pension as guest of the sultan. Jamāl ad-Dīn's continued attacks on the Persian Shāh may well have been a factor in the assassination of the Persian ruler in 1896. Jamāl ad-Dīn's Pan-Islāmism was useful to Abdül Hamid II only as a means of winning support of his people. Actually, Abdül Hamid's enthusiasm for Pan-Islāmism was in direct proportion to his increasing unpopularity. Through Jamāl ad-Dīn he expected to win more prestige not only inside the boundaries of his empire but also in other Muslim lands.

Jamāl ad-Dīn was unhappy in Istanbul. During his last years he was kept in virtual house arrest and under observation by the authorities. Enmeshed in endless court machinations, he tried again and again to escape or get permission to leave, but he was unsuccessful. He died at Istanbul on March 8,

1897, reportedly of cancer, but some claimed that he was poisoned by agents of the sultan. In 1944, on the assumption that he was an Afghan, his body was transferred to Kabul and a memorial mausoleum was erected in his honor.

As the leading propagandist for Pan-Islāmism, Jamāl ad-Dīn urged the unity of all Muslims in their struggle against the West.[11] To win prestige for the movement, he proposed to combine religion, politics, and culture in one all-embracing movement. Muslims must awake. They must achieve definite goals: (1) liberate themselves from Western domination; (2) support necessary reforms to win regeneration with strength; (3) get behind popular and stable government; and (4) cultivate modern scientific and philosophic knowledge.

His followers regarded Jamāl ad-Dīn as the chief exponent of modernism in Islām. Although not an intellectual of great caliber and although he was often unscrupulous in his activities, he made an indelible impression on the Islāmic world. His insistence that Pan-Islāmism must champion humanism, emphasized the call for religion to serve human ends. As a populist sympathizing with the poor and unprivileged, he preached help for the have-nots. However, despite a lifetime of enthusiastic propaganda, he was never to see his ideal of Islāmic unity achieved.

In contrast to the peripatetic Jamāl ad-Dīn, who roamed throughout Arab lands in pursuit of Pan-Islāmism, his disciple, Muḥammad ʿAbduh (1845–1905) preferred to remain in Egypt, his native country, to work for the same goal. A student of Jamāl ad-Dīn, Muḥammad ʿAbduh was depressed by the decadence he saw in Islāmic society. What was needed, he said, was the revivification of religion together with political unification under one supreme head. Above all, there must be needed reforms.

Muḥammad ʿAbduh was exiled to Syria for complicity in an uprising. In his mid-thirties he went to Paris, where for a time he edited a newspaper with Jamāl ad-Dīn. In writings and speeches, he maintained that there was no conflict between Islām and science. He interpreted passages in the Koran from a rational point of view and recognized that Islāmic scholasticism had its limitations.[12] He rose eventually to the highest religious post in Egypt, that of mufti.

While his master Jamāl ad-Dīn was a political activist who believed that only through revolution could needed reforms be brought to Islām, Muḥammad ʿAbduh held that only through a genuine religious awakening could the ground be prepared for necessary reforms. Jamāl ad-Dīn saw political agitation as the only effective course, but Muḥammad ʿAbduh preferred to limit himself to religious reforms in such areas as polygamy, divorce, and wearing the veil. It was necessary first of all, in Muḥammad ʿAbduh's view, to rid Islām of its medieval scholasticism. Islām must be reconciled with modernism, and Muslim society must be reconstructed on a democratic political basis while maintaining the basic tenets of religion. Once these prerequisites were met, Muḥammad ʿAbduh argued, a vigorous Pan-Islāmic world would come into being.

Jamāl ad-Dīn and Muḥammad ʿAbduh, working respectively from political and religious approaches, saw Pan-Islāmism as a distant but attainable goal. Both expressed the familiar enthusiasm of the pan-theorist. Both were unaware that the movement they sponsored was fading away in the shadow of local particularisms. In a world of national states, religion could not overcome the demands of nationalism.

Role of Abdül-Hamid II

The first patron of Pan-Islāmism was Abdül-Hamid II, who as sultan-caliph, appropriated the budding Pan-Islāmic movement to justify his own tyrannical hold on the Turkish Empire. The first "constitutional sultan," he abolished the constitution after it had served his purposes. He pronounced himself the defender of the Islāmic social system against Western imperialism, especially against the British in the Near East and the French in Morocco. Calling for Muslim unity, he urged a fanatical defense of Pan-Islām. It was an article of Muslim faith, he claimed, for all in Islām to combine in a holy war for the spread of Islāmic ideals. He was not averse to using Pan-Islāmic goals in international intrigue, behind which he was able to hold control of his empire for a third of a century. Exploiting Muslim fanaticism, he urged every Muslim, no matter where he lived, to combine with his fellow Muslims in what would be a *jihād* against the West.

The Western world, influenced by Abdül-Hamid's propaganda, tended to regard him as the Muslim pope, as a purely spiritual authority. What was misunderstood in the West was that Abdül-Hamid regarded himself not merely as a sultan but as the caliph of the entire Islāmic world, and also as its temporal authority. Westerners regarded Abdül-Hamid's treaties with Islāmic states as a renunciation upon the part of the caliph of temporal authority in the country concerned, but he, himself, saw such treaties as a recognition of his position. To confuse the West, he pretended to support constitutionalism, but actually maintained a rigid dictatorship. For him, Pan-Islāmism was the key to tyrannical power.

Collapse of the Caliphate

The Islāmic religion went beyond the boundaries of Christianity, which by force of circumstances in the modern era was limited mostly to creed and culture. Islām, it must be stressed again, called also for a central sovereignty with temporal connotations, a special kind of social system, and a common law. These unifying features helped provide for a common alliance of scattered adherents. Whereas Western Christian states managed to break up the polity of medieval Christendom during the economic drives of the Commercial and Industrial Revolutions, the political particularism of the Reformation, the cultural impact of the Enlightenment, and the social changes of the French Revolution, Islām seemed to have solid foundations for unity in all these fields.

It was the goal of Pan-Islāmism to buttress these apparently unifying foundations, but it turned out to be a hopeless task. The caliphate was already in collapse.[13] The story of the caliphate from its beginning was one of continuing feuds, dissent, and warfare. The term "caliph," from the Arabian *khalīfah*, meaning "successor," was the title given to the head of Islām. Theoretically, Islām was a theocracy, and its caliph was considered the vice-regent of God. The name "caliphate" denoted the rank, dominion, or office of a caliph. When Muḥammad the Prophet died, the caliph, his successor, was chosen to rule in his place.

The caliph was supposed to have both spiritual and temporal powers, but not prophetic power, which was reserved for Muḥammad. The first caliph, Abu Bakr, was succeeded by Omar, Athman, and Ali, all considered to be orthodox caliphs. The first major division in Islām occurred after Ali's death. The Umayyad dynasty set up its capital at Damascus, chiefly by force of arms. But the Shīʿites continued to recognize the descendants of Ali, and in 750 A.D. won the caliphate after massacring members of the Umayyad family. The Shīʿite caliphs set up the ʿAbbāsid family with its headquarters at Baghdad.

From then on, the caliphate descended into a maelstrom of conflicting claims. Abdul Abbas (750–750 A.D.), the first caliph under the ʿAbbāsid regime, was also called Saffah, meaning "shedder of his enemies' blood." Struggle for control of the caliphate became traditional, replete with feuds and confrontations, including assassinations. In 1520 the title was taken over by Turkish sultans, who kept it until the last caliph, Muḥammad VI, was deposed. In March 1924 the Turkish parliament decided to abolish the caliphate completely. Members of the house of Osman were expelled from Turkey at a time when Mustafa Kemal was re-elected President of the Turkish Republic.

This story of decline indicates that the caliph's authority, whether spiritual or temporal, had never been accepted universally without dispute. The Ottoman caliph was supposed to be the "sword of Islām," but that claim was never recognized throughout the Islāmic world, from Cairo to Calcutta. Turkish nationalism turned out to be incompatible with claims for an international Pan-Islāmism. The clash between the Pan-Islāmism of Caliph Muḥammad VI and the nationalism of Mustafa Kemal led eventually to the collapse of the caliphate. Muḥammad VI excommunicated Mustafa Kemal as an infidel, and Kemal expelled Muḥammad VI as a traitor.

With the collapse of the caliphate, the Pan-Islāmic movement found itself in eclipse, and Pan-Islāmism was lost in hopeless disputes about the future of the caliphate. Pan-Islāmic congresses were held in attempts to re-establish the "rightful" caliph, but invariably they ended in dissension and acrimony. In 1926, rival congresses were held in Mecca and Cairo—with no tangible results. Internecine disputes continued throughout the Islāmic world.

Recrudescence of Islāmic Militancy

Despite the decline of the caliphate, Islāmic militancy continued. Orthodox Muslim extremists, convinced that they alone had access to the godhead, denounced other religions as faulty and as inferior to the one true faith. They had little use for the principle of tolerance. *Jihād*, holy war, was to be emphasized in its literal sense, and many lives were to be lost in this fetish of fanatical orthodoxy.

In its early days a proselytizing religion, Islām spread westward across North Africa. Enemies were given the choice of accepting Islām or the sword. Islāmic orthodoxy was simple; only God is sovereign. No people could have sovereignty in an Islāmic state. Therefore, to speak of an Islāmic republic was a contradiction in terms. There could be no democratic lawmaking, because legislation had already been accomplished through the Prophet Muḥammad in the Koran.

Such Islāmic premises meant that there was an insurmountable conflict between the religion and the contemporary world of sovereign nation-states. The religious umbrella was supposed to cover all Muslims, whose first loyalty was considered to be to the chosen religion of God and not to an artificial state-structure. If there was to be nationalism it had to be based on Islāmic religion.

This was the solidified ideology behind Pan-Islāmic militancy and its rebirth in the 20th century. In the 19th century, Muslim rulers sought to keep pace with the contemporary development of nationalism by introducing secular legislation and reducing the jurisdiction of religious law. Orthodox Muslims resented this procedure as a dangerous abnegation of the word of God passed on through Muḥammad the Prophet. They opposed any Western-minded secular ruler who sought to adopt ways alien to Islām. For them, the proposed abolition of the veil for women was an unbelievable atrocity.

The religious issue was complicated by oil, the black gold of an industrialized society. Fantastic wealth, flowing into Islāmic coffers, brought with it unprecedented prosperity. But Muslim leaders found it difficult to cope with the economic changes that accompanied the flow of oil. Oil profits tended to be converted into Cadillacs for the chosen few, while the masses had little share in material abundance.

The extent of Islāmic militancy was revealed in Iran, where the revival of

Pan-Islāmism was especially strong. The Iranian revolution, starting in 1979, was marked by a bitter struggle between clerical forces and Westernized intellectuals and liberals. From his house of exile in Paris, the Ayatollah Ruhollah Khomeini, Islāmic religious leader, called for resistance to Muḥammad Rezā Shāh Pahlavi and his brutal security police. Khomeini preached fire and brimstone; the Iranian people, he charged, had turned from the true faith to the false ministrations of a secular-minded and Western-oriented Shāh. They had succumbed, he said, to the blandishments of the "American Devils," and they should beware of the Kremlin bear bringing gifts of honey. They should reject the accoutrements of the 20th century, and return to the one true faith. He, Khomeini, would lead the way and awaken Iran from its long sleep. Moreover, he would set a standard for the entire Islāmic world. Pan-Islāmism was seen as the only way to achieve a rebirth of the true religion.

The words of Khomeini sparked a religious revolution. The Shāh left Iran on January 16, 1979, and at the end of the month Khomeini returned to his homeland to lead its regeneration. Millions of Iranians took to the streets as Islāmic zealots at last had their day. Women who had bared their bodies in swim suits in Western fashion were forced to return to the veil. The country descended into near anarchy as the ruling Islāmic Party sought to stifle opposition. The Islāmic Constitution, drafted under clerical domination, placed final authority in Khomeini. Turmoil continued with revolts among varied minorities, and there was a wave of executions. Members of the Majahedeen-i-Khalq and the smaller Marxist-Leninist-Maoist factions died before revolutionary firing squads. American diplomats were arrested and held in an extraordinary incident.[14]

It was not clear whether the Islāmic power structure could be maintained. Neighboring Iraq took advantage of the chaos in Iran to assert its control over disputed oil lands, and for a time seemed to triumph. But Iranians, striking back in anger, forced Iraqi troops from their soil in a continuing confrontation.

Khomeini wanted Iran to have a powerful Muslim establishment with all non-Muslims reduced to second-class citizenship. Even more, he hoped for an integrated Pan-Islāmic society, which would return to the original precepts of Muḥammad. This goal, he was certain, could be achieved only through the rebirth of Islāmic militancy. There was, however, a formidable obstacle—the factionalism of Islāmic society. Chaotic was the web of national rivalries, which went far beyond a sense of religious unity. Here was additional proof of the strength of nationalism—neither religion nor class could drown out the appeal of nationalism in the age of nation-states. Khomeini's brand of Pan-Islāmism could not possibly thrive in a society where nationalism, not religion, was the key attachment. The deadly Iran-Iraq conflict, still raging in the year 1984, gives evidence of the continuing strength of nationalism in human affairs.

Libya's Muammar Kaddafi

To Khomeini's clarion call for Pan-Islāmic unity can be added the brooding fanaticism of Libyan dictator Muammar Kaddafi. To the world, Kaddafi was a dangerous eccentric, a mystical religious zealot bent on exporting terrorism. Egyptian President Anwar Sadat called him "a vicious criminal, 100 percent sick and possessed of the demon," and Sudan's President diagnosed him as "a split personality—both evil."[15] For more than a decade, this extraordinary individual ruled his desert country with a simplistic blend of Islāmic austerity and revolutionary zeal.

The son of a Bedouin peasant, Kaddafi was born in a goatskin tent in northern Libya. As a young boy he was taught by an itinerant teacher to read and write and to recite the Koran by rote. He studied the works of Michelle Aflaq, Marxist founder of the Baᶜath Party, Sun Yat-sen, and Kemal Atatürk. By the age of 16, his revolutionary fervor made him a leader. Using as a model Egypt's Gamal Abdel Nasser, he persuaded schoolmates in a military school to seek power by deposing King Idris, and then fighting for Arab unity. By 1969, the young rebels were ready for a coup. The Free Officers Movement, led by Kaddafi, overthrew King Idris by an Arabian Nights ruse. Inviting the king's police to a party, the rebels took them prisoner at the peak of festivities. At the age of 27, the Bedouin nomad became the ruler of Libya at a time when the Western-installed monarch was vacationing in Turkey.

Once in power, Kaddafi began to chart a new course for the Arab world. He presented his ideology of the "Third Universal Theory," an alternative to capitalism, which he denounced as exploitative, and communism, which he saw as godless. In his *Green Book*, modeled on Mao Tse-tung's *Little Red Book*, Kaddafi gave his plan for government as a kind of nationwide town meeting. Instead of parliaments, he formed 173 people's congresses. "The era of the *Jamahiriyah* [State of the Masses]," he said, "will be established everywhere. Governments will disappear. Police will disappear. Regular armies, capitalism, salaries, wages, commerce, trade, profit, interest—all these things will disappear and man will be free."[16]

Despite this promised new system of government, Kaddafi became the nation's dictator. Opponents to the regime were arrested and thrown into prison. Those who criticized the leader were eliminated, and defectors who went abroad were tracked down by the dictator's agents. Widespread nationalization, currency regulations, and wholesale conscription of civil servants into the army weakened the country's economy. Nevertheless, with oil money flowing in, Kaddafi was said to have financed and armed revolutionary groups throughout the Arab world, and to have helped terrorists of various nationalities, especially in the Middle East and Africa. He was accused of plotting and dealing with revolutionaries from Ulster to Latin America.[17] He supported "national liberation movements" in some 45 countries.

Behind Kaddafi's activities was the portrait of a brooding fanatic, a man with a mercurial temper, suffering from a host of painful physical ailments from stomach ulcers to kidney colic. Critics denounced his fanatic extremism, boastful pronouncements, and periodic fits of deep depression, during which he retreated to the desert and brooded in a tent.

Kaddafi saw himself as a Pan-Islāmic missionary of messianic proportions. He was "a simple man" from the desert chosen to lead Islām to days of glory. From his early days, he was a devout zealot, reciting all the prayers required by Islāmic law, drinking no liquor, and following a tribal custom of eating no fish. Inclined to periods of silence, he would disappear from the public for long periods of self-imposed isolation in the desert. Most of all, he regarded himself as the moulder of Islāmic unity: "I am the leader of a revolution that expresses the feelings of the whole Arab nation and the whole Islāmic world. We in Libya are responsible for the whole Arab nation [and] our behavior must be respectable."[18]

Kaddafi's Pan-Islāmism envisioned a unity of the Muslim tribes of North Africa into a Sahelian empire stretching as far south as Zaïre. The presidents of Niger, Mali, and the Sudan, all accused the Libyan dictator of plots to overthrow them. In November 1980, Libyan troops invaded neighboring Chad professedly to bolster the regime of President Goukouni Oueddei, but more accurately to occupy its uranium-rich northern region.

Unfortunately for him, Kaddafi's Pan-Islāmic vision attracted little support among the very leaders he supposed to be his intimate allies. His continuing threats and aggressions alienated Muslim leaders, who shared his piety but not his political ambitions. In November 1983 his troops fought alongside Syrians in Lebanon against Yasser Arafat's remnant Palestine Liberation Organization. Pan-Islāmism could not flourish with Muslims killing Muslims.

Despite his lack of support, Kaddafi persisted in preaching the gospel of Pan-Islāmism. He described himself as its natural leader, and used his oil billions to bolster his implacable hostility to Israel. With this kind of dangerous support Pan-Islāmism had little chance of progressing beyond the point of colorful eccentricity.

The Failed Macro-Nationalism

Even the Koran could not prevail in a society dominated by divisive nationalism. Pan-Islāmism turned out to be a Utopian idea which never bore fruit. Though the idea attracted support in the more powerful Muslim states, it was never implemented as a working ideology. There were far too many imponderables.

1. *Nationalism.* Unfortunately for its advocates, Pan-Islāmism called for a union of disparate elements in the Age of Nationalism. The intensi-

fication of nationalism in the 20th century and the ambitions of individual rulers of Muslim nation-states once again proved to be more powerful than the internationalization of religion. Islām, no more than Christianity, was unable to unite its followers along religious lines. Pan-Islāmism preached a supranational movement at a time when the idea of Western nationalism had penetrated into Muslim states. Persians, Turks, Syrians, Iranians, Egyptians, Libyans, all were enticed by the slogans of nationalism.

2. *Religious Animosity.* Added to political nationalism were deep-rooted rivalries within Islām itself. Pan-Islāmists never were able to overcome the traditional enmity between Sunnīte and Shīʿite factions. Efforts to heal differences between the two major sects of Islām were unsuccessful. Pan-Islāmism could not thrive in this atmosphere of mutual hatreds.

3. *Weak Leadership.* Neither the early nor later leaders of Pan-Islāmism were effective in welding a transnational unity. The intellectual leadership of Jamāl ad-Dīn and Muḥammad ʿAbduh was ineffective despite their call for modernism and their emphasis on lack of conflict between Islām and science. These apostles spoke loudly for the idea, but little action for unity followed their enthusiastic words. Their advocacy remained religious minded without political or revolutionary drives.

Leadership of Abdül-Hamid II from Constantinople was suspect throughout the Islāmic world. At a time when nationalism was getting more and more powerful, Pan-Islāmists sought leadership from a ruler, who despite his claims, remained half-feudal in aspirations. In reality, the Turkish sultan used the Pan-Islāmic movement primarily as a weapon against rising national liberation forces. He had little use for Muslims in other Islāmic states. He was motivated not by the idea of Pan-Islāmism, but by the necessity of maintaining his own absolute rule, in short, by nationalism instead of an overall macro-nationalism.

Later Pan-Islāmists were self-appointed missionaries of messianic zeal who called for the unity of Islām under their own leadership. Iran's Ayatollah Ruhollah Khomeini proclaimed his own Islāmic authority in his state, and urged other Muslims to join him in a religious revolution throughout the Islāmic world. Similarly, Libya's Muammar Kaddafi presented himself in the image of a "first among equals." In the Muslim world rent by national rivalries, neither Khomeini nor Kaddafi was taken seriously as a respected leader of the Islāmic movement.

4. *End of the Caliphate.* In 1918 the Ottoman Empire fell along with the Hohenzollern and Hapsburg Empires. The caliphate, which supposed a wide religious unity, officially ended in 1924 with the formation of the Turkish national state. After this development, other Muslim states turned more and more to their own interests. There was disappointment throughout the Islāmic world on the fall of the caliphate, and there were

many calls for a restoration. But the voice of Pan-Islāmism became weaker and weaker.

5. *Competition from Pan-Arabism and Pan-Turkism.* Pan-Islāmism had to endure the competition of two other macro-nationalisms, the strongly linguistic Pan-Arabism and the zealously nationalistic Pan-Turkism. Pan-Arabism moved away from the Pan-Islāmic idea. Young Turks, attracted by Western ideology, actually weakened Pan-Islāmism by calling for Europeanization to strengthen their own state. Transnational religion could not compete with such powerful national drives.

6. *Organizational Failure.* Efforts to revive the caliphate as well as the shadowy Pan-Islāmic movement proved to be unsuccessful. The 1924 Pan-Islāmic Conference held in Cairo and Mecca called for a new caliphate led from Mecca. It failed. The 1932 Pan-Islāmic Congress held at Jerusalem was adjourned with no practical results. From then on, there was no more reference to a revived caliphate.

7. *Lack of Mass Appeal.* Pan-Islāmism failed to win grass-roots support throughout the Islāmic world. There was little mass interest for it in the Middle East. The large Muslim populations of Russia and India, failing to respond to Pan-Islāmic propaganda from Istanbul, suspected it of being a means of supporting Turkish leadership in the Muslim world. Religious leadership from Mecca—yes; political control from Istanbul—no.

CHAPTER 8

PAN-ARABISM: INTEGRATION VERSUS DIFFERENTIATION ____

Whether, if maintained in its present peak, the All-Arab nationalist movement will result in the emergence of a common nationality, even overcoming the divisive effects of separate states, is not
yet certain.

—Benjamin Aksin

The Unstable Unity

Where the Pan-Islāmic movement was dominantly religious, the closely
related Pan-Arabism was primarily political in context, but with religious,
linguistic, and cultural overtones.[1] Pan-Arabism sought union of all Arabs
in a giant supranational secular state. It emphasized historical and cultural
ties between all Arabs, linguistic affinity in the Arabic tongue, and
observance of the traditions, customs, and laws of Islām. It was especially
sensitive to Islām, which it regarded as a cohesive factor in confrontation
with the non-Arab world.

The goal of Pan-Arabism was always integration. It would consolidate all
the varied nationalist movements in Arab-speaking countries to produce
one solid front. The entire Arab world—the precious "All" of the pan-
movements—would be fused into one community conscious of its power
and political assertiveness. Arabs would be united in a common territory as
a people with one distinctive language, religion, and culture. Ruling Arab
elites everywhere were expected to join the movement, and to sacrifice
parochial loyalties in favor of All-Arab integration.

Such was the dream. But here, too, as elsewhere among the macro-
nationalisms, a pan-movement was beset by disruption, irreconcilable
motivations, and differentiation. Pan-Arab proto-nationalism was weakened by the prevalent trend to hetero-nationalism. The longed-for unity
was frustrated by political particularism, economic imbalance, and the
opposition of non-Arab and non-Muslim minorities in Arab states. Unfortunately for Pan-Arabic theorists, Arabs, too, tended to give their primal
loyalty to the national state, a common occurrence in the Age of Nationalism. There was little support for the proposed all-encompassing political
unity. Pan-Arabist leaders were to learn, as others elsewhere, that it was no

simple matter to overcome regional interests. True, there was an abiding love for Islām and its tenets, but even this religious motivation was not enough to overcome particularistic political, economic, and military loyalties.

Though closely related Pan-Islāmism remained a binding force in the Arab world, it was not strong enough politically to revive the caliphate.[2] Islām gave Arab nationalism its special character, but did not displace it. Rivalries were so intense that the whole Arab world split into disparate units. Neither Pan-Islāmism nor Pan-Arabism, neither the religious nor the secular aspect, could overcome the appeal of nationalism. Neither a universalist religion nor a secular-minded pan-movement could change the attractiveness of nationalism, the most powerful ism on the contemporary scene.

The Geopolitical Argument

For Pan-Arabists, the geopolitical situation was basic. They called for a union or federation of all Arab-speaking peoples from Arabia proper westward across North Africa to the Atlantic. Arabia proper and Yemen, however, form only a small portion of the Arab-speaking world. The proposed Arab superstate would include all Arab-speaking peoples living in Arabia and the Middle East (Iraq, Lebanon, Syria, Jordan, and stateless Palestine, the latter without a geographical center since the emergence of Israel), Egypt, and the Arabic-speaking peoples in countries west of Egypt (Libya, Tunisia, Algeria, and Morocco).

The Arab connotation consisted of eastern and western halves. The eastern half, centered in the Middle East, comprised a compact group of territories, which over the course of centuries, became not only Islāmic in religion but Arabic in language and culture. The western half of the Arabic world, extending from the borders of Egypt to Morocco, consisted of Muslims who also saw themselves as Arabic. However, the farther away they were from Arabia proper, the less was the urge for Arabic union.

Both spheres, east and west, were divided by jealousies and suspicions. All Arabs, as Muslims, turned to Mecca for holy prayers, but they had no intention of yielding to political domination from Arabia proper. Intellectual champions of Pan-Arab unity faced a herculean task in seeking to unite peoples torn by differentiation. So deep-seated were these animosities that Pan-Arabism turned out to be one of the least effective of all the pan-movements. Not even the opposition of Arabs everywhere to the existence of the state of Israel was sufficient to unite them in a supranational political organism.

The geopolitical claim to unity did not serve the Pan-Islāmic cause. Pan-movements generally tried to minimize the importance of strong national or tribal identification in favor of supranationalism. Pan-Arabism, too, sought to overcome such traditional loyalties in favor of the larger one but was unsuccessful. Nationalism, supported by both the educated elite and the masses in separate states, had the stronger appeal precisely because it had freed the Arab world from European control. Once in momentum, it took on a xenophobic character. It reflected the needs of a secular-oriented society, which accepted Islām as its religion but not the idea of a supra-theocratic state.

Although some scholarly theoreticians opted for a proto-national Arab state, there was little support at the grass-roots level. The warriors of both Iraq and Iran believed deeply in the tenets of Islām, including the prospect of a delightful heaven reserved for those who fell in battle, but they attempted to kill each other to preserve their own national interests—in this case, a matter of valuable oil wells.

Historical Continuum

Following the death of Muḥammad in 632 A.D., his followers moved swiftly westward across North Africa, sweeping ahead in a *jihād*, a holy war, which eventually made Islām one of the world's great religions. In religious ecstasy they crossed the Strait of Gibraltar, and headed up the Iberian peninsula with Western Europe as a prized goal. It seemed that nothing could stop this relentless drive. For a time, the Muslim conquest seemed to be on the verge of success, until, as mentioned before, Charles Martel stopped them at the Battle of Tours in 732. The Arab tide receded thereafter, leaving traces of Muslim culture in a Spain held for Christianity.

Elsewhere, throughout North Africa, Islām and Arabic culture retained powerful footholds. Only in the east, however, was the Arab hold secure. The nucleus of a larger Arab state never extended beyond Arabia proper.[3] The Umayyad caliphs of Damascus managed to hold Arab countries in a loose union for a time, but in the middle of the 9th century their successors had to recognize the virtual independence of local dynasties in Syria and Egypt. Later, these two states would work together under a single monarch, an almost unique development in the Arab world. Even this tenuous unity, however, did not last in the face of mutual antagonisms.

The issue of Arab solidarity became complex in the 16th century when Ottoman Turks, claiming leadership of the entire Islāmic world, united much of the Middle East under Turkish control. Turks insisted that the capital of the Arabic world should be transferred to Constantinople. There were rumblings of discontent among Arabs elsewhere, but no national consciousness for a time appeared sufficient to rescue Arabs from Ottoman power.

During the first decade of the 20th century, Arab-speaking peoples became increasingly hostile to Turkish overlordship. Admittedly, the Turks were fellow Muslims, but in the eyes of Arabs they were political strangers. World War I, with its explosive effect on four great empires, including the Ottoman Empire, gave Arab-speaking peoples the opportunity for which they were waiting. They would break away from the Turkish grip, and express their own growing national sentiment.

The Pan-Arab movement was not only a protest against Turkish domination, but also against European imperialism. The movement, from intellectual awakening to political activity, fed upon resistance to European imperialism. During the war, Lawrence of Arabia and other British agents worked with Arabs to overthrow the Turkish yoke. Once freed from Turkish control, Arabs suddenly found themselves mandated to Western powers. Although for a time crippled by inertia and indifference, Arabs began to adopt the trappings and mythology of a proto-national movement. They would be freed from both Turkish and Western domination.

The budding Pan-Arab movement, however, was confronted with difficult local problems. In Egypt, where the main obstacle was British occupation, Pan-Arabs began openly to oppose British rule. At the same time, came the birth of Egyptian nationalism, parting company with Pan-Arabism and developing provincial aspects.[4] Moreover, there was additional fragmentation of the Arab East. Syria rose in anger against French mandates. There was rising particularist sentiment in Lebanon. Similarly, in Palestine hostility to the British mandate and to its adjunct, political Zionism, generated a local type of national sentiment.[5]

World War I severed the Arab components of the Ottoman Empire and sent them on the way to semi-nationhood.[6] After the war, the old Ottoman Empire was abolished. On November 1, 1922, the Grand National Assembly abolished the sultanate. Sixteen days later, Muḥammad VI (1861–1926), the last sultan of the Ottoman Empire, boarded a British warship and fled to Malta. Later, he attempted to install himself as caliph in the Hejaz, but he failed.

The effort to unite freed Arab states in a greater union supported by Pan-Arabic ideology was also unsuccessful. There was little desire for such a union. At the end of the war, London told the Arabs that Britain would favor the formation of a larger Arab state, but the offer aroused little enthusiasm.

Arab hatred of Turkish domination turned out to be only a superficial bond of unity. There were far too many diversities in the Arab world, far too much differentiation. New, fanatically independent Arab states emerged after World War I: Arabia proper (Saudi Arabia and Yemen), and later Egypt, Iraq, Syria, and Lebanon. In each case, nationalistic demands were far stronger than the call for a supranational Arab identity. National flag and patriotic anthem came first. Pan-Arab propaganda was well received, but particularistic nationalism was infinitely more appealing.

There were two opposing tendencies at work in the Middle East: the urge to centralization under Pan-Arabism, and the lure of regional separateness. Pan-Arab intellectuals boasted of Islāmic universalism and the unity of Arab language and culture. But this call for unity was not strong enough to overcome the formation of ten sovereign states with a population of 70 million, living on four million square miles of Middle Eastern territory. Although the establishment of the state of Israel in 1948 sent a shock wave throughout the Arab world, there was only a temporary unity in the effort to throttle the Jewish state at its birth. Egypt, Jordan, Syria, Lebanon, Iraq, and Saudi Arabia went to war against Israel, but failed to destroy it. Indeed, when the fighting ended in 1949, Israel was in possession of 50 percent more territory than it had been granted originally. Nor were later Arab attempts any more successful in obliterating Israel.

The cause of Pan-Arabism was weakened further by the problem of oil. The discovery of oil, the precious fluid of modern industrialized society, led to bitter squabbling among Arab states and additional differentiation. The bonds of economic nationalism were strengthened. Oil-producing Arab states joined in the creation of the Organization of Petroleum Exporting Countries (OPEC) in the goal of determining world oil prices and in advancing members' interests in trade and development dealings with industrialized oil-consuming nations, but the aim was strictly economic.[7] Arab members of OPEC, just like the members of the European Economic Union, did not have the least intention of merging their political sovereignty. Iran and Iraq, both members of OPEC, even went to war in 1982–1984 because of differences over disputed oil territory, including the crucial Iranian port city of Khorramshahr. Rivalry between Sunnīte and Shīʿite Muslims added fuel to the confrontation.

Earlier efforts at political union were equally ineffective. The Arab League (AL), formed in 1945, with its headquarters at Cairo, dedicated itself to strengthening member ties and to furthering Arab aspirations.[8] From its beginning, however, the League was hampered by habitual dissension. After the lightning Israeli victory in the Six-Day Arab-Israeli war of June 1967, militant and dissatisfied League members continued to search for varied means of retaliation. They even sought Soviet aid for their continued struggle against Israel. But the old rivalries persisted.[9] Israel's greatest asset in its struggle for existence remained the Arab sense of differentiation.

Nasser as Charismatic Pan-Arabist

Pan-Arabism was no exception to the general rule that macro-nationalisms tend to attract the attention of self-appointed champions who regard themselves as logical leaders destined to assume command of the movement. No other Arab leader succeeded more than Nasser in winning the support of Arab masses throughout the Middle East. Under his aggressive and sometimes opportunist leadership, Egypt surged to the forefront of the Pan-Arabist movement. Even the loss of two wars did not dim the popularity of this charismatic leader. Yet, in the long run, he failed in his aim to create a unified Arab world.

Gamal Abdel Nasser was born on January 15, 1918, in the Bacos section of Alexandria, the son of the local postal administrator.[10] As a young student he was constantly in trouble with his schoolteachers, some of them British. He took part in many anti-British street demonstrations. With other youngsters he chanted, "Oh, Almighty God, may disaster take the English!" After attending a law college for several months, he entered the Royal Military Academy, from which he was graduated as a second lieutenant. He then worked with the Free Officers movement to overthrow the Farouk government.

In 1948 Nasser took part in the Arab war against the newly created state of Israel. On July 23, 1952, together with some 89 other Free Officers. Nasser led an almost bloodless *coup d'état*, which ended the monarchy. In the ensuing struggle for power, he outmaneuvered the popular General Muḥammad Naguib, and became premier on February 1, 1954. In January 1956 he promulgated a constitution under which Egypt became an Islāmic Arab welfare state with a one-party political system. As Prime Minister and later President of Egypt, he sought a populist foundation for his regime, confiscating land from wealthy landowners, and turning it over to the poverty-stricken *fellahin*. As first President of the United Arab Republic, he tried to make himself the unchallenged spokesman for all African states. Despite the opposition of dispossessed landowners, rival military cliques, Naguib's supporters, Communists, and others, Nasser managed to maintain his grip as Egypt's political leader for some 18 years until his death in 1970. He demonstrated a remarkable ability to hold the reins of power.

In his *The Philosophy of the Revolution* (1955), Nasser described his hopes of becoming the leader first of 55 million Arabs, then 224 million Africans, and eventually 420 million followers of Islām. He aspired to be the leader not only of Pan-Arabism, but of Pan-Africanism and Pan-Islāmism. His first step was the formation in 1958, together with Syria, of the United Arab Republic, which he hoped some day would include the entire Arab world. This union, which never worked effectively, was as close as Nasser could come to his triple dream of Pan-Arabism, Pan-Africanism, and Pan-Islāmism.

Nasser explained his goal in simple terms:

There are no limits beyond which we will not go. Our task is the removal of rocks and obstacles from off the way. This is our only duty. The future and all its challenge is work that is open to all patriots with ideas and experience. This is a duty and a privilege demanded of them. We cannot perform the whole task. It is our cherished duty, our moment of historical responsibility, thus to bring our people at long last together, and meld them in units for the future—the future of Egypt—strong and free.[11]

Egypt, indeed, was at the heart of Nasser's philosophy. In the struggle for unity, he saw his own country as the center of three surrounding circles.

The first Arab circle was "a part of us, and we are a part of it, our history being inextricably part of its history." Nasser's second circle, enclosing the Arab circle, was the continent of Africa. Egyptians could not remain aloof. They were in Africa; they gave Africans their northern gate; they were the link with the outside world; and they would never relinquish responsibility for it. Africa, in Nasser's view, was vital for Egypt—the life-giving waters of the Nile flowed through Egypt from the heart of the continent.

Nasser's third great circle, circumscribing all the continents and oceans, was Islām, "the domain of our brothers in faith." Islām, the common religion, linked together all Arabs, with centers of Islāmic learning at Mecca, Damascus, Baghdad, and Cairo. Cairo was the true center of the concentric circles.

Nasser claimed that there were 'heroic and glorious roles which never found heroes to perform them." All three circles surrounding Cairo were distinguished by "a wandering mission in search of a hero." With little concern for modesty, he nominated himself: "We alone, by virtue of our place, can perform the role." He would lead all ten sovereignties in the Pan-Arab world.

Nasser never deviated from this theme during his entire political life. On March 11, 1959, he delivered a speech at Damascus in which he hammered away at the idea of Pan-Arabism under his own leadership:

Fellow Countrymen: When we took it upon ourselves to raise high the banner of Arab nationalism and defend its call; when we chose the difficult, hard way, the way of defending the whole of the Arab nation, working for it in its entirety, of Arab unity and Arab nationalism, we knew that this might be a rough one to travel, that it might be easier if we chose one of an isolationist policy, a road with a policy that was indeed selfish, a policy that was based largely on ignoring whatever happened in other Arab countries. We knew that such a policy would be easier at the outset, but that eventually it would hand over one Arab country after another to its enemies, that such a divided Arab nation would not achieve solidarity, would inevitably surrender to imperialism; so all of us, each and every one of the sons of this nation, preferred the rough, hard way, the way to Arab unity and solidarity, and resolved to raise the banner of Arab nationalism and exert every effort thoroughly to consolidate it.[12]

These were eloquent words, but scarcely effective in the fragmented Arab world. It was too much to expect jealous Arab chieftains to heal their historic rivalries and submit to Nasser's leadership. Most of all, Nasser misjudged economic realities by regarding his leadership in purely institutional and political terms. He failed to understand the powerful economic factors at work in the Middle East. His political slogans were insufficient to meet economic realities. Egypt had won her independence, and had emerged as a full-blown national state with proper institutions in the Western tradition—flag, anthem, coins, and stamps. But behind the facade of Egyptian independence were all the economic miseries of the past. Nationalism had not solved the persistent problems of exploitation, poverty, and illiteracy. To expect Arab oil barons, as Nasser did, to accept the domination of impoverished Egypt was too much.

Nasser had some accomplishments to his credit, including land reform, increased industrialization, a campaign against corruption, and more women's rights. Arab leaders elsewhere, however, were not impressed. For them, Egypt was a police state, replete with the accoutrements of dictatorship, including censorship, lack of privacy, and control of the media. It was a common practice in Egypt to send political enemies to prison camps in the desert. There was little improvement in the everyday life of the *fellahin*, who were as impoverished as ever. Though other Arab leaders could scarcely claim the benefits of Western democracy, still they had little desire to endanger their sovereignty by submission to Nasser. With their oil billions, they had no intention of awarding leadership of the Arab-Muslim world to a Cairo politician whom they believed to be subject to delusions of grandeur.

Nasser's enemies coined the word *al-Nasiriyyh*, Nasserism, to refer to the movement created by Nasser in the Arab world. The term was used sarcastically to describe the belief that Pan-Arabism could succeed only under Nasser's leadership. Nasserism, existing mainly outside Egypt, lacked any form of central organization; it really represented an emotional cause rather than a regimented and coordinated movement.[13]

Nasser died on September 28, 1970, from a heart attack. Although he had managed to give some dignity to a people resentful under foreign control, he was never able to realize his ambition of creating a unified Arab world under his own leadership.

The Pan-Arab Ba'ath Party

Macro-nationalisms generally attract the support not only of charismatic leaders but also of central organizations which seek to give them political strength and coordination. Relations between leaders and organizations are usually close. But in the case of Pan-Arabism, Gamal Abdel Nasser and the Ba'ath Party both proclaimed their support for Arab unity. Both worked to achieve that objective, but they still remained enemies.

By the early 1960s, the Arab Middle East was divided into three kinds of states. The first, the monarchical, consisted of anti-revolutionary and anti-socialist monarchies—Saudi Arabia, Jordan, Libya, and Morocco. In the intermediate group, with varying ideologies and political structures, were Lebanon, Yemen, Kuwait, the Sudan, and Tunisia. The third group, comprising the revolutionary states of Egypt, Algeria, Syria, and Iraq, called for radical political reform and supported the ideas of Arab nationalism and socialism. These socialist states differed widely in their interpretations of both revolution and socialism.

In this complicated superstructure, the Ba'ath Party became the leading organization for the promotion of Pan-Arabism. It called for 'urubah, a semi-mystical term denoting the essence of being Arab, belonging to the Arab "nation," speaking Arabic, born a Muslim in an Arab land, and holding to the precepts of Islām. It involved an awareness of a special destiny:

The Arab nation has an important mission which has manifested itself in renewed and complete forms in the different stages of history, and which aims at reviving human values, encouraging human developments, and promoting harmony and cooperation among nations [of the world].[14]

This basic principle extended Arabism beyond the narrow limits of state, and enabled Ba'ath theorists to claim universalism and humanism as their ultimate goals.

Michel 'Aflaq, founder of the Ba'ath Party, called for a militant Arab nationalism based on socialism. "The battle for unity," he said, "according to our doctrine and our view and our struggle—cannot be separated from the battle for freedom and liberation and socialism, nor should it be under any circumstances."[15] Europe, in his view, was as fearful of Islām as in the past. Europeans realized that the strength of Islām had been reborn and had emerged in the new form of Arab nationalism. "We see Europe befriending traditional Islām and giving it support. That kind of Islām—superficial worship, vague and colorless values—is being gradually Europeanized. The day will come when the nationalists will find themselves the only defenders of the true Islām, and they will have to create in it new meaning if they are determined to preserve good reason for the survival of the Arab nation."[16] With this stand, the Ba'ath Party placed Pan-Arabism above Pan-Islāmism. Islām was to be retained, of course, but in its proper place.

The Ba'ath Party was critical of Nasser's regime. At the Sixth National Conference of the Ba'ath Party held on October 5, 1963, at a time when the Ba'ath Party was in power in both Syria and Iraq, political leaders carefully discussed the role of Nasser's Egyptian regime. Their resolution 10 was explicit:

The positive aspects of Abdel Nasser's regime in Egypt induce the party to accept the principle of unity with Egypt; but its negative aspects require that Abdel Nasser be received only as a partner [in the union] so that the union will not be based on the same principles as his regime. . . . It was Abdel Nasser who forced upon the party a struggle which, from the party's standpoint, has no other cause than Abdel Nasser's dictatorial tendencies.[17]

In other words, the Ba'ath Party had no intention of accepting the Egyptian strong man as the leader of the Pan-Arab movement.

In November 1963, only a month after the Sixth National Conference, the Ba'ath leadership was overthrown in Iraq. The proposed Syria-Iraqi union, a critical step on the way to Pan-Arab unity, failed to materialize. From then on, Ba'ath influence began to wane, and its once strident call for Arab unity became muted. Neither Nasser, with his pretension to leadership, nor the Ba'ath Party, with its claim of political regimentation for the movement, was successful in advancing the cause. Neither the charismatic leader nor the party organization was able to surmount the internal divisions of the Arab world—monarchy versus socialism, Shi'ite versus Sunnite sects, oil-rich Arab sheiks versus poverty-stricken *fellahin*.

As elsewhere, the theory of Arab unity was expressed in eloquent phraseology, but on a practical scale the possibility of Pan-Arab union was shattered by irreconcilable differences. These differences, persisting to the present day, react to the advantage of tiny Israel surrounded by squabbling Arab states.

Debate on Vitality

Reality or myth? Is the idea of Arab unity actual, not potential? Is it a present reality or a distant goal? Is it a battered but still-standing idea? Or is it a political concept turned to ashes, beset by problems not foreseen by creators of the myth, a weak pan-movement in process of dissolution? A fascinating debate on these conflicting positions took place in the pages of *Foreign Affairs* in 1978–1979.

For Walid Khalidi, one-time Professor of Political Studies at the American University in Beirut, Lebanon, the Arab system of states is first and foremost a "Pan" system.[18] It postulates the existence of a single Arab nation behind the facade of a multiplicity of sovereign states. In Khalidi's view, the manifest failure even to approximate unity does not negate the empirical reality of the Arab nation. "It merely adds nominative and prescriptive dimensions to the ideology of Pan-Arabism. The Arab nation both *is*, and *should be,* one."[19]

According to Khalidi, individual Arab states are deviant and transient entities, their frontiers illusory and permeable, the rulers interim caretakers, or obstacles to be removed. Champions of Pan-Arabism, speaking in the name of *vox populi*, have a mandate from the entire Arab nation. "Before such super-legitimacy, the legitimacy of the individual states shrinks into irrelevance."[20] Khalidi claimed that the oneness of the Arab nation has corollaries in concepts of the dignity of the nation, and the oneness and therefore the inviolability of its territory "from the [*Atlantic*] Ocean to the [Arab] Persian Gulf." For historical and cultural reasons, these ideas find powerful resonance among the vast majority of Arabs at every level of society in the five great regimes that make up the Arab world—the Fertile Crescent, the Gulf, the Peninsula, the Nile Valley, and the Maghreb. This reasoning gives sanctity to the parallelograms of *"raisons"* that make up the result stuff of the Arab political process—*raison d'état, raison de status quo, raison de la révolution,* and *raison de la nation.*

Unlike the four seasons of the universe, Khalidi saw the four *raisons* of the Arab political universe operating concurrently, diagonally, and dialectically, and not in two compartments in opposition to one another. "Irrespective of the degree or kind of commitment to them, the concepts of Pan-Arabism are functionally the most effective tool of change and legimitation in the hands of the Arab political elite."[21]

In essence, Khalidi's argument expressed in scholarly tones the case for Pan-Arabism. His presentation was challenged in the next issue of *Foreign Affairs* by Fouad Ajami, of the Department of Politics at Princeton University.[22] According to Ajami, the "myth" of Pan-Arabism, an idea that had dominated the political consciousness of modern Arabs, is nearing its end. At the height of its power, Pan-Arabism could make regimes look small and petty—disembodied structures headed by selfish rulers, who resisted the sweeping mission of Arabism and who were supported by outside powers which supposedly feared the one idea that could resurrect the classical golden age of the Arabs.

Ajami saw Khalidi's argument as flawed. "Now, however, *raison d'état*, once an alien and illegal doctrine, is gaining ground. Slowly and grimly, with a great deal of anguish and of outright violence, a 'normal' state system is becoming a fact of life."[23] According to Ajami, Pan-Arabism's retreat began in 1967 after the Six-Day War with Israel, "which marked the Waterloo of Pan-Arabism."[24] This defeat dishonored virtually all Arabs, and in particular the Pan-Arabs in Cairo and Damascus. "The defeat had underlined the vulnerability of the Arab system of states, the bankruptcy of the Arab border and its guardians, whether radical or conservative. The champions of Pan-Arabism were defeated in the Arab system; the idea had lost its magic."[25] Subsequently, leaders of Arab states read their interests differently and independently.

Ajami described the diplomacy of Anwar Sadat of Egypt as the most dramatic example of the weakness of Pan-Arabism, if only because Egypt had been the mainstay of the Arab system. But there were additional revolts and separatist attacks against monolithic Pan-Arabism. Another crack in the Pan-Arab edifice was the virtual end of the Ba'ath Party, which had taken seriously its mission of establishing one Arab nation. Still another challenge to Pan-Arabism was the threat of a partitioned Lebanon, only one of a decade of setbacks. Neither the fire and passion of the Libyan Revolution nor the leadership of dictator Muammar Kaddafi in an attempt to combine oil and Pan-Arabism, could assure the universality of the movement. Oil money could not turn history around and revive an exhausted idea.

Ajami saw Arab universalism as far too slender an idea:

The Arabs who had once seemed whole—both to themselves and to others—suddenly look as diverse as they had been all along. The differences, smothered over by ideology and by a universalistic designation, can in no way be ignored or suppressed. Indeed, the more they are blanketed over by a thin veneer of superficial universalism, the more dangerous they become, if only because they create resentment on the part of those who do not feel the designation and who judge that Arabism places them at a disadvantage—that is, it used to ask some of them to fight and die while others did not, or to use their territory as sanctuary for guerrilla raids while others were safely insulated by ceasefire lines and U.N. troops or to pay for the economic inefficiency and large populations of sister states.[26]

In Ajami's view, whether the Arabs liked it or not, what they were left with and what increasingly they must acknowledge is the profound fragmentation of the Arab existential and political crisis. They have shared themes and concerns which must not obscure the fragmentation. The day of Pan-Arabism has passed. Many problems must be worked out in the Arab system of national states: the "responsibility" of the rich states; the "rights" of the small states; the usual struggle for primacy and advantage among the resourceful and skilled states; the Palestinian quest for self-determination; restoration of order in Lebanon; and the struggle of the pre-eminent Arab state, Egypt, for economic solvency and viability. In conclusion, Ajami described the passing of Pan-Arabism as just the ending of one sea of troubles.

What should we conclude about diametrically opposed positions of these two experts on the Pan-Arabic movement? Khalidi sought to revive the sagging momentum of Pan-Arabism, while Ajami, hewing to the line of scholarly objectivity, was willing to admit the bankruptcy of Pan-Arabism as a viable historical movement. Such differences persist to the present day.

The Myth of Pan-Arabism

The idea of Pan-Arabism, of the *Umma Arabiyya Wahida Dhat Risala Khalida*, "the one Arab nation with an immortal mission," never won its way to fruition in the Arab world. Arab unity had been the sole publicly acceptable idea of statesmen and ideologies alike,[27] but slowly the Arab world broke down into what has been called the "normal" system of states.

Pan-Arabism was beset by enormous obstacles, both internal and external. Like other pan-movements, it was long on promises, short on performance. From its beginning, it was destined for failure. Once the opportunity came with the defeat of Turkey in World War I, Arabs of the Middle East, far from uniting to achieve their "immortal mission," fell to squabbling among themselves. There were far too many differences among the Arab-speaking peoples.

There were insurmountable weaknesses. The Arabs of North Africa west of Egypt felt no sense of loyalty to their fellow Arabs in the east, and had little inclination to respond to propagandistic appeals. As the state system became a fact of life in the Arab world, most champions of Pan-Arabism were exiles who sought to promote their cause from abroad. To Arab intellectuals living in other countries, distinctions between their people in the Middle East seemed unimportant, almost non-existent. These were literary intellectuals who dealt in grandiloquent abstractions, but it was something else to move from metaphysical praise of "the Arab nation" to a strong Pan-Arab political order.

At one time the Arabs were united in their opposition to colonialism. They were annoyed by both the Sykes-Picot agreement[28] and the Balfour Declaration.[29] The retreat of British and French imperialism in Arab countries, and the growing sympathy in London and Paris for the Arab cause tended to remove the binding cement of anti-colonialism. Individual Arab states began to go their own way.

The Israeli victory in 1948–1949 traumatized the entire Arab world, and dealt a tremendous blow to Arab pride. Arabs saw the emergence of Israel not simply as a Palestinian defeat, but as a grievous setback for the Pan-Arab mission. They regarded their weakness *vis-à-vis* Israel as out of line with past Arab glory and achievements. For a time, Arabs everywhere were united in their hatred for the Jewish state, but this sense of unity began to evaporate in the face of nationalist goals. One Israeli victory after another made discouraging blows on the idea of Pan-Arabism.

Like Pan-Islāmism, Pan-Arabism failed to become a popular movement, despite zealous propaganda appeals. There were far too many disparities among Arab peoples. Lebanese felt little in common with Yemenites, Tunisians with Saudi Arabians. While intellectuals continued to boast of the great potentials of Arab unity, the masses were unimpressed. Neither the Arab League nor the United Arab Republic found much popular support. Islām was acceptable, but a loss of sovereignty was not. Mecca, yes; a politically unified caliphate, no! Pan Arabism, like other macro-nationalisms, was destined to remain an unimplemented myth.

Still, there were intermittent attempts to revive Pan-Arabism. Reporting from Cairo in June 1982, correspondents Rowland Evans and Robert Novak wrote that Israel's invasion of Lebanon had encouraged Pan-Arabism, which had been held in check in Egypt since the assassination of Anwar Sadat in October 1981.[30] But the fact remained that the Arabs could not seem to stop fighting among themselves.

Some 140 million Arabs seemed united by their common historical origin, traditions, language, religion, and their access to much of the world's oil. Behind this facade of unity, however, remained profound political, territorial, and economic rivalries which made the cause of Pan-Arabism a hopeless one. The differences were insurmountable: the existence of artificial boundaries inherited from European colonialism; the continuation of tribal allegiances; the class struggle between holders of oil wealth and poverty-stricken masses; rivalries between Islāmic sects; and divergent approaches to solving the Palestinian problem. There were far too many bitter inter-Arab conflicts: Egypt versus Libya; Soviet-supported Algeria versus

Western-supported Morocco and Mauretania; the civil war in Lebanon, a battleground for inter-Arab views on the Palestinian question; the power struggle between Syria and Iraq for the control of Greater Syria; border disputes between Iraq and Kuwait; an armed conflict between the conservative North Yemen Republic backed by Saudi Arabia and the Marxist, Soviet-supported, regime in the South.[31] Given all these conflicts and rivalries, to speak of "the one Arab nation with an immortal mission" becomes a contradiction in terms.

CHAPTER 9

ZIONISM AS MACRO-NATIONALISM

The land of Israel was the birthplace of the Jewish people. Here their spiritual, religious and national identity was formed. Here they achieved independence and created a culture of national and universal significance. Here they wrote and gave the Bible to the world.

Proclamation of Independence of Israel, May 15, 1948

The Pan-Religious Impulse

Pan-movements, emphasizing the "all," "every," or "entire," take on a cultural and political character aiming to promote the solidarity of peoples bound by combinations of kindred languages, historical traditions, geographical proximity, race, religion, or other postulated ties. In the more restricted sense, they may be classified as pan-national, pan-continental, or pan-religious.

There were three major pan-religious movements, all of which sought to combine those of one religious faith in a union transcending national boundary lines. Pan-Christianity reached its apogee in the Middle Ages. In the modern era, despite efforts at conciliation in ecumenical drives, Christianity was divided into major and minor sects, thereby losing its former political unity. Pan-Islāmism, similarly grounded in the belief that all its followers belonged together in one giant union, was hampered not only by ecclesiastical differences, such as those between Sunnītes and Shīʿites, but also by irreconcilable national antagonisms.

Zionism, claiming to represent the third major religion, sought to transform its religious goals into some semblance of political unity. The Jewish national movement had as its goal the re-establishment of Palestine as a Jewish national state. From its inception, it was designed as a global movement for inclusion of all Jews, wherever they might be, in a reversal of the *Diaspora*,[1] and the reoccupation of the Holy Land as the homeland of all Jews. It was supported intellectually and financially by Jews throughout the world. Wherever Jews were oppressed, as in Tsarist Russia, the Third Reich, and Soviet Russia, the impulse to return to the Holy Land was strong. In democratic countries, however, in the United States, Britain,

France, Italy, Switzerland, and elsewhere, where Jews have been granted equal citizenship, there was little urge to emigrate to Israel.[2] They would give financial support, but they had no intention of relinquishing their citizenship. They reserved first loyalty for their own state, and felt a secondary attachment to their religion, together with sympathy and understanding for the state of Israel. American Jews, like American Catholics, reserved political loyalty for their own country. They would practice their religion in their own national homeland.

For strict Zionists, this attitude was a mistaken one. They saw no distinction between religion and politics. They fashioned their own political state in Israel, nurtured its existence through war after war, and beckoned to Jews everywhere to join them in implementating the Zionist ideal. They argued that Jews would never be accepted or allowed complete freedom in states dominated by other religions. This was an unconvincing argument for Jews who played a major role in building American society. They objected to being included in a movement which they felt violated their status as citizens of an already established national state.

Although Zionism provided a new spiritual and historic homeland for many Jews, although it created for the Jewish people their first large and active organization, and while it revived the sense of Jewish nationalism in many assimilated Jews, it did not achieve its goal of a unified global supranationalism. Zionism has not won the common bond necessary to transcend national obligations, and whether it will be able to satisfy its claim that it is the solution for "the Jewish problem" remains an open question.

Jews and Palestine

Although Zionism is a modern nationalist movement, it is in a very real sense a continuation of the century-old sentiment of Jews for a restoration of their homeland.[3] Jews have identified themselves with Palestine, the Land of Israel, since their patriarchal beginnings. The Jews were one of the few peoples in the ancient world who had a strong sense of national consciousness.

The Old Testament tells the story of how the ancient Hebrews were associated with Palestine. The land of Canaan was conquered by Moses and Joshua (c. 1000 B.C.), and Hebrew power was consolidated there. In 721 B.C., Israel, the northern kingdom, was taken by the Assyrians. In 580 B.C., Babylonians conquered Judea with its capital at Jerusalem, in the process destroying the Temple built by Solomon. After the destruction of this short-lived Jewish state in Palestine, the Jews of the *Diaspora* moved to Babylonia and elsewhere. Toward the end of the 6th century B.C., exiled Jews returned to rebuild the Temple, and set up the Second Jewish Commonwealth. In 70 A.D., conquering Romans sacked Jerusalem, and burned the Second Temple. The dispersion continued with Jewish communities settling in the Middle East, Asia Minor, the Balkans, Russia, and later in Western Europe.

The original intense nationalistic fervor of the Jewish people survived with undiminished zeal for two thousand years. Jews of the *Diaspora* never forgot the Land of Israel. Those in exile remained faithful to their early nationalist ideal. In daily prayers, in teaching the young, in literature and law, in philosophical speculation, there was always the lure of Palestine. For Jews dispersed over the globe, the Holy Land symbolized the glory of ancient days, as well as the hope for redemption of a people. Messianic leaders appeared with the call for union of all Jews from the ends of the earth to return and claim that national heritage. Religion and national life, they said, formed an unbreakable bond demanding a return to Zion. The distant past should be combined with the elusive future, "the end of days," when all Jews would belong to the Land of Israel. "It was the cradle of their early peoplehood. There they were welded into what we call today a nation. National triumphs and catastrophes, perpetuated in religious lore, remained associated with the hills and valleys of the little country. Above all the religious and literary genius of the Jews blossomed in the Land of Israel."[4]

This Jewish sense of national consciousness clashed with the goals of others. The little narrow strip of land, about the size of Vermont on the eastern end of the Mediterranean, had seen centuries of conflict between Jews, Christians, and Muslims. Many peoples had contended for its possession, including Hebrews, Philistines, Babylonians, Persians, Syrians, Romans, Arabs, and Turks. Nevertheless, Jews in the Middle Ages never ceased to yearn for a return to what they regarded as their own homeland. They would leave it to the will of God to be led back to their old home. For generations, pious Jews made pilgrimages to the Holy Land. Some settled there permanently in order to be buried in holy soil.

In the modern era, Zionism emerged as a continuum of the deeply-rooted Jewish sense of national consciousness. Based on religious sentiment, it was also a political and secular movement rising in Central Europe as a reaction to politico-economic ills. Jews were politically humiliated, economically deprived, socially rejected, ghettoized, and persecuted. *Diaspora* Jews, financiers as well as scholars and devotees, contributed money and learning to what they believed to be the self-rejuvenating remnant in Zion.[5]

During the first half of the 19th century, it was believed that the Jews of Central and Western Europe would be politically emancipated and assimilated into the social and cultural life of the varied European states. Toward the end of the century, however, it became increasingly clear that the rewards of assimilation extended to only a very few, and that the vast majority of Jews still suffered the slings of misfortune, oppression, and humiliation. Persecution, especially in Tsarist Russia, gave additional impetus for a return to the homeland, the spiritual haven where Jews could live in peace and prosperity. They wanted to become "normal"—like all other peoples, and enjoy their own nation. The great problem was that the land for which they yearned was not only the scene of recurring religious rivalries, but also of conflicting national aspirations.

Return to Zion

In the late 19th century there was a strong revival of the "back to Zion" ideal. Stimulus for organization came from varied sources—from coffee shops in anti-Semitic Vienna, cafés of anti-Dreyfusard Paris, and cellars of the Jewish Pale in pogrom-minded Russia. Strongly nationalistic in tone, the move for a return to Zion was stimulated by the ongoing nationalism in Western Europe. It was a kind of derivative national sentiment encouraged by primary nationalisms already existing throughout the European continent. There was a powerful base: where the extension of national sentiment to Africa and Asia was a reaction to colonial exploitation, Zionism—the demand of an ancient people for its long-suppressed rights, was the last product of European nationalism. It was "a product which, since it is a national sentiment, not a colonial exploitation, is the more solid and therefore the more formidable."[6]

Hans Kohn, who during his lifetime as a pioneer specialist on nationalism devoted much attention to the history of Zionism, pointed out that the general European scene was favorable to its development. In the first third of the 19th century, the dominant elements had been liberal individualism, the struggle against traditionalism, and the belief in humanitarianism; the second third (from about 1848 to 1878) was dominated by nationalism, the attempt to liberate and unite peoples as corporate bodies; and the third period (from 1878 to 1914) was an era of expanding imperialization and colonization.[7] The national movement came comparatively late for Jews, for Zionism as an organized movement belonged almost wholly to the last third of the 19th century.

The Kohn analysis is valid. Indeed, until the late 19th century, the yearning of Jews for the Land of Israel had been strictly religious in concept. Until then, Jews throughout the world saw the Holy Land as the scene of universal ethical monotheism. They were proud of it as the homeland dedicated to ideals of peace, justice, and brotherhood, as described by the prophets and expressed in the *Mishna* and Palestinian *Talmud*. However, with the quickening of national sentiment everywhere, the critical ism began to supersede religion as the dominant urge for a Return to Zion. A new national movement was in the process of formation.

Two important forces contributed to the strength of the Return to Zion movement—assimilation and anti-Semitism. During the late 18th century, reaction against medieval institutions—the core of the Enlightenment—included the integration of Jews into the larger community, a tendency favored by both the American and French Revolutions, Napoleonic rule, and the new liberalism. Jews of the early and mid-19th century began to see advantages in emancipation and assimilation. Orthodox Judaism, long the object of persecution, saw hope in the new secularism and the new world of science. Throughout world society, Jews began to relinquish their old distinctive traditional way of life. Many saw sanctuary in becoming assimilated in Christian lands. Others, converting to Christianity, entered the stream of Christian life. Those who adhered to ancient Jewish ritual began to enjoy the benefits of the new liberalism: they were given a status of equality unheard of in the Middle Ages. Thus they could enter the professions and the business world as they wished, and the onus of century-old legal discrimination seemed to have been lifted. Assimilation appeared to have solved the age-old "Jewish problem."

However, the lack of discrimination and assimilation was an exaggerated hope. Toward the end of the 19th century, the process of emancipation and assimilation began to face the threat of a steadily increasing anti-Semitism. Intensified national sentiment throughout the continent reacted to the disadvantage of Jews. Russians began to call for a country limited to Russians and Slavs, Germans for a nation of Germans and Aryans, French for a state purely French and Latin.

In Russia, especially, the status of Jews degenerated to a dangerous point in the era of pogroms.[8] Because of centuries of socio-economic discrimination, Russian Jews were concentrated in commercial and intellectual professions. They were prominent both as businessmen and political radicals, hated as both socialists and capitalists. In the early 1880s, they were subjected to legal discrimination, including laws forbidding them to own land and restricting them to mercantile pursuits and the lending of money. Regarded as an alien element on the Russian scene and as the people responsible for the crucifixion of Christ, they were made targets of religious passion, economic discrimination, and distrust.

At this time, the Russian police began the practice of pogroms (Russian "devastations"), officially sponsored riots which led to physical assaults on Jews and even killings. The first widespread pogroms followed the assassination of Tsar Alexander II in 1881, even though the assassin was not a Jew. Russian mobs in more than 200 cities attacked Jews and destroyed their property. Pogroms were common during the early part of the 20th century. Although the Russian government did not organize the riots, its anti-Semitic policy made them possible. Authorities were reluctant either to stop pograms or punish those who were responsible for them. For those Jews caught in the web, the rising Zionist sentiment seemed to provide a way out of their real dilemma.

Almost as traumatic for Jews was the isolated incident of the Dreyfus case in France, which, although promoted by no organized party, committed

French conservatives to an official program of anti-Semitism. The details are familiar:[9] In October 1894 Captain Alfred Dreyfus (1859-1935), an Alsatian Jewish officer serving on the French General Staff, was court-martialed for treason, officially degraded, and sentenced to imprisonment on Devil's Island. Clericals, royalists, and the military denounced Dreyfus as a Jewish traitor; bourgeois anti-clericalists and Socialists came to his defense. Dreyfusards accused the anti-Dreyfusards of discrediting the Republic and seeking an excuse for an authoritarian regime.

The problem was that Dreyfus was innocent. It was found that his original accuser had forged evidence. Retried at Rennes in September 1899, he was found "guilty with extenuating circumstances," but pardoned. After pressure for his acquittal, the court-martial verdict was quashed in July 1906. Dreyfus was readmitted to the Army and awarded the French Legion of Honor.

As a side issue to the conflict between clericalism and anti-clericalism, French anti-Semitism was emotional in content, but less enduring than anti-Semitism in Imperial Russia. French clericals, who denounced Jews as "a devouring canker," demanded that they be transported to some distant country where they would "reform their habits or die of want." Paul Lapeyre, author of a history of Social Catholicism, excoriated Jews as "descendants of those who had crucified Jesus."[10]

Anti-Semitic parties arose in Germany and Austria, where the archetypes of modern anti-Semitism were to be found.[11] Here, large parties were formed to restrict the liberties and political rights of Jews. Anti-Semitism in Germany and Austria developed not only as ideology, but also as a political movement. Despite the abolition of religious disabilities, anti-Semitism emerged in increasing vigor there, because the burden of the New Industrial Revolution had fallen heavily on old handicraftsmen and peasants, making them bitter against the Jews in Germany and Austria who seemed to be in the vanguard of the new capitalist bourgeoisie. Anti-Semitism also drew support from the disgust which middle-class Germans and Austrians had for excesses of financial capitalism, as well as for the demands of advanced radicalism.

Added to the generating economic factor was a philosophical racialism which gave strength to the doctrine of anti-Semitism. The innocent philological theories of Friedrich Max Müller[12] were used to construct the pseudo-scientific doctrine of superiority of the Indo-European-Aryan-Nordic "race" as against the Semitic "race." Jews were denounced as corrupt, the Jewish character as wickedly devoted to the necessity for obtaining material advantage.

European anti-Semitism was bolstered by a forgery, *The Protocols of the Elders of Zion*, which presented the story of an extensive Jewish conspiracy to bring the world under Jewish domination.[13] In 1903, during the pogrom in Kishinev, a short form of the *Protocols* appeared in the Russian newspaper, *Znamia*. In 1905, the *Protocols* were published in book form by

Sergei Nilus. The editor claimed that the material was obtained by a woman who stole them from an eminent French leader of Freemasonry. In the 1917 edition, Nilus claimed that the manuscript had been given him by a Russian official, and that it consisted of notes of a plan submitted to the "Council of Elders" by Theodor Herzl at the First Zionist Congress held at Basel in 1897. The notes described a conspiracy to blow up the major capitals of Europe, destroy the Aryan race as well as Christian civilization, and erect a Jewish-Freemason world-state.

The *Protocols* were obviously a clumsy and slanderous forgery.[14] Nevertheless, they were used with telling effect, playing an important role in stimulating anti-Jewish sentiment, even in England and the United States, hitherto relatively free from public anti-Semitism. They led to a wave of feeling against Jews everywhere.

The depths of anti-Semitic fury promoted by the *Protocols* forced many Jews, who until then had thought in terms of emancipation and assimilation, to seek a new sense of Jewish identity. Those who wished above all to be absorbed anonymously into the civic life of their countries, began to despair of ever attaining that goal. Many began to pay more and more attention to the aims and aspirations of a movement designed to free them from irrational and unfair tactics. Zionism might possibly help to maintain their sense of dignity in a hostile climate. Perhaps the Zionists were right in their contention that "the whole of Jewry" must organize in a campaign to counteract the false claims of the *Protocols*.

From this time on, there began an ideological struggle among Jews themselves. One side saw in the Jewish renascence promised by Zionism the solution to what had become known as "the Jewish problem." The other side, rejecting the idea that the Jews were a nationality, held fast to the belief that Judaism was a religious faith and that Jews and non-Jews alike inside the same country shared exactly the same nationality, citizenship, and political and social ideals. The struggle between these two contrasting views was a long one, lasting through the establishment of the state of Israel. Zionists, who saw themselves as a strong supranationalism, urged all Jews, scattered throughout the world, to heed the call of a Return to Zion. Non-Zionists and anti-Zionists, while recognizing the importance of Israel as a homeland, persisted in their contention that all those of the Jewish faith, already emancipated by the traditions of the 18th-century Enlightenment and 19th-century liberalism and democracy, should be integrated into their own community, precisely as other peoples. The conflict, unresolved, continued to the end of the 20th century.

From Moses Hess to Theodor Herzl

Zionism was fortunate in the progenitors who fashioned its theories and nurtured its development. Dedicated and able strategists paved the way.

Moses Hess. Among the early precursors of modern Zionism in Western

Europe was the political philosopher Moses Hess (1812-1875), generally recognized as the father of Zionist Socialism.[15] Prominent in the days of Marx and Engels, Hess had fled from his native German homeland after the Revolution of 1848. For the rest of his life, he lived in exile, mostly in Paris. He had two lifelong interests: philosophical socialism (what he called "ethical" or "true" socialism), and the plight of his fellow Jews.

Hess's attitude toward his religion underwent several changes. In his twenties, he believed that Jews, already accomplishing their mission in history, should turn to assimilation. He felt himself to be thoroughly German. After the death of his father in 1851, he married his Christian companion, Sybille Pesch of Aachen. Filled with compassion for the suffering of his fellow Jews, he gradually became convinced that their emancipation was not worth the price of assimilation.

In 1862 Hess published a book titled *Rom und Jerusalem*, which eventually became a classic in Zionist literature. In moving prose, he described the inner transformation that had taken place in his own life. Although in the past he saw his own path as remote from Judaism, he was sure of a clear road for Jews. For 2,000 years they had lived in lands in which organically they could not coalesce. Hess, like his fellow Jews, was beginning to think of his nationality as "inseparable from the inheritance of my ancestors, the Holy Land and the eternal city, the birthplace of belief in the divine unity of life and the brotherhood of all men."

Hess's views on the future of Judaism were partly naïve and partly clear-cut in reasoning. His understanding of "race" was unscientific and fallacious. He saw all past history as a combination of the primal "race" struggle and the secondary class struggle. He wrote about two "world-historical races" which shaped modern society—the Aryan and Semitic, the Aryans aiming at explaining and beautifying life, the Semites in moralizing and sanctifying it. In falsely identifying his fellow Jews as a "race," Hess made the same error as Count Arthur de Gobineau, whose *Essay on the Inequality of Human Races* (1853-1855) was a pseudo-scientific study devoted to extolling Aryanism. The difference was that where Hess praised both Aryan and Semitic "races," Gobineau laid the foundation for the persecution of Jews as a non-Aryan race.

In his accounts of political aspects of Jewish life, Hess set a standard for Zionist ideology. He called on his fellow Jews to preserve their nationality while in exile, and to work for the political restoration of Palestine. Again and again, he referred to his underlying theme—the indestructability of Jewish nationality. Jews, he said, must assure a "center of action," around which Jewish leaders could pursue their religious mission. They must try to create a future Jewish state based on acquisition of territory by the Jewish "nation" *as a whole*, and create legal conditions under which work could flourish. They must be certain to construct a Jewish society in accordance with Mosaic (in Hess's view "socialist") principles. Politically, Jews must learn to combine Spinozaistic-Jewish beliefs, national elements, and socialist principles.

Leo Pinsker. Theories expressed by Moses Hess in Western Europe received additional emphasis in Tsarist Russia. Here, persecution of Jews had reached a climax in the early 1880s when murderous pogroms occurred throughout the Jewish Pale. The pioneer Zionist in Imperial Russia was Lev Semenovich Pinsker (1821-1891), born in Thomaszów, Russian Poland (now the Ukrainian S.S.R.), the son of a Hebrew scholar.[16] After studying law, Pinsker turned to the practice of medicine. Like Hess, he initially supported secular assimilation of Jews into the society in which they lived, as an offshoot of the Enlightenment (*Haskala*). He changed his mind after a vicious pogrom in Odessa in 1881, which he believed had taken place only with governmental complicity. Again like Hess, he began to see Jewish nationalism as the only solution for Jewish suffering.

In 1882 Pinsker published an extraordinary pamphlet titled *Auto-Emancipation: A Warning of a Russian Jew to his Brethren.* As a physician, he thought in terms of diagnosis. The Jews, he was certain, were burdened with the virus of anti-Semitism, a social pathology. The Jews were hated, he said, because even though they had no national existence, they continued to display the spiritual characteristics of a national entity. In his view, the hatred of Jews was a psychosis, a disease which in two thousand years of Jewish history had become incurable. They could never really find a true home in a non-Jewish country, because they would be persecuted as soon as they became too populous.

Pinsker's cure for the ills of Judaism became the essence of Zionism. The only possible restorative for Jewish health and dignity, he warned, lay in finding a home in which they would not be strangers. They must emigrate with the consent of European governments to some territory, not necessarily Palestine, where they could live the national life of a "normal people." That goal, he said, was favored by historical circumstance. History was an ally because new states were rising which, at an earlier time, would not have dared to dream of resurrection.[17] Jews, he warned, must not rely on humanitarianism of a civilized society, but on their own inner strength, their own historic will—on self-help, or auto-emancipation.

During the same year (1882) in which Pinsker's pamphlet appeared, a new Zionist group called *Hibbet Ziyon* (Love of Zion) emerged, later named *Chovevi Ziyyon* (Lovers of Zion), with its members pledged to work for emigration to Palestine. Pinsker, who until then had not stressed Palestine as a homeland, was converted to the idea; he became leader and chief theorist of the Zionist organization. The movement then represented a combination of religious longing for a messianic restoration of Zion and 19th-century nationalism. Pioneers began to move from Russia and Eastern Europe to "redeem" (*gelulah*) the Holy Land.[18] The first Zionist colonies were established: *Rishon le Sion* in Judea; *Zichron Jakob* in Samaria; and *Eosh Pina* in Galilee.

At this time, Pinsker's appeal to Western European Jewry went unheeded. Instead, he concentrated on sending his small group of older Orthodox Jews and young students, the latter known as the *Bilu*, to start Jewish agricultural colonies in the wilderness of Palestine. Untrained for a way of life which they had never known before, and without sufficient funds, Pinsker's pioneers in the Holy Land were soon faced with bankruptcy. They were saved by the intervention of Baron Edmond de Rothschild (1845-1934), who provided financial and some political support. Pinsker did not hesitate to seek help from such Jewish benefactors. The first settlers worked surreptitiously, relying on Arab laborers for assistance. Pinsker was rebuffed when he tried to win political concessions from the Sublime Porte for colonization. The Turks moved to stop immigration to Palestine by setting up legal and administrative obstacles.

Faced with what seemed to be insurmountable barriers, Pinsker became pessimistic in the closing years of his life. He began to doubt whether *Eretz Israel* would ever serve as a solution for saving Jews from persecution. He now believed that the Jewish problem might possibly be solved through Baron Maurice de Hirsch, whose Jewish Colonization Association (JCA) called for the settlement of Jews in Argentina. Before Pinsker died, he reached the conclusion that Palestine would remain only the spiritual center of the Jewish people.

Achad Ha-am. Pinsker's earlier reliance on Baron de Rothschild and other Western philanthropists led to the emergence of an opposing faction in the budding Zionist movement. It was led by the writer Achad Ha-am (1856-1927), a pseudonym meaning "One of the People" for Asher Ginzberg. A political essayist, Ha-am played an important role in extending Pinsker's attempt at a fusion of traditional Zionism with modern nationalism.[19]

In Ha-am's view, it was a mistaken Utopian idea to seek a solution of the Jewish problem by sending masses of Jews to Palestine. Therefore, he opposed Jewish colonization in Palestine, and criticized what he called Rothschild's paternalism. Zionism, he said, could never contribute a quantitative solution nor a remedy against anti-Semitism. Instead, the first Zionist concern should be qualitative and metaphysical. Jews for too long had been isolated from their national heritage, from their original national community. Thus, Palestine should be seen only as a Jewish cultural center, the spiritual home of Jewish civilization. Jews who went there—farmers, scholars, artisans, and students—should revive Hebrew culture in the spirit of the ancient prophets. This selective community would exert its influence on Jews scattered throughout the world, and in this way, would lead to an intellectual and moral rebirth of Judaism. Zionism, said Ha-am, had little to do with the economic betterment of Jews or their individual happiness, but would remain a metaphysical and spiritual idea designed to reverse the tendency toward loss of Jewish faith and identity.

Ha-am's version of Zionism never attracted the support of masses of Jews, precisely because it did not offer any satisfactory solution to the pressing political and economic needs of Jews in countries suffused with anti-Semitism. However, his strong support for the idea of Hebrew culture permeated and influenced Zionist circles. By emphasizing ties with the historic Jewish past, he gave direction to the entire Zionist concept, and helped turn it into a modern nationalist movement.

Theodor Herzl. Thus far Zionism had been a small movement arising in East European ghettoes, and supported by Western Jewish philanthropy. A new and vital impulse came to the movement with Theodor Herzl (1860-1904), father of political Zionism and founder of the World Zionist Organization.[20] By strength of will and leadership, Herzl lifted Zionism from its small cultural boundaries, and fashioned it into a political movement of global significance. Born in Budapest on May 2, 1860, he studied law and later turned to journalism, acting as a correspondent for the Vienna *Neue Frei Presse.* Attending the Dreyfus trial as a reporter, he witnessed the riotous behavior of a Parisian mob when the innocent Jewish officer was humiliated publicly, and stripped of his military rank. Shaken by the experience, Herzl came to the conclusion that the only solution for rampant anti-Semitism would be the mass exodus of Jews from the European continent, and their settlement in a land of their own. Until this traumatic experience in Paris, he had been an assimilationist, but his mind then changed. Against their own wishes, he now believed, Jews had been forced by outside pressure to form a nation of their own.

In 1896 Herzl published a pamphlet titled *Der Judenstaat (The Jewish State),*[21] in which he presented his own version of political Zionism. Although he was not aware of Pinsker's work in Odessa, Herzl, in effect, came to the same conclusions. Anti-Semitism would always exist. The Jewish problem was a national one that could be solved only by making it a global political question to be discussed and settled by the civilized world. "The distinctive nationality of the Jews neither can, will, nor must be destroyed."[22] And again: "Our national character is too historically famous and in spite of every degradation, too fine to make the annihilation desirable."[23]

Herzl advised his fellow Jews to seek international sanction for creation of a Jewish state. He recommended the founding of a "Society of Jews" to make necessary preparations, as well as a "Jewish Company" to promote colonization. He was sharply critical of that form of colonization favored by philanthropist Baron de Rothschild and the *Chovevi Ziyyon* movement. Philanthropy was fine, he said, but what was needed was Jewish action to win a homeland with international approval. In his estimation, this was the first and vital task of Zionism.

In 1897 Herzl founded *Die Welt,* which became the official organ of the Zionist movement. That same year he convoked the First Zionist Congress at Basel, which drew some 200 delegates from all over the world. Herzl was responsible for the clear-cut terms of the Basel Program:

> Zionism strives to create for the Jewish people a Home in Palestine secured by public law. The Congress contemplates the following means to the attainment of this end:
>
> 1. The promotion on suitable lines of the colonization of Palestine by Jewish agricultural and industrial workers;
> 2. The organization and binding together of the whole of Jewry by means of appropriate institutions, local and international, in accordance with the laws of each country;
> 3. The strengthening and fostering of Jewish national sentiment and consciousness;
> 4. Preparatory steps toward obtaining Government consent, where necessary to the attainment of the aim of Zionism.[24]

With this proposal, Herzl moved Zionism from its limited Odessa version to an inter-territorial, democratic-nationalist movement, the first of its kind in Jewish history. In his Basel Program, Herzl brought Zionism into the mainstream of modern nationalism, and even more, from the very beginning, conceived of it in macro-nationalistic terms—"binding together the whole of Jewry." He would bring together homeless and landless Jews, who had been subjected to abnormal political, economic, and spiritual conditions, and re-establish them in their historic homeland through uninterrupted and unrestricted immigration and settlement. He would appeal not simply to the poor and oppressed, but to *all* Jews, wherever they were, to come to *Eretz Israel* to take part in a resurrected Jewish national life.

Creation of the World Zionist Organization was Herzl's greatest achievement. As its President, he tried to win from Turkish Sultan Abdül Hamid II permission to found a Jewish charter company for settlement in Palestine. Similar attempts to obtain help from Wilhelm II and other rulers were unsuccessful. The only public offer came in 1903, when British Colonial Minister Joseph Chamberlain suggested the uninhabited highlands of the East African protectorate of Uganda as a possible Jewish homeland, an offer which met with an angry refusal.

Herzl's role in the story of Zionism was vital. Until his time, Zionist activity had been primarily religious and historical, with modest steps toward colonization in Palestine. His secular national program marked a powerful forward step. He spoke highly of Hebrew culture and the Hebrew national language, but in his view, metaphysical speculations and Hebrew folklore must take second place to the all-important political goal of a national homeland. He led the World Zionist Organization for only seven years, from 1897 to his death in 1904 at the age of 44. Burdened by overwork, he died in the belief that his work was a diplomatic failure.

Herzl failed to understand his own enormous influence on the Zionist movement. The series of Zionist congresses that he initiated gave his fellow Jews their first unity since ancient times. His work at Vienna[25] stimulated masses of Jews to look to Palestine as their true homeland. He transformed Zionism successfully from a vague sentiment into a world secular organization with political strength. After his death, he became a legendary figure in the Jewish world. In August 1949, shortly after the establishment of Israel, his remains were transferred from Vienna, and reinterred on Mount Herzl in Jerusalem. A Herzl museum was constructed nearby. The anniversary of Herzl's death, the 20th of Tammuz in the Jewish calendar, was made a national memorial holiday in Israel.

Internal Schisms and Anti-Zionism

From its inception, Zionism produced various schools of thought, stressing differences of opinion and approaches to the national problems facing the Jewish people. As one of many rival Jewish ideologies, it was divided by a wide diversity of internal factions.[26] Thus, while Herzl called for a viable Jewish state, Achad Ha-am proposed only a spiritual or cultural center in Palestine. There were differences between those who supported political Zionism and those who placed prime emphasis upon the religious base of Jewry.[27]

Where political Zionists saw the Jewish people's inalienable right to its ancient land as central to national striving, practical Zionists saw the territorial question as one capable of compromise. Political Zionists received the support of a series of Zionist leaders, who carried on in the tradition of Herzl. These included Max Nordau (1849-1923), David Wolff-sohn (1856-1914), and Vladimir Jabotinsky (1880-1940). All argued that Zionist strategy must seek to win adequate political conditions for its national aims before turning to such subsidiary activities as extensive colonization.

Political Zionism was opposed by "practical Zionism," led by Chaim Weizmann (1874-1952). Practical Zionism insisted that such nationalist goals as cultural regeneration and settlement in Palestine must occur simultaneously with political diplomacy. Only by eventual settlement in Palestine could the historical continuum of Judaism be maintained. As leader of the "practicals," Weizmann held that Zionism should concern itself not only with Jewish cultural rebirth but also with diplomacy to fashion a legal foundation for ultimate settlement in Palestine. It was Weizmann who obtained from the British Government the Balfour Declaration promising support for the establishment of Palestine as a national homeland for the Jewish people.[28]

In his strategy for Zionism, Weizmann looked for supporters everywhere, including those who advocated the "mission" idea, those who preferred the prospect of a binational state, non-Zionist Jews, and the divided Zionist-Socialists. He wanted help from both wealthy and poor Jews. He formed the Jewish Agency for Palestine in 1929 in agreement with Louis Marshall (1856-1929) and Felix Warburg (1871-1937). He was a strong champion of the idea of gradualism.

Labor Zionist factions, which differed among themselves, eventually became Weizmann's most reliable allies. In general, labor Zionists believed that the primary task of Zionism was to create in Palestine a Jewish farmer-worker class, and thereby eliminate the erroneous occupational distribution in Western Europe and elsewhere. They would synthesize socialism and Zionism. Only in Palestine, they said, could there be a strategic base for achieving socialism. They differed among themselves on subsidiary issues. Prominent among the Zionist-Socialists were Ber Borochov (1881-1917), leader of Marxist Zionism; Nachman Syrkin (1868-1924), non-Marxist Socialist; and Aaron David Gordon (1856-1922), advocate of "Hebraic Socialism."

The road of Zionism was a rocky one. Added to these internal schisms was the opposition of anti-Zionists of varying shades of opinion. Anti-Zionists argued that Judaism was a religion and not a nationality, and must be preserved as such. *Diaspora* Jews, they said, were content to retain their religion while living as emancipated citizens in civilized states. Above all, they resented the implication that Zionism was a pan-ideology including all Jews in its aims and aspirations.

Anti-Zionist sentiment existed both in Western and Eastern Europe. Critics in Western Europe argued that only enemies of liberty, equality, and fraternity held the position that Jews were a nation, and that Jews in general wanted to see a homeland restored in Zion. Anti-Zionists would work to promote the Hebrew language and culture, but they emphatically would not relinquish their nationality in favor of an ephemeral Jewish nationalism. Anti-Zionist Jewish assimilationists believed that the best solution for the Jewish problem would be intermarriage with the Christian community.

Anti-Zionists also emerged in Eastern Europe, where some traditionalist Jews supported the settlement of small numbers in Palestine as a religious duty, especially those who wanted to end their days in the Holy Land. But others considered Zionism to be false messianism to resettle Palestine as a means of ending the Exile. These anti-Zionists saw Zionism not only as a false religious idea, but also as an irrational secular design.

Some Jewish Socialists denounced the proposed synthesis of Zionism and Socialism as a perversion of Marxian ideology. Socialism, they claimed, was a movement to unite the workers of the world against the evils of capitalism, not a limited attempt to end the *Diaspora* and bring Jews back to the Holy Land. The Jewish question, they argued, was but one facet of the global class conflict. These anti-Zionists argued that the battle for Jewish redemption should be fought at the barricades everywhere, not merely in the Holy Land.

Among the most vociferous critics of Zionists were ultra-orthodox Jews both inside and outside Israel. These Jews took a militant anti-Zionist stand in accusing the Israeli national administration of betraying the Jewish cause. Zionism, they said, had departed from Jewish orthodoxy. Therefore, they refused on religious grounds to recognize the authority of the state.[29]

Ultra-orthodox anti-Zionists categorically refused to accept Zionists as spokesmen for the Jewish people. Recognition of Zionism, they charged, has inflicted more harm on the authentic people of Israel, its Torah, and its faith than upon the Arab people. "Actually, the Zionist atheists have no intrinsic connection with the Jewish People. There is no fact so axiomatic of the Jewish People as their adherence to the Torah. The Jewish People have no interest in Zionists or Zionism, or in temporal power; we eschew nationalism and its political implications."[30] Before the advent of political Zionism, Jews lived in Palestine side by side with Arab neighbors in complete tranquillity. The fight between Jews and Arabs began only with the Balfour Declaration. The Old *Yishuv* (the Jewish community), predating Zionism, found itself caught in this conflict against its will. Thus argued orthodox anti-Zionists.

Ultra-orthodox anti-Zionists turned to history to support their cause. They denounced Zionists as "the proud reincarnation of the infamous hoodlums who were responsible for the genocide of the Jewish people at the time of the First Temple."[31] The Prophet Jeremiah, they claimed, had pleaded with them to lay down their arms in the face of insurmountable odds and certain defeat, and to surrender the city of Nebuchadnezzar, King of Babylonia. Jeremiah proclaimed the will of God that the city of Jerusalem and the Holy Temple be destroyed as punishment for sin, and that if the Jewish people accepted this decree their lives would be spared. Jeremiah was labeled a traitor by these early Zionists, and, as a result, not only was the Temple destroyed, but almost the entire population slaughtered. These Zionists were responsible also for the destruction of the Second Temple. Although advised by their leaders to lay down their arms and surrender to the Romans, they refused and brought upon themselves the second exile. In their surge for power and victory at all costs, the "Zionists" proclaimed alternate suicide. This Masada complex,[32] said the ultra-orthodox anti-Zionists, condemned the Jewish people to complete physical annihilation. They survived because they rejected the national suicide implicit in the days of Masada.

These anti-Zionists, including the *Neturei Karta* (Friends of Jerusalem) and Agudath Israel (Society of Israel) held that any solution of the Jewish problem should come through divine intervention and not through temporal agencies. It was a religious duty of Jews to remain in states where they lived: "By command of the Torah, the Jew is obliged to further the welfare of the state wherein he dwells. He entertains no thought of rebellion. The Torah forbids us to retake the Holy Land by force of arms.

Jews abhor the murder of any human being for any reason whatsoever. In our entire long exile, there has never been an instance where the Torah justifies the use of murder, as the Sages point out with particular reference to *Genesis Rabba* 93."[33]

The *Neturei Karta* bitterly condemned the "State of Israel" for obstructionism, delaying tactics, ambiguity, threats, covert operations, and provocations. It asserted that the Torah—until the advent of Judaism—is ruled out by the Zionist state as a vital and fundamental factor. It accused the creation of the Jewish state before the coming of the *Mōshīah* (Messiah) as blasphemous and heretic. "The basic aim of Zionism is the ingathering of all Jews from all countries into the Zionist state. The Jews of the world, however, give no sign of complying. Under-cover anti-Jewish acts may be used by Zionist agents from time to time to speed the lagging *'Aliya'* [immigration to the Zionist state]. . . . The Jews have no territorial aims or claims."[34] The *Neturei Karta* proclaimed an unbridgeable gap between Judaism and Zionism.

In Britain and the United States, where there was much support for Zionism, there were evidences of anti-Zionism. On May 24, 1917, C. J. Montefiore, president of the Anglo-Jewish Association in England, attacked political Zionism as incompatible with the religious basis of Jewry. It formulated, he charged, "a secular Jewish nationality, recruited on some loose and obscure principle of race and ethnographic peculiarity."[35] Similar protests were made in the United States by Jacob H. Schiff and Louis Marshall, then heads of the American Jewish Committee. "I believe I am not far wrong," Schiff said, "if I say from fifty to seventy percent of the so-called Jewish nationalists are either atheists or agnostics and that the great majority of Jewish nationalist leaders have absolutely no interest in the Jewish religion."[36]

Opposition to Zionism continued in the United States during World War II. Outside the Jewish consensus and strongly inimical to its goals, the American Council for Judaism denounced Zionism as unacceptable nationalist dogma. It charged that newly created Israel, in conjunction with the World Zionist Organization, unrealistically called for the political allegiance of all Jews, a goal that could never be achieved. The small organization, like the ultra-orthodox *Neturei Karta*, refused to recognize the political claims of Zionism, and urged a sharp distinction between religious beliefs and political adherence. The differences persist to the present day though the dissenters have had little success in embarrassing the Israeli government.

Achievements and Failures

Convinced Zionists saw their goal, the solving of the Jewish problem, as won by the establishment of the state of Israel. In their view, the Jews of all the world at long last had their sovereign national state. Hebrew had been revived as a national language; Jewish culture had been reborn in its national home; and appropriate military strength had been created to defend the homeland against surrounding Arab enemies. For Zionists, *Diaspora* Judaism had now sustained its existence against what had seemed to be insurmountable odds. What had begun as a utopian, messianic movement had won its way to reality.

These were, indeed, positive achievements. At the same time, however, the claim of Zionism as a macro-nationalism had not been fulfilled. The 1897 Basel Program called specifically for "the organization and binding together of *the whole of Jewry.*" Unlike other nationalist liberation movements, which could count on mass support, Zionism, weakened by a conglomeration of internal dissensions, never managed to win the mass support it desired.

Zionist prediction that the Jewish problem would be solved by the Return to Zion turned out to be somewhat flawed. Zionist ideology held that anti-Semitism, attributable to Jewish homelessness, would disappear in the solvent of a sovereign Jewish state. That hope remained unfulfilled. Anti-Semitism took on what seemed to be official governmental policy in the Soviet Union, where Jews were subjected to oppression, and at the same time forbidden to emigrate to Israel. Even in democratic countries, where Jews lived under modern conditions of equal citizenship, declining economic conditions led to increasing anti-Jewish sentiment. Here assimilation and acculturation were not successful altogether in dissolving Jewish identity or opposing it.

Since its rebirth in 1948, the state of Israel has maintained a precarious existence. Surrounded by implacable Arab enemies, the little country has been forced to fight its way against those who had no intention of recognizing its existence. Condemned by majorities in the United Nations, and harried by PLO terrorists who were supported by Arab oil money, Israel saw its only salvation in aggressive reaction against would-be exterminators. It endured wars in 1948-1949, 1956, 1967, and 1982. Yet it received worldwide condemnation in June 1982 when it invaded Lebanon in an effort to root out PLO terrorists. Critics charged that a supranationalist zealotry was all there was to Israel, that she intended by territorial aggrandizement to push her way to a military dominance of the entire Middle East. Before his resignation in 1983, Prime Minister Menachem Begin was accused of believing that anyone who did not share his goal of a Greater Israel, ruling captives by force, was anti-Israel.[37]

Reconciliation of the Arab world to the existence of Israel remains but a pious hope. Confrontation between two macro-nationalisms in the heart of the Middle East persists as an obstacle to world peace. Zionist and Pan-Arab views remain irreconcilable: Zionists continue to see Israel as confirmation of the prophetic vitality of an ancient homeland; Arabs reject the idea absolutely as a violation of their own historic rights.

With its limited success, Zionism reveals the problem facing all macro-nationalisms. Invariably, pan-movements seek to impose supranationality upon peoples who are divided into many factions, and who are not ready to cast aside their established nationality in favor of a wider loyalty. People who share a common language, culture, or religion may feel a sense of affinity, but at the same time they are not willing to merge their political existence into a larger nationalism of unknown value. Global Jewry, like the world's Slavs, Germans, Africans, or Latin Americans, are subject to a kind of historical law—nationalisms thrive in the contemporary world in the Age of Sovereignty, while the idea of larger macro-nationalisms invariably succumbs to the fetish of fixed territorial borders.

CHAPTER 10

PAN-AFRICANISM: THE BLACK MAN'S BURDEN _____

Until Africa is one economic unit it will remain the plaything of
the great powers of the world and the only way for a people to
keep control of one economic unit is to have one representative
political power controlling the whole area.

—J. Nyerere (1973)

Continental Black Unity

All macro-nationalisms, from Pan-Slavism to Pan-Arabism, are motivated by
a combination of aspirations, including the urge to win independence and
political power, assurance of security, the obtaining of economic advantages,
and extension of the prestige of a people considered to belong together in a
common union. Such movements generally reveal a kind of contempt for
smaller and weaker states. There are also many differences among the macro-
nationalisms. Some are bound mostly by territorial claims, others by linguistic
and cultural similarities, some by religious goals, still others by bonds of
common historical traditions. Each one has its own combination of goals, but
all are motivated by the desire to cross the boundaries of established states.

  Pan-Africanism is somewhat difficult to classify. Firstly, its goals were
dictated by geography. Pan-Africanism has been a continental movement,
based on a desire to unite the peoples of that vast continent. Secondly, the
movement has reflected a racial component, the proposal to unite all black
peoples (but also including non-black Arabs) of the vast continent.[1] The call of
race has been primal. The black men of Africa, at one time subjected to
overwhelming control by white entrepreneurs, were not motivated by a
common history nor by historical traditions. They were divided by strong
tribal differences, which tended to merge into a strong sense of racial
consciousness. The racial connotation was directed at the white man, the
foreign oppressor.

  In some respects, Pan-Africanism resembled Pan-Europeanism. Both were
geographical-continental in scope, with the goal of bringing together an entire
continent in one great, powerful union. Linguistic and cultural dimensions were
lacking in both Pan-Europeanism and Pan-Africanism. Neither one shared a

common language nor a common culture. Neither recognized one dominant political state. Both emphasized politico-economic power and prestige, the demands of security, and a common defense. Both, however, as ideological movements, tended to remain in an embryonic stage, unable to overcome divisivé negative factors, national sovereignty in the case of Pan-Europeanism and tribal consciousness in Pan-Africanism. The possibility of a really effective African unity, despite high-sounding calls from the Organization of African Unity (OAU), became increasingly remote.

There were two stages in the development of Pan-Africanism. Its earlier form was shaped by the leadership of blacks residing in the United States and the West Indies. Starting as a movement for worldwide unity of blacks, this early stage was dominated by American and West Indian radicals devoted to black separatism, and demanding a home in Africa for all blacks no matter where they lived. Though not religious in content, this early Pan-African sentiment was similar in motivation to the Jewish Return to Zion movement. It was grounded in the belief that those blacks who had been brought in slavery to the United States and the Caribbean, starting in the early 17th century, had a homeland to which they should return.

The second stage of Pan-Africanism began with the gradual decolonization of Africa after World War II, when the character and leadership of Pan-Africanism became really African, not American or Caribbean. Educated blacks who had come into close contact with Western civilization through study in universities in Berlin, Oxford, Paris, and Stanford, returned to their homes to provide leadership for a new drive for continental unity. These students of Western culture suffered much more from racial intolerance than tribal natives who had remained behind on the steppes of Africa. On their return to Africa, the students were determined to win real political emancipation, as well as economic prosperity and industrial modernization for their people.

The new Pan-African movement began in 1945 at the Pan-African Congress held at Manchester, England. Under the leadership of Kwame Nkrumah, a Ghanian militant, and George Padmore, a West Indian ideologist, the Congress called for African independence from its white masters and a new deal for Africa. After its masses were organized, Ghana won its independence in 1957, to be followed by most other African states by 1963.

Like its European counterpart, Pan-Africanism never was able to overcome fragmentation throughout the continent, despite its champions' efforts. New African states were set up on the same basis as the geographical hodgepodge created by earlier white colonialists. The main obstacle to Pan-African unity was unwillingness of the new states to surrender their sovereignty to political union. It was the same familiar story—a lack of agreement on any common form of political structure or leadership. Revolutionary Pan-Africanists repeatedly called for political unity among those who had little understanding of any kind of political organization. Furthermore, the desire for continental union was frustrated by the persistence of tribalism, which tended to become the decisive factor in African political life.

New African leaders were caught unprepared by the receding tide of colonialism and the emergence of new African states. The road to political independence was eased for them by the heady wines of patriotism, but the matter of fashioning a working economy was an entirely different and considerably more difficult business. Influenced by European experience, they tried such solutions as common markets, coordination of production, and experiments with labor unions. Perhaps economic unity, as tried in Europe, might lead to eventual coalescing of political sovereignties and a working Pan-Africanism.

Here again one can see the familiar story of the macro-nationalisms—established nationalisms strongly resist any attempt to obliterate their sovereignty in favor of a larger union of a portion of the world's population believed to be ready for a common politico-economic life.

The Spoliation of Africa

The opening up and partition of Africa was a classic story of gold, glory, and God, compounded of greed, adventure and missionary zeal.[2] In the process, imperialist invaders squeezed the Dark Continent of its wealth, while announcing to the world that they were suppressing slavery, tribal warfare, superstition, and disease. They insisted that they were bringing the benefits of civilization to backward peoples, but actually they were more interested in gold, rubber, diamonds, ivory, ebony, copra, cocoa, oil, coffee, and cotton. Africans were well aware of what was happening. Resenting this pious paternalism and exploitation, they later would turn the tools of nationalism on their occupiers.

Actually, there were five Africas, not merely one. Along the northern coastline, bordering the Mediterranean, was a temperate area, historically an adjunct of European civilization. Just south of this area was the belt of the Sahara, Libyan, and Nubian deserts, where white and black strains blended. The next belt below stretched across the continent from Guinea to the Sudan—the "land of the blacks." Central, or Equatorial Africa was a land of dense jungle inhabited by blacks. At the southern tip was the temperate zone of South Africa, with a dominantly black population under white control.

During the early part of the 19th century, French, British, and Portuguese traders held small posts in Africa, but none had penetrated into the interior. In November 1855, a Scottish missionary, David Livingstone (1813-1873), exploring East and Central Africa, discovered Victoria Falls. In March 1866, he returned to the area "to blaze a trail for the gospel." When the outside world lost contact with Livingstone, James Gordon Bennett, owner of the New York *Herald*, sent Henry Morton Stanley (1841-1904), a British journalist, to find the missionary-turned-explorer. The two men, missionary and journalist, finally met at Ujiji on Lake Tanganyika in November 1871 in a memorable meeting since identified by the understated: "Dr. Livingstone, I presume!"[3]

The highly publicized story of Livingstone and Stanley and their subsequent explorations had a extraordinary effect throughout Europe.[4] Tales of untold riches in the vast continent stimulated the imagination of European businessmen, adventurers, and clerics. For many bored by life at home, Africa beckoned as a promised land. Fired with enthusiasm, hundreds hit the African trail. Burton, Speke, Baker, Schweinfurth, and Grant explored the sources of the Nile; Nachtigal, Barth, Laing, and Denham went to the Sahara and Sudan; Caillé, Clapperton, and Lander traveled to the Niger; Livingstone toured the Zambesi valley; and Stanley and Brazza toured the Congo area. There were great possibilities here for gold, trade, and national expansion. For men of the cloth there were literally millions of Africans waiting to be converted to Christianity.

The result was the carving up of the great continent into segments. Belgian, French, British, Portuguese, Spanish, Italian, Dutch, and later German businessmen, adventurers, and missionaries moved in. There was no planning—all was chaos and confusion as boundaries were settled by power and might. No attention was paid to tribal patterns: natives were mixed indiscriminately in the hectic grab-all as territory and prestige shifted toward the strongest and most powerful.

Explorers, traders, and promoters appeared in the wilderness, bringing with them a handful of treaties, sometimes merely printed forms. The intruders would seek out a willing chief who appeared to have some influence over his people and who would relinquish the right of sovereignty, sell land, or grant concessions.[5] After control was gained from tribal chieftains, the area was subjected to forced labor and exploitation of natives.

Among the earliest of European exploiters was Leopold II (c. 1865-1909), King of the Belgians. Organizing his own private Congo Free State, reluctantly recognized by the Great Powers, he amassed an enormous fortune from rubber and ivory. He so mistreated the natives in his quest for profit that he aroused universal condemnation. His private domain in the heart of Central Africa was abolished in 1908. The region was annexed by Belgium as the Belgian Congo.

The British were more circumspect, working quietly, efficiently, and with tact in the business of obtaining the greater share of profits in the great continent. In a series of possessions along the eastern seaboard running from Egypt in the north to Cape Colony in the south, the British brought with them cricket, steak-and-kidney pie, magistrate courts, and an abiding interest in Africa's wealth. After acquiring Cape Colony, they seized Egypt in 1882, and took virtual sovereignty over the Sudan in 1889. In South Africa they went to war from 1899 to 1902 with the pastoral-minded Dutch settlers, and for a time won the whole of South Africa. In the west, the British acquired the Gold Coast, Nigeria, Sierra Leone, and the lower

Cambian region. In the east, they annexed Uganda, Kenya, and a part of Somaliland. Wherever there was profit to be made for The City, British traders appeared as if by magic.

The French, too, transferred much of their national character to the African scene. They encouraged natives to speak French and wear red military pantaloons, but at the same time demanded subservience to French administration. They had maintained a foothold in Algeria as early as 1830. With the opening up of Africa, they extended their control into Morocco and Tunisia along the Mediterranean coast, and annexed most of West Africa from Algeria south to the Congo. In East Africa, they acquired a part of Somaliland and the island of Madagascar (1885).

British and French acquisitive instincts in Africa were bound to end in confrontation. The British took on a string of possessions from northeast to south, the French from west to east. In March 1898, British General Herbert Kitchener led a force of British and Egyptian troops up the Nile, reaching the small town of Fashoda on September 10. The problem was that Fashoda had been occupied since July 10 by French troops commanded by Major Jean Baptiste Marchand. Kitchener blandly invited Marchand to withdraw. The French officer declined to move without authorization from Paris.

The crisis nearly led to war between the two colonial powers. The British refused even to begin negotiations unless Marchand withdrew. The French, unwilling to risk war, yielded to London, and on November 4 ordered Marchand to withdraw. The affair was settled finally in March 1899 when the French relinquished their claims to land along the Nile, and in turn the British recognized French possession of territories in the Sahara Desert. There was wealth enough in Africa for both British and French entrepreneurs.

Germany was a late starter in the African hunt, but she managed to obtain her share of the booty. In the mid-1880s, Bismarck reversed his lifetime policy, and gave the green signal for a German share of African spoils. German traders and missionaries belatedly took what was left in Africa, acquiring such vacant areas as Togoland (1884); German East Africa (1884-1889); German South-West Africa (1884-1890); and the Cameroons (1884-1911). Although these were large areas, they were comparatively poor in natural resources compared to other territories on the continent. The German public was attracted by the idea that Germany, like Britain, could be a colonial power. But there were shadows: administrators in their African colonies, like those representing Leopold II earlier, were so heavy-handed in their treatment of their African wards that there were embittered protests throughout the world. German publicists heatedly denied the charges.

Italians, after unification of their country, sought new prestige as well as material benefits by annexing Eritrea and Italian Somaliland, both coastal districts in East Africa. When they attempted to acquire Ethiopia, they received a crushing defeat at Adowa (1896). But they managed to wrest Tripoli and Cyrenaica from the Turks. The Italian excuse for penetration into Africa was "population pressure." Rome brought quick-stepping troops, spaghetti, and a concern for profits to its African colonies.

Portuguese, too, wanted a share of the spoils. They subsequently held Angola and portions of Guinea and East Africa. The Spanish also were land-hungry: they acquired Rio de Oro on the west coast, the northern coast of Morocco, and several small offshore islands.

So chaotic was the drive for African land that ground rules had to be set up for division of the continent. At the Berlin Conference on African Affairs, held from November 15, 1884 to February 26, 1885, the signatories promised "to protect the natives in their moral and material well-being, to cooperate in the suppression of slavery and the slave trade, to further the education of the natives, and to protect missionaries and explorers." These were beautiful words filled with hypocrisy. There was an opportunity to prevent greedy aggression and land-grabbing, but it was lost. Profits came first, the well-being of Africans a poor second. Fifteen years later, the only non-colonial lands remaining in Africa were Ethiopia and Liberia, the latter founded in 1822 as a colony for emancipated American slaves.

The real lure was African gold, diamonds, and rubber. Were not magnificent white men bringing with them the blessings of civilization to natives, strong legal systems, superior customs and traditions, modern technology, and a proper God? White intruders said little or nothing about the accompanying curses of syphilis, related diseases, and lashes of the whip to assure satisfactory production. The vast undertaking was simply bare-faced exploitation. One day, the black man of Africa would seek relief through nationalism of his own and an attempted Pan-Africanism.

Decline of Colonialism

To American criticism of African partition, Europeans replied with a "look-who's-talking" argument. Americans, they charged, had subjugated with utmost cruelty the native Indian population, encouraged slavery, and practiced discrimination against blacks even after the Civil War. Europeans, on the other hand, after decades of exploitation in Africa, pointed out that they began to relinquish authority there after the middle of the 20th century.

Throughout the great continent, Europeans set up administrative structures corresponding to their own philosophies of government. The British, ruling indirectly through native chieftains, hoped to combine traditional tribal with modern institutions. This left little place for young educated Africans, who reacted by setting up their own nationalist political parties. The French pursued a different policy of direct rule, introducing natives to French culture with the ultimate aim of complete assimilation.

There were some flaws in this process: by direct rule, native chieftains were subordinated to Paris, and only a small proportion of natives was assimilated into the French system.

Belgian paternalism left a political vacuum in the Congo so wide that when independence was granted in 1960, the natives were unprepared for the sudden change. The new Congo was plunged into chaos. The Portuguese, like the French, called for political control and assimilation, but with even more arbitrary methods. Unreconciled to the trend of decolonization, Lisbon held on until 1974, longer than any other European colonial power. Portugal finally gave in to the demands of nationalists in Angola and Mozambique. Germany lost her colonial possessions in Africa after World War I, Italy after World War II.

African nationalist agitation began between the two World Wars, when educated Nigerians and Ghanians organized movements for more participation in administration of their own countries. A sense of national consciousness began to spread throughout the continent. Modest calls for more participation in government were succeeded by increasing demands for independence. The trend to liberation gathered momentum.

By the opening of World War II, colonialism in Africa was well on the way to collapse. During the war, Africans, who previously had been much impressed by European political ability and military invincibility, began to have second thoughts after observing Europeans in action. Black administrators began to take the place of Europeans called home for war service. By the end of the war, nationalist parties began to emerge everywhere. Natives went to the polls to express their newly found political strength.

After World War II there occurred a rare phenomenon—the transformation of an entire continent from foreign to local control. One independent African state after another emerged. Most preferred a republican form of government and full legal independence, but at the same time many new states retained loose connections with the former mother country.

Africans educated either in missionary schools at home or in the West became leaders of new political party organizations. Among them were Milton Obote of Uganda, Kenneth Kaunda of Zambia, Jomo Kenyatta of Kenya, Joseph Mobutu of Congo, Julius Nyerere of Tanzania, Leopold Binar of Burundi, and Fidele Nkundabagenzi of Rwanda. All preached the gospel of nationalism.

The new African nationalism was not without serious political and economic problems. The political union of unrelated and rival tribes based on the old order was bound to have serious consequences. Although the original trend was toward republican governments, there came increasing pressure from both Right and Left, leading on the one hand to military dictatorship and on the other to Communist infiltration. In the mid-1960s, the system of political parties was challenged by a series of military coups. In some cases, the military coups were forestalled by concessions and reforms, but there were far too many problems to be solved.

On the left, Communists sought to take advantage of the political chaos by advancing their own cause. Denouncing Western capitalist-fascist-imperialism, the Kremlin supported African guerrilla movements with the excuse that the Soviet Union was supporting the liberation of oppressed peoples. Eventually, Moscow would send Cuban and East European satellite military advisers and troops to assist in the process of Communist liberation.[6] Ironically, with the decline of Western European imperialism, the Soviet Union sought to move into the vacuum by promoting what it called a humanitarian crusade to free Africans from the tentacles of Western democracy in favor of a new "People's Democracy" directed from Moscow.

Added to political confusion were pressing economic problems. Natives who flocked to cities from the hinterlands in search of new opportunities found themselves beset with ills of modernization. For many Africans, the standard of living actually fell below that existing during the colonial regimes. New governments failed to exploit their rich natural resources; there was a lessening demand in world markets for African products; and most states were burdened by a runaway inflation. Economic prosperity did not necessarily follow political emancipation.

It was too much to expect that new African nation-states, already burdened with their own problems, could see much benefit in a larger nationalism covering the entire continent. As new members of the international community, they joined the United Nations and its subsidiary organizations. They sent delegates to all-African organizations, such as the African Development Bank, the Economic Commission for Africa, and the Organization of African Unity (OAU). Such participation, however, was more automatic than meaningful. There were far too many problems to be solved at the national level without risking the complexities of a continental union. Pan-Africanism would be used by the new African states for political purposes, but it had no real influence on their policies. It called for a union that in fact could not be achieved.

Origins of Pan-Africanism

The idea of one Africa uniting the thought and ideals of all peoples on the Dark Continent, and those taken from Africa elsewhere to a life in demeaning circumstances, had its origin in the United States and the West Indies. There groups of blacks, though separate in origin, became exposed to a new culture, but at the same time thought of their homeland as one idea and one land. In the late 18th century, a separate Negro Church formed in Philadelphia calling itself "African." There were also various "African" societies in many parts of the United States.[7]

During the late 1870s, following the era of Reconstruction, blacks in the United States were alienated by growing racism and economic depression. Some among them began to think in terms of returning to Africa.

Benjamin F. Porter, President of the Liberia Joint Stock Company of Charleston, South Carolina, claimed that he had 150,000 "exiles" enrolled. In a letter dated November 6, 1877, addressed to the President of the Republic of Liberia, he wrote:

Dear Sir,—This will inform you that the colored people of American and especially of the Southern States desire to return to the fatherland.

We wish to come bringing our wives and little ones with what wealth and education, arts and refinement we have been able to acquire in the land of our exile and in the house of bondage. . . .

We are now in a position to say, if you will grant us a home in your Republic where we can live and aid in building up a nationality of Africans, we will come, and in coming we will be prepared to take care of ourselves and not be burdensome to the Government.[8]

Outstanding among other advocates of African colonization was Bishop Henry M. Turner, who demanded an indemnity "to go home to Africa." He adopted a polemical tone in criticizing his fellow Negroes. They had remained in slavery, he said, for 250 years, and had been free for a mere 50 years. They had been dominated by the "buckra," or white race, and were denied civil and political rights while enriching a country and helping to give it a standing among the powers of the earth. "The fool Negro has no more sense than a jackass, . . . ridicules the idea of asking for a hundred million dollars to go home, for Africa is our home, and the one place that offers us manhood and freedom, though we are subjects of nations that have claimed a part of Africa by conquest. . . . Every man that has the sense of an animal must see there is no future in this country for the Negro."[9]

Turner denounced black emigration to the West. Negroes were sacrificing their property at a mere song. They would be far better off moving to Africa, where they would have a permanent home. "The white people are all alike and the same conditions that drive [Negroes] from Georgia will prevail in Mississippi, Arkansas and the western states." When nearly a thousand blacks assembled at the depot in Athens, Georgia, in late March 1900, they had to wait and take freight trains and cattle cars. "The fools appear to have nothing to say or nothing to do with this emigration, but the moment Africa is mentioned they swarm like bees and pour the vituperation and scandal upon the only spot that offers manhood and freedom."[10]

That same year, 1900, a black West Indian barrister, H. Sylvester-Williams of Trinidad, who practiced law in London, called a "Pan-African" Conference there. Some 30 delegates, mostly from Britain and the West Indies, with a few from the United States, attended the meeting. The term "Pan-African" was used for the first time at this conference. The delegates were welcomed by the Lord

Bishop of London, and a promise was won through Joseph Chamberlain not to "overlook the interests and welfare of the native races."[11]

This first meeting of Pan-African enthusiasts had no deep roots in Africa, and had little impact at the time. For nearly two decades thereafter, the movement remained quiescent. Then it was revived under two leaders, the flamboyant Marcus Garvey and the quiet intellectual W. E. Burghardt Du Bois, who sparked the future independence movement in Africa and the promotion of Pan-Africanism.

The Garvey Movement

The most important movement for black territorial separatism and a return to Africa began in 1914 under the leadership of a Jamaican, who promised a black nation in the African homeland. In a brief but scintillating career, he led a highly popular mass movement, whose goal was the wholesale migration of American blacks to Africa.

Marcus Manasseh Garvey was born on August 17, 1887, at St. Ann's Bay, Jamaica, of Koromantee stock.[12] He was educated at local elementary schools until his family's financial problems forced him to work as a printer's apprentice.[13] Moving to Kingston in 1904, he worked for a printer, and helped lead an unsuccessful strike in 1907. From 1909 to 1911, he worked and traveled in Costa Rica, Panama, and other Central American countries, where he was angered by the harsh treatment of black workers. In 1912 he went to London, where he worked at his trade of printer.

In London, Garvey came into contact with native Africans, who described to him the exploitation and squalor of Africa amidst immense riches. As the grandson of an African slave, he, too, had felt the burden of prejudice and oppression. He had grown up under a color caste system—white, mulatto, and black—which even when he was young aroused his resentment, not only against whites but against mulattoes as well. Embittered, he decided that it was his task to lead his fellow blacks in the Western Hemisphere back to the promised land of Africa.

Regarding himself as a Negro Moses, Garvey in 1916 sailed to New York City to seek support for his crystallizing ideas. Inspired by the career of Napoleon, he would lead his people to assert their legitimate rights and return to their homeland. A short, squat man with piercing eyes and large head, he began to speak to small audiences on Lenox Avenue in Harlem in New York City. At first, he was ignored and dismissed as an immigrant carpetbagger. In 1919 he was shot by an insane man, the bullet grazing his forehead. He rushed to the street from his brownstone home "with the blood of the martyr" coursing down his cheeks. The next day his assailant leaped to his death from a prison window. This affair, involving a woman (later his wife) who attempted to shield him from his attacker, was given extensive coverage in the local press. Soon all the people of Harlem would know about Marcus Garvey.

Several years earlier, while in Jamaica, Garvey had founded his Universal Negro Improvement Association (UNIA) as a black self-help organization. Using the motto "One God, One Aim, One Destiny," he claimed that whites would always be racist, and insisted that the black man must develop a distinct racial civilization of his own. Moreover, he must work out his salvation in his motherland. He proposed many slogans: "Africa for the Africans, at Home and Abroad!" "Renaissance of the Black Race." "Ethiopia Awake!"

Garvey came into Harlem at a timely moment, when black unhappiness was at its peak. Blacks were humiliated by Jim Crow treatment in the armed forces in World War I and even violence at the hands of the civilian population. The resurgence of the Ku Klux Klan in the immediate postwar years added to black resentment. Garvey's propagandistic skills soon brought him favorable attention not only among the blacks of Harlem, but also throughout every corner of the country's Black Belt. The vigorous leader swept through the states to be acclaimed everywhere.

In 1918 Garvey built Liberty Hall, a great zinc-roofed shed where he held his meetings. At the same time, he founded a weekly newspaper called the *Negro World*, which soon had a wide circulation. In bombastic editorials, he referred to the glorious history of the Negro, with special attention to Nat Turner's slave revolt and Toussaint L'Ouverture's leadership of the Haitian Rebellion. He devoted special emphasis to Africa's past regal splendor. The pages of the *Negro World* were filled with the philosophy and opinion of Marcus Garvey. *The Negro World* soon had an international circulation.

Garvey was soon leading a proliferating movement. However, his career began to take on a bizarre twist, which aroused the uncomfortable opposition of moderate black leaders, but which endeared him to an ever-increasing multitude of followers. He proclaimed himself "Provisional President of Africa." He adopted an anthem: "Ethiopia, Thou Land of Our Fathers." He presented an official flag for his movement: black (for Negro skin), green (for Negro hopes), and red (for Negro blood). He spoke to huge meetings at Liberty Hall and heard himself described as "greater than Jesus Christ." After such meetings tens of thousands of Garveyites would parade through Harlem, led by "His Excellency, Marcus Garvey, Provisional President of Africa," bedecked in a dazzling uniform with gold braid and a hat with white plumes, while riding in a huge black Packard automobile.

Garvey proposed to seek an economic solution to black problems by establishing black-run businesses. It was important, he said, for Negroes to become independent of white capital and white employers. He would set up an independent "Black Economy," which would function inside the white capitalistic world. Among such enterprises was his Black Star Line, which he regarded as the beginning of a Negro merchant marine. Through it he would set up trade relations between the blacks of all the world. To finance the line, he sold shares to followers for five dollars each. He purchased his first boat, the *Yarmouth*, from the North American Steamship Company, and renamed it the

Frederick Douglass.[14] The ship, loaded with a cargo of liquor, foundered on its first trip to Cuba. Garvey excoriated the crew for becoming drunk on the voyage.

Garvey's movement took on odd and extravagant overtones. He created what he called a "Black Religion with a Black God." He set up a social order with a feudal hierarchy of dukes, duchesses, and ladies-in-waiting. His "Black Nobility" included Knight Commanders of the Distinguished Order of the Nile. His Universal African Legion was outfitted in blue and red uniforms. The Universal Black Cross paraded in white uniforms. He promoted the manufacture of black baby dolls for children.

Negroes were thrilled by the man whom many regarded as their Black Moses. Roi Ottley described the reaction: "Harlem was spellbound. For the first time white New York became aware of the proportions of the movement, its implications, and indeed its divertissements. Marcus Garvey had become a world figure, and his movements and utterances were noted by every European Power with possessions in Africa."[15]

In early 1923 the federal government, investigating the Black Star Line, indicted Garvey for using the mails to defraud people. Evidence was introduced to reveal that there were 40,000 stockholders, that millions of dollars were involved, and yet there were no tangible assets. Handling his own defense, Garvey was ultimately convicted. After losing his appeal, he was fined a thousand dollars, and sentenced to five years in prison. In 1927 he was pardoned by President Calvin Coolidge, but was deported as an undesirable alien. Moving to London, he died there in obscurity, while holding fast to his Pan-African dream.

Without its dynamic leader, Marcus's Pan-Africanism collapsed. Its temporary success was due in large part to support by tens of thousands, who desperately sought a solution to their social ills. Blacks, who saw themselves as victims of prejudice and without work, regarded the stocky little leader as a Messiah who would lead them to a better life. But in the long run, the vast majority had no intention whatever of leaving the United States. The dream of an all-black nation was fine for a sorely beset people, but most blacks considered themselves to be far removed from the African scene. Their homeland was America, and many of their sons had fought in all of America's wars. If they lagged behind in enjoying the country's riches, the day would surely come in this democracy, they felt, when they would be accepted on an equal plane.

In his brief career, Garvey was able to transform hopes for a black community into the largest secular organization in black American history. With his flair for the dramatic, he lent a sense of pride and dignity to a people deeply wounded by prejudice and injustice. Nonetheless, he was considerably less successful in promoting the idea of Pan-Africanism, and his attempts to establish branches of his movement in Africa met the active opposition of both African and European political leaders.[16]

Although Garveyism collapsed, its vision inspired emulation among later African nationalists. Future leaders of the independence movement in Anglophone West Africa were well aware of the Garvey movement. Francophone West Africans joined French-speaking West Indians to promote the parallel doctrine of *négritude*.[17]

W. E. Burghardt Du Bois

Black American intellectuals were alienated by Garvey's bizarre behavior. Not only did he make a sharp distinction between whites and blacks, but also between blacks and mulattoes. He had grown up in Jamaica under a color caste system—white, mulatto, and black, and he never relinquished his resentment against both mulattoes and whites. He criticized the "near-white" leaders of the National Association for the Advancement of Colored People (NAACP), whom he accused of reflecting the desire of bourgeois blacks to win social acceptance from whites. The NAACP, he charged, encouraged participation in existing white institutions at a time when blacks desperately needed to create their own communities. For a time, Garvey succeeded in driving a wedge between dark and light-complexioned blacks, but most American blacks and whites made no distinction between mulattoes and blacks.

Black American intellectuals pointed out that Garvey's racialism brought him the open support of the Ku Klux Klan.[18] Ku Klux Klan leaders, they charged, spoke from Garvey's platform at Liberty Hall, and praised the Back-to-Africa Movement. Garvey had replied: "I regard the Klan as a better friend of the race than all the groups of hypocritical white men put together. You may call me a Klansman if you will, but, potentially, every white man is a Klansman, as far as the Negro in competition with whites socially, economically, and politically is concerned, and there is no use lying about it."[19]

Pan-Africanism received its most powerful stimulus from the work of a black intellectual whose approach was far removed from the flamboyance and eccentricities of Marcus Garvey. William Edward Burghardt Du Bois was born at Great Barrington, Massachusetts, on February 23, 1868.[20] His academic career was brilliant: B.A., Fisk University (1888); B.A. in philosophy, Harvard (1890); and a Harvard Ph.D. in history (1895).[21] After teaching at Wilberforce and the University of Pennsylvania from 1894 to 1896, he became Professor of Economics and History at Atlanta University (1907-1910). Meanwhile, he began a prolific writing career.[22]

As historian, Du Bois contributed much to the documentation of black history. As sociologist, he opposed the racial theories associated with Social Darwinism. As propagandist, he used novels, plays, poems, and essays to advance the cause of Pan-Africanism. Typical of his work was his denunciation of the "separate but equal doctrine," which another black leader, Booker T. Washington, had accepted in the so-called Atlanta Compromise. To Du Bois, this was an abdication of the claim of full equality guaranteed in the Fourteenth and Fifteenth Amendments of the United States Constitution.

In opposition to the Atlanta Compromise, Du Bois in 1905 became a founding member, along with William Monroe Taylor, of the Niagara Movement. That organization agitated for full civil rights for blacks, including the franchise, abolition of any color bar, advanced education, and opposition to segregation in railroad trains. In 1909 he joined other blacks and liberal whites in forming the National Association for the Advancement of Colored People (NAACP), for which he became director of publicity and research. He was also editor of *The Crisis*, the NAACP's monthly paper, which he edited from 1910 to 1934, and in whose pages he repeatedly supported economic cooperation among black consumers and producers.

In his prolific writings, Du Bois described the Negro as a sort of seventh son, born with a veil and gifted with second sight in the American world. He had two needs—as American, as Negro: two souls, two thoughts, two unreconciled strivings, two warring ideals in one dark body. He had ambivalent loyalties—toward race and nation. Du Bois saw himself as integrally a part of Western civilization and "yet, more significant, one of its rejected parts, one who expressed in life and action and made vocal to many, a single whirlpool of social entanglement and inner psychological paradox."[23]

Throughout his career Du Bois concentrated on several themes: (1) The Negro people as a race have a contribution to make to civilization which no other race could make; (2) American Negroes were in the vanguard of blacks all over the world in promoting Pan-Negroism, the idea that no matter where they lived they should feel an emotional commitment to one another; (3) Negroes could solve their problem only by promoting their own organizations, including businesses, newspapers, and schools; salvation would come only with the leadership of an educated black elite, the "Talented Tenth" of college-educated and professional Negroes; and blacks throughout the world have a special attachment to the great continent of Africa as their "greater fatherland."[24] With cogent presentation of these views Du Bois urged American blacks to demand egalitarianism on the domestic scene and to work for the Pan-African movement. At a time when most American blacks were embarrassed by what was called the "primitiveness" of their ancestral African societies, Du Bois called attention to the great medieval kingdoms on the continent, praised the sophisticated cultures of African tribes, and suggested that New World blacks owed a debt of gratitude to earlier African cultures.

Du Bois attended the first African conference held in London in 1906 and the First Universal Race Congress held there in 1911. By the time of World War I, his ideas had crystallized into a determined agitation for black rights throughout the world. The war spelled opportunity. At the beginning of the conflict, popular opinion held that it would last at most four months, because the weapons of modern warfare would take such a ghastly toll that there would be an overwhelming demand for the end of such barbarism. Instead, there was an avalanche of destruction and slaughter, which went on for four years.

From a local conflict it had spread to world proportions. At its end, thrones toppled and four empires were destroyed, republics were formed, and the whole face of the world was transformed. In these extraordinary changes Du Bois saw the possibility of a new deal for the oppressed black man.

Obtaining passage on the Creel press boat, the *Orizaba*, Du Bois landed in France in December 1918.[25] His aim was to impress upon delegates of the Peace Congress sitting at Versailles the importance of Africa in the future world. He tried to have a conference with President Woodrow Wilson, but was able to get only as far as Colonel Edward M. House, the president's private diplomatic adviser. House was sympathetic, but noncommittal. In a memorandum sent to the President, Du Bois urged that the prevailing sentiment of "self-determination" be applied to Africa. The Peace Conference should form an international nationalized Africa, to have as its basis the former German colonies. "This Africa for the Africans could be under the guidance of international organization. The governing international commission should represent not simply Government, but modern culture, science, commerce, social reform, and religious philanthropy. It must represent not simply the white world but the civilized Negro world."[26] This would inaugurate on the Dark Continent "a last great crusade for humanity."

At the same time, Du Bois hoped to promote a Pan-African Congress during the winter when the Peace Conference was in full session. The Congress would embrace black leaders from throughout the world, including America, Abyssinia, Liberia, Haiti, and the French and British colonies. Its goal would be to press the Peace Conference to help modernize Africa, and in the reconstruction of the world to provide international machinery leading toward the civilization of African natives.

The correspondent for the Chicago *Tribune* reported details of Du Bois's memorandum in a dispatch describing his dream of "an Ethiopian Utopia." "It is quite Utopian, and it has less than a Chinaman's chance of getting anywhere in the Peace Conference, but it is nevertheless interesting."[27]

Pan-African Congresses

Convinced that blacks throughout the world should work together, Du Bois, between 1919 and 1927, called four Pan-African Congresses in Europe and the United States. The theme of all four Congresses was the condition of the black race in Africa. Each meeting emphasized the "absolute equality of races."[28]

While in Paris at the Peace Conference, Du Bois was told that no Pan-African Congress could be held there because France was still under martial law. He turned for help to Blaise Diagne, a black deputy from Senegal and *Commissaire-Général* in charge of recruiting native African help. French Premier Georges Clemenceau, who owed a debt of gratitude to Diagne, finally gave permission to hold the Congress in Paris. The U. S. State

Department, advised officially by the French Government that no such Conference would be held, informed American blacks that there would be no Paris meeting.

The First Pan-African Congress. Meeting in Paris in late February 1919,[29] the Congress was composed of 57 delegates from 15 countries; 12 were from nine African countries. The West Indies were represented by 21 delegates, the United States by 16. The assembly drafted an appeal to the Peace Conference to give the Negroes of Africa a chance to develop unhindered by other races. In a series of resolutions the delegates requested and demanded:

1. That the Allied and Associated Powers establish a code of laws for the international protection of the natives of Africa.
2. That the League of Nations establish a permanent bureau for this purpose.
3. The Negroes of the world demand that the natives of Africa and all peoples of African descent be governed according to these principles:
   (a) The *land* and its natural resources be held in trust for the natives.
   (b) *Capital.* The investment of capital and granting of concessions shall be so regulated as to prevent exploitation of the natives and exhaustion of the natural wealth of the country.
   (c) *Labor.* Slavery and corporal punishment should be abolished.
   (d) *Education.* It was the right of every native child to read and write. The State should be responsible for higher education.
   (e) *The State.* The natives of Africa must have the right to participate in Government. If any State excludes citizens or subjects of Negro descent from its body politic, it was the duty of the League of Nations to bring the matter to the civilized world.[30]

Second Pan-African Congress. Having thus set up the idea of Pan-Africanism, Du Bois went ahead with the task of building a real organization, and assembling what he called "a more authentic Congress and movement." Corresponding with blacks in all parts of Africa and throughout the world, he finally arranged for a Congress to meet in London, Brussels, and Paris in August and September 1921.

Du Bois faced difficulties. Diehard imperialists in England, Belgium, and elsewhere, he felt, hoped to recoup their war losses by intensified exploitation of colonies, and they were suspicious of native movements of any kind. Moreover, there was competition from the Garvey movement, originating in the West Indies and accounting for the small West Indian representation in the Du Bois movement. To Du Bois, Garvey's Pan-Africanism was a poorly conceived, if intensely earnest, determination to unite the blacks of the world. It was a peoples' movement rather than one supported by intellectuals. Du Bois admitted the appeal of its popular agitation, and that it had strong backing among masses of West Indians and increasing numbers of American blacks. "Its weakness lay in its demagogic leadership, its intemperate propaganda, and the natural fear which it threw into the colonial powers."[31]

The opening London meeting of the Second Pan-African Congress was held on August 28, 1921. Of the 113 delegates, 41 were from Africa, 35 from the United States, 24 from Europe, and seven from the West Indies. Beatrice Webb, Leonard Woolf, and other Fabian Socialists were present at the gathering.

A second meeting was held at Brussels. The selection of Brussels was deliberate, because the Belgian Congo, one of the richest African colonies, was amassing enormous profits for Belgian entrepreneurs, and there had been accusations about the abuse of native laborers there. Annoyed Belgian officials accused the delegates of being in the pay of the Soviet Union, and preaching political chaos as a means of ending Belgian rule in the Congo. Even before the meeting, a Belgian newspaper denounced the forthcoming Congress: "It is interesting to note that the association is directed by personages who it is said in the United States have received remuneration from Moscow (Bolshevik). The association has already organized its propaganda in the lower Congo, and we must not be astonished if some day it causes grave difficulties in the Negro village of Kinshasa composed of all the ne'er-do-wells of the various tribes of the Colony, aside from some hundreds of laborers."[32] Belgain fears were exaggerated. Actually, the Kremlin opposed the Pan-African Congress as evidence of "Negro bourgeois nationalism," and condemned it as violating proletarian international unity.

The third session in Paris requested the League of Nations to place a Negro on the Mandates Commission.

Du Bois played a leading role in all the sessions. He was responsible for the wording of the theme of the Congress in its Manifesto:

The world must face two eventualities: either the complete assimilation of Africa with two or three of the great world states, with political, civil and social power equal for its black and white citizens, or the use of a great black African state founded in Peace and Good Will based on popular education, natural art and industry and freedom of trade; autonomous and sovereign in its internal policy, but from its beginning a part of a great society of people in which it takes its place with others as co-rulers of the world.[33]

Du Bois made it plain that the absolute equality of races—physical, political and social—was the foundation stone of world peace and human advancement. No one denied, he said, great differences of gift, capacity, and attainment among individuals of all races, but the voice of science, religion, and practical politics was one in denying the God-appointed existence of super-races, or of races naturally and inevitably and eternally inferior. It was the shame of the world, he said, that the relation between the main groups of mankind and their mutual estimate and respect was determined chiefly by the degree in which one could subject the other to its service, enslaving labor, making ignorance compulsory, uprooting religion and customs, and destroying government. All this, so that the favored few could luxuriate in the toil of the tortured many.

Du Bois accused England with her *Pax Britannica*, her law courts, established commerce, and "a certain apparent recognition of native law and customs," of nevertheless systematically fostering ignorance among natives, enslaving them, and declining even to train black and brown men in real self-government. Belgium had taken some steps in assuming responsiblity for her colonies and to lift them from the worst abuses of an autocratic regime, but she did not give Africans possession of their land, any voice in their own government, or any provisions for their political future. Portugal and Spain had never drawn a legal caste line against Negroes, but the industrial concessions of Portuguese Africa were almost wholly in the hands of foreigners whom Portugal could not or would not control. Alone among the great colonial powers, France sought to place her cultured black citizens on a plane of legal and social equality with whites, while giving them representation in her highest legislature. It was a splendid beginning, but one that needed to be completed by widening the political basis of native government, by restoring to the indigenes the ownership of the soil, by protecting native labor against capitalistic aggressions, and by asking that no man, black or white, be forced to be a soldier unless the country gave him a voice in his own government.

Du Bois had polemical words for his own country. The United States of America, he said, after brutally enslaving millions of blacks, suddenly emancipated them and began their education, but did not act with any system of forethought. It threw freedmen upon the world penniless and landless, educated them without thoroughness and system, and subjected them to lynching, lawlessness, discrimination, insult, and slander, such as human beings had seldom endured and survived. The government gave the franchise to the Negro only when danger had passed, and allowed hundreds of educated and civilized blacks to be disfranchised. Moreover, in 1776, 1812, 1898, and 1917, it asked and allowed thousands of black men to offer their lives as a sacrifice to a country which despised them.

In his Manifesto, Du Bois urged that the Negro, through his "thinking intelligentsia," make these demands:

1. The recognition of civilized men as civilized despite their race or color;
2. Local self-government for backward groups, deliberately rising as experience and knowledge grow to complete self-government under the limitations of a self-governed world;
3. Education in self-knowledge and in scientific truth and in industrial technique, undivorced from the art of beauty;
4. Freedom in their own religion and social customs, and with the right to be different and non-conformist;
5. Cooperation with the rest of the world in government, industry, and art on the basis of Justice, Freedom, and Peace;

6. The ancient common ownership of land and its natural fruits and defence against the unrestrained greed of invested capital;

7. The establishment under the League of Nations of an international institution for the study of Negro problems; and

8. The establishment of an international section in the Labor Bureau of the League of Nations, charged with the protection of native labor.[34]

Third Pan-African Congress. Critical differences of aim and method between those in the Paris office and Du Bois's American blacks interested in the movement nearly led to its dissolution. The Third Pan-African Congress met in London in 1923 and was continued in Lisbon later in the year. The small London session, attended by H. G. Wells, was addressed by Harold Laski. The Lisbon meeting was more successful. Eleven countries were represented there, including Portuguese Africa.

The Congress in Lisbon turned more directly to African affairs. The Liga Africana, with headquarters in Portugal and representing indigenous associations scattered through the five provinces of Portuguese Africa, was in charge of the Congress. Here demands were made specifically for Africans (*italics as in original text):*

1. A *voice* in their own government.

2. The *right* of access to land and its resources.

3. *Trial by juries* of their peers and under established forms of law.

4. *Free elementary* education for all; broad training in modern industrial technique; and higher training of selected talent.

5. *The development* of Africa for the benefit of Africans, and not merely for the profit of Europeans.

6. *The abolition* of the slave trade and of the liquor traffic.

7. *World disarmament* and the abolition of war; but failing this, and as long as white folk bear arms against black folk, the right of blacks to bear arms in their own defense.

8. *The organization* of commerce and industry so as to make the main objects of capital and labor the welfare of the many rather than the enriching of the few.[35]

Fourth Pan-African Congress. Thus far, the Pan-African idea was more American than African. In order to place direction of the movement nearer other African centers of population, Du Bois planned a Fourth African Congress in the West Indies in 1925, with meetings in Jamaica, Haiti, Cuba, and the French islands. Accommodations, however, could not be found on any steamship line except at the price of $50,000. Du Bois suspected that "colonial powers spiked this plan."

The Fourth Pan-African Congress was finally held in New York in 1927, with 13 countries participating and little direct African representation. There were 208 delegates from 22 American states and 10 foreign countries. A resolution stressed six points:

Negroes everywhere need (*italics as in original text*):

1. *A voice* in their own government.
2. *Native rights* to the land and its natural resources.
3. *Modern education* for all children.
4. *The development* of Africa for the Africans and not merely for the profit of Europeans.
5. *The reorganization* of commerce and industry so as to make the main object of capital and labor the welfare of the many rather than the enriching of the few.
6. The treatment of civilized men as civilized despite differences of birth, race, or color.[36]

Although Du Bois worked zealously, the Pan-African movement was losing ground. As a remedy, he proposed in 1929 to hold a Fifth Pan-African Congress on the continent of Africa itself. He selected Tunis because of its accessibility. Elaborate preparations to make the movement at last geographically acceptable came to naught with two insuperable difficulties: the French Government insisted that a possible Fifth Pan-African Congress proposed by Du Bois could take place at Marseilles or any other French city, but not in Africa. Secondly, there was the handicap of the Great Depression of 1929. It was some years before the movement could be revived.

Fifth Pan-African Congress. The Pan-African idea lay dormant for 15 years. Neither the eccentric Garvey nor the intellectual Du Bois had been successful in maintaining momentum for the Return-to-Africa movement. Once again, the end of a major war provided new opportunity. Black labor representatives from Africa and the West Indies, attending a Trades Union Congress in London in the winter of 1945, convened at Manchester to form a Pan-African Federation. Again, a Congress devoted to Pan-Africanism was held outside Africa. Some delegates demanded that any future meeting take place not in Europe but in some African country such as Liberia.

Meanwhile, there was another kind of "Pan-African" movement, proposed by Jan Smuts of South Africa. Black critics complained that Smuts was hoping to unite the white rulers of Kenya, Rhodesia, and the Union of South Africa in a scheme to rule the entire African continent in the interests of white investors and exploiters. The plan, proposed as early as 1921, was discouraged by the British Colonial Office. It was suggested again at the San Francisco Conference beginning on April 25, 1945. Du Bois denounced the proposal: "We may yet live to see Pan-Africa as a real movement."[37]

In 1934 Du Bois had resigned from the directorate of the NAACP after charging that it was dedicated too much to the interests of the black bourgeoisie, and that it ignored the masses. Later, he rejoined the organization as director of research, but this, too, ended in a bitter quarrel. Meanwhile, motivated by his lifelong interest in Marxian ideology, he moved steadily leftward in his political sympathies. In 1951, because of his identification with pro-Russian causes, he was indicted as an unregistered agent for a foreign power. Although acquitted, he became more and more disillusioned with the United States. In 1961 he joined the Communist Party, denounced his citizenship, and moved to Ghana, where he worked on the *Encyclopedia Africana* until his death in Accra on August 27, 1963, at the age of 95.

As propagandist and polemicist, Du Bois was a pioneer spokesman for the idea of Pan-Africanism. Blacks in the United States, the Caribbean, and Africa were influenced by his work, but in none of these areas was he able to win mass support. Most American blacks were alienated by his proposal that a tiny group of black intellectuals, the "Talented Tenth," like the philosophers of Plato's *Republic*, should lead and uplift the masses. Where flamboyant Marcus Garvey had sought and even won mass support for a time, Du Bois's activism won relatively few converts.

Nor did African leaders respond favorably to Du Bois's version of Pan-Africanism. They were impressed by his enthusiastic support of black culture, but they were much more interested in the immediate business of liberation and the creation of sovereign nation-states. They saw the good doctor as a visionary with his dream of a future United States of Africa. He may well have been a prophet ahead of his time, but he was an impractical idealist. In their view, there could be no nationalism writ large until national consciousness was stimulated at the local level throughout Africa.

Pan-Africanism Revived

The idea of Pan-Africanism was revived after World War II with the withdrawal of European imperialist powers from the continent, and the subsequent formation of new African nation-states. The first Conference of Independent African States was convened in April 1958 at Accra, capital of Ghana. Eight nations, including five from the Arab north, sent delegates. Prime Minister Kwame Nkrumah of Ghana, who played a leading role at the meeting, called it the most significant event for many centuries in the history of Africa. He deprecated the idea of economic unity as time-delaying; only a political union could assure uniformity of foreign policy projecting the African personality and presenting Africa as an important force in world affairs. Delegates denounced colonialism, warned the French to get out of Algeria, condemned South Africa as racist and Portugal as imperialist, and urged the creation of a permanent machinery dedicated to African unity. The conference ended with the hymn "God Bless Africa."

Kwame Nkrumah's skepticism about African economic unity was directed at the Economic Commission for Africa (ECA), founded by the United Nations that same year—1958. The ECA encouraged regional economic groupings, acted in an advisory economic capacity for African states, and produced statistical and other information related to resources and commerce.[38]

From 1958 on, the search for continental unity degenerated into opposing factions. Just as Eurocrats turned to a plethora of organizations to coordinate their economic and political policies, so did Pan-Africans seek unity through a variety of regional groupings. Typical of these regional organizations was the Council of the Entente, established in 1959 as an informal body representing five West African states, with the object of coordinating their foreign and fiscal policies and public services. In Africa, as elsewhere, continental unity was sacrificed in favor of a regional combination.

At the Second Conference of Independent African States, meeting at Addis Ababa, Ethiopia, in 1960, the Pan-African movement split into two major factions. The conservative Monrovia bloc, consisting of the Brazzaville Twelve (all former French colonies) plus Liberia, Nigeria, Somalia, Sierre Leone, Togo, Libya, and Ethiopia, favored a "Community" of African nations rather than a union ("Africans should respect one another's sovereignty.") Supporting the principle of gradualism, the Monrovia bloc was neutralist with leanings toward the West.

On the radical side was the Casablanca bloc, consisting of Morocco, the United Arab Republic, the Mali-Guinea-Ghana group, and the Algerian rebel FLN. Convening in 1961 to coordinate its policies, the Casablanca bloc considered itself more Pan-African than the Monrovia bloc. It was anti-French, Socialist, and willing to cooperate with the Soviet Union and her satellites. It urged African economic and cultural unity as well as a joint military command.

By 1963 the Monrovia and Casablanca blocs formed the two poles of Pan-Africanism. In that year the Organization of African Unity (OAU) was founded. Consisting of delegates from 32 states, the organization convened under the chairmanship of President Sékou Touré of Guinea. A permanent Secretariat was set up in Addis Ababa, where heads of African states would meet each year to discuss common problems. Its goals were to resolve differences between the Monrovia and Casablanca blocs, promote unity among all African states, and eradicate all forms of colonialism. Eventually, all independent nations of Africa except South Africa became members.

From its beginning, the OAU had to face the problem of maintaining borders originally set up during the colonial era. Many such frontiers could not be justified on a tribal basis. It was almost an impossible situation, for any suggested rectification of borders immediately resulted in additional complaints. If a part of one state were to be granted adjustment, other sections would seek similar changes. The only chance for any kind of international stability was to retain borders as they existed.

This delicate situation invited Soviet interference. The Kremlin saw an enticing vacuum in the enormously rich continent now freed of "Western capitalistic colonialism." Arguing that "liberation forces" were entitled to freedom, the Russians sent Cubans and East European satellite troops into such widely separated areas as Ethiopia and Angola to enhance Soviet prestige. The

Kremlin explained its own imperialism as a humane effort to rid Africans of the coils of evil capitalism. Most African leaders were aware of Soviet pretensions. They were not attracted by an economic system already in disarray, nor were they willing to tolerate Soviet interference in their political affairs.

Otherwise, the OAU rarely managed to act in concert. Like its European counterpart, it presented a dramatic case on paper, but was weak in action. There were far too many differences between individual member states controlled by ambitious rulers. Many complained that benefits supposed to be derived from customs unions were not distributed evenly. There were some minor successes. In 1966-1967, for example, the OAU assisted Somalia and Kenya in resolving a border dispute. It helped liberation movements in Portuguese territories. These accomplishments, however, were limited.

The prestige of the OAU declined precipitously when Idi Amin, deposed dictator of Uganda, pushed his way to temporary leadership in its affairs. Denounced as "the black Hitler," he had been condemned throughout the world for uncivilized behavior when in power. He was accused of the murder of at least 200,000 Ugandans in a barbaric blood bath.[39] Another African leader who aspired unsuccessfully to the chairmanship of OAU was Colonel Muammar Kaddafi, Islāmic fundamentalist, who was accused of using his country's vast oil income to support terrorists everywhere. With two such "statesmen" at its helm, the OAU could merit little respect either in Africa or elsewhere as a responsible organization in world affairs.

By tradition, the annual meeting of OAU heads of state was a kind of celebration to reaffirm that a continent, once run by foreigners, could solve its own problems, and at least present an image of unity. In July 1982, delegates meeting in Tripoli, Libya, to prepare the year's conference, promptly broke down into squabbling factions over a dispute which threatened to divide the continent into those who looked East for ideological inspiration and those who favored association with the West. Foreign ministers of African member states met informally, but were not able to muster the required quorum of 34 countries. Nearly 20 nations boycotted the meeting; others withdrew their delegations, leaving fewer than 30. The issue at hand was a dispute over the Western Sahara. In the preceding February, 26 African countries meeting in Addis Ababa, Ethiopia, supported a move to award membership to the Polisario guerrillas who were fighting Morocco's control of Western Sahara.

Also at stake was the role of Colonel Kaddafi in OAU affairs. By tradition, the post of OAU chairman was usually given to the leader of the conference's host nation. The quarrel meant that the Libyan strong man would not get the chairmanship he wanted. He implied that he would go ahead with a "rump" meeting, which would, in effect, cripple the organization. He did nothing, however, and retired in disgust.

The gradual deterioration of the OAU meant that Africa would again be divided into hostile ideological camps, and that the organization would lose its credibility as a force in international diplomacy. Thus there was growing concern that an openly divided Africa would invite a renewed scramble for influence by foreign powers.[40]

Embryonic Pan-Africanism

Despite the efforts of the Garvey and Du Bois movements and the subsequent post-World War II revival, Pan-Africanism remained divided into inarticulated and ineffective parts. Throughout its existence, it was burdened by bitter differences in leadership, political orientation, and national ideology. There was little agreement among its supporters. Despite the emotional calls of its proponents, there was little chance of a continental-wide union and a Return-to-Africa trek from the New World.

In the United States and the Caribbean, where the idea of Pan-Africanism originated, the movement collapsed under the eccentricities of Garvey and the unpopular intellectualism of Du Bois. Nor did the idea gain firm ground in Africa itself, where too many contending factions were distributed throughout the continent. The Muslim North was drawn to Pan-Arabism, the tribal center of the South to Pan-Africanism and its concomitant négritude. The idea of Pan-Africanism did help somewhat to prevent the Balkanization of all Africa, but the continent remained in a ferment of change as each artificial newly created state sought in its own way to determine its political future.

Again we see the handicaps of the macro-nationalisms. It was always easy to involve common ideals in the call for supranationality, but it was an entirely different matter to overcome divisive factors among peoples seemingly of similar backgrounds. In Africa, as elsewhere, there were the same protestations of harmony in eloquent speeches at international congresses. But at the critical point—where national sovereignty would have to be sacrificed in the cause of a greater unity, the new African states, like their European counterparts, retreated into the confines of nationalism. Pan-Africanism, too, remained a shadowy dream. The new forces of national consciousness in Africa chose to consolidate and strengthen territorial separateness. This trend toward diversity proved to be far stronger than the spirit of Pan-Africanism with its demand for a large-scale unity.

The new African leaders had enough of their own problems at home without considering the urge for the larger supranational entity. National boundaries had been largely non-existent when European imperialists moved in during the late 19th century. The continental borders set up remained arbitrary and artificial. When the Europeans left, Africans were more responsive to their indigenous tribal loyalties than to the imperialists' boundaries. New African leaders were faced with the enormous task of developing a sense of nationhood above and beyond the loyalties of the past. It was difficult enough to transcend tribal loyalties without resorting to the lure of Pan-Africanism.

CHAPTER 11

PAN-ASIANISM: RACIAL XENOPHOBIA

China's four hundred millions are the foundation of Asia's cosmopolitanism. As a foundation is essential to expansion, so we must talk nationalism if we want to talk cosmopolitanism. "Those desiring to pacify the world must first govern their own state." Let us revive our lost nationalism and make it shine with greater splendor, then we will have some ground for discussing internationalism.

—Sun Yat-sen (1924)

Transition: Asian Nationalism

Nationalism in Asia was by no means merely an imitation of the modern historical phenomenon beginning in the late 18th century with the French Revolution. On the contrary, it was mainly a rebirth, rediscovery, or renaissance, in which Asians in various countries began to find for themselves an awakening of what they felt to be their distinct national souls. Certainly, the revolt against Western imperialism played a major role in the emergence of Asian nationalism. In the second half of the 19th century, the West had shown itself to be superior to Asia in modern political organization, commercial ability, scientific and technical achievement, and military skill. As a result, Asian civilizations and cultures had fallen under the heel of Western imperialists. Asia, like Africa, became subservient to the West. Partly in response to this aggression, Asians turned to their brilliant past to justify their own national goals. It was a reflex historical action to foreign intervention.

Asian leaders were well aware of what was happening. Sun Yat-sen pointed out that when one spoke of Europe's scientific progress and of the advance of European material civilization, he was talking only about some two hundred years of history. In his view, Europe a few hundred years ago could not be compared with China. "Cosmopolitanism has just flowed out of Europe in this generation, but it was talked of two thousand years ago in China. Europeans cannot yet discern our ancient civilization."[1] China, said Sun Yat-sen, must revive her "lost nationalism," and re-create it in revolutionary form, far removed from the old monarchical Manchu state and society.

The origins and development of the new nationalisms in modern Asia varied from country to country. In general, Asian nationalism began in the late 19th century, at a time when the continent was being overrun by foreigners. It reached a crescendo at the turn of the century, and continued apace throughout the 20th century. As in Europe, it began as an ideological movement among bourgeois lawyers, journalists, merchants, poets, and philosophers, all of whom reflected the desires of, and spoke for, the masses—workers and peasants. Far Eastern nationalism, like its European counterpart, was filled with inconsistencies, contradictions, paradoxes, and complexities. Though similar in basics to Western nationalism, there were some differences. All variations of Asian nationalism were influenced by events outside Asia, and each had its own characteristic impulses and drives. With the two World Wars, Asian nationalists began to break the chains of Western domination, and seek their own destiny without foreign interference.

There were five major areas forming the pattern of Asian nationalism: China, Japan, the Indian subcontinent, South-East Asia, and Western Asia. Each had its own regional and particularistic characteristics. Each took its own special form, and there were few links between them.

There was, however, one emotional link among Asian nations: they were uniformly sick and tired of white domination. It was in the most simple sense of the term a racial confrontation—the yellow versus the white race. Although hundreds of different peoples of diverse origins formed the amalgam of China, they were predominantly yellow in race. From the earliest days of nomadic hunters and fishermen to the time of the Mongols and Manchus, there was a steady intermixture of peoples across the heart of China. Northern Chinese came to bear a physical resemblance to Tatars, with narrow Mongolian eyelids, yellow skin, and a lack of hair on the face, while those in the south, related to the Indo-Chinese, had skins more nearly Caucasian and black beards. No matter—they saw themselves as a distinct yellow race.

The Japanese, too, regarded themselves as a yellow race, descendants of the race of Yamatos. Shinto priests spoke of the Japanese "race" as forming "the root of the world." Although their ancestry had been described as everything from Melanesian, Malayan, Mongolian, Semitic, Hamitic, to Aryan, they saw themselves as ethnically yellow and in conflict with the dominant white race. They had an emotional link with other Asians, but always with the understanding that others in Asia must subject themselves to Japanese leadership. They expected Asians to "cooperate" with them in driving the whites out of the continent, but only under Japanese direction.

There were two trends in Asian nationalism. Firstly, was the solidification of distinct nationalisms, by which the continent was fragmented into a number of nation-states. Secondly, was the appearance of a vague, unorganized Pan-Asianism, by which all Asians were to combine to confront the invading white race. The goal of Pan-Asianism was expressed succinctly in 1938 by Japanese Admiral Nobumasa Suetsugu, retired naval officer and Japanese Home Minister, when he asserted that the domination of Asia by the white race must cease:

Whether or not this will mean the ejection of the white race from East Asia is a very serious problem. From the standpoint of world peace, unless the colored peoples are liberated so that they can receive the benefits of heaven equally with the whites, and unless the white domination of the world is ended, justice and humanity, so often invoked by the white peoples will remain empty phrases. Unless the colored races are rescued from their miserable slavery under the yoke of the whites there can be no world peace. If we try to bring it about suddenly there will be bitter friction and our aims might be defeated. But the goal is clear and things must end in that direction.[2]

There were humiliations from the West. On February 24, 1913, by Presidential proclamation in the United States, Japanese laborers in Hawaii were forbidden to emigrate to the United States mainland. With certain exceptions (governmental officials, ministers, professors, students, and Chinese wives of American citizens), all others were excluded after being rated as idiots, diseased persons, anarchists, or those convicted of moral turpitude. Humiliated, the Japanese interpreted such laws as a direct, intolerable insult to their race. Pan-Asianism was one form of response to this kind of bigotry.

The Idea of Pan-Asianism

In a sense, Pan-Asianism was one of the oldest pan-movements. The idea originated in the mind of Genghis Khan (1162-1227), undisputed emperor of Mongolia.[3] Starting from obscure beginnings, he brought all the nomadic tribes of Mongolia under his control, and set up a strongly disciplined military state. He then turned his attention beyond his own borders, and began a series of campaigns carrying his influence as far as the Adriatic Sea in the west and the Pacific Ocean in the east. Subjugating defeated peoples, he used terror to maintain his rule. His Mongol Empire was among the greatest continental unions of medieval and modern times. Holding tight rein over the land mass from Peking to the Caspian Sea, he sent his generals to raid Persia and Russia. Always his goal was to mold all Asia into one vast union—the eventual mission of Pan-Asianism.

The idea of Pan-Asianism was revived in the late 19th century, partly as a response of the Asian yellow race against the unwanted invasion of white imperialists. The Chinese saw Pan-Asianism as a rebirth of the old "Celestial Empire," the Japanese regarded it as a manifestation of the "Imperial Principle." Like Pan-Africanism, with its accent on black unity, Pan-Asianism sought to counter white pressure by uniting Asians of yellow race in common opposition to white foreigners. It was a deep-rooted anger and hatred for intruders, who had little or no understanding of native pride and dignity.

Despite the huge size of Asia and its combination of different cultures, the idea of Pan-Asianism gained ground in the late 19th century. It never became an organized movement, nor did it take on a political complexion. It remained a vague sentiment, supported mainly by intellectuals. It never managed to win a mass base. Its positive aspect, that is, the aim of reviving the glory of ancient cultures, remained quiescent. Like Pan-Africanism, it was essentially a negative movement directed against economic exploitation by white foreigners and their territorial acquisitions. It protested strongly against the color bar, which it regarded as insulting and demeaning.

Pan-Asian intellectuals saw unity where there was none. There was, indeed, a *tendency* toward continental union, but it never became a political reality. Like most pan-movements, Pan-Asianism called for a macro-nationalism which never managed to overcome the jealous sovereignties of established nationalisms.

The Spoliation of China

For centuries Western Europe had to contend with invasions from Asia. One notable example was Attila, King of the Huns from 434 to 453.[4] Known as the "Scourge of God," Attila led his nomadic people from north central Asia to conquer much of Europe in the 5th century A.D. After overcoming the Eastern Roman Empire and forcing it to pay heavy tribute, he invaded Gaul in 451, with the objective of defeating the Germanic Visigoths. In 452, the Huns invaded Italy, sacking several cities, but had to leave because of famine and pestilence. Before he could attack the Eastern Empire, Attila died in his sleep.

The process of Asian invasions was reversed in the latter half of the 19th century, when European imperialists turned their eyes to China, the largest of Asian countries and larger than all Europe. For centuries, the Chinese had been isolated from the West, despite efforts by Venetian travelers, such as Marco Polo (1254-1324), Catholic missionaries, and Portuguese merchants to establish fruitful contacts. The Chinese saw the West as inhabited by inferior peoples. The Chinese saw themselves as culturally creative, a gifted people who knew about paper and printing long before their introduction to the West. Meticulously following Confucian ethical codes, including ancestor worship, they produced a rich treasure of art, philosophy, and poetry. Their wealth in natural resources, however, remained largely untapped, until it received the acquisitive attention of Westerners.

Meanwhile, before the era of Western penetration, the Chinese were undergoing a serious upheaval of their own. For two thousand years, dynasties came and went in a kind of cycle. In the 18th century, the Manchu dynasty, faced with extortion and corruption at upper levels and by poverty and misery at the lower strata, was clearly nearing its end. Militant war lords, with armed forces of their own, obeyed no government. The country sank into chronic disorder, and there was widespread banditry. The Manchus sought European assistance to meet such chaotic conditions caused by social confusion and greed of absentee landlords. The weakened country was ripe for foreign penetration.

European explorers, adventurers, merchants, and missionaries moved into a continent in disarray. They would obtain concessions from the beleaguered Manchu rulers, while at the same time offering to protect them against internal opposition.[5]

It is a familiar story—how an entire continent became the scene of ruthless Western exploitation. The process was similar to that of the partition of Africa. Pleading altruism, advanced education, and the advantages of modern science and technology, Europeans, later joined by Americans and Japanese, became absorbed in the China trade. European invaders carved the vast country into "spheres of influence," which meant virtual control of huge areas of Chinese territory. They would "open" China to the West for mutual benefit.

The beginning of the spoliation of China revealed the ambivalence of the British national character. Nineteenth-century Britain set a standard with its progress toward a workable democracy and a sophisticated legal system. The British public contemptuously denounced, as uncivilized barbarism, the slave traffic carried on by Arab merchants. But at the same time, the British man-in-the-street showed little concern about the extent of the opium trade carried on by British merchants with the connivance of Chinese officials. The business of Britain (with a bow to Calvin Coolidge's remark later) was business.

At issue was the annoying problem of the opium trade. Westerners were interested in Chinese products, but the Chinese had no reciprocal interest in the output of the Industrial Revolution. This made for difficulties in trading. For some time, the East India Company had tried to redress the balance by bringing Chinese tea to Europe in exchange for Indian-grown opium. British merchants gathered the opium poppy in India for sale in the huge Chinese market.[6] Local Chinese officials used this illegal trade as a pretext for collecting bribes from would-be importers.

Eventually, this trade in opium became a source of contention for the Chinese government. Ravages caused by the opium trade led Chinese officials to undertake a major effort to suppress the evil business altogether. However, London reacted violently. Surprisingly, the British public succumbed to war fever.

Thus began the notorious Opium War (1841-1842), one of the lesser credits of British history. The Chinese were quickly defeated. By the Treaty of Nanking (Nan-jing), the Chinese were required to pay a heavy indemnity, cede Hong Kong to Britain, and open five ports (Canton, Ningpo, Foochow, Shanghai, and Amoy) to British trade. They were also forced to recognize the principle of extraterritoriality granting foreign residents in China the rights they enjoyed at home, and exempting them from the jurisdiction of native courts (capitulations).

Thus was set up the treaty system which caught the Chinese in an intricate and ever-augmented web. The original round of treaties, which opened five Chinese ports to Western trade, was extended until, eventually, the number would rise to more than 80. These treaty ports, plus tariffs and extraterritoriality, clearly infringed on China's sovereignty. Western merchants wanted their businesses sheltered by their own laws and contracts.

Along with commerce, the Western-Chinese relationship was characterized by a search for souls, an evangelism which sought converts among the millions of Chinese. For a time, the desire for profits and for souls proceeded together. The difference was that the traders were consumed with greed, the missionaries with humanitarian motives to do something for Asians. Both movements were to result in confrontation with Asians. But while Western and Asian merchants shared the common profit motive, missionaries and local inhabitants had no such joint interests. Missionaries played a largely unwitting role as catalytic agents for the eventual Chinese revolution. "The knowledge they brought with them and simply by their presence in China, they inevitably hastened the breakdown of the Chinese order and helped to kindle Chinese nationalism in all its many forms."[7]

Defeat in the Opium War was a humiliating blow to Chinese dignity and pride. It also contributed to the later rise of Pan-Asianism. Convinced that they had granted concessions only under extreme pressure, the Chinese tried to discourage trade with the West, and avoided diplomatic contact. Western businessmen reacted with dissatisfaction and anger. In 1857, Britain and France, annoyed by Chinese refusal to recognize their diplomats and deal with their traders, combined in a second war against China. The Chinese again suffered defeat. In 1858, the Treaty of Tientsin once more required China to pay a large indemnity, open additional ports to foreign trade, protect Christian missionaries, accept foreign diplomats, and guarantee Westerners the right of travel in China. The Imperial Government had second thoughts about this, and refused to ratify the treaty. In an appalling act of vandalism in 1860, some 17,000 British and French troops entered Peking and deliberately burned the Emperor's extensive Summer Palace. Loot-laden British and French soldiers brought back so many tapestries, enamels, porcelains, wood carvings, and vases that a new fashion for Chinese art was set in the West.

Meanwhile, a new process of spoliation ensued. While central China was permeated by extraterritoriality and treaty rights, Western nations were busily penetrating into the outside rims of the great country. These territories really had never been integral parts of China proper, but they had political and cultural ties with China, and paid tribute to the Chinese Empire. Russians moved down the Amur River, set up a Maritime

Province, took over the peninsula of Liaotung with Port Arthur, and founded Vladivostok in 1860. In 1883, the French, despite Chinese protests, assumed a protectorate over Annam, and combined it with other states to form a large empire in French Indo-China. In 1885, the British, already holding Hong Kong, annexed Burma.

These aggressions stimulated the appetite of neighboring Japanese, by this time sufficiently Westernized to act like European imperialists. Using as an excuse a dispute over recognition of Korean independence, Japan went to war with China. With a combination of modern weapons and superb training, the Japanese were soon victorious. By the treaty of Shimonoseki (1895), China ceded Formosa and the Liaotung Peninsula to Japan, and had to recognize the independence of Korea.

The unexpected Japanese victory stunned Western imperialists. A non-European, non-white people had revealed extraordinary capability in modern warfare. The Russians, especially, who had begun to construct the Trans-Siberian Railway in 1891 with its intended terminus at Vladivostok, were concerned lest Japan have designs on Manchuria. Moscow, joined by Paris and Berlin (the Germans by this time were looking for an opportunity to take advantage of the Chinese grab-bag), sent a joint protest to Tokyo. The Japanese, angered but realistic, relinquished the Liaotung Peninsula to China.

For the Chinese, already humiliated by Western tactics, this was additional mortification. The Western Powers then began another scramble for concessions. The Germans extorted a 99-year lease on Kiaochow Bay and exclusive rights in the Shantung Peninsula. They took also a lease on the Liaotung Peninsula, from which they had been successful in excluding Japan. Moscow acquired Port Arthur, and the right to build railways in Manchuria to meet the Pan-Siberian system. The British took Wei-hai-wei. The French acquired Kwangchow. The Italians, too, sought acquisitions, but they were rebuffed.

The United States, fearing exclusion from the lucrative Chinese trade, enunciated the Open Door Policy, holding that China should remain territorially intact and independent but at the same time businessmen of all nations should be able to trade there without discrimination. American interests in China had been less than those of Britain, under whose leadership they had been initiated. The Open Door Policy, supported by Britain, allowed Americans the luxury of denouncing British imperialism, while at the same time participating in its benefits.

The Chinese people were faced with an unbearable situation. The country was in chaos with large areas infested by bandits, guerrillas, and revolutionary secret societies conspiring against the helpless government. Meanwhile, the country was being chopped into foreign concessions, while its peripheries were being grabbed by imperialists. In 1895, one of the secret societies, the Order of Literary Patriotic Harmonious Fists, the Boxers, broke out in rebellion.[8] Murdering Chinese Christians and European missionaries, and besieging foreign legations, the Boxers killed some three hundred foreigners, including the German Minister Baron von Ketteler (June 20, 1900). Angry European Powers, joined by Japan, sent an international force against the insurgents, and put them down. The Chinese were forced to pay a large indemnity.[9]

The experience of the Boxer Rebellion led Manchu officials to emulate Japan and strengthen China through a process of Westernization. In 1902, the Empress-Dowager announced a new reform campaign. It was too late. In 1911, revolutionaries led by Dr. Sun Yat-sen overthrew the old Manchu dynasty, and set up a republic.

The spoliation of China presents a classic case of how nationalism was stimulated by outside interference. Western penetration of China had been impelled not by professed humanitarian motives, but primarily by simple greed. Little wonder that the word imperialism began to be called an obnoxious abomination by most of the world's people. Taking advantage of the Chinese divided by internal dissension, and depriving them of the fruits of their own land could not be justified by hypocritical claims of advancing the cause of civilization. Not only did the process result in intensified nationalism in China, but it also stimulated anti-European sentiment throughout the continent. An eventual Pan-Asian reaction to this exercise in might-and-power was to be expected. In the eyes of millions of the yellow race, the white man was responsible for the shameful treatment of fellow human beings. When Pan-Asianism emerged as an ideology, it was certain to be accompanied by a distinct racial connotation.

The Japanese Connection

Where the reaction of China to foreign infiltration was negative in tone, that of Japan was positive, in the sense that it reacted vigorously against the West, and tended to take a leading position in the flowering of Pan-Asianism. The Japanese saw advantages in the medley of cross-currents making up the somewhat ephemeral Pan-Asian movement.

Throughout their history, the Japanese revealed a strong sense of racial pride, though it was not until their country was opened to the West that they began to emphasize their own ethnic distinctiveness. Japanese mythology held that the gods Izanagi and Izanami married and begot the Japanese islands, at the same time giving birth to the Sun Goddess Amaterasu. The descendants of Amaterasu ruled Japan, it was believed, in an unbroken line, the oldest reigning dynasty on earth. Like other peoples, the Japanese saw themselves as a Chosen People, of divine descent. A Japanese scholar made the claim that "from the fact of the divine descent of the Japanese people proceeds their immeasurable superiority to the natives of other countries in courage and intelligence."[10] Because the earliest inhabitants of the islands were gods, all those living in Japan were descendants of the race of Yamatos, "Seed of the Sun."[11] It was the mission of the Yamato race to prevent the human race from becoming devilish, to rescue it from destruction, and lead it to the world of light. Eventually, the Japanese War Office deemed it to be "the great mission of the Japanese race to bring all the races of the world into one happy accord."[12]

The Japanese contention of being a "pure" race is, of course, fallacious. They belong, indeed, to the general biological classification of the yellow race, and are distinctly recognizable as members of that ethnic group. But they, like all other mixed peoples, vary so much in physical characteristics, from height to form of skull, and bodily proportions, that it is unreasonable to set them apart as a "pure race." Europeans see them as small men, possessing abnormally large heads, short legs, Mongolian eyelids, large and prominent cheek bones, and straight hair. But these characteristics are variable: there are Japanese more than six feet tall.

There is no unanimity among scholars on the matter of Japanese origins. They have been described as related to nearly every people in the world, from Hottentots to Irish.[13] Western scholars offered some strange theories—that the Japanese built the Tower of Babel; that they can be identified with Turano-Africans; that they were one of the lost tribes of Israel; that they have a Caucasian ancestry; or that the parent race was Hittite.[14]

Nor could Japanese scholars agree on the matter of origins. Some turned to the classics for origins: the Japanese were descendants of the Kami (god) who lived in Takamagahara (heaven); they originated in Judea; or they came from Greece. Other Japanese scholars turned to ethnology: the ancestors of the Japanese were Huns; Japanese and Koreans were of the same stock; or there were Malaysian forbears. Still others based their theories on anthropology: prehistoric men and the present Ainu were one group and the Pan-Ainu plus Asians equalled contemporary Japanese.[15] One theory held that prehistoric peoples of Japan were Eskimo; another found racial origins in the early Ainus; still another concluded that the Japanese had Turkish blood, because the Chosus in Japan "are robust in health and have long noses."[16]

There were also conflicting schools of opinion as to whether the Japanese originated in northern or southern Asia. Those who held the theory of northern Asian origin believed that the earliest dwellers of the Japanese islands were cave dwellers (koro-pok-guru), an aboriginal people, who were either annihilated or assimilated by the Ainu, a flat-faced, hirsute people who came from the north.[17] The Ainus were overwhelmed in turn by two successive waves of invaders, who although of different origin, united to form "the distinctive racial group from which the present Japanese are descended."[18] Those who believed in the theory of southern Asian origin found an Indonesian or Polynesian connection.

For centuries, Japan remained closed to the West. In the 16th century, in either 1542 or 1543, Portuguese and Spaniards, attracted by the possibilities of profits, as well as a means of planting their Christian faith, brought firearms, sponge cake, and gonorrhea to the Japanese.[19] The main legacy of this Iberian intrusion was intense fear in Japan. The Tokugawa seclusion edicts, enacted early in the 17th century, forbade the practice of Christianity, and did not allow Japanese to travel abroad legally. Some Dutchmen, who were interested in their account books and not religious conversion, were allowed to stay. The Chinese were the only foreigners regularly allowed entry into Japan.

Until the mid-19th century the Japanese remained isolated from the West, and retreated into what historians called a "centralized feudalism." The emperor (*mikado*) was regarded as sacred and too aloof to mingle in everyday affairs. Executive power was vested in a *shogun*, a hereditary prime minister. The great lords of the realm, the *daimyo*, were bound to the *shogun* by a pledge of fealty. Confucianism, the preferred religion in the Tokugawa state, placed emphasis on education, loyalty, and filial piety.

In 1853 the American Commodore Matthew Calbraith Perry visited Japan with several impressive battleships and a letter from President Millard Fillmore to the Japanese Emperor requesting a treaty.[20] Perry would return the next year with a large squadron. Ultimately, he negotiated a treaty opening Japanese ports to American commerce. In 1858, Townsend Harris, the first American representative to Japan, negotiated a commercial treaty.[21] European Powers, envious of the success of noisy and active Americans, quickly sought treaties and extraterritorial privileges. When conservative Japanese protested, they were taught a lesson in Western diplomacy by the bombardment of the town of Shimonoseki in 1864. The Japanese concluded that Western military strength was more powerful than their own. Adaptable and strongly nationalistic, in contrast to the disunited Chinese, they resisted Western imperialism, fashioning an imperialism of their own.

The Japanese already had a sense of national identity, based upon supposed racial affinity, linguistic distinction, historical traditions, and the Shinto religion, while supported by imperial institutions. Regarding the predatory West as a serious threat, they responded to it in quite different fashion from the Chinese. The people were highly intelligent and educated, government officials trained and sophisticated. The *samurai* leadership was well versed in military matters. When it became obvious that change was necessary to meet the demands of the West, the challenge was met head-on and with success.

The shogunate had been unable to solve pressing political, economic, and social problems. To meet the unwelcome probing power of the West, it was necessary that the Japanese people place their own house in order, especially to put an end to the bickering, violence, and bloodshed, and bring about a profound change in government. That is exactly what happened in 1867, when the discredited shogunate was overthrown, and the empire restored. The vigorous young Emperor Mitsuhito, who reigned from 1867 to 1912, broke down the old feudal order and instituted startling changes. Seven centuries of military rule came to an end. Feudal Japan was transformed into a modern constitutional state, an industrial society, and a world power. In fewer than 50 years, the Japanese progressed from wonder and curiosity about Commodore Perry's "black ships" to an amazing victory over the Russians.

The reforms were extraordinary and effective. In 1871, an imperial decree abolished the old fiefs and divided the land among independent farmers. The next year saw the opening of the first railroad in Japan, and also the introduction of compulsory elementary education. Universal military service, under German direction, was introduced. A modern navy, under British guidance, was constructed. Japanese students were sent abroad to study Western culture and science; new civil and criminal legal codes were drafted; religious liberty was guaranteed; and trade and industry were promoted. In 1889, a constitution was adopted, which guarded the emperor's powers, and provided for a bicameral diet consisting of an upper house of peers (363 members) and a lower house elected through limited suffrage (463 members).

In this extraordinary transformation, Japanese nationalism merged into imperialism. If the West was intent on extending its influence in East Asia, then why could not the Japanese do the same thing? If the West wanted raw materials, markets, and places to invest capital in Asia, why not the Japanese? Besides, they could protect and guide Oriental civilization against intrusion by the white man.

Tokyo looked west and saw an impotent Chinese giant already in the process of dismemberment. In 1876 Japan recognized Korea and subsequently sought to bring it under control. The subsequent Sino-Japanese War (1894-1895) resulted in a quick Japanese victory. The giant Russian bear entered the scene next. Moscow established a Russo-Chinese Bank (1896) to help pay the Chinese indemnity; won a concession for the Chinese Eastern Railway to Vladivostok; leased the Liaotung Peninsula and Port Arthur coveted by Japan; and sent agents into Korea and Manchuria.

In response to what they saw as Russian aggression, the Japanese were careful first to obtain a Western ally in the Anglo-Japanese Alliance of 1902. In 1904 they insisted that Russians withdraw from Manchuria and Korea, a demand contemptuously refused by Moscow. The Russo-Japanese War of 1904-1905 followed. To the amazement of the entire world, the war ended with the rout of Russian armies at Mukden, and the annihilation of the Russian fleet at the Battle of Tsushima (1905). At the suggestion of American President Theodore Roosevelt, the peace concluded in the Treaty of Portsmouth (New Hampshire) required both belligerents to evacuate

Manchuria, but recognized their spheres of influence there. It also awarded Port Arthur, a lease on the Liaotung Peninsula, and the southern half of the island of Sakhalin to Japan. The treaty recognized Japanese rights in Korea.

Japanese national pride was stimulated by this extraordinary triumph over a great Western power. The earlier alliance with Great Britain in 1902, based on mutual needs, indicated Japanese parity with an advanced Western state, and provided a sharp contrast to the "unequal treaties" which had plagued China. In Europe and the Western Hemisphere, Japan was thus regarded as a country to be reckoned with in world affairs.

The significance of the Japanese victory was understood throughout Asia. The effect was dramatic in the vast continent: by clever modernization and industrialization, an Asian people of yellow race had resisted successfully the domination of the West.

Despite its victory, the Japanese Government at this time did not seek a position as a leader of Asia, nor did it seek directly to promote Pan-Asian feelings.[22] It was concerned with a world position rather than an Asian one. Nevertheless, in Japan there were already intellectuals who were thinking in terms of Pan-Asian sentiment. They resented the humiliating pose of the white man, and insisted that far too many concessions were being made, not only by Chinese but by Japanese officials. Already, extremist national societies were being formed to call for rejection of ideas foreign not only to Japan but to Asia, and to promote Japanese expansion throughout the continent. These ultra-nationalists supported the idea of political murder to advance their cause. They would extend Japanese nationalism beyond its localized peripheries, and then take the lead in promoting a great Pan-Asianism under Japanese auspices.

During the years immediately following the Russo-Japanese War, the Japanese increased their hold on Korea and their interests in China. The outbreak of World War I gave Japan, ally of Great Britain, the opportunity of seizing Shantung and German holdings in China. When China attempted to nationalize her iron mines and ironworks in central China, where Japanese businessmen had many financial interests, Tokyo reacted in 1915 with the Twenty-One Demands. These included extension of Japanese concerns in Manchuria, transfer of German leaseholds in Shantung to Japan, acceptance by China of Japanese "advisers," and, in general, placing unwanted Japanese controls on the Chinese economy. To the resentment of China, many of these demands were adopted at the Versailles Peace Conference in 1919. For humiliated Chinese, Japanese imperialism was no more desirable than that of the Western Powers.

Japan's position as a world power was recognized at the Washington Naval Conference of 1921-1922, which set the ratio of naval shipping (5:5:3) between the United States, Britain, and Japan. Tokyo saw this agreement as a basis for its own naval supremacy in the Far East. The Japanese could be satisfied in national pride; they controlled Korea, had extensive interests in China, and had begun national expansion by appropriating former German colonies in the Pacific, north of the Equator. It was time to think of Pan-Asian leadership.

Indian Subcontinent

The third major area forming the pattern of Asian nationalism was the Indian subcontinent in south central Asia. In this vast area of 1,261,483 square miles, peoples of varying origins, religions, and cultures pulled violently in opposite directions. At times, some seemed to be on the verge of political disintegration. But despite the many differing peoples, the force of nationalism has been strong enough to hold the country together.

India's ethnic history is quite different from that of China and Japan. The Chinese and Japanese, dominantly Mongoloid, structured their Pan-Asianism on a confrontation between yellow and white races. A racially distinct division cannot be drawn for India. Several strains are discernible: the main Caucasoid elements include the dark-skinned Dravidians in the south and lighter-skinned peoples in the north; there are Negroid, Australoid, and Mongoloid stocks in the south. Hindi is the official language, with English as an associate tongue. The constitution recognizes only 14 national languages, but there are as many as 1,652 languages and dialects spoken in the country. Religion is 83 percent Hindu, 10 percent Muslim.

At the dawn of the 20th century, one paramount Western power, Britain, exercised control over the vast subcontinent. British penetration began as early as the 17th century under the auspices of the East India Company.[23] The rival French, also attracted by a rich source for raw materials and markets, were defeated in the Seven Years War (1756-1763), mostly through the efforts of Robert Clive and Warren Hastings. Using a combination of treaty-making and conquest, the East India Company gradually extended its control to the borders of China and Afghanistan. British mastery was eased by political, cultural, and religious factionalism among hundreds of petty states. By the India Act of 1784, London granted a measure of local autonomy, but power remained in the hands of British officials named by Parliament to succeed the often corrupt East India Company agents.

From the beginning of British control, the peoples of India resented attempts to change their social and religious customs. In 1857, Sepoys, local soldiers in British service, protested against the use of cartridges greased with animal fat, and refused to bite the cartridges as a violation of their religion. The subsequent mutiny was quickly suppressed.

In 1876, Prime Minister Benjamin Disraeli saw to it that Queen Victoria was crowned Empress of India, a new jewel in the British crown. About three-fifths of India was under British rule, while about two-fifths, divided into many states and principalities, remained under the control of Indian princes who accepted British supremacy. The British claimed that their rule in India was extremely effective. They pointed to improvements in the codification of laws and the administration of justice, the establishment of schools and universities, and the construction of roads and railways.

Indian patriots had other views. They accused the British of failing to solve such problems as infanticide, illiteracy, poverty, famine, and disease. The first tangible expression of Indian nationalism came in 1885 with the formation of the Indian National Congress, which called attention to the basic problem of Indian poverty. It urged governmental reforms to provide for more Indian representation, and called for better opportunities for Indians in the civil service and armed forces. Only a government of India by Indians, it was argued, could solve the country's complex problems. Leaders of the Indian National Congress had differing views varying from accommodation with Britain to revolutionary nationalist idealism.

The Indian viewpoint on relations with Britain was expressed in 1881 by Dadabhai Naoroji, an intellectual who held that the impoverishment and destruction of India were caused mainly by the unnatural treatment it received at the hands of British rulers. He accused the British of being a crushing foreign agency in India, displacing its children and depriving them of their natural rights and means of subsistence in their own country. An exhaustion of the very life-blood of the country was going on unnecessarily. Unless this disastrous drain was duly checked, said Naoroji, and until the people of India were restored to their natural rights in their own country, there was no hope for the material amelioration of India's problems.

In a memorandum submitted to the Secretary of State for India, Naoroji wrote about the material exhaustion of India and the no less sad and lamentable moral loss. He ended his memorandum with a dramatic appeal:

By all means, let Englishmen be proud of the past. We accord them every credit for the order and law they brought about, and are deeply thankful to them, but let them now face the present, let them clearly realize and manfully acknowledge the many shortcomings of omission and commission, by which, with the best of intentions, they have reduced India to material and moral wretchedness: and let them, in a way worthy of their name and history, repair the injury they have inflicted, and a benefit and glory to England, by allowing India her own administration under their superior, controlling and guiding hand—or in their oft repeated profession and words, "by governing India for the Indian's good."
May the God of all nations lead the English to a right sense of their duty to India, is my humble and earnest prayer.[24]

The British were willing to make political concessions to meet Indian demands, as long as their own control was maintained. The Indian Councils Act of 1892 provided for greater Indian representation in central and provincial councils. Lord Curzon, Viceroy from 1899 to 1905, offended Congress leaders by his measure to partition the large province of Bengal for its better administration.

Meanwhile, Indian nationalism broke into two confronting factions in a development that was to have major repercussions. The problem of Bengal led Indian Muslims to form a political organization of their own. The All-India Muslim League, founded in 1906, was dedicated to the achievement of Muslim rights. Leaders of the Indian National Congress claimed that a divided nationalist movement gave the British political ammunition to play off one party against the other as a means of solidifying British control. The Congress, therefore, called for self-government for India.

The British responded with what Indian nationalists called the usual mixture of promises of constitutional reform, together with further repressive measures. The 1909 Indian Councils Act (Morley-Minto Reforms) took into account the separate interests of Muslims. The Montagu-Chelmsford Report (1918) proclaimed a greater degree of self-government for India. The Rowlatt Acts (1919), decreed as an answer to riots, further restricted liberties of the people. The Simon Report (1930) again recommended a gradual increase in self-government, but emphasized the necessity for continued British control.

The story of the subsequent development and triumph of Indian nationalism needs little attention here. As early as 1919, Mohandas K. Gandhi organized the first of many passive resistance campaigns against British rule. Seer and mystic, his frail body emaciated by fasting and asceticism, this enigmatic but charismatic leader promoted a campaign which eventually led to Indian independence in 1947. The subcontinent was then partitioned into the states of India and Pakistan, and bloody riots broke out between Hindus and Muslims as millions fled in crisscross migrations to new states.

Pan-Asianism could not flourish in this maze of conflicting interests. India had too many worries of her own without seeking either leadership of or attachment to a Pan-Asian movement. Indian leaders were absorbed by the needs of self-sufficiency, not the goal of uniting all Asians in a continental-wide union. The country was still split by disputatious and diverse interests. Even after the state of Pakistan was bloodily cut away, India's large Muslim minority remained unhappy and fearful. Moreover, factionalism within the Congress itself continued to clutter the sometimes chaotic political scene. The differences persist to the present day. India had her own pressing problems without taking on those of all Asia.

South-East Asia

South-East Asia, the third major area forming the pattern of Asian nationalism, was under some form of Western political control before the opening of the 20th century. There, too, as in China, Japan, and India, a proud and defiant people looked upon the Western white man as an intruder in their affairs. There, too, the response was a quickening of national consciousness in the Age of Nationalism.

Burma, on the mainland in South-East Asia, in an area nearly the size of Texas, attracted the acquisitive instincts of the English, Dutch, and French. There were many different sub-groups, including the dominant Burmese (related to Tibetans and forming 72 percent of the population), the Chins, Karens, Lachins, Kayahs, Mons, and Shans. The people, of Mongoloid stock, were related to others in East Asia. In religion the Burmese were 85 percent Buddhist.

English and Dutch traders were active in Burma as early as the 17th century.[25] The French came to Burma in the 18th century. As the power of the British grew in India, it came into conflict with the expansion of Burmese frontiers. The result was a series of wars from 1824 to 1884. On March 5, 1824, the Governor of India declared war, and the British invaded Lower Burma by sea. Burmese troops, only half of whom had muskets, repulsed initial British advances but finally succumbed. The victorious British took parcels of Burmese land and imposed a heavy indemnity.

Again, in 1852, the British found a pretext for war to combat local extortions. This time they added Lower Burma to the British Empire. The situation in Burma deteriorated gradually, until, in 1885, it was conquered and came under control by London as a part of the Indian Empire. In 1937 Burma became self-governing. Independence outside the Commonwealth was achieved on January 4, 1948. Nationalism was the driving force of Burmese opinion, initially directed against the British, who were accused of having no real intention of conferring autonomy on the country, and then against the Japanese who invaded Burma in 1941 during World War II. The Burmese "patriot army" finally won the hotly desired independence.

The French, using a combination of diplomacy and force, gradually extended their control over what was loosely known as French Indo-China.[26] French missionary interest in the area went back to the 17th century. In the 1850s, the French used the excuse of Christian persecutions to intervene in southern Vietnam. From 1883 to 1885 a war with China ensued when the Chinese claimed sovereignty over the country. Then known as Annam, Vietnam had a long tradition of national identity and a period of national revolt before the era of French penetration. The conquering French set up a series of protectorates in their *Union Indochinoise*, by which native rulers—the emperor of Vietnam and the kings of Laos and Cambodia—were allowed to retain their thrones. The people would be Gallicized and assimilated. French culture would be brought to new French subjects.

French policy was designed to frustrate Indo-Chinese nationalism, but it was not successful. It soon became obvious that the formal native structure of government was little more than a sham. The French expected to eliminate local institutions and at the same time retain the loyalty of the people. Added to political problems were economic difficulties. Indo-Chinese businessmen complained about French tariff policies, because French concepts of property tended to break down the structure of village landholding, and throw economic power into the hands of landlords and moneylenders.[27]

Vietnamese nationalism was stimulated by Chinese and Japanese resistance to Western imperialism. Japan's victory over Russia in 1905 and the budding movement of "Asia for the Asians," added to the Chinese Revolution of 1911, led to increasing demands for a Vietnamese republic. The French managed to contain the Vietnamese through the two world wars, even though Vietnamese opinion was alienated by French rule. Nationalist aims gathered force in 1940, when Vietnam was occupied by Japan. With defeat impending, Tokyo granted the country independence under a puppet government. After Japan's surrender, Communist Viet Minh guerrillas, under the leadership of Ho Chi Minh, seized Hanoi and set up the Democratic Republic of Vietnam.

From 1946 to 1954 the Viet Minh waged war, finally defeating the French forces at Dienbienphu. The country was divided along the 17th parallel, with the North going to the Communists and the South to the control of the Bao Dai government.

It was an old and familiar story. Western powers were feeling the impact of a rising Asian nationalism. The French, who had initiated the urge of nationalism in Europe in the late 18th century, found themselves stimulating nationalism in their colonial territories in South-East Asia.

After three centuries, the Dutch controlled the most widespread colonial empire in South-East Asia.[28] In an archipelago of great beauty and rich natural resources, consisting of some 3,000 fertile islands strung like jewels along the equator, more than one hundred million Indonesians endured a bitter experience under foreign rule. In a complex brown-white racial mixture, Malayans and Papuans constituted the main ethnic groups, with the Chinese as the largest non-indigenous people. Some 2,000 years ago, Hindu and Buddhist civilizations came to the area from India, but both were replaced by Islām in the 16th century as the dominant religion.

The Dutch emerged as a major power in the area in the 17th century, maintaining their rule until World War II, when Japan occupied the islands. At the turn of the century, the Netherlands East Indies comprised a vast island area, stretching from northern Sumatra to western New Guinea. Java was its political center. For the Dutch, this colonial area provided a source of riches: on occasion, almost half the Dutch national budget was met by what was called a "surplus" from Indonesian revenues. Like the British, the Dutch used a carrot-and-stick technique in governing the archipelago. The Dutch carefully extended their political, economic, and military control. Dutch forces, engaged in a long struggle for the conquest of northern Sumatra, exerted pressure on those who did not take kindly to alien rule. When resentment became too great, the Dutch responded with "ethical reforms," designed to give a measure of relief but no meaningful autonomy.

Toward the end of the 19th century, there was growing opposition to Dutch rule. Native discontent was fanned by the exploitation of the peasants. Indonesians were angered by the Dutch custom, geared to emphasize white supremacy, of requiring natives to drop to their knees in the presence of their masters. Increasing discontent led Dutch officials to a change in attitude. In 1901 they inaugurated a policy of decentralization, designed to achieve improvement through local village administration. The program, however, turned out to be so paternalistic that it aroused even more hostility.

Indonesian nationalists, inspired by events in India, formed a political association in 1908 to train its members for educational and social leadership. Three years later, an Islāmic association was founded. At this time, Javanese nationalists were as concerned about Chinese traders in their homeland as by Dutch repressive rule. In 1911, Indonesian nationalists began to call for autonomy, while remaining in union with the Netherlands. The next year came the first call for independence with the formation of a freedom party. Concerned even more, the Dutch turned again to the carrot: they would meet nationalist demands by authorizing a parliament with limited powers.

From then on, the situation followed the familiar pattern of Asia for the Asians. The nationalist movement became widespread when the archipelago was occupied by the Japanese in World War II. In 1945, Nationalist leaders Achmed Sukarno and Mohammad Hatta proclaimed Indonesia an independent republic. Attempts to re-establish Dutch rule met with strong resistance. An agreement was reached by the creation of a United States of Indonesia, linked in union with the Netherlands. This union was dissolved in 1954 as the Republic of Indonesia was proclaimed.

Indonesian independence, as elsewhere in Asia, was followed by unrest and tragic upheaval. The white man had been forced out, but symptoms of internal dissension multiplied. Demands for regional autonomy grew. In 1950 Java and Borneo revolted; two years later there was a major revolt in Atjeh, followed by rebellions in 1955 and 1957 in the Celebes and Moluccas. In 1965-1966, more than 300,000 Indonesians were killed in anti-Communist riots in a macabre blood bath. The nation, freed of Western colonialism, degenerated into political upheaval, poverty, and massive slaughter. There was some improvement after Sukarno was forced out of power in 1968. Much of the discontent was due to his overblown ambitions and his near-alliance with Communist China.

Western Asia

The story of Western Asia overlaps that of Eastern Europe. Here nationalist symptoms were displayed in the 19th century, along with the development of nationalism in Western Europe. The Ottoman Turkish Empire, holding territories in both Europe and in Asia, began gradually to lose its western provinces.

The old Ottoman Empire was affected by two nationalist drives. Turkish nationalism came to be more concerned with Turks than with the Ottoman Empire as a whole or with Islām. At the same time, Arab national sentiment began to grow among those who were Muslim but not Ottoman. Arabs in general remained loyal to the Ottoman Empire until it was defeated. Attention has been given in a previous chapter to these developments.[29]

Efforts at Organization

Nationalism throughout the five major areas of Asia followed a similar basic pattern, although each had its own special regional characteristics. As in Africa, resentment for the white foreigner built up in a crescendo of hatred. Despite their conglomeration of cultures, Asian intellectuals spoke of a unifying common past, a common destiny, and a common enemy in Western imperialism.

At the opening of the 20th century, however, Asian nationalism was not yet based on popular organization. There was a tendency toward union, but no political reality. The Pan-Asian idea was in the air as an observable trend, but it lacked organization. The ideals of individual freedom and economic well-being had led to the flowering of Asian nationalism. Having adopted the political and economic models of the West, Asian leaders began to think in Western terms. This included the idea of a continental-wide unity, of Asia for the Asians.

Strangely enough, the first proposal for Asian unity came not from Asia itself but from Moscow. After the Bolshevik Revolution of October 1917, the Russians, enamored of the vision that theirs was the primary step toward world revolution, suggested that all Asia also could throw off the capitalist yoke. For this reason, they organized in 1920 a Congress of Oriental Nations at Baku. Asian intellectuals, already thinking in terms of a Pan-Asianism of their own, but as suspicious of Bolsheviks as of Western imperialists, stayed away from the conference. It was conspicuously unsuccessful.

Inside Asia, the first attempt to give substance to a vague Pan-Asian sentiment was made by the Japanese. World War I had much to do with the pace of change. The Japanese, observant and calculating, stood aside as the West was drenched with blood in cruel, massive warfare. In 1920 the Japanese convened the first Pan-Asian Conference at Nagasaki, under the auspices of their Pan-Asian Society. The delegates discussed plans for economic cooperation, but were careful not to go beyond economics into the political sphere. From the beginning, there was tension between Chinese and Japanese delegates, both of whom expected to be leaders in any proposed Pan-Asiatic union. The Indian representatives were carefully noncommittal. No decisions of import were made, beyond one to establish a permanent Pan-Asian bureau at either Peking, Shanghai, or Tokyo.

Until this time, Pan-Asian feelings in Japan had had little positive content, and had been more a negative reaction against the West. But with the defeat of Russia and the success of the modernization program, there was a hesitant return to old established Japanese values. Each time, this swing of the pendulum was accompanied by a rise in Pan-Asian sentiment.[30] Japanese intellectuals were already speaking in terms of "Asia is One," and "Asian roots and Asian cultural solidarity." The implication, of course, was that any such Pan-Asianism would be directed from Tokyo.

Japan's new aggressive policy was promoted by Baron Giichi Tanaka (1863-1929), Prime Minister and advocate of Japanese expansion. Distinguishing himself in the Russo-Japanese War, he advocated Japanese involvement in a Siberian expedition against the new Soviet regime in Russia. Minister of War in 1918 and Prime Minister in 1927, he adopted an aggressive tone toward China. However, the "Tanaka Memorial," a document in which he supposedly advised the Emperor to adopt an expansionist policy in China, was charged to be a forgery.[31] Forgery or not, the "Tanaka Memorial" reflected an existing urge for expansion culminating in the formation of the "Greater East Asia Co-Prosperity Sphere" advocated by Japanese militarists in the World War II era.

The conference of Nagasaki revealed that the Japanese had little understanding of, or sympathy for, other Asian peoples. From their viewpoint, Pan-Asianism meant simply Japanese domination of Asian society. That sentiment annoyed the Chinese, who distrusted the Japanese and who later had dramatic and tragic confrontations with them. Other Asians, too, who expected a possible union based on equality, were suspicious of Japanese motives. For the Japanese, Pan-Asianism was senseless without Japanese leadership. For other Asians, this interpretation was an anathema. Under the circumstances, a workable Pan-Asianism could scarcely be expected.

The next attempt at organization came under Chinese auspices, when the Second Pan-Asian Conference was convened in 1928 near Shanghai. Again, there were irreconcilable differences between Chinese and Japanese delegates, to such a degree that the meeting was doomed to failure. Continental union could scarcely be won in the face of mutual recriminations, hostile speeches, and angry exchanges. There were the usual expressions of contempt for the Western intruder, and affirmations of Asia's cultural heritages, but there was little support for the idea of Asian unity among peoples literally at each other's throats.

Already, both Asian and African leaders were thinking in terms of an Afro-Asian consciousness instead of continental pan-movements. In January 1929, at the instigation of Jawaharlal Nehru, delegates of nineteen countries met at Delhi, including the representatives from India, Australia, and New Zealand, as well as from Egypt and Ethiopia. The conference condemned Dutch military activities in Java. It also passed resolutions supporting the theme of national liberation.

The conference at Delhi revealed a retrogression in the Pan-Asian idea. Both Japanese and Chinese intellectuals continued to speak in terms of Pan-Asian organization, but both were motivated primarily by national identity and national aspirations. When the Japanese invaded Manchuria in 1931, efforts to promote Pan-Asianism vanished amid the clouds of war. Pan-Asianism virtually disappeared in the solvent of Japanese militarism.

The Bandung Conference

When the idea of Pan-Asianism was revived in the mid-1950s, it was allied with Pan-Africanism in an attempt to express something of the common spirit of the new, re-born states of Asia and Africa. Half the peoples of the world were moved by a similar xenophobia, opposition to colonialism, and fear of and contempt for the white man. A conference of Afro-Asian states would meet to discuss the political and economic problems which faced new and developing nations.

From April 15 to 24, 1955, representatives of 29 Asian and African nations met at Bandung, West Java, in Indonesia.[32] This was the first celebration of the existence of independent Asian and African "unaligned" nations. Among the leaders present were Chou En-lai of China, Jawaharlal Nehru of India, and Gamal Abdel Nasser of Egypt. Communist China, which had an interest in promoting relations with other Asian and African states, assumed an important role in the proceedings. Pointedly not invited were South Africa, Nationalist China, and Korea.

Although the delegates represented varying views, they agreed on the fundamental principles of human rights as expressed in the Charter of the United Nations. They condemned the policies of racial segregation and discrimination. They agreed:

(a) in declaring that colonialism in all its manifestations is an evil which should speedily be brought to an end;

(b) in affirming that the subjection of peoples to alien subjugation, domination, and exploitation constitutes a denial of fundamental human rights, is contrary to the Charter of the United Nations, and is an impediment to the protection of world peace and cooperation;

(c) in declaring its support of the cause of freedom and independence for all such peoples; and

(d) in calling upon the powers concerned to grant freedom and independence to all such peoples.[33]

The delegates then specifically declared their support for the rights of Algerians, Moroccans, Tunisians, and Arabs of Palestine to self-determination and independence; for the government of Indonesia in the case of West Irian; and for the position of Yemen in respect to Aden.[34] Delegates spoke glowingly of the "Bandung spirit of conciliation."[35] Though there were differences among the Bandung countries, they began to operate as a loose bloc in the United Nations. By 1962, Asian and African countries composed half the membership of the United Nations where they called for immediate steps to grant independence to the remaining trust territories and dependencies. Asian-African congresses became annual events in New York, home of the United Nations.

Both Asian and African states were entering their second stage of nationalism. Their revolutions and civil wars of the first stage had ended. Now, in the second stage, they had to deal with disruptive forces inside their own boundaries. There were major divisions on both continents: in Africa there were differences between Casablanca and Monrovia blocs; in Asia there were similar factions. All the new countries were confronted also with economic problems. In their search for security, they turned either to the United States or the Soviet Union for aid.

As elsewhere, however, the impulse for projection into the third stage of nationalism—the larger macro-nationalism—faltered. Early Pan-Asianism had been strongly racial in content. Now the old xenophobia had run its course. There was less reason to hate the white man in the new Asia. Western representatives of business and industry, once feared and angrily rejected, were now welcomed. There were more Englishmen in the new India and Pakistan than in the colonial era, but they were there on Indian and Pakistani terms. There was more flexibility in the new Asian nationalism, as well as less interest in the ideology of Pan-Asianism.

There were some minor efforts at unity, notably the Asian and Pacific Council (ASPAC), formed in 1966. Ten Asian states (including Japan and Taiwan) were devoted to fostering economic, social, and political cooperation specifically among non-Communist countries of the area. Such unions were far removed from the goals of Pan-Asianism.

The Failed Macro-Nationalism

Pan-Asianism never achieved effective organization or recognition as a political reality. At one time, it represented a common cause against the exploiting white race, but with the recession of colonialism it lost much of its *raison d'être*. It still retained some appeal in its attempt to end the final remnants of imperialism, but its insistence on a common destiny for all Asian peoples attracted only lukewarm support. Communist China and capitalist Japan had little interest in a common destiny. The days of possible union against white domination were past.

Pan-Asianism was another example of how projected larger nationalisms founder on the rock of sovereignty. Like Pan-Europeanism or Pan-Africanism, Pan-Asianism remains a hazy sentiment supported by idealists who see common cause where there is no common identity. Efforts to give it dynamic force failed. Champions of Pan-Asianism continued to minimize differences between continental peoples, but realists in Tokyo and Peking learned that days of negative protest against the color bar were gone. In the vast areas of Asia, the mixture of cultures and the cross currents of political goals did not help extend the macro-nationalisms, despite zealous efforts of well-meaning theorists.

CHAPTER 12

PAN-AMERICANISM: DRIVE FOR HEMISPHERIC SOLIDARITY

> In the spirit of Christopher Columbus all of the Americas have an eternal bond of unity, a common heritage bequeathed to us alone. Unless we together redeem the promise which his voyage held for humanity, it must remain forever void. This is the destiny which Pan-Americanism has chosen to fulfill.
>
> —Calvin Coolidge

Meaning of Pan-Americanism

The general movement of Pan-Americanism consists of three phases, at times in rivalry with one another. The original form, introduced in the early 19th century, was Pan-Hispanism, a continental movement which aimed to unite the Spanish-American states of South America in a common union. This attempt at synthesis was later given the name of *la patria grande* ("the great Fatherland") by the Peruvian writer and political leader, Victor Raúl Haya de la Torre.[1]

The second form of continental union took on another dimension when, during the course of the 19th century, an attempt was made to close the gap that had existed between the Spanish-American states and others, such as Brazil and Haiti. Pan-Americanism developed both right- and left-wing phases.[2]

The third form, and the one that is best known, emerged gradually toward the end of the 19th century, when the United States took over leadership in the drive for solidarity. In this phase, an attempt was made to extend the ism beyond its earlier purely South American form.

Pan-Americanism as a macro-nationalism has many differences from, but some similarities with, other pan-movements:

1. Unlike Pan-Europeanism or Pan-Africanism, and alone among the macro-nationalisms, Pan-Americanism is hemispheric rather than continental. Aiming to cover the entire Western Hemisphere, it seeks to combine a large portion of the world's surface in a strong unity.

2. Unlike Pan-Slavism or Pan-Germanism, Pan-Americanism has no distinct linguistic base. The major languages include Spanish, French, Portuguese, and English.

3. Unlike Pan-Islāmism and Zionism, Pan-Americanism has no distinct religious affinity. It is dominantly Protestant in the North and Catholic in the South. The trend to unity has no solid ecclesiastical base.

4. Pan-Americanism has few historical traditions which make for unity. The hemisphere is divided into heterogeneous, multi-cultural peoples, dominantly Anglo-Saxon in the North and largely Hispanic in the South. The type of nationhood that exists in Europe is not found in Latin America. Mexican author and diplomat Carlos Fuentes explained it succinctly: "Nationalism represents a profound value for Latin Americans simply because of the fact that our nationhood is still in question. In New York, Paris, or London, no one loses sleep asking himself whether the nation exists. In Latin America you can wake up and find that the nation is no longer there, usurped by a military junta, a multinational corporation or an American ambassador surrounded by a bevy of technical advisers."[3] To Fuentes, destabilization and a perverted sense of nationalism were sorry facts.

5. Like Pan-Europeanism, Pan-Americanism is largely economic in tone. Hemispheric solidarity was conceived as a means of promoting the economic well-being of all member states. There is little desire to venture into the political sphere, and certainly there is no effort to limit sovereignty. The political urge was and is devoted to the major task of keeping imperialists out of South American territory.

6. Far from promoting political solidarity, Pan-Americanism has remained a loose union ready for political action only in the event that acquisitive Europeans seek to Balkanize the Western Hemisphere. The tenuous nature of political solidarity was revealed in the Spring of 1982, when an Argentine military junta, faced with economic difficulties, decided to win national support by invading the Falkland Islands, several hundred miles off the Argentine coast. Insisting that the "Malvern Islands" were Argentine since the early 1820s, the junta expected no British resistance. It was certain of hemispheric support. It was both right and wrong in its expectations—right in believing that Argentine national consciousness would be aroused, but wrong in its estimate of British reaction.

With an eye on Gibraltar, North Ireland, and what remained of the British Empire, the British struck back. Although 8,000 miles from home base, seasoned British troops defeated bewildered Argentine conscripts. The Falkland Islands remained British.

The Argentine junta was mistaken also in assuming that the entire hemisphere would unite in opposition to British imperialism. Brazilians were coldly indifferent. Washington, with an eye on the North Atlantic Treaty Organization, in which Britain was an important member, and very much worried about Soviet imperialism, denounced Argentine aggression and gave active support to Britain. Argentines, suffering a humiliating defeat, denounced the United States as only a fair weather friend for the cause of Pan-Americanism. The incident revealed the unsubstantial and flimsy nature of nationalism writ large. Here, as elsewhere, the attempt to combine nationalisms was shattered on the rock of sovereignty.

The Monroe Doctrine

In his Farewell Address in 1796, George Washington stated that the security of the United States rested in the Western Hemisphere. In 1811, when there were fears that Spanish Florida might be transferred to England, Congress passed a "No Transfer" resolution supporting Washington's view. In 1820 Henry Clay proposed the early principles of Pan-Americanism. In 1823 President James Monroe announced a doctrine opposing European intervention to control the destiny of Latin American countries which had gained their independence.

The Monroe Doctrine presented four major points: (1) the American continent no longer was to be considered as open for future colonization by European powers; (2) the American political system was essentially different from that of Europe; (3) the United States considered it dangerous to its peace and safety if any attempts were made by European powers to extend their system to any part of the Western Hemisphere; and (4) the United States would not interfere with existing colonies or dependencies of European powers in the New World nor would she interfere in the internal affairs of European nations.[4]

In effect, the Monroe Doctrine was a unilateral declaration coming from Washington without approval of concerned Latin-American states. It represented a blend of United States self-interest, commercial design, and neighborly altruism. Tinged with idealism, it saw the New World as a haven of liberty and democracy, in contrast to the tyrannical monarchies of decadent Europe.

The British uneasily professed support for the Monroe Doctrine. They gave moral and naval aid to South American countries that broke away from the Spanish Empire. Foreign Minister George Canning held that he had called the New World into existence to redress the balance of the Old World. The United States and Britain, he proposed, should issue a joint statement opposing other European powers from interfering in South America. President James Monroe, however, on the advice of Secretary of State John Quincy Adams, decided on a unilateral statement aimed at Britain as well as other European states. Britain, in fact, was the only European power which, with its command of the seas, could threaten the independence of South American states. In the awkward negotiations, the British actually were outmaneuvered diplomatically by the United States.

Throughout the 19th century, the United States regarded the Monroe Doctrine as a unilateral proclamation, and paid little attention to Latin-American requests for clarification or explanation.[5] The attitude was that only the United States could consider its own need for security. The Olney Corollary of 1895 declared that no European power would be allowed to take any action in the Western Hemisphere without consulting the United States. One outcome of this policy was the Spanish-American War of 1898. In 1904, when Britain, Germany, and Italy blockaded Venezuela to force it to meet its debts, President Theodore Roosevelt replied with the Roosevelt Corollary, which will be discussed later.

At first, Latin Americans welcomed the Monroe Doctrine, even though it seemed to establish a kind of United States hegemony. Later, however, it was denounced increasingly as an arm of United States imperialism. Latin Americans remained unimpressed, even though they were spared the kind of spoliation occurring in both Africa and Asia. Criticism of the Monroe Doctrine and United States policy mounted steadily in the 19th and 20th centuries. Latin Americans resented what they regarded as intrusion in their affairs. Despite Washington's cautious diplomacy, they resented preachings from the North, and preferred their own variegated patterns of political change. Economically, they saw evil effects in "dollar diplomacy." Culturally, they revealed a strong anti-Yankee sentiment. Receptive to European forms, they preferred the mystique of a spiritual affinity with the Old World, at least in cultural affairs. They were reluctant to yield their national individualism to what they saw as North American control. Pan-Americanism modeled on the Monroe Doctrine was not to their liking.

Origins

Angered by Spanish colonial rule and inflamed by the ideology of the Enlightenment as well as by the American and French Revolutions, South Americans decided to cut themselves free from Spain. Taking advantage of Napoleonic domination of Spain, they launched rebellions. In the years after 1815, the movement, gathering momentum, spread throughout the continent. While rejecting Spain, the newly liberated peoples of South America retained a Spanish cultural heritage.

The outstanding figure in this drive for independence was Simón Bolívar (1783-1830), whose name is always invoked as the father of Pan-Americanism.[6] He is given credit for the basic conception of New World separateness and the specific ideas that developed from it, including, especially, the Organization of American States. Latin-American historians see this as far-fetched, that Bolívar really desired only a confederation of Spanish-American states, which, with British support, would resist the encroachments of the United States and Brazil. Historian John Edwin Fagg notes that Bolívar's own statements and actions were prolific but inconsistent. "His fertile brain and eloquent pen were constantly pouring out ideas. Honest scholars can truly differ as to his real and ultimate thoughts. Perhaps he did not know himself."[7]

In the view of Latin American scholars, Bolívar's views wavered between idealistic visions of a world order and more realistic local nationalisms, but in the long run what he hoped for was a confederacy of Spanish-American states. His idea of New World separateness appeared as early as September 6, 1815, when his "Jamaica letter" was composed in exile at a time when strong Spanish forces were arriving to stifle the independence movement. In this letter, Bolívar presented an eloquent case for South American freedom. His people, he said, were opposed to Old World absolutism, and they would defend themselves against Spanish tyranny. Keeping the issue alive during his military campaigns, he succeeded in winning much support. Although he welcomed the Monroe Doctrine, he remained suspicious of United States' motives.

Bolívar began to call for united action for security. Under his auspices, invitations were sent out for the first Pan-American Congress to meet in Panama. Delegations arrived from Peru, Mexico, Colombia (then consisting of the present republics of Colombia, Venezuela, Panama, and Ecuador), and Central America (what are now Guatemala, El Salvador, Honduras, Nicaragua, and Costa Rica). Bolivia and Chile accepted invitations, but sent no delegates. Brazil, Argentina, and Paraguay declined. Britain and the Netherlands sent observers. France was not invited.

Bolívar was opposed to inviting the United States, because he felt that it would dominate the conference. Nevertheless, President Francisco de Paula Santander of Colombia issued the invitation. Henry Clay, already a strong champion of Pan-Americanism, worked zealously, despite strong opposition, for congressional approval. It was agreed finally to send two delegates with careful instructions. One died on the way to Panama, the other arrived too late for the meeting.

The "First Congress of the American States" met in Panama from June 22 to July 25, 1826.[8] One delegate after another rose to make enthusiastic speeches about the necessity for cooperation among the former Spanish colonies, and the need for a common citizenship. All the Americas must be defended against conquest and colonization by European powers. The delegates proposed a treaty of Perpetual Union. They called for a future general assembly and regular meetings to arbitrate differences, especially boundary and citizenship problems. They would meet at Mexico City because of unsatisfactory health conditions in Panama. They called for a multinational force of 60,000 men, as well as, unified naval command to keep Spain out of the Americas.

Grandiloquent speeches were one thing, but mass support was another. In fact, little interest had been aroused in Latin America for Pan-Spanish Americanism. The goverments concerned showed little enthusiasm for the proposed treaties of alliance and mutual assistance. Most were more motivated by defense of their national interests than by the prospect of confederation. Even Bolívar, losing interest, became skeptical about the possibility of Pan-American union.

Another conference was called at Lima, Peru, from 1847 to 1848, at a time when the United States was at war with Mexico. Five Pacific nations of South America drew up a Treaty of American Confederation, calling for common action against aggression. In 1856, delegates of Peru, Chile, and Ecuador met at Santiago to consider the British-American proposal for a canal across Panama. The conferees signed a treaty calling for a "union of the great American family," from which the United States was pointedly excluded. Other South American states declined to sign the treaty. In November of the same year, delegates of several South American states, meeting in Washington, signed a treaty of alliance.

The idea of Pan-American unity was affected strongly by the beginning in 1861 of the American Civil War. There were also bitter conflicts in South America. From 1864 to 1870, Paraguay was at war with Uruguay, Argentina, and Brazil. Spain took advantage of the situation by seizing islands off Peru. In this precarious situation, another conference was called at Lima (1864-1865), which drew up a Treaty of Union and Defensive Alliance. When the Civil War in the United States ended, Spain withdrew from South America.

Two conferences followed, one at Lima at 1877 and another at Montevideo in 1886-1889. Hoping to promote Pan-Spanish Americanism, the delegates at these meetings signed agreements to simplify the principles of public and private law, and to regulate practices in trade marks, property rights, and patents. The United States declined to participate.

Results of all these conferences were unimpressive. Most Latin-American states were concerned primarily by the desire to maintain their own national existence, hold their borders against grasping neighbors, thwart any attempts at recolonization by Spain, and counter United States influence. Continental solidarity of former Spanish-controlled peoples was a fine idea for theorists, it was said, but national sovereignty was more important than the urge for continental unity. Jealously independent national states in South America were not attracted by uncharted waters.

United States' Initiative

Little had been accomplished under Hispanic-American auspices for the implementation of Pan-American ideals. Representation at Hispanic-American conferences had been sporadic. There was some limited accord on such aspects of international law as rights of neutrals, status of aliens, and economic and social relationships, but otherwise these gatherings showed little concrete results.

New leadership for Pan-Americanism was provided toward the end of the

19th century by the United States, which was taking an increasingly important role in world politics. While European nations were engaged in a scramble for territory or concessions in Africa and Asia, the United States, forging to the lead in the Second Industrial Revolution, began to turn its attention southward. There was no need for additional land, but the lure of rich markets and economic advantage was most attractive.

Initiative was provided by Secretary of State James G. Blaine. No friend of Britain, he suspected her of having improper designs in South America despite the Monroe Doctrine. He was also concerned by the possibility that France might obtain a strategic foothold in the New World if the projected Ferdinand de Lesseps canal across Panama were completed. In Blaine's estimation, the time was ripe for assuming leadership of South American affairs.

As early as 1881, Blaine called for a hemispheric conference under United States sponsorship. In August 1882, his successor, Frederick T. Frelinghuysen, concerned that European powers might object, called off the proposed meeting. Meanwhile, Blaine, who had run unsuccessfully for the presidency, persisted in his support for a conference. By this time, use of the term "Pan-Americanism" had gained some public support, partly because it was suggestive of the then popular Pan-German and Pan-Slavic movements.

Eventually, in May 1888, Congress authorized the convening of a Pan-American Congress to be held in October 1889 in Washington. The meeting was financed by the United States. Canada, as a part of the British Empire, was not invited. It was agreed that the conference would be devoted primarily to the promotion of commerce and preservation of peace, and that political matters would be avoided. It was proposed that attention be given to such items as uniform regulations for weights and measures, patents, copyrights, trademarks, and the inauguration of steamship lines between North and South America.

When they arrived in the United States, delegates were entertained lavishly with all-paid excursions to see the natural wonders of the country, such as Niagara Falls and the Grand Canyon, but also to observe the increasing industrial might of the United States. Some seventy sessions were held until April 19, 1890. The delegates agreed only on a few issues, such as a common metric system, port dues, an inter-American bank, and an international monetary fund. They approved new shipping lines as well as a future Pan-American railway. Proposal for a customs union was dropped. Argentine representatives, who obstructed the meeting from its beginning, denounced it as a scheme by Washington to corner Latin-American raw materials in competition with more lucrative European offers.

Before it adjourned, the Washington conference created the International Union of American Republics, which was supposed to gather and distribute commercial information to all member states. This was far from Blaine's original intention of replacing European economic advantages in favor of the United

States. None of the agreements negotiated in Washington was ratified by the required number of states.

The first conference under United States auspices was both praised and condemned. The New York *Tribune* saw it accomplishing most important indirect results: "The ground has been leveled, the way has been opened for securing united action upon the part of the eighteen commonwealths which will promote the enlightened interests of each and the common welfare of all, and it now remains for the United States to take the initiative and complete a great work of high civilization. By conciliatory diplomacy, by the opportune negotiation of treaties, by energetic and intelligent action and by perseverence and patience and tact, the State Department can accomplish great and memorable results for American civilization."[9] Other newspapers and journals expressed similar views. At long last, it was said, the Monroe Doctrine was passing by process of diplomatic evolution into a stage of higher development. Blaine and his followers were encouraged by what seemed to them to be an outstanding success.

The claim for success was not unanimous, certainly not in Latin America. José Martí, Cuban patriot, denounced it as "a worthless meeting, or a presidential campaign banner, or a pretext for a subsidy hunt."[10] He saw the independent states of Latin America as being admitted on their knees to a new master. There was a danger that Central America would be divided in half by the Panama Canal, "the Canal blade slicing through its heart." The United States was a juggernaut, an imperialistic monster, a dreadful foreigner, which was fixing its eyes upon the entire American family of nations. This attitude, popular in Latin America, did not help promote the idea of strong Pan-Americanism.

Pan-American Conferences, 1901–1919

Despite the meager results of the first conference in Washington in 1889, a permanent organization was formed. A series of ten conferences followed. Until the ninth gathering, they were known officially as Inter-American Conferences. At Bogotá in 1948, the name was changed to the Organization of American States. At successive meetings, representatives of approximately 21 American republics discussed a variety of subjects: codification of international law, financial, industrial, and commercial problems; transportation and communication; conciliation and arbitration; highway journalism; trademarks; the Red Cross and sanitation and health questions; and promotion of cultural relations. There was a notable absence of political discussion: each nation jealously guarded its sovereignty.

In the decade after the first conference at Washington, Pan-American sentiment was dampened by a quarrel between the United States and Chile over damages when sailors from the cruiser *Baltimore* were killed in a bar fight.

There was additional acrimony when Secretary of State Richard Olney in 1895, at the time of the Venezuela boundary dispute with British Guiana, declared that the United States was "practically sovereign" in the Americas and that its fiat was law.[11]

Sentiment was growing in Latin America that the United States regarded its own interests as paramount in the Western Hemisphere at the expense of its southern neighbors. Sanitation agreements were well and good, but Latin Americans began to regard them as subsidiary to trade, investments, and prosperity, to be won with the proposed Panama Canal. Indeed, North American diplomats were concerned with the interests of the United States. They would discuss conciliation and arbitration because they wanted to limit the influence of European powers in American disputes. In their view, inter-American solidarity hinged on maintaining the Monroe Doctrine. Therefore, they sought to take a strong position, if not a domineering role, in the series of Pan-American conferences. Meanwhile, Latin Americans were troubled by the McKinley Tariff Act enacted in 1890, the annexation of Puerto Rico, and the protectorate established over Cuba in 1898.

Washington saw its version of Pan-Americanism as altruistic, while Latin Americans regarded it as North American domination. At the conferences, there remained a residue of Hispanic-American sentiment, which sought guarantees of security against both non-American powers and the United States. Pan-Americanism versus Pan-Hispanic Americanism continued to be an awkward theme at the series of conferences.

In 1899, President William McKinley urged that a second conference be called in Mexico. It was held finally from October 22, 1901, to January 31, 1902, with nineteen nations represented. President Theodore Roosevelt, who had succeeded the assassinated McKinley and who had not yet become the champion of the Big Stick, instructed his delegates to remain inconspicious. The conferees agreed to endorse the American plan for a canal across Panama; recommended the creation of an inter-American bank; approved further work on the planned Pan-American Railway; authorized a Pan-American Health Organization; and passed resolutions on patents and literary rights. There were some differences on matters of arbitration. Delegates dropped the word "International" from the official name of the conference, and instead, took the designation Union of American States.

By this time, Theodore Roosevelt was ready for his Big Stick diplomacy, and the issue revolved around Venezuela. During the rule of dictator Cipriano Castro, Venezuela had plunged into heavy debt to European investors. When Castro became unwilling and unable to meet these obligations, he had to face forcible action by Europeans. Concerned European governments, however, mindful of the Monroe Doctrine, disclaimed any intention of permanent occupation. Roosevelt at first was inclined to agree with them.

When Castro refused to submit foreign financial claims to the Hague

Tribunal, Great Britain, Germany, and Italy imposed a blockade, bombarded Venezuelan ports, and destroyed Venezuelan naval craft. Roosevelt intervened, got Britain and Germany to agree to limited arbitration, and the matter was settled by the Hague Tribunal in 1904.

Meanwhile, trouble arose in the Dominican Republic, when debts payable to an American firm were given a preferred position over other creditors. European investors protested. Again, there was a possibility, as in Venezuela, of armed intervention. Roosevelt, seeking to forestall threats to United States' interests in the Caribbean, proclaimed what later became known as the Roosevelt Corollary to the Monroe Doctrine. With this proclamation, the American President transformed the Monroe Doctrine from one of nonintervention by European powers to one of intervention by the United States: "Chronic wrongdoing, or an impotence which results in a general loosening of the ties of civilized society, may in America as elsewhere, ultimately require intervention by some civilized nation, and in the Western Hemisphere the adherence of the United States to the Monroe Doctrine may force the United States, however reluctantly, in flagrant cases of such wrongdoing or impotence, to the exercise of an international police power."[12] The era of Big Stick diplomacy was at hand.

Aware that his actions were causing anger and dismay in Latin America, Theodore Roosevelt was anxious that the next conference avoid political questions altogether. The Third Pan-American Conference was held at Rio de Janeiro from July 23-August 26, 1906. Roosevelt favored Brazil as a meeting place because he regarded the United States and Brazil as natural allies in confrontation with Spanish-speaking Latin American peoples. Secretary of State Elihu Root, who was to play a leading role in the Pan-American movement, managed to counteract much of the criticism that was being leveled at Washington. He was most careful in his address at the meeting to soothe Latin-American sensitiveness: "We wish for no victories but those of peace; for no territory except our own; for no sovereignty except the sovereignty over ourselves. . . . We wish to increase our prosperity, to expand our trade, to grow in wealth, in wisdom, and in spirit, but our conception of the true way to accomplish this is not to pull down others and profit by their ruin, but to help all friends in a common prosperity and common growth, that we may all become greater and stronger together."[13]

Somewhat mollified by Root's diplomatic phraseology, the delegates called for a new codification of inter-American law, discussed matters of arbitration, and welcomed Panama to the inter-American family. It seemed that for a time at least there was a strengthening of inter-American solidarity.

The Fourth Pan-American Conference met in Buenos Aires from July 12 to August 30, 1910. This meeting also was lacking in controversy. The American delegation was instructed to be most cordial and unobtrusive, and to do what it could to promote solidarity between North and South America. In an atmosphere of good will, the conferees proposed an exchange of professors and students. At this meeting, the name of the Bureau of American Republics was changed to Pan-American Union. One announcement made at the conference was greeted with enthusiasm: Andrew Carnegie had made a gift of $750,000 to complete the Pan-American building, one of the most beautiful edifices in Washington. The Fifth Conference was scheduled to meet in 1914, but was postponed due to increasing world conflict.

Meanwhile, Pan-Hispanists, already angered by Roosevelt's Big Stick diplomacy, became even more resentful of what they called "dollar diplomacy," the furtherance of U.S. business interests, especially in the Caribbean. They reacted angrily against the intervention in Nicaragua of U.S. Marines, who were sent there in 1911, and who remained there until 1933. They also denounced United States pressure in Haiti, the Dominican Republic, Honduras, and Puerto Rico. They were partially mollified when President Woodrow Wilson took office in 1913 because in his campaign for election he had criticized the practice of "dollar diplomacy." They were additionally appeased after the outbreak of World War I, when Wilson proposed a Pan-American security system with a mutual guarantee of territorial integrity. Pan-Hispanists were pleased with the idea that the Monroe Doctrine should be regarded as a multilateral agreement instead of a symbol of U.S. paternalism.

Despite these favorable developments, Latin-American faith in Wilson's idealism began to plunge dramatically. The American President seemed to be undergoing a change of heart, as he became the most interventionist of American executives. In April 1914 he ordered U.S. naval forces to bombard and occupy Vera Cruz, the Mexican seaport. In December 1915, fearing that Germany had designs in the area, he sent troops to occupy Haiti, and set up a puppet regime there. In 1916 he dispatched a miitary force under General John J. Pershing into Mexico. The Americans, failing to find Pancho Villa and his makeshift army, eventually withdrew. Outraged Latin Americans by this time had more than serious doubts about Wilson's friendly regional system.

During the early years of World War I, Latin Americans were angered when the British Royal Navy cut off their trade, a move which allowed American commerce and investments to soar to great heights. When the United States entered the war in 1917, eight Latin-American countries followed suit; five broke off relations with the Central Powers. But few Latin-American countries, with the exception of Brazil, where Pan-American sentiment was strongest, felt inclined to help the United States. The result was that Latin-Americans were excluded from decision-making at the Versailles Peace Conference after the war.

The Fifth Pan-American Conference met at Santiago from March 25 to May 3, 1923. There was a tone of skepticism in the atmosphere. The meeting, in the words of Secretary of State Charles Evans Hughes, was "an assembly of mice presided over by a cat." This time an open clash occurred between Pan-Hispanists and Pan-Americans. The United States vetoed a proposal to create an all-American League of Nations with a "multilateral Monroe Doctrine."

Delegates vied with one another in denouncing the United States. Argentinians caustically noted that Pan-Americanism did not exist outside of a grandiose building in Washington. There was tension not only between Latin Americans and North Americans, but also between the previously friendly ABC-powers—Argentina, Brazil, and Chile. The entire Pan-American movement descended to a new low.

The Sixth Pan-American Conference was held at Havana from January 10 to February 20, 1928. Aware of Latin-American resentment, the United States sent President Calvin Coolidge with the delegation on a battleship. Included among the party were Colonel Charles Lindbergh, the national hero, and Will Rogers, the popular humorist. The Americans hoped to smooth relations with their southern neighbors, but their efforts were frustrated. At the closing session, Latin-Americans, nursing anger compounded over the years, began to denounce the United States in bitter speeches. There had been an underground of resentment in previous conferences, but nothing to compare with these open expressions of disapproval. Crowds in the galleries, roaring approval of critical remarks, hissed pro-American speakers.

The American press reacted acidly against what it regarded as unfair attacks. The *Wall Street Journal* remarked: "Here in the United States as well as throughout the Latin republics there has been a campaign as dishonest as it is determined, to picture this country as the aggressor of the other republics. No proof has been adduced; the parties, instead, have relied upon the constant repetition of the falsehood."[14] "Our Pan-American policy," stated the New York *Herald Tribune*, "is subject to attack, either at Havana or in this country, only by those who innocently or malevolently misunderstand it."[15] *La Nacion,* of Buenos Aires, replied that "the high-sounding declarations heard in Havana do not serve to erase the inexcusable acts committed in Central America which still weigh overwhelmingly and paralyze real Pan-Americanism."[16]

A new approach to the entire problem of Pan-Americanism came with the accession of President Franklin D. Roosevelt in 1933. By that time, the United States was in the process of liquidating most of the troop occupations that had infuriated Latin Americans, and new attempts were made to remove old grievances. In his inaugural address on March 4, 1933, Roosevelt proposed a Good Neighbor policy, a multilateral concern for security which took into account the feelings of Latin Americans:

In the field of world politics, I would dedicate this nation to the policy of the Good Neighbor—the neighbor who resolutely respects himself and because he does so, respects the rights of others—the neighbor who respects the sanctity of his agreements in and with a world of neighbors.[17]

Roosevelt underscored his Good Neighbor policy in a notable address to the Pan-American Union on April 12, 1933, "Pan-American Day." There was a unity of thought, he said, among the people of this hemisphere, a manifestation of the common ideal of mutual helpfulness, sympathetic understanding, and spiritual solidarity. The citizens of the twenty-one republics had common ties—historically, economically, and socially, which bound them to one another. The well-being of one nation depended in large measure upon the well-being of its neighbors. "The essential qualities of a true Pan-Americanism must be the same as those which constitute a good neighbor, namely, mutual understanding, and through such understanding, a sympathetic appreciation of the other's point of view. It is only in this manner that we can hope to build up a system of which confidence, friendship and good-will are the cornerstones."[18]

Roosevelt defended the Monroe Doctrine as directed at the maintenance of independence by the peoples of the continent. Hand-in-hand with the Pan-American doctrine of continental defense, the peoples of the American Republics understood more clearly with the passing years, that the independence of each Republic must recognize the independence of every other Republic. "Your Americanism and mine must be a structure built of confidence, cemented by a sympathy which recognizes only equality and fraternity. It finds its source and being in the hearts of men and dwells in the temple of the intellect."[19]

These were fine words spoken by a consummate politician. Roosevelt was thinking in global terms. The international situation was aggravated by Japanese aggression in China, Mussolini's designs in Africa, and the growing possibility of Hitlerite aggression on the European scene. It was necessary, Roosevelt said, to put the house of the Western Hemisphere in order to meet possible dangerous days ahead. As a prerequisite, due attention must be given to the grievances of Latin Americans, and especially to halting American intervention in the Caribbean area.

Roosevelt's decision meant an abrupt about-face in his own attitude. As Assistant Secretary of the Navy, he had supported the landing in Vera Cruz and the occupation of Haiti and the Dominican Republic. In his revised view, that kind of intervention had to stop. He was sustained in this goal by his new Secretary of State, Cordell Hull, who had long opposed what he regarded as an overbearing United States' attitude in hemispheric relations.

The new Good Neighbor policy nearly foundered in its early days when a chaotic situation arose in Cuba. Under-Secretary of State Sumner Welles went to Cuba in the summer of 1933 to help resolve a precarious situation. There was bitter popular opposition to dictator Gerardo Machado. Welles attempted to intervene by sponsoring a replacement, but his efforts came to naught when Sergeant Fulgencio Batista, supported by leftist elements and students, took control with an anti-American professor, Romón Grau San Martin, as Provisional President. Welles urged Roosevelt to intervene militarily, but the President declined. Roosevelt had no desire for an intensification of Yankeephobe sentiment.

The Seventh Pan-American Conference took place from December 3 to 26, 1933, in Montevideo in an atmosphere of what was regarded as hemispheric danger. Japan had delivered a serious blow to the United Nations, and Hitler represented an immediate danger. Both the Geneva Disarmament Conference and the London Economic Conference had failed. Hull had some good arguments for Western Hemisphere solidarity in the face of ever-increasing dangers.

Again, there were the familiar pleas for unity, plus the traditional truculence of the Argentines, who were anxious to establish themselves as leaders in the Western Hemisphere. The American delegation, taking little part in the discussions, declined major committee assignments, and took care not to give an impression of leadership or dictation. Hull astonished the Latin-American delegates by quietly accepting a proposal that Washington had always resisted—a ban on intervention in the internal or external affairs of all the American states. This marked an important turning point in relations among states of the Western Hemisphere.

The United States followed with action: a treaty with Cuba ended the Platt Amendment and the protectorate; Panama's status as protectorate was abrogated; and U. S. Marines were withdrawn from Haiti and Nicaragua. The result was a decided stimulus to the idea of Pan-Americanism. The Good Neighbor policy seemed to be working. Hull negotiated tariff reciprocity treaties with Latin-American states. U.S. Government funds began to flow to South America. Academic exchanges burgeoned and travel increased in an atmosphere of good will.

The Eighth Pan-American Conference, now called the Inter-American Conference, met at Lima from December 9 to December 27, 1938. Once again, Hull sought an expression of hemispheric solidarity, but the situation was ominous. There were many German, Italian, and Japanese businessmen in Lima, all of whom had little intention of subscribing to democratic resolutions. They decked the city in their national flags. The Argentines, again disruptive, boasted of their close economic and cultural relations with Europe. The meeting was short and ineffective. Hull managed to obtain a vague resolution of solidarity, a modest victory under the circumstances.

Pan-Americanism in World War II

Inter-American unity, with some breaches, was maintained during World War II. Despite the tradition of Latin-American hostility to the United States, as well as fear of and resentment for Yankee diplomacy, inter-American collaboration bore fruit during the war. Throughout Central and South America, with some exceptions, there was widespread opposition to the ideology and actions of Hitler and Nazism. In the mid-1930s, there was much indignation against Nazi efforts to strengthen the Brown Network among Germans in Brazil and especially in Argentina. Axis agents were active in South America before and after 1939.

Within seven months after Pearl Harbor, twelve Latin-American states declared war on the Axis. All the rest, with the exception of Argentina and Chile, severed relations with Germany and Italy. In August 1942, Brazil, after six of her ships were sunk by German U-boats, declared war; later she sent an expeditionary force of 25,000 men to join the Allies in the difficult Italian campaign. With her strategic location, Brazil became enormously valuable to the United States in its war effort, and gave the United States temporary use of naval and air bases, important for American operations in the Pacific. Peru provided similar bases, and Mexico provided an air squadron for combat.

Argentina, with a tradition of obstruction at Pan-American conferences, became strongly anti-British and turned to the Fascist powers. Other Latin American and South American countries opposed Axis aggression. Fear of Nazi Germany acted as a stimulant for a temporary sense of Pan-American solidarity.

The Organization of American States

The Ninth Conference of American States was supposed to meet in Bogotá in 1943, but it was postponed because of the war. Eventually, the conference began on March 9, 1948. Its purpose again was to stabilize relations in the Western Hemisphere during the dangerous era of the Cold War.

The Ninth Conference marked the culmination of the Pan-American movement. What had been previously known as the Inter-American System was changed to the Organization of American States (OAS). The word "States" was used in the title to keep the way open for Canada, even though Canadians showed little interest. The United States also hesitated because of Canada's commitment to the British Empire and Commonwealth.

The OAS Charter expressed the results of decades of meetings and negotiations:

Convinced that the historic mission of America is to offer man a land of liberty, and a favorable environment for the development of his personality and the realization of his just aspirations;

Conscious that that mission has already inspired numerous agreements, whose essential value lies in the desire of the American peoples to live together in peace, and, through their mutual understanding and respect for the sovereignty of each one, to provide for the betterment of all, in independence, in equality and under law;

Confident that the true significance of American solidarity and good neighborliness can only mean the consolidation of the continent, within the framework of democratic institutions, of a system of individual liberty and social justice based on respect for the essential rights of man;

Persuaded that their welfare and their contribution to the progress and the civilization of the world will increasingly require intense continental cooperation;

Resolved to persevere in the noble undertaking that humanity has conferred on the United Nations, whose principles and purposes they solemnly reaffirm;

Convinced that juridical organization is a necessary condition for security and peace founded on moral order and on justice. . . .[20]

The headquarters of the Organization of American States was located in Washington, D.C. A permanent Council was composed of a representative, with ambassadorial rank, from each of the 21 republics. The organization was supported by quotas from each member government.

The primary function of the OAS was to implement the various resolutions passed by the preceding international conferences. It would seek ratification of all treaties and conventions signed by member states at each of the preceding congresses. Emphasis was placed on economic, social, and cultural relations, but there was much interest in political affiliations. The term "Continental Solidarity" appeared again and again in the everyday work of the organization. More than a century of effort had been devoted to this ideal, and it was hoped that the OAS would be successful in promoting the sense of international community desired by its proponents.

The OAS leadership was guided by a basic philosophy: in the modern world there are bound to be conflicts, especially territorial, between nations living in close proximity to one another. The so-called Pact of Bogotá, concluded in 1948, was designed especially for the purpose of solving such disputes. All the American republics pledged themselves to settle any differences by using pacific means. On the occasion of any friction or confrontation, any member state could call a meeting of the Ministers of Foreign Affairs to consider the problem and seek to solve it.

The OAS set up technical agencies for special economic, social, and cultural programs. The more prosperous states were expected to assist less advanced countries in matters of living standards, sanitation, illiteracy, or other obstacles to progress. The Pan-American Union, the much-praised white marble building in Washington, became a clearing house for information for all member states. The OAS issued some three dozen special periodicals devoted to such subjects as agriculture, education, housing, natural resources, and child welfare.

On the surface, it seemed that tremendous progress was being made in the movement toward hemispheric harmony. Perhaps much of the urge toward territorial aggression and unrestrained nationalism typical of the 20th century had been overcome. But despite the successes of the elaborate paper organization, many Latin Americans continued to interpret Pan-Americanism as merely a manifestation of the imperialistic ambitions of the United States. They charged that Central and South America had been mortgaged to the United States in a series of intricate loans and capital investments. Their governments, they said, had sold out to Washington. They urged adherence to a rival *Unión Latino-Americana* which would resist a Pan-Americanism dominated from Washington.

Troubled Partnership

There were three opposing pan-movements in the Western Hemisphere, all stimulated from outside sources. France sought to promote Pan-Latinism;

Spain tried to encourage a Pan-Hispanic sentiment; and the United States eventually took the lead in supporting its version of Pan-Americanism.

Of the three pan-movements, Pan-Latinism was much the weakest. It managed to win little support. Pan-Hispanism emerged early in the 19th century. Simón Bolívar, *El Libertador*, hero of the independence movement, was politically anti-Spain,[21] but once freedom was won he lent the weight of his leadership and popularity to a cultural Pan-Hispanism for the New World. Though stronger than its rival Pan-Latinism, Pan-Hispanism never was able to achieve its goal of continental solidarity.

Although United States' interest in hemispheric affairs was indicated as early as 1823 in the Monroe Doctrine, for most of the rest of the century, Washington showed little concern for an inter-American partnership. North Americans were not attracted by the series of conferences held under Hispanic-American leadership from 1826 to 1888-1889. Nor were Latin Americans convinced that the Monroe Doctrine would really protect them from serious European aggression. At a time when Africa and Asia were being despoiled by greedy Europeans, South America was free of this kind of spoliation. Yet, Latin Americans were unwilling to attribute their good fortune to the Monroe Doctrine.

The attitude of the United States began to change toward the end of the 19th century, as it began to forge ahead in the Second Industrial Revolution. Central and South America now began to assume a new importance in the eyes of American financiers, industrialists, and businessmen. Here was a huge continent wide open for sales and investment opportunities. It had been saved from European imperialists. Now was the time for real hemispheric solidarity, for a new kind of Pan-Americanism which would cover the entire Western Hemisphere. From 1889 on, the United States took the lead in the Pan-American movement in a series of conferences devoted to economic, social, and cultural matters of concern to all the American republics.

At first, the United States tried to limit its interests in Central and South America to economic relations. It was a difficult problem inside the maze of international relations. Relations between the American republics in the North and South began to shift like a pendulum back and forth between economic cooperation and political and military intervention.

United States military action, beginning in Venezuela in the 1890s, culminated with the war with Spain in 1898, the annexation of Puerto Rico and a protectorate over Cuba. Latin American intellectuals began to criticize the "colossus of the north." Their anger was increased when Theodore Roosevelt issued his Corollary to the Monroe Doctrine, introduced his Big Stick diplomacy, and intervened in Panama. There was further resentment in 1904, when the United States officially arrogated the word "American" to itself.

Attracted at first by the idealism of Woodrow Wilson and his criticism of "dollar diplomacy," Latin Americans were irritated when he turned out to be the most interventionist of presidents. When Wilson sent his military force into

Mexico (but failed to apprehend Villa and withdrew), both Mexican and much Latin American opinion was outraged. Other blows at Pan-Americanism were struck by a supposedly sympathetic Wilson, such as the occupation of Haiti in 1915 because of defaults, the seizure of the Dominican Republic and establishment of a United States military government there, and the campaign to make Nicaragua a protectorate.[22]

The pendulum began to swing back in 1933 with Franklin D. Roosevelt's Good Neighbor policy. Cordell Hull's famous declaration: "No state has the right to intervene in the internal or external affairs of another" was received with much satisfaction by Latin Americans. The definite United States policy from then on was opposition to armed intervention. But, instead of support, Latin-American sentiment, motivated by a combination of pride, resentment, and national egoism, began to waver. Discontented with their own economic problems, Latin Americans resented more than ever the activities of North American firms, from IBM to Ford to Coca-Cola, in their countries.

Anti-Yankee sentiment was illustrated dramatically in 1958, when Vice President Richard M. Nixon made what was supposed to be a good-will tour in Central America. In Venezuela he was insulted and spat upon by young hotheads. After the incident, José Figueres, former President of Costa Rica, appearing before a Congressional Committee, issued a blunt statement to the American people revealing why Mr. Nixon had been received in so unfriendly a fashion. The highly emotional tone represented the attitude of many Latin Americans:

As a citizen of the Hemisphere, as a man who had dedicated his public life to the cultivation of inter-American understanding, as a student who knows and esteems the United States, and who has never tried to conceal that esteem from anyone, no matter how hostile, I deplore the fact that the people of Latin America, as represented by a handful of over-excited Venezuelans, should have spat at a worthy functionary, who represents the greatest nation of our times. But I must speak frankly, even rudely because I believe that the situation requires it: people cannot spit at a foreign policy, which is what they wanted to do. And when they have run out of other ways of making themselves understood their only remaining recourse is to spit. . . .

Of course, you have made certain investments in the American dictatorships. The aluminum companies extract bauxite almost gratis. Your generals, your admirals, your civil functionaries, and your magnates receive royal treatment there. As your Senate verified yesterday, some concessionaires bribe the reigning dynasties with millions for the privilege of hunting on their grounds. . . .

Meanwhile, our women are raped by gangsters, our men castrated in the torture chambers, and our illustrious professors disappear lugubriously from the halls of Columbia University in New York. When one of your legislators calls this "collaboration to combat communism," 180 million Latin Americans want to spit.

Spitting is a despicable practice, when it is physically performed. But what about moral spitting? When your government invited Pedro Estrada, the Himmler of the Western Hemisphere, to Washington, did you not spit in the face of all democrats of America? . . .

We Latin Americans are tired of pointing out [your] mistakes. . . . We are not asking for handouts except in cases of emergency. We are not people who would spit for money. We have inherited all the defects of the Spanish character, but also some of its virtues. Our poverty does not abate our pride. We have our dignity.

What we want is to be paid a just price for the sweat of our people, the sap of our soil, when we supply some needed product to another country. This would be enough for us to live, and to raise our own capital, and to pursue their own development.[23]

Figueres's remarks are quoted at some length here because they embody the sentiments of millions of Latin Americans, their sense of frustration, aggrieved pride and dignity, and contempt for their Yankee neighbors. Most of all, his strictures reveal why the course of Pan-Americanism under United States sponsorship has been a thorny one, unable to overcome the recurring outbursts of anti-Yankee sentiment.

The United States tried again in 1961, when President John F. Kennedy, in his inaugural address, formally proposed a ten-year Alliance for Progress to promote economic relations and social reform. The President put young idealists of the newly organized Peace Corps to work on a popular level. He also sent advocates of Pan-Americanism south to heal the wounds. On a more practical plane, he ordered foodstuffs under the Food for Peace program. He also encouraged loans to good neighbors. To many Latin Americans, Kennedy became an instant hero.

Some 1,400 representatives of the American Republics met in August 1961 at the Uruguayan seaside resort of Punta del Este to draw up a charter for the Alliance for Progress. The Declaration of Punta del Este, emphasizing the virtues of democracy, called for accelerated economic progress and broadened social justice.[24] The United States promised to contribute $1 billion of public funds for use in Latin America and to promote an equivalent amount for private investment. It was an extraordinary effort to win back the good will and friendship of an entire continent. President Kennedy made triumphant tours in Latin American states.

Disillusionment quickly set in. Throughout Latin America, the sentiment gathered force that the United States was seeking to buy its way in making Latin America immune to communism. Ruling juntas were reluctant to sponsor reforms that might endanger their status. Everywhere, the Left, stiffly anti-American, charged that the Alliance for Progress was in reality a scheme to promote United States imperialism. Democracy had hard going: military coups displaced civilian governments in nine countries during the first four years of the Alliance.[25] In 1962 an attempt was made to improve the Alliance for Progress by creating a new Inter-American Committee for the Alliance of Progress (CIAP). Cooperation moved from a general alliance to bilateral agreements. The assassination of President Kennedy on November 22, 1963, removed much of the impetus from this movement.

By this time, the United States, which had pledged non-interference in Latin American affairs under the Good Neighbor policy of Franklin D. Roosevelt, began to have second thoughts about relinquishing its police power in an increasingly dangerous situation. Americans had gone to war in Korea and Vietnam to block Communist expansion through a circular line of demarcation set up in the Far East. Now a considerably greater danger was appearing closer to home in the Castro dictatorship in Cuba. If the United States could sacrifice the blood of its youth on the battlefields of far-away Asia, it was not likely that it would allow further Communist penetration in the Caribbean and South America. The new situation called for a radical readjustment in the attitude of Washington toward interference in Latin America.

The matter became urgent when on February 16, 1959, former student leader Fidel Castro led his rebel band against the harsh and corrupt Batista dictatorship, and in the resulting political vacuum took power as premier. At first, the American public was lulled into indifference by reports by seemingly able journalists that Castro was merely an "agrarian reformer." By 1960 it became uncomfortably apparent that Castro, far from being a moderate, was beginning to transform Cuba into a Communist state modeled on the Soviet pattern. The bearded dictator nationalized U.S.-owned property without compensation. He turned increasingly toward Moscow for supplies of arms and oil. In 1961, Cuban exiles in the United States, trained and equipped by the U.S. Central Intelligence Agency (CIA), landed an invasion force of 1,400 men at the Bay of Pigs in an abortive attempt to overthrow Castro. When, in 1962, the Soviets installed missiles in Cuba, President Kennedy, in confrontation with Nikita Khrushchev, demanded their removal, with an implied threat of atomic warfare. The Russians, backing down, withdrew their missiles.

In Washington's eyes there was another grave danger which had to be met. After the Bay of Pigs fiasco, a confident Castro began a process of revolutionizing a half-dozen Latin American nations. The Organization of American States in 1962 excluded Cuba from membership, but this had little effect on the Cuban dictator. Six delegations with representatives of two-thirds of the population of Latin America, including Brazil, Argentina, and Mexico, voted against the ban. Castro replied by castigating OAS as a "house of prostitution."

From this point on, the attitude of the United States to intervention in Latin America began to undergo a significant change. Washington began to recast its interests with objectives consistent with the global imperative of containing Soviet power.[26] Its central aim became the reassertion of United States influence in its own backyard. To implement this goal it supported friendly governments, especially in Central America, and took active steps to keep less pliant leftists from power. Through increased economic and military aid, it supported "client" regimes in El Salvador, Honduras, and Costa Rica. Honduras agreed to construct military facilities for United States use, and to allow anti-Sandinista paramilitary forces to operate from its territory.

In 1933 Franklin D. Roosevelt had proclaimed: "The definite policy of the United States from now on is one opposed to armed intervention" [in Latin

America]. Nearly a half century later, faced with the ever-present danger of Communist expansion, Washington had a change of heart. In 1978 the Carter administration authorized the Central Intelligence Agency to support moderate opposition to dictatorships in Central America. In March 1980 the junta in El Salvador was faced with an upsurge in left- and right-wing violence, whereupon Congress froze American aid to Nicaragua, which was backing Salvadoran leftists. A year later, the Reagan administration declared that Washington would not remain passive in the face of Communist subversion. It threatened to "go to the source"—Cuba. The United States sent more military advisers and increased military aid to El Salvador. In December 1981 the Reagan administration announced that it was going to train 1,500 Salvadoran government troops. It also secretly authorized a $20 million CIA plan to create a 500-man paramilitary force based in Honduras to cut off Nicaraguan supplies to Salvadoran leftists.[27] In August 1982, U.S. Air Force C-130s ferried Honduran troops to the Nicaraguan border to protect the anti-Sandinista force from Nicaraguan retaliation.[28]

Washington believed that its intervention was helping to check leftist expansion in Central and South America. But many Central and South Americans saw a completely different picture. In their estimation, this was by no means Latin-American solidarity, but rather a renewal of United States economic and military intervention in the affairs of its southern neighbors. They recognized the rising violence (the death toll passed 30,000 in El Salvador), as well as political polarization and increased tensions in Latin American states, but the old cry was heard again—Washington had no right to interfere in what were local problems. The intervention of the United States in Grenada in late October 1983 to rescue medical students and to prevent construction of a Cuban-Soviet forward base in the Caribbean, was denounced as new American "gunboat diplomacy." But even this "invasion" had little effect in promoting a sense of Pan-Americanism directed against the United States.

Pan-Americanism in Decline

Despite its paper successes, with its plethora of international agencies, Pan-Americanism, like virtually all other pan-movements, revealed weaknesses which it was not able to overcome. Seeking to extend the boundaries of nationalism in favor of nationalism writ large, it, too, foundered on the rock of national sovereignty. Like Pan-Europa, it had limited success along the lines of economic union, but the moment it entered into the political sphere it lost its *raison d'être*.

Unlike other pan-movements, which based their appeal on language, religion, or supposed ethnicity, Pan-Americanism included peoples of diverse speech and faiths. There are enormous differences between Latin Americans and North Americans, with different ideas about individuals and society, government, justice, law, and morality. Such differences led to the emergence of societies which were more unlike than like one another. In the long run, the conflict between Pan-Hispanism (based on *Hispanidad*, the pride of being Spanish) and Pan-Americanism has never, and probably never will, be resolved. For Pan-Hispanists, it was essential that their own security be protected against both Europe and the United States. They complained that the Monroe Doctrine never was defined adequately, and that it was questionable whether it gave Latin Americans the security they wanted. The United States, on the other hand, saw the Monroe Doctrine as eminently successful in warding off the greedy hands of European imperialists. It regarded Pan-Americanism as a friendly neighbor policy valuable for both North and South America.

The prospects of a viable Pan-Americanism under United States leadership grow ever dimmer, despite the optimism of its champions. The United States is a superpower which is feared, envied, and unloved in Latin America, and the anti-Yankee sentiment in Latin America is much more than a normal reaction to superior wealth and power. Latin American politicians have learned through experience that to be successful they must become loud critics of the United States, knowing that their publics resent what is regarded as overexpansion of United States interests in Latin America. Efforts of Americans to ingratiate themselves are regarded as a sign of weakness. Moreover, Latin Americans regard North American liberalism and democratic ideals as unsuited to Latin American traditions and their way of life.

Pan-Americanism has not thrived in this atmosphere. Lawrence E. Harrison sees the movement not only in decline, but on the verge of extinction:

Pan-Americanism, at least under U.S. leadership as it was understood by Presidents from Franklin D. Roosevelt to Lyndon Johnson, is in its death throes, if, indeed, it ever lived. The ties that bind together the nations of North and South America became fewer and weaker; the policies and actions of the countries south of the Rio Grande became increasingly independent of U.S. influence. The vision of two great continents joined by common liberal values and aspirations as well as by geography, marching hand-in-hand into a better future for all is distorted almost beyond recognition by the events of the last several years. Many idealists and pragmatists alike among U.S. observers are alarmed, feel frustrated, and are searching for explanations.[29]

CHAPTER 13

*RETROSPECT AND PROSPECT_*

The vision of Europa—a community to replace the rivalries of a
bloody millenium—has faded. . . . The expectation of political
unity, of common economic policies to deal with inflation and
unemployment, of a real parliament and a common currency—all
that has receded from the realm of the concrete.
     —Flora Lewis, in *The New York Times*, March 23, 1975

Realm of the Evanescent Dream

What conclusions can be drawn about the meaning, characteristics, and
development of the macro-nationalisms, the pan-movements, in the
contemporary world? It is axiomatic that nothing in history is permanent.
Fifty-century B.C. pre-Socratic cosmologist Heraclitus of Ephesus was correct
in his belief that, while the world is eternal, it is in a constant state of change.
"Everything flows, nothing abides." It should follow that nationalism and
national consciousness in the modern nation-state have served their historical
sentence, and are now on the way out in favor of nationalism writ large. That
is the judgment of champions of the pan-movements, who see historical
change as favorable to their cause.

Unfortunately, nationalism refuses to conform to this exact pattern as the
20th century approaches its close. It persists and flourishes at the center level,
while the peripheries—the larger macro-nationalisms and the smaller mini-
nationalisms—are either in decline or enjoy strictly limited success. The nation-
state and the consciousness of nationalism stay in focus as historical
phenomena, while efforts to combine nationalisms in a larger state, or to break
them down into smaller regional nationalisms, remain blurred and indistinct.

One needs only observe current trends. The Marxist-Leninist-Stalinist goal
for world society was an internationalism based on a shifting of class controls.
World proletarians had nothing to lose but their chains. Evil capitalism with its
bourgeois nationalism would be overthrown, and there would emerge a global
egalitarian society to succeed the Age of Nationalism. This was the seemingly
realistic goal. But it has been relegated to the realm of vague hopes. After more
than 65 years of the Soviet experiment, the masters of the Kremlin have settled
for maintenance of as rigid a nationalism as there is on earth. The Red Star of

Moscow flies over *national* tanks, *national* submarines, *national* Olympic athletes. The Russian citizen in his monolithic state is trained to recognize Mother Russia, not Mother World.

The persistent preference for nation above class continues to exist everywhere throughout the Communist world. It came early when Yugoslavia's Tito, successfully defying the Kremlin, set up his own brand of national communism. It appeared on a major scale when the "People's Republic of China" turned up its collective nose and refused to bow to the kind of "workers' internationalism" dictated from Moscow. It came to the surface in recent years in satellite Poland, where Communist mismanagement resulted in the appearance of the nationalist Solidarity movement with a slogan: "A hungry nation can eat its government."

The fact remains that macro-nationalisms retreat before the realities of persistent nationalism. The experience of Germany is a good example. The impact of two World Wars finally convinced the German people that Pan-Germanism was an unrealistic delusion, not worth its weight in feathers. The mighty effort to promote Pan-Germanism led only to the tragic loss of millions of lives and a country nearly destroyed as if by giant earthquakes. The sense of German macro-nationalism vanished when it became obvious at long last that a tragic mistake had been made. Neither Germany nor the world was ready for an expanded Pan-Germanism. The German people decided that there was more profit to be made in a stabilized mark and the distribution of millions of *Volkswagens* throughout the world. The goose-step had brought only ruin, degradation, and shame. Only a few wild-eyed dreamers still accept the Pan-Germanic line. Like the Japanese, the Germans have found more profitable outlets for their creative energy.

Pan-Slavism, too, foundered on the rock of nationalism. Soviet policy is no longer geared to the leadership of a Pan-Slavic movement designed to enfold all the Slavs of the world in the embrace of the Russian bear. There are now other worlds to conquer. The Kremlin is enticed by the prospect of stepping into the vacuum left by the decline of Western colonialism. Instead of combining all Slavs in its new empire, it looks to North Koreans, Vietnamese, Cubans, Afghans, and varied African peoples as possible subjects in a mighty new empire. While condemning remnants of Western colonialism in Africa and Asia, the men of the Kremlin go about the business of creating a new Soviet imperialism of their own, while at the same time declaring that they are only in the altruistic business of supporting local "liberation" movements. The old Pan-Slavism with its limited goals has vanished, to be succeeded by a realistic grab-for-empire. The focus is both inward and outward—to strengthen the national state, expand its influence, and forget the Pan-Slavic panegyrics of Pushkin and Dostoevsky.

Similarly, the religious impulse of Pan-Islāmism and the political drive of Pan-Arabism take second place to the existing nationalisms. Islāmic Egypt and Islāmic Libya face one another in snarling contempt. Islāmic Iraq goes to war

RETROSPECT AND PROSPECT 249

with Islāmic Iran. Ousting their Shāh and his program of modernization, Iranians turned to an aged, fanatical Ayatollah, who saw his country's salvation in a return to medieval orthodoxy. Muslims throughout the Islāmic world made their daily obeisance to Muḥammad, and many took the pilgrimage to Mecca, but common religious ideals could not overcome the call of nationalism.

The trend is also continental and hemispheric. Africans dutifully attend Pan-African Congresses and speak the language of continental unity, only to return home to face raging national and tribal conflicts in their artificially structured nation-states. Pan-Asianism in the Far East remains hazy and unfulfilled. Here, too, the larger nationalism is rejected in favor of established nationalisms. Pan-Americanism, conceived of as hemispheric unity, has not progressed far: Latin Americans, despite the show of unity, still look with a mixture of envy and contempt upon the rich giant country to the north. The sentiment here is much the same as elsewhere: xenophobia is infinitely preferable to dangerous subservience to a powerful neighbor.

The pattern is not only local, continental, and hemispheric, but global. Everywhere countries with set borders look increasingly inward, despite the growing uniformity in many aspects of current life. American rock-and-roll music has conquered the youth of the world from Tokyo to Moscow, the German *Volkswagen* is popular from Brisbane to Rio de Janeiro, Japanese transistors are preferred from Manila to London, but these evidences of common preferences do not necessarily make for common political ideals.

As the twentieth century moves into its final decades, every country continues to focus on its own special problems. The troubles are much the same everywhere—inflation, unemployment, financial ills, chaos in production and distribution—but such difficulties are seldom attached to the broader question of regional, continental, or hemispheric solidarity. In administrative circles, longing eyes are cast at the International Monetary Fund for help in warding off national bankruptcy, but even here, money is accepted with the understanding that national sovereignty will not be affected in any way. As a result of this accented inward focus, the differences between countries continue to be stressed at the expense of international unity.

The vision of extended pan-movements, once so attractive, has faded. Statesmen everywhere preach the virtues of internationalism, peoples everywhere continue to feed and clothe themselves with products imported from all over the world, and champions of national solidarity optimistically promote pan-congresses. But statesmen have no intention of implementing what they preach. People blame anyone but themselves for the failure of international cooperation. Champions of the pan-movements continue to operate in an unrealistic dream world.

Meanwhile, international conferences continue in an atmosphere of cordiality, with long discussions on fishing rights, energy, food, raw materials, medical problems, populations, poverty, *et al.* But little effort is made on the critical matter of international action. There seems little prospect of macro-nationalistic unity, unless human beings are willing to drop flag-and-anthem in favor of a workable global citizenship.

A Matter of Sovereignty

Central to the problem is a key factor: national sovereignty remains the hub of international relations in contemporary society. In the ebb-and-flow of the historical process, the nation-state remains paramount as the institution retaining the loyalty of peoples. The appeal of national sovereignty appears to be stronger than either emotional propaganda for the super-state or the bombs of terrorists calling for the rights of mini-nationalisms.

The infrastructure of modern nation-states became solidified through wars and revolution. Once boundaries became set and relatively secure, there were critics who looked beyond the peripheries of what had already been established. Their ideology was simple—like belongs to like. They presented race, language, common historical traditions, and geography as reasons for extending solidarity beyond existing frontiers. These advocates of the larger nationalism saw in the pan-movements a natural development for peoples of similar backgrounds.

It was no simple matter, however, to achieve the goal of nationalism writ large. There were far too many domestic quarrels in the family of nations which were supposed to live in harmony. It was not easy to convince a people inured to flag-and-anthem to take on a higher loyalty, even if it meant solidarity with those of common religion, culture, or historical tradition.

The idea of national sovereignty has tremendous appeal precisely because it is geared to one of the most important of human instincts—the need for security. The infant finds security in its mother, the child in the family, the citizen in the state. In a dangerous world the individual seeks comfort by adhering to the code of like-needs-like. This is the essence of national sovereignty. Where it exists, it is regarded as a precious heritage never to be relinquished. Any attempt to dilute it in favor of a larger sovereignty is regarded with suspicion, even as treason. Patriotism is hinged to the national entity—the country comes first, love it or leave it.

Where national sovereignty does not exist among a people of similar background, history, and traditions, there generally is a hard core of self-appointed patriots who would cast out the foreign devil and satisfy their own craving for national identity. Here one sees the essence of unsatisfied mini-nationalisms.

An example is the Caribbean island of Puerto Rico, with its 3.4 million people, currently having the status of a U.S. Commonwealth. Most Puerto Ricans are satisfied with their ties to the United States, but a small group of dedicated fanatics carry on a campaign of terror and sabotage to win independence. The miniscule minority has won attention far beyond its actual strength. Puerto Rican nationalists hold that they are kept in bondage by the United States, that the Hispanic roots of their culture have been violated, that North American values have supplanted their own, and that their economic situation has worsened under United States control. Most of all, they are angered by what they see as an unwanted process of Anglo-Saxon acculturation.

Puerto Rican nationalists punctuated their demands with acts of violence. They began a campaign of terror to end political ties with Washington and economic control by "foreigners." A series of nuisance raids soon turned into violent confrontation. On November 1, 1950, while President Harry Truman was in the Blair House across the street during the remodeling of the White House, Puerto Rican nationalists opened fire on guards stationed there. On March 1, 1954, other nationalists in the visitors' gallery of the U.S. House of Representatives sprayed the House floor with bullets, wounding five Congressmen.

Most Puerto Ricans did not share the sentiment of extremists. Assimilationists believed that it was essential to cast their lot with the United States. Others favored statehood. In 1952, some 67 percent of the island's population supported the commonwealth status that went into effect that year. Only 13 percent favored statehood, while 19 percent wanted independence. The will of the people was given in the referendum of July 23, 1967, when the vote was: commonwealth 425,481; statehood 273,315; and independence 4,205.

This was a democratic decision, but it was unsatisfactory to unreconciled dissenters. The *Fuerzas Armadas de Liberación Naçional* (Armed Forces of National Liberation), known as FALN, claimed responsibility for more than a hundred bombings in the United States and Puerto Rico. Far from achieving a favorable result, the FALN saw its support decline precipitously: sentiment for statehood soared to 55 percent.

Puerto Rican nationalists refuse to accept this democratic decision. They regard themselves as heroic guerrilla fighters, saintly liberators who refuse to compromise with Yankee tyranny. One day, they insisted, they would be looked upon as genuine heroes, who had won the fight for liberation for their country. Then their misguided brothers would give them the acclaim they deserved.

A similar spirit exists among the IRA, the PLO, Basques, Ukrainians, and Armenians, all of whom use weapons of terror, but at the same time deny that they are terrorists. They see themselves as true patriots who want only the national sovereignty to which they are entitled.

Behind these demands is a powerful historical tradition. The process is a familiar one since the formation of national states in modern times. Once the boundaries of the nation-state were fixed, a sense of territorial imperative (euphemism for nationalism) came into existence. "This is our land, our turf, keep off!" The primary goal was to maintain the established national sovereignty. The most heinous crime of all was disloyalty to the state, equated with treason.

At the same time, this centripetal force looked askance at any attempt to extend the nation-state into a larger entity. This urge, while regarded as perhaps legitimate and desirable, was seen as dangerous because it might lessen the already established sense of security. For Russians, the idea of Pan-Slavism was attractive, as long as it did not challenge the existing national sovereignty.

Such are the limits surrounding the idea of national sovereignty. It is a philosophy of let-well-enough-alone. If there is a "normal" expansion of territory, well and good, especially if kindred peoples are concerned. But never dilute the nation by seeking a questionable solidarity. Never tamper with existing national sovereignty.

The Dynamics of Nationalism

The lack of success of both peripheries of nationalism—the macro-nationalisms and the mini-nationalisms—testifies to the staying power of nationalism itself as the most powerful of political emotions on the contemporary scene. The ever-present need for security is gratified more by nationalism than by its offshoots. It persists because it satisfies a persistent need. Lewis Namier described it accurately as "a mass movement, centralizing and levelling, dynamic and ruthless, akin in nature to the horde."[1] It is the kind of historical phenomenon which responds to the needs of a changing society.

After the Renaissance there was enormous progress in the natural sciences, a development which resulted in the rapid transformation of human lives. With the new technology came large-scale industry and the simultaneous rise of a vigorous middle class. Meanwhile, the medieval union of Church and State deteriorated with the rise of the national state. To justify the existence of new nation-states, bourgeois nationalists turned to the real or imaginary past in a search for common pedigrees and traditions. The new sense of national consciousness became solidified in the French Revolution and its aftermath, ten years that shook the fabric of society. The medieval ecclesiastical community gave way to a collection of jealously independent nation-states.

Nationalism, the focus of collective loyalty, became the dominant political, economic, cultural and psychological movement of the new age. Its special form was noted by Isaiah Berlin: "It emerged particularly in France in the form of the defense of the customs and privileges of localities, regions, corporations and, of course, states, and then of the nation itself, against the encroachments of some external power—Roman law or Papal authority, or against related forms of universalism—natural law and other claims of supranational authority."[2] The strength of the new movement was indicated by its resistance against external powers of any kind.

European nationalism, which served as a model for the world, was given coherence, perhaps unconsciously, by Napoleon Bonaparte, the French conqueror, who stimulated national sentiment wherever he led his armies. In Germany, the new movement was given credence by Johann Gottfried Herder, who called attention to the *Volksgeist* and the *Nationalgeist*, the spirit of the community which lay at the heart of nationalism. Among the basic needs of man, Herder said, as important as food, communication, or procreation, was his elemental desire to belong to a group. This became, indeed, the dominant political idea of the 19th and 20th centuries.

Unfortunately, Herder's plea for a cultural or spiritual autonomy was transformed into an integral, aggressive movement characterized by embittered rivalries and clashes of national interest. What was originally conceived as a desirable cultural ideal turned into an inflamed sense of national consciousness. Human beings everywhere, exaggerating their own national virtues, began to show a patronizing contempt for their neighbors. Nationalism became clothed with a veneer of xenophobia, fear of the stranger. Peaceful coexistence was rejected in favor of resentment and hostility. "We" became noble and sublime, "they" were inferior, superficial, and morally empty. The new sentiment extended beyond the boundaries of Europe to all the world.

It was, indeed, a deplorable way to run world society. Emotional nationalism was responsible in large part for the two tragic World Wars of the 20th century, in which millions of lives were snuffed out in barbaric fashion. In vain have men of good will spoken against it. Historian Hans Kohn warned that nationalism was a deeply divisive force if it was not tempered by a liberal spirit of tolerance and compromise or the humanitarian universalism of a non-political religion. "Its stress upon national sovereignty and cultural distinctiveness hardly helps to promote cooperation among peoples at the very time when for technological and economic reasons they become more and more interdependent."[3]

Even as a young man, the great physicist, Albert Einstein, expressed his opposition to nationalism. He spoke out with particular bitterness while living in Berlin during World War I. At the beginning of the war, Einstein was asked by the Goethe Society of Berlin to write an essay. The resulting exchange brought Einstein, the internationalist, face to face with German nationalism. He was forced to make deletions from his own article. What he submitted dismayed the Goethe Society. He equated patriotism with the worst of aggressive animal instincts. He assessed the concept of aggression: "The psychological roots of war, in my view, lie in a biologically based, aggressive peculiarity of the human being. We 'masters of creation' are not the only ones who may claim the glory of this gift; we are surpassed in this respect by many animals, such as the bull or rooster."[4]

Einstein went on to denounce the shrine of patriotism. "It is beyond me to keep secret my international orientation, to keep anything secret. The state to which I belong as a citizen does not play the least role in my spiritual life; I regard allegiance to the government as a business matter, somewhat like the relationship with an insurance company."[5]

Einstein saw a human being as a part of the whole, the Universe, a part limited in time and space. Each individual experiences himself, his thoughts and feelings, as something separated from the rest—"a kind of optical delusion of his consciousness." This delusion, which expresses itself in nationalism, is a kind of prison which restricts individuals in personal desires. Einstein regarded it as a major task to free ourselves from this prison by widening our circle of compassion to embrace all living creatures. The distinguished physicist saw the bankruptcy of nationalism and the necessity of liberating human society from its shackles.

Estimate of the Macro-Nationalisms

Little can be said about the future of the macro-nationalisms. The historian must avoid the pitfalls of prophecy—that is not his function. It is unreasonable to predict coming historical trends. There are far too many accidental factors in the historical process which do not lend themselves to prophecy. Anything can happen—from the disappearance of nationalism to suffocation of the world's population by an atomic blast. Neither quanitification, predictability, nor computerization can give any exact indication of what is going to take place in the 21st century. It is best to leave this area to high-powered and financially sensitive think-tanks with their corps of "experts" engaged in elaborate guesswork. The effort to transform the social sciences into pure sciences has been a flat failure.

What we do know about the macro-nationalisms is that they have not been able to supersede the current system of national states. One after another, the pan-movements could not solidify into a workable extended nationalism— neither Pan-Germanism, Pan-Slavism, Pan-Europeanism, Pan-Africanism, Pan-Asianism, nor Pan-Americanism. In each case, despite the claims of advocates at pan-congresses, the larger movements of nationalism have remained vague and ephemeral. Nationalism itself still exists as a dominant historical force, but efforts to extend it into regional, continental, or hemispheric status have never attained even a modicum of success.

In the final analysis, nationalism writ large fails because it does not give human beings the security they want. Macro-nationalisms lose their appeal because they are too thinly spread to satisfy the always present feeling of safety. Supposed "brothers" tend to be regarded as foreigners. In common parlance, for most people the pan-movements are regarded as too much of a good thing.

The pattern is not regional, but global and universal. Not one of the existing macro-nationalisms has been able to overcome the sense of national sovereignty. The next century, with a new combination of historical values, may well tell a different story. One can only wait and see.

NOTES _____

Chapter 1
Nationalism Writ Large

1. See Carlton J. H. Hayes, *Essays on Nationalism* (New York, 1926), pp. 245, 250.

2. The three classic studies of nationalism are: Carlton J. H. Hayes, *The Historical Evolution of Modern Nationalism* (New York, 1931); Hans Kohn, *The Idea of Nationalism* (New York, 1944); and Boyd C. Shafer, *Faces of Nationalism: New Realities and Old Myths* (New York, 1972). See also Louis L. Snyder, *The Meaning of Nationalism* (New Brunswick, N.J., 1954); *The Dynamics of Nationalism* (Princeton, N.J., 1964); *The New Nationalism* (Ithaca, N.Y., 1968); and *Varieties of Nationalism: A Comparative Study* (New York, 1976).

The most productive work on nationalism in the United States came out of Professor Hayes's seminar at Columbia University in the 1930s. In Europe excellent work has been done in Theodor Schieder's seminar at the University of Cologne, Federal Republic of West Germany. The best scholarly journal devoted exclusively to nationalism is the *Canadian Review of Studies in Nationalism,* supported in part by the Canadian Government, and edited by Thomas Spira of the University of Prince Edward Island, Charlottetown, Canada.

3. See the companion volume to this study: Louis L. Snyder, *Global Mini-Nationalisms: Autonomy or Independence* (Westport, Ct., 1982).

4. For a geopolitical treatment of continental pan-movements, see Karl Haushofer, *Geopolitik der Pan-Ideen* (Berlin, 1931).

5. This idea was projected in the first edition of my textbook, *A Survey of European Civilization* (Harrisburg, Pa., 1941), and developed in the succeeding editions.

6. See Robert O. Keohane and Joseph S. Nye, Jr. (eds.), *Transnational Relations and World Politics* (Cambridge, Mass., 1972).

7. Seyom Brown, in *Saturday Review*, May 20, 1972, p. 65.

8. *Ibid.*

9. Quoted by Frank T. Cary, chairman of the International Business Machine Corporation (IBM), in *The New York Times*, November 8, 1975.

10. Hugh Stephenson, *The Coming Clash* (London, 1972). See also Stephenson's article, "The Coming Clash of the Nation State and the New Leviathans," in *The Times* (London), August 25, 1972.

11. For a summary of these points of view. See Joseph S. Nye, "Multinational Enterprises and Prospects for Regional and Social Integration," in *Annals of the American Academy of Political and Social Science*, vol. CCCCIII (September 1972), pp. 116-26.

12. *Ibid.*

13. Robert S. Walters, "International Organizations and the Multinational Corporations: An Overview and Observations," in *Annals of the American Academy of Political and Social Science*, vol. 403 (September 1972), p. 121.

14. See Raymond Vernon, "The Future of the Multinational Enterprise," in Charles Kindleberger (ed.), *The International Corporation* (Cambridge, Mass., 1970).

15. *The New York Times*, December 6, 1972, in an interview with James Reston.

16. See "Collective Parataxis," a paper delivered by Nelson Foote at a conference on "Psychoanalysis 1980: Converging Views," held at the Barbizon Plaza Hotel, New York, January 27, 1980.

17. *Ibid.*

Chapter 2
Pan-Slavism: The Urge for Union

1. Hans Kohn, *Pan-Slavism: Its History and Ideology* (Notre Dame, Ind., 1953), p. 251.

2. On Herder's role in the development of German nationalism, see Robert R. Ergang, *Herder and the Foundations of German Nationalism* (New York, 1931).

3. The précis here is from Herder's *Gesammelte Werke*, ed. by Bernhard Suphan (Berlin, 1909), vol. XIV, pp. 277-80.

4. *Ibid.*, p. 27.

5. Kohn, *Pan-Slavism, op.cit.*, p. 2.

6. Palacký's most important work, *Geschichte Böhmens* (in German, 5 vols., 1836-1867; in Czech, 5 vols., 1858-1867), was of the utmost significance in stimulating Czech national consciousness. It was the result of laborious research in the local archives of Bohemia and in various libraries in main European cities. Publication of the work was hindered by police censorship based on Palacký's account of the Hussite movement.

Among Palacký's additional works were *Würdigung der alten Bömischen Geschichtsschreiber* (Prague, 1930), which dealt with publications then inaccessible to Czech students; *Archiv česky* (6 vols., Prague, 1840-1872); *Urkundliche Beiträge zur Geschichte des Hussitenkriege* (2 vols., Prague, 1872-1874); and *Radnorst* (3 vols., Prague, 1871-1973), a collection of articles and essays written in

Czech. For an estimate of Palacký, see Count Lützow, *Lectures on the Historians of Bohemia* (London, 1905).

7. Palacký's letter was reprinted in *Radhorst, op.cit.*, vol. III, pp. 11-17. Translation in Kohn, *Pan-Slavism, op.cit.*, pp. 65-69.

8. On Bakunin, see E. H. Carr. *Michael Bakunin* (London, 1937). Bakunin's views on Pan-Slavism were opposed to those of the moderates who had called the meeting. To the radical Bakunin, Palacký's sense of loyalty to the Austrian monarchy was insufferable.

9. Kohn, *Pan-Slavism, op.cit.*, pp. 70-71.

10. *Ibid.*, p, 71.

11. *Ibid.*, p. 73.

12. For an excellent examination of Russia's role in Pan-Slavism, see Joseph S. Roucek, "Pan Slavism: An Ideological Weapon," *Central European Journal*, vol. XVII (May 5, 1969), pp. 163-83, and its sequel, "Pan-Slavism in Our Day," *ibid.* (September 9, 1969), pp. 256-64.

13. Roucek, "Pan Slavism: An Ideological Weapon," p. 170.

14. On Danilevsky, see *Die Politisierung und Radikalisierung Problems: Russland und Europa bei N.Y. Danilevsky, Forschung zur europäischen Geschichte*, vol. 1 (1864).

15. The full title was *Russia and Europe: An Inquiry into the Cultural and Political Relations of the Slav World and the German-Roman World* (*Russland und Europa: Eine Untersuchung über die kulturellen und politischen Beziehungen der slawischen zur Germanisch-romanischen Welt*). See the 1926 German edition (Stuttgart, 1920), especially pp. 278-79, 326.

16. On Dostoevsky, see Abraham Yarmolinsky, *Dostoevski, A Life* (New York, 1934); E. J. Simmons, *Dostoevsky, The Making of a Novelist* (New York, 1940); J. Lavrin, *Dostoevsky* (New York, 1943); J. A. Lloyd, *Fyodor Dostoevsky* (New York, 1947); and Ronald Kingsley, *The Undiscovered Dostoevsky* (London, 1962).

17. See Feodor Mikhailovich Dostoevsky, *The Possessed*, trans. by Constance Garnett, Modern Library edition (New York, n.d.), part II, chap. VII, pp. 250-56.

18. *Ibid.*

19. *Ibid.*

20. *Ibid.*

21. Feodor Mikhailovich Dostoevski, *The Diary of a Writer*, trans. by Boris Brasol (2 vols., New York, 1949), vol. II, p. 780. The original edition appeared in Russian in January 1877.

22. Dostoevsky's address was in response to a talk delivered the day before by Turgenev, in which the latter admitted that he was unable to decide the question as to whether or not Pushkin was to be considered the supreme Russian national poet, in the sense that Shakespeare, Racine, and Goethe were national poets in their respective countries.

23. Dostoevsky, *The Diary of a Writer, op.cit.*, vol. II, pp. 960-61. This excerpt is from Dostoevsky's "Explanatory Word Concerning the Address on Pushkin," which he used as an introduction to the printed version of his speech.

24. Kohn, *Pan-Slavism, op.cit.*, pp. 140-41.

25. *Ibid.*, p. 142.

26. Quoted by Roucek in "Pan-Slavism: An Ideological Weapon," *op.cit.*, p. 163.

27. *Ibid.*

Chapter 3

Pan-Germanism: The Teutonic Mission

1. On German nationalism in general, see Louis L. Snyder, *German Nationalism: The Tragedy of a People* (Harrisburg, Pa., 1952; Port Washington, N.Y., 1969); and *Roots of German Nationalism* (Indianapolis, Ind., 1978).

2. On Fichte, see Snyder, *German Nationalism, op.cit., passim,* xi, 16, 18, 19, 32, 43, 49, 102, 130, 142, 145, 150, 184, 199, 210, 231, 238, 240, 252, 266, 267, 268.

3. *Ibid.,* p. 130.

4. *Ibid.,* pp. 21-44.

5. *Ibid.,* p. 33.

6. See *ibid., passim.*

7. On List, see Louis L. Snyder, *Roots of German Nationalism, op.cit.,* pp. 1-34. This chapter was based on a paper originally delivered before The American Historical Association in Chicago, December 28, 1950.

8. Hans Kohn, *The Idea of Nationalism* (New York, 1944), p. 322.

9. Koppel Pinson, *Modern Germany: Its History and Civilization* (New York, 1954), p. 120.

10. On Lagarde, see R. W. Louger, *Paul Anton de Lagarde* (Cambridge, Mass., 1962).

11. On biological racialism, see Louis L. Snyder, *Race: A History of Modern Ethnic Theories* (New York, 1939), and *The Idea of Racialism* (Princeton, N.J., 1962).

12. On Adolf Stoecker, see chapter 2 of Louis L. Snyder, *From Bismarck to Hitler* (Williamsport, Pa., 1935), pp. 13-24.

13. Lueger had a strong influence on Hitler. In *Mein Kampf,* Hitler told how he was at first unimpressed by Lueger, but later came to admire him for his views. (Adolf Hitler, *Mein Kampf* [Munich, 1943], pp. 58-59).

14. H. von Poschinger, *Fürst Bismarck als Volkswirt* (Berlin, 1889), vol. I, Pt. 4, p. 63, note 9.

15. On Bismarck's conversion to imperialism, see Louis L. Snyder, "The Role of Herbert Bismarck in the Angra Pequena Negotiations between Germany and Britain, 1881-1885," *The Journal of Negro History,* vol. XXXV, no. 4 (October 1950), pp. 435-53.

16. Quoted in Hans Kohl, *Dreissig Jahre preussische-deutsche Geschichte* (Giessen, 1888), pp. 277 ff.

17. According to the Zanzibar Treaty of 1890 between Britain and Germany (the two chief rivals in East Africa), Zanzibar and the future Tanganyika were divided: Britain obtained the future Uganda and recognition of its paramount interest in Zanzibar and Pemba in exchange for ceding the strategic North Sea Island of Heligoland (Helgoland), and noninterference in Germany's acquisitions in Tanganyika, Ruanda, and Urundi.

18. *The Pan-Germanic Doctrine, Being a Study of German Political Aims and Aspirations* (London and New York, 1904), pp. 25-26. (Hereafter referred to as P.G.D.)

19. P.G.D., p. 27.

20. *Handbuch der Alldeutschen Verbandes* (Munich, 1914), p. 7.

21. *Alldeutscher Blätter* (1898), p. 17 ff.

22. Mildred S. Wertheimer, *The Pan-German League* (New York, 1924), p. 65 ff. See also P.G.D., pp. 30-31.

23. P.G.D., pp. 30-31.

24. Among these ancillary organizations were the German Colonial Society, the Central Association for Commercial Geography; the General School Association for the Preservation of *Deutschtum* Abroad, the General German Language Association; the German Navy League; the East Mark Association (for Germanization of the Poles); the Pan-German Language Association; the Young German League; The League of National German Associations; the German People's League; the Central Association for the Union of Navy Leagues Abroad; the National German League of Apprentices; the German Health Association; the Central Committee for Promoting German National Games; the Association for Dissemination of Popular Literature; the German Association for North Schleswig; the Loan and Trust Banking Society of Scjerrebek in Schleswig; the German Settlers' Association in Schleswig; the Protestant Association for the Care of Orphans in Posen; the German Protestant Association in Kobissau; the Protestant Orphans' Home of Bethlehem in West Prussia; the German Settlers' Association in West Prussia; the German Loan Bank in East Prussia; the German Association for the Preservation of the German Language in Belgium; the German School Association of Vienna; The German League in Bohemia; the German Bohemian Forest League; the Germania Association in Trebaitz; the German People's Bank in Bohemia; the North Mark Association; the German League in North Moravia; the South Mark Association; the South Mark People's Savings Bank in Graz; the Ulrich Miners' League; the Germanic League in Vienna; the German National Association in Austria; The East Mark Self-Help Association; the German People's Union in South Tyrol; the Protestant Central Association for German Emigrants; the German Brazilian Emigrants' Association; the German Colonial School Association; the Catholic St. Raphael Association; the Colonial Economic League, the Central Association of Germans in North America; the Union of German Associations in Chicago; and the Society for Discussing the Central European Union under the Presidency of the Duke of Schleswig-Holstein. This array of associations was Pan-Germanic in kind, and all were engaged actively in promoting *Deutschtum* by various means.

25. P.G.D., p. 60.

26. *Ibid.*, pp. 28 ff.

27. *Zwanzig Jahre alldeutscher Arbeit und Kämpfe* (Leipzig, 1910), p. 78. (Hereafter noted as Z.J.A.)

28. Z.J.A., p. 342.

29. *Ibid.*, pp. 48-59.

30. *Ibid.*, pp. 308-9.

31. *Ibid.*, pp. 358-60.

32. *Ibid.*, pp. 400-404.

33. *Ibid.*, p. 1.

34. The term H.K.T. Verein referred to the three founders of the East Mark Society—Hansemann, Kennemann, and von Tiedemann.

35. P.G.D., pp. 40-41.

36. The United States had the oldest treaty with Samoa dating from 1878, the Germans from 1879. For a treatment in-depth of the clash between the United States

and Germany, see Alfred Vagts, *Deutschland und die Vereinigten Staaten in der Weltpolitik* (2 vols., New York, 1935), vol. 1, pp. 636-98.

37. In France and England, Wilhelm II's visit to Tangier was regarded as an effort to test or break the newly formed Entente Cordiale. The French dismissed M. Théophile Delcassé, Minister for Foreign Affairs, who had been responsible for the Anglo-French Agreement, and disturbed by the German "challenge," agreed to an international conference on Morocco.

38. Z.J.A., p. 2.

39. For the definitive study on Schoenerer and his work, see Andrew C. Whiteside, *The Socialism of Fools: Georg Ritter von Schoenerer and Austrian Pan-Germanism* (Berkeley, Calif., 1975).

40. *Ibid.*, p. 6.

41. "Anti-Semitism had a long history in Germany going back to the Crusades, to Luther and Eisenmenger, but it found its modern ideology in Fichte, Führing, Lagarde, Stoecker, and Houston Stewart Chamberlain, re-enforced by their Austrian allies Schoenerer and Lueger." (Pinson, *Modern Germany, op.cit.*, p. 504).

42. Whiteside, *The Socialism of Fools, op.cit.*, p. 6.

43. From the *Stenographische Berichte*, as quoted in I. Suval, *The Anschluss Question in the Weimar Era: A Study of Nationalism in Germany and Austria, 1918-1936* (Baltimore, Md., 1971), pp. 3-4.

44. P.G.D., p. 29.

45. Wertheimer, *The Pan-German League, op.cit.*, pp. 164-65.

46. See Z.J.A., pp. 58, 96, 109, 133, 149, 219, 255, and 399, for resolutions of the annual meetings of the Pan-German League.

47. On the origins of World War I, see Sidney B. Fay, *The Origins of the World War* (2 vols., New York, 1930); Philip Nicholas Mansergh, *The Coming of the First World War, 1878-1914* (London, 1947); and Bernadotte Schmitt, *The Coming of the War, 1914* (2 vols., New York, 1930). For a much criticized revisionist view, see Harry Elmer Barnes, *The Genesis of the World War* (New York, 1926), which placed chief blame on France and Russia for the origins of the war.

48. Especially in the League of Agriculturalists, the German Peasants' League; the Christian German Peasants' Union; the Central Association of German Manufacturers; the Manufacturers' League; and the League of Middle Class Citizens in the German Empire.

49. The précis here of the memorandum of May 20, 1915, is from the full text in *The Pan-German Programme*, trans. with an introduction by Edwyn Bevan (London, 1918), pp. 6-18.

50. In foreign countries the complete text of the petition was published originally in the Parisian Socialist newspaper *Humanité* on August 11, 1915, after the Socialist *Berner Tagwacht* had published an abridged version on June 22, 1915.

51. The manifesto of June 20, 1915, contained 1,341 signatures in all, including 352 professors of universities and colleges; 158 schoolmasters and clergymen; 145 superior administrative officials, mayors, and town councillors; 148 judges, magistrates, and lawyers; 40 members of the *Reichstag* and the Prussian *Landtag*; 18 retired admirals and generals; 182 manufacturers, businessmen, and bankers; 52 agriculturalists; and 252 artists, authors, and publishers. It was truly a manifesto of German intellectuals. After the 1,341 signatures had been appended to the petition, the Government stepped in to prevent further canvassing, apparently in the belief that its Pan-German spirit might be of propaganda value to the Allies.

52. From the text in Bevan, *The Pan-German Programme, op.cit.,* pp. 19-31.

53. *Ibid.*, p. 31.

54. Among British publications devoted in large part to denunciations of Pan-Germanism were Charles Robert Leslie Fletcher, *The Germans: What They Covet* (London, 1914); Austin Harrison, *The Kaiser's War* (London, 1914); John C. Powys, *The Menace of German Culture* (London, 1914); Emil Reich, *Germany's Swelled Head* (London, 1914); and Gabriel de Wesselitsky, *The German Peril and the Grand Alliance* (London, 1916).

There were similar books in France: Paul Palant, *Le péril allemand* (Paris, 1914); Charles Phillippe Théodore Andler, *Pan-Germanism: Its Plans for German Expansion in the World* (Paris, 1915); Georges Blondel, *La guerre européene et la doctrine pangermaniste* (Paris, 1915); P. H. Michel, *Les origines du pangermanisme* (Paris, 1915); and Jules Freilich, *Le délire pangermanique* (Paris, 1918).

Publications denouncing Pan-Germanism also appeared in the United States: Solomon Grumbach, *Germany's Annextionist Aims* (New York, 1917); and Henry Pratt Judson, *The Threat of German World-Politics* (Chicago, 1918).

The French author and publicist André Chéradame published books in several cities attacking Pan-Germanism as a menace: *La querre européene et la paix voudrait allemagne* (Paris, 1915); *The Pan-German Plot Unmasked* (London, 1917); *Pan-Germany: The Disease and Cure* (Boston, 1918); and *The United States and Pan-Germanism* (New York, 1918).

55. Roland G. Usher, *Pan-Germanism,* was published in its original edition by Houghton Mifflin in 1913.

56. The new edition: Roland G. Usher, *Pan-Germanism: From Its Inception to the Outbreak of the War: A Critical Study* (New York, 1914). Meanwhile, Usher had been promoted to full professor.

57. *Ibid.*, p. 1.

58. *Ibid.*, pp. 2-3.

59. *Ibid.*, pp. 14-15.

60. For the full text of this manifesto of the intellectuals, see Ralph Haswell Lutz (ed.), *Fall of the German Empire, 1914-1918* (Stanford, Calif., 1932), vol. 1, pp. 74-78.

61. Quoted in Sigmund Freud and W. C. Bullitt, *Thomas Woodrow Wilson: A Psychological Study* (London, 1967), p. 247. The authors, Freud, the father of psychoanalysis, and Bullitt, assistant in the U.S. Department of State and delegate of the American delegation at Versailles, commented on Wilson's statement: "The ignorance of geography revealed by these sentences is so astonishing, especially in view of the fact that Wilson had been studying maps for months in Paris, that it seems further evidence that he was striving to forget and succeeding in forgetting the map he had arranged" (p. 248).

Parenthetically, it should be observed that the Freud-Bullitt study is a combination of impressive insight and wild guesswork. The authors psychoanalyzed the wartime American leader without benefit of couch, and relied specifically on his speeches, letters, private papers, and political actions. They show him as a vain, arrogant, indecisive, weak leader, motivated by a love-hate complex toward his "incomparable father." They depicted Wilson as a fanatical religious zealot: "It was God's treaty given to mankind by God's son Woodrow" (p. 249). They accused Wilson of "betraying the trust of the world as a matter of principle" (p. 228), and charged him with an unconscious identification with Christ: "He decided he would be the Saviour" (p. 188).

This book originally written in 1938, a year before Freud's death, by the 80-year-old psychoanalyst and an American diplomat, was filled with ridicule of, and contempt for Wilson. Freud admitted his bias: "[Wilson] was from the beginning unsympathetic to me, and this aversion increased in the course of years the more I learned about him and the more severely we suffered from the consequences of his intrusion into our destiny." (p. xi)

This study may be regarded as one of Freud's lesser contributions to the discipline of psychoanalysis.

62. Alfred Kruck, *Geschichte des Alldeutschen Verbandes* (Wiesbaden, 1954), pp. 192, 203. Quoted in George L. Mosse, *The Crisis of German Ideology* (New York, 1964), p. 225.

63. Konrad Heiden, *Geschichte des Nationalsozialismus* (Berlin, 1932), p. 6.

64. Hannah Arendt, *The Origins of Totalitarianism* (New York, 1966), p. 222.

65. Werner Masur, *Hitler's Letters and Notes* (New York, 1973), p. 29.

66. Quoted by Werner Masur, in *Adolf Hitler: Legende, Mythos, Wirklichkeit* (Munich, 1971), p. 176.

67. Adolf Hitler, *Mein Kampf*, 805th-809th ed. (Munich, 1943), p. 133.

68. *Ibid.*, pp. 12-13.

69. *Ibid.*, p. 11.

70. *Ibid.*, p. 10

71. On Haushofer, see Hans Werner Weigert, *German Geopolitics* (New York, 1941); Andreas Dorpalen, *The World of General Haushofer: Geopolitics in Action* (New York, 1942); A. Grabowsky, *Raum, Staat und Geschichte* (Berlin, 1966); and Hans Adolf Jacobsen, *Karl Haushofer: Leben und Werk* (2 vols., Boppard am Rhein, 1979).

Among Haushofer's major works were: *Geopolitik des Pazifischen Ozeans* (Berlin, 1925); *Bausteine zur Geopolitik* (Berlin-Grünewald, 1928); *Weltpolitik von Heute* (Berlin, 1934); and *Geopolitik der Pan-Ideen* (Berlin, 1935).

72. In his *Essay on the Inequality of Human Races*, originally published in 1853-1855, Gobineau maintained that "without the slightest doubt a people's language corresponds to its mentality and it is furthermore a universal maxim that the hierarchy of languages is in strict accordance with the hierarchy of races." (Arthur de Gobineau, *Essay on the Inequality of Human Races*, trans. by Adrian Collins [New York, 1915]), vol. 1, p. 203. This principle became a favorite one among "racial scientists" in Nazi Germany.

73. "Chamberlain had created a fusion of the racial mysticism of Wagner, Gobineau, and of the new anti-Semitism; he was copied by Alfred Rosenberg, and Hitler and Himmler drew the consequences." (Karl Dietrich Bracher, *Die deutsche Diktatur* [Cologne, 1969] p. 31.)

For Houston Stewart Chamberlain's works, see *Die Grundlagen des 19. Jahrhunderts* (Munich, 1899); and George Schott (ed.), *Houston Stewart Chamberlain, der Seher des Dritten Reichs: Das Vermächtnis Houston Stewart Chamberlains an das Deutsche Volk in einer Auslese aus seinen Werken* (Munich, 1934, 1941).

74. Ewald Banse, *Germany Prepares for War: A Nazi Theory of "National Defense,"* trans. by Alan Harris (London and New York, 1934), p. xix.

75. See Roman Rome, "The Origins of the Second World War and the A.J.P. Taylor Controversy," *Intellect* (September-October 1975), pp. 126-29, for an excellent treatment of the confrontation.

76. See William Roger Lewis (ed.), *The Origins of the Second World War: A.J.P. Taylor and His Critics* (New York, 1972), p. 39.

77. *Ibid.*, p. 6.

Chapter 4
Pan-Europa: Distant and Fragile Dream

1. Colin Clark, *British Trade in the Common Market* (London, 1962), pp. 1-2.

2. R. C. Mowat, *Creating the European Community* (London, 1973), p. 2.

3. From Robert Southey, *Ode*.

4. Exactly what these "elemental instincts of man" are remains a subject of dispute among anthropologists, biologists, and historians.

5. Walter Hallstein, address to a joint meeting at Harvard University and the Massachusetts Institute of Technology, May 22, 1961.

6. According to Carlton J. H. Hayes, pioneer scholar in the study of nationalism, the phenomenon moved from an originally positive to a negative form, from "blessing to curse," through several stages of development: humanitarian, Jacobin, traditional, liberal, and integral—from a liberal tone during the time of Metternich to a dynastic conservatism in the Bismarck era to a tragic descent into aggression and expansion in the 20th century. The Hayes's formula has remained basic in the study of nationalism. (See Carlton J. H. Hayes, *The Historical Evolution of Modern Nationalism* [New York, 1931].)

7. The pertinent extract from Bismarck's "Iron and Blood" speech follows: "It is true that we can hardly escape complications in Germany, although we do not seek them. Germany does not look to Prussia's liberalism, but to her power. The South German states—Bavaria, Württemberg, and Baden—would like to indulge in liberalism, and because of that no one will assign Prussia's role to them! Prussia must collect her forces and hold them in reserve for an opportune moment, which has already come and gone several times. Since the Treaty of Vienna, our frontiers have not been favorably designed for a healthy body politic. Not by speeches and majorities will the great questions of the day be decided—that was the mistake of 1848 and 1849—but by iron and blood." (Horst Kohl [ed.], *Die politischen Reden des Fürsten Bismarck: historisch-kritische Gesammtausgabe* [Stuttgart, 1892-1904], vol. II, pp. 29-30, translated by Louis L. Snyder). This speech, delivered on September 30, 1862, before some 30 members of the budget commission of the lower house of the Prussian parliament, the *Landtag*, was made when Bismarck was Minister-President of Prussia. His words soon spread throughout the Germanies, with the rhythm of the phrase changed to "blood-and-iron."

8. On European integration, see Arnold J. Zurcher, *The Struggle to Unite Europe, 1940-1958* (New York, 1958); Richard Mayne, *The Community of Europe* (New York, 1963); Uwe Kitzinger, *The Politics and Economics of European Economic Integration* (New York, 1963); Ernest B. Haas, *The Uniting of Europe* (Stanford, Calif., 1964); and Henri K. Brugmans, *L'Idée européene* (Bruges, 1970).

9. Hugh Thomas, *Europe: The Radical Challenge* (London, 1973), p. 5ff.

10. Here again there was a split. One group of functionalists supported the idea of international cooperation, such as joint secretariats under the control of the governments concerned. Other functionalists wanted bodies that would integrate fully their varied economies as a step to complete political unity. The latter argued that such inter-governmental cooperation would not work because any single government could break the agreements in much the same way as the old military alliances were fractured.

11. In all probability, Churchill's unexpected change of view was due to the feeling that Britain, and much of Europe, had begun an economic recovery with the assistance of the American Marshall Plan. The British had stood alone during much of the war, and the idea persisted that she should continue to remain aloof from Continental affairs.

12. Thomas, *Europe, op.cit.*, p. 10.

13. Among Richard N. Coudenhove-Kalergi's prolific writings on Pan-Europeanism were: *Europa Erwacht* (Paris, 1934); *Europe Must Unite* (Glarus, Switzerland, 1939); *Crusade for Pan-Europe* (New York, 1943); *Kampf um Pan-Europa* (Zürich, 1949); *Die europäische Nation* (Stuttgart, 1953); *Eine Idee erobert Europa* (Munich, 1958); *Pan-Europa* (Munich, 1966); and *Ein Leben für Europa* (Cologne, 1966). He also edited the *Pan-European Review*, and contributed many articles to journals in Europe and the United States.

14. In 1942, in the midst of World War II, the American Cooperative Committee for the Pan-American Union became the American Committee for a Free and United Europe.

15. The proposal of French Foreign Minister Aristide Briand in 1929 for the formation of the United States of Europe was rejected by the national governments to which it was addressed.

16. At this time the Pan-European Union had 20,000 members.

17. Mowat, *European Community, op.cit.*, p. 208.

18. *Ibid.*

19. From 1958 to 1960 Schuman was President of the European Parliamentary Assembly.

20. Quoted in Mowat, *European Community, op.cit.*, p. 61.

21. European federalists, who greeted Churchill's words with delight, were dismayed when, returned to office in 1951, he made it clear that his vision of a federated Europe, which he declared while in the Opposition, was a union of nations on the Continent itself.

22. Soviet rejection of the Marshall Plan marked the end of efforts to win economic cooperation for Europe as a whole. The Plan was accepted readily, however, by Western European nations. This was the first step in the development of an integrated economy in Western Europe.

23. Quoted in Walter Farr, *Guide to the Common Market* (London, 1972), p. 24.

24. On ECSC, see L. Lister, *Europe's Coal and Steel Community* (New York, 1960).

25. On EEC, see Kitzinger, *European Economic Integration, op.cit.*

26. Text in Farr, *Common Market, op.cit.*, p. 33.

27. *Ibid.*, p. 27.

28. Although Britain joined the Common Market, there remained much opposition in the country to its membership.

29. *Daily Telegraph* (London), August 14, 1981.

30. Quoted in Farr, *Common Market, op.cit.,* pp. 28-29.

31. *Ibid.* An even more passionate German advocate of European unity was Walter Hallstein, the first president of the European Common Market, and its head for nine years. Hallstein died in April 1982 at the age of 80.

32. *The New York Times,* March 23, 1982.

33. *Ibid.*

34. *Ibid.*

35. Quoted in *Time,* February 8, 1963, p. 23.

36. *The War Memoirs of Charles de Gaulle: Salvation, 1944-1946,* trans. by Richard Howard (New York, 1960), p. 269.

37. *Ibid.,* p. 320.

38. On French relations with the Common Market, see Henry W. Ehrmann, *Organized Business in France* (Princeton, N.J., 1957); Warren Baum, *The French Economy and the State* (Princeton, N.J., 1958); and William Diebold, Jr., *The Schuman Plan: A Study in Economic Cooperation in 1950-1959* (New York, 1959). See also H. I. MacDonald, "European Common Market," *Behind the Headlines,* vol. XVIII, no. 4 (1958); and J. Hasbrouck, "Will the Common Market Succeed?" in *Foreign Policy Bulletin,* October 1, 1959.

39. *Time,* International edition, September 17, 1965, p. 66.

40. New York *Herald-Tribune,* Paris edition, September 11-12, 1965.

41. The distribution of seats was decided before the election: Britain, France, West Germany, and Italy would have 81 each; the Netherlands 25; Belgium 24; Denmark 16; Ireland 15; and Luxembourg 6.

42. Another eight countries joined later—Austria, Cyprus, Greece, Iceland, Malta, Switzerland, Turkey, and West Germany.

43. Barnett Cocks, *The European Parliament: Structure, Procedure, and Practice* (London, 1973), p. 7.

44. See Robert Jackson and John Fitzmaurice, *The European Parliament* (London, 1979), pp. 139-40, 147-50.

45. The Euratom Treaty entered into force on January 1, 1958. Britain, Ireland, and Denmark became members of Euratom in 1973.

46. European technical collaboration was extended in 1962 with the formation of the European Space Research Organization, and in 1964 with the European Space Vehicle Launching Development Organization (ELDO), dedicated to the development of European rockets for launching space vehicles.

47. For a discussion of this thesis of European duality, see Max Kohnstamm and Wolfgang Hager, *A Nation Writ Large: The Policy Problems of the European Community* (London, 1973), pp. 6-13.

48. A leader of the Italian Resistance against Mussolini, Spinelli, while in prison, insisted that he and his comrades were working for "a free and united Europe." (See Thomas, *Europe, The Radical Challenge, op.cit.,* p. 8. See also Altiero Spinelli, *Manifesto dei Federalisti Europei* (Parma, c. 1957).

49. Quoted in *Time,* International edition, August 24, 1981, pp. 11-12.

50. An opinion poll on the number of West Germans favoring the European Community showed a drop from 62 percent to 49 percent, the lowest figure ever recorded during West Germany's membership in the Common Market. (*Time,* International edition, August 24, 1981, p. 12).

51. For development of the theme of legislative power in Europe, see Valentin and Juliet Lange, *The European Parliament and the European Community* (London, 1978), pp. 5-9.

52. See K. von Lindeiner-Wildau, *Le Supranationalité en tant que Principe de Droit* (Leiden, 1970), pp. 137 ff.

53. On COMECON, see D. Michael Kaser, *COMECON* (Oxford, 1965). Comecon was later joined by East Germany and Albania. Albania was expelled in 1961 because of her support for China in the Sino-Soviet confrontation. In 1962 the Mongolian People's Republic was added as a new member of Comecon.

Chapter 5
The Tribes of Europe: From Anglo-Saxonism
to Pan-Scandinavianism

1. On Macaulay, see George Otto Trevelyan, *The Life and Letters of Macaulay* (London and New York, 1876, 1908, 1959).

2. On Froude, see George F. Gooch, *History and Historians in the Nineteenth Century* (London and New York, 1913).

3. On Freeman, see W.R.W. Stephens, *The Life and Letters of E. A. Freeman* (London, 1895).

4. Thomas Carlyle, *Past and Present* (New York, 1918), pp. 300-309.

5. *Ibid.*, p. 309.

6, Because Charles Kingsley had written three historical novels, Lord Palmerston invited him to become Professor of Modern History at Oxford. Kingsley soon showed that he was not suited to the chair. On Kingsley, see the biography by Una Pope-Hennesey, *Canon Charles Kingsley* (London, 1948).

7. C. W. Stubbs, *Charles Kingsley* (New York, 1899), p. 111.

8. From the preface to Dilke's *Greater Britain* (London, 1868).

9. From Rudyard Kipling's "The White Man's Burden" (London, 1899).

10. R. Marshall, "Rudyard Kipling and Racial Instinct," in *Century Illustrated Monthly* (July 1899), vol. 58, pp. 375-77.

11. C. D. Platt, "The Cult of Kipling," *The Month* (January 1900).

12. E. T. Raymond, *Disraeli, Alien Patriot* (New York, 1925), p. 244.

13. Lord Rosebery's explanation was in reply to a challenge issued when he addressed the Imperialist Institute in 1898 on "The English-Speaking Brotherhood."

14. From a speech delivered by Lord Curzon at a banquet held at the Chamber of Commerce in London on February 12, 1903. Quoted in Earl of Ronaldshay, *The Life of Lord Curzon* (London, 1928), p. 418.

15. B.E.C. Dugdale, *Arthur James Balfour* (New York, 1937), vol. 2, p. 287.

16. Quoted in Michael Kraus, *A History of American History* (New York, 1937), p. 360.

17. John Fiske, "Manifest Destiny," *Harper's New Monthly Magazine* (March 1885), p. 588.

18. Josiah Strong, *Our Country: Its Possible Future and Its Present Crisis* (New York, 1891), pp. 208 ff.

19. Madison Grant, *The Passing of the Great Race* (New York, 1918), p. 145.

20. Henry Fairfield Osborn, *Man Rises to Parnassus* (New York, 1927), p. 185.

21. Henry Fairfield Osborn in the preface to Grant, *The Passing of the Great Race, op.cit.*

22. Lothrop Stoddard's books include *The Rising of Color Against White Supremacy* (New York, 1920); *The Revolt Against Civilization* (New York, 1922); *Racial Realities in Europe* (New York, 1924); and *Re-forging America* (New York, 1927).

23. For a fuller discussion of the fallacies of race, see Louis L. Snyder, *Race: A History of Modern Ethnic Theories* (New York and Toronto, 1939); and Ashley Montagu's excellent *Man's Most Dangerous Myth: The Fallacy of Race* (New York, 1942).

24. Karl Pearson, "The Problems of Anthropology," *Scientific Monthly* (November 1920), p. 45.

25. On the history of Portugal, see Harold V. Livermore, *A History of Portugal* (Cambridge, Eng., 1947); and Charles E. Nowell, *A History of Portugal* (New York, 1952).

26. For the best documented work on the life of Prince Henry the Navigator, see José I. F. da Costa Brochade, *Infante d. Henrique* (Lisbon, 1942).

27. In 1493 a papal Bull of Demarcation assigned to Spain all the land west of a line from the Arctic Pole to the Antarctic at a point "a hundred leagues toward the west and south of the Azores and Cape Verde Islands." Portugal was to have all lands discovered east of the line. England and France, whose claims were excluded in this papal document, paid no attention to the award.

28. Quoted in Boyd C. Shafer, *Faces of Nationalism: New Realities and Old Myths* (New York, 1972), p. 128.

29. For discussions of early Spanish nationalism, see Edward J. Goodman, "Spanish Nationalism in the Struggle Against Napoleon," *Review of Politics* (1958), vol. XX, pp. 330-40; and Richard Herr, "Good, Evil, and Spain's Rising Against Napoleon," in Richard Herr and Harold T. Parker, (eds.), *Ideas in History: Essays Presented to Louis Gottschalk by His Former Students* (Durham, N.C., 1965).

30. On Spanish explorations and the Spanish empire, see Roger B. Merriman, *The Rise of the Spanish Empire in the Old World and the New* (4 vols., New York, 1918); Martin A. S. Hume, *Spain: Its Greatness and Decay, 1479-1788* (Cambridge, Eng., 1913, 1940); and Reginald Trevor Davies, *The Golden Century of Spain, 1501-1621* (London, 1937, 1954).

31. Shafer, *Faces of Nationalism, op.cit.*, p. 115.

32. For the classic history of the Netherlands from the 16th to 18th centuries, see John Lothrop Motley, *The Rise of the Dutch Republic, 1555-1584* (3 vols., New York, 1856), and *History of the United Netherlands, 1584-1609* (4 vols., The Hague, 1860-1863). For a treatment of Dutch colonialism, see Herman T. Colenbrander, *Koloniale Geschiedenis* (3 vols., The Hague, 1925); and J. J. van Klaveren, *The Dutch Colonial System* (Rotterdam, 1953).

33. For general histories of Scandinavia, see Brynjolf J. Hovde, *The Scandinavian Countries, 1720-1863* (2 vols., Boston, 1943); and Royal Institute of International Affairs, *The Scandinavian States and Finland: A Political and Economic Survey* (London, 1951).

34. A plan to create Nordek, a sort of northern European Common Market, failed.

Chapter 6
Turkish Dilemma: Pan-Ottomanism, Pan-Turkism, and Pan-Turanism

1. On the history of Turkey, see Herbert A. Gibbons, *The Foundations of the Ottoman Empire* (Oxford, 1916); Mehmed F. Köprülü, *Les origines de l'Empire Ottoman* (Paris, 1935); and Paul Wittek, *The Rise of the Ottoman Empire* (London, 1938). See also William L. Langer and K. R. Blake, "The Rise of the Ottoman Turks and Its Historical Background," in *American Historical Review* (April, 1932), pp. 468-505.

2. On the Young Turks, see Harry Stuermer, *Two War Years in Constantinople: Sketches of German and Young Turkish Politics,* trans. by E. Allen and the author (New York, 1917); and Ernest E. Ramsaur, Jr., *The Young Turks: Prelude to the Revolution of 1908* (Princeton, N.J., 1957).

3. See Ramsaur, *The Young Turks, op.cit.,* for an analysis of Young Turk ideology.

4. Hans Kohn, *Nationalism: Its Meaning and History* (Princeton, N.J., 1955), p. 63.

5. The analysis here is from Ziyā Gökalp, *Turkish Nationalism and Western Civilization,* trans. and ed. by N. Berkes (London and New York, 1959), pp. 71-85.

6. Elie Kedouri (ed.), *Nationalism in Asia and Africa* (New York and Cleveland, 1970), p. 52.

7. Ziyā Gökalp, *Turish Nationalism, op.cit.,* pp. 78-79.

8. Quoted in Kedourie, *Nationalism in Asia and Africa, op.cit.,* p. 192.

9. *Ibid.,* p. 52.

10. On Mustafa Kemal, see Dagobert von Mikusch, *Mustapha Kemal* (New York, 1931); and Harold C. Armstrong, *Grey Wolf: Mustafa Kemal* (London, 1932).

11. On the restoration in Turkish history, see the analysis by Tekin Alp, *Le Kémalisme* (Paris, 1937), pp. 109-29.

12. From Tekin Alp's chapter reproduced in Kedourie, *Nationalism in Asia and Africa, op.cit.,* p. 214.

13. *Ibid.,* p. 219.

14. *Ibid.,* p. 221.

15. Though Pittard spoke plainly about the Turks being an "anthropological amalgam," Tekin Alp quoted Pittard as affirming that "the Turkish race represents, without any doubt, one of the most beautiful types at the point of juncture between Europe and Asia." (See Kedourie, *Nationalism in Asia and Africa, op.cit.,* p. 214.)

16. Kedourie, *Nationalism in Asia and Africa, op.cit.,* p. 50.

17. From Gökalp, *Turkish Nationalism and Western Civilization, op.cit.,* pp. 71ff.

18. For a more balanced discussion of the differences between state and nation, see George Schwab, "State and Nation: Toward a Further Clarification," in Michael Palumbo and William O. Shanahan, *Nationalism: Essays in Honor of Louis L. Snyder* (Westport, Ct., 1981), pp. 60-67.

Chapter 7
Pan-Islāmism: Search for Religious Unity

1. On the Islāmic religion, see Ameer, Ali Syed, *The Spirit of Islam* (London, 1922); D. S. Margoliouth *Mohammed and the Rise of Islam* (New York, 1927); A. J.

Wensinck, *The Muslim Creed* (Cambridge, Eng., 1932); T. W. Arnold, *The Preaching of Islam* (London, 1935); A. S. Tritton, *Islam: Belief and Practice* (London, 1951); A. J. Arberry, *The Koran Interpreted* (New York, 1955); K. W. Morgan (ed.), *Islam* (New York, 1958); and *The Koran*, trans. by M. M. Pickthal, in *The Meaning of the Glorious Koran* (New York, 1956).

2. From *The Koran*, trans. by J. M. Radwell (New York, 1948).

3. Sūrah III, *Al' Imram* ("The Family of Imram").

4. Sūrah XXI, *Al-Arbia* ("The Prophet").

5. Hazim Zaki Nussibeh, *The Idea of Arab Nationalism* (Ithaca, N.Y., 1956), p. 32.

6. See *Cambridge History of Islam* (Cambridge, Eng., 1979), vol. 2, pp. 98-99.

7. Philip Hitti, *History of the Arabs* (London, 1964), pp. 753-54.

8. *Cambridge History of England, op.cit.*, vol. 2, p. 172.

9. *Ibid.*, vol. II, pp. 179, 180, 187.

10. Philip Hitti, *The Near East in History* (Princeton, N.J., 1961), p. 405.

11. This anti-Western attitude was typical of Jamāl ad-Dīn's thinking. He presented the theory of modernization and internal development of Muslim states, during which they could adopt Western customs for their own benefit. But he always insisted that this type of combination made the caliphate capable of coping with European powers and resisting their exploitation and influence. (Hitti, *The Near East in History, op.cit.*, p. 406).

12. Hitti, *History of the Arabs, op.cit.*, p. 754.

13. On the caliphate, see Haroun al-Raschid, *Caliph of Baghdad* (London), 1881); William Muir, *The Caliphate: Its Rise, Decline and Fall* (Edinburgh, 1915); Bernard Lewis, *The Origins of Ismailism* (Cambridge, Eng., 1945); and C. Brockelman, *History of the Islamic People*, trans. by J. Carmichael, *et al.* (New York, 1947).

14. The chaotic situation in Iran was indicated on November 4, 1979, when Iranian militants took 90 hostages, including 65 Americans. The excited students vowed to remain in the U.S. Embassy until the deposed Shāh was returned to Iran to stand trial. Despite international denunciations and American efforts, including an abortive rescue attempt in April 1980, the crisis continued. The drama ended on January 21, 1981, when Washington agreed to an accord involving the release of frozen Iranian assets. Fifty-two Americans were flown to freedom.

15. *Newsweek*, July 20, 1940.

16. *Newsweek*, July 20, 1981, p. 42.

17. Among Kaddafi's plots and deals were: an abortive alliance with Algeria (1975); proposed merger and occupation of Chad (1980-1981); plot against Anwar Sadat of Egypt (1974); interference in Ethiopia (1977); training of insurgents in Gambia (1980); incitement of tribal strife in Ghana (1981); aid and training of the PLO in Lebanon (1970 on); plot against King Hassan in Morocco (1971); attempt to annex territory in Niger (1976); financing for an Islāmic nuclear bomb for Pakistan (1975-1976); campaign to overthrow the government of Somalia (1981); subversion in the Sudan (1974); proposed mergers with Syria (1971, 1980); proposed merger with Tunisia (1974) and support for guerrillas there (1980); futile military intervention to save Idi Amin in Uganda (1979) and interference in national elections there (1980); and support for Polisario rebels in Western Sahara (1975 on). (List compiled by *Newsweek*, July 20, 1981, p. 41).

18. Kaddafi in an interview with Elaine Sciolini, *Newsweek*, July 20, 1981, p. 46.

Chapter 8
Pan-Arabism: Integration versus Differentiation

1. On Pan-Arabism, see Eugene Jung, *La révolte Arabe* (2 vols., Paris, 1924-1925); George Antonius, *The Arab Awakening: The Story of the Arab National Movement* (Philadelphia, 1939); Hazem Z. Nusseibeh, *The Idea of Pan-Arabism* (Ithaca, N.Y., 1956); Walter Z. Laqueur, *Communism and Nationalism in the Middle East* (New York, 1956); F. A. Sayegh, *Arab Unity: Hope and Fulfillment* (New York, 1958); Morroe Berger, *The Arab World Today* (London, 1962): and S.G. Haim, *Arab Nationalism,* (Berkeley and Los Angeles, Calif., 1962).

2. See Chapter 7.

3. On the history of the Arabs, see Philip Hitti, *History of the Arabs* (London, 1956); Francesco Gabrieli, *Gil Arabi* (Florence, 1957); and Bernard Lewis, *The Arabs in History* (London, 1958).

4. Hitti, *History of the Arabs, op.cit.,* p. 755.

5. *Ibid.*

6. *Ibid.,* p. 756.

7. The Organization of Petroleum Exporting Countries (OPEC) was created November 14, 1960, on Venezuelan initiative. Members in 1984 were Algeria, Ecuador, Gabon, Indonesia, Iran, Iraq, Kuwait, Libya, Nigeria, Qatar, Saudi Arabia, United Arab Emirates, and Venezuela.

8. Members of the Arab League formed in 1945 were Algeria, Eqypt, Iraq, Jordan, Kuwait, Lebanon, Libya, Morocco, Saudi Arabia, Sudan, Syria, Tunisia, and Yemen.

9. Dissension became habitual inside the Arab League. In 1968 Tunisia disrupted a League meeting by voting against a resolution barring peace with Israel. In 1969, Iraq, after the public execution of 14 accused Israeli spies, complained that the press in other Arab countries had shown insufficient sympathy for its action. The chaotic situation in Lebanon, running into 1984, caused further dissension among Arabs.

10. On Nasser, see Wilton Wynn, *Nasser of Egypt: The Search for Dignity* (New York, 1959); Robert St. John, *The Boss* (New York, 1960); and Miles Copeland, *The Game of Nations* (New York, 1969).

11. Gamal Abdel Nasser, *Egypt Liberated: The Philosophy of the Revolution* (Washington, D.C., 1956), p. 77.

12. From the full text in Muhammad Khalili, *The Arab States and the Arab League* (Beirut, 1962), vol. 2, p. 946.

13. Hisham B. Sharabi, *Nationalism and Revolution in the Arab World* (Princeton, N.J., 1966), p. 97.

14. From the Constitution of the Socialist Arab Resurrection Party, text in Khalili, *Arab States, op.cit.,* Article 10, Third Principle, vol. 1, pp. 663-70.

15. Michel ʿAflaq, *For the Resurrection* (Beirut, 1959), p. 243.

16. *Ibid.,* p. 47.

17. From the text in the resolution of the Sixth National Congress of the Baʿath Party, quoted in Sharabi, *Nationalism and Revolution in the Arab World., op.cit.,* p. 138.

18. Walid Khalidi, "Toward the Unthinkable: A Sovereign Palestinian State," *Foreign Affairs* (July 1978), pp. 695-713.

19. *Ibid.,* p. 695

20. *Ibid.*

21. *Ibid.*, p. 696.

22. Fouad Ajami, "The End of Arabism," *Foreign Affairs* (Winter, 1978-1979), pp. 354-73.

23. *Ibid.*, p. 355.

24. *Ibid.*, p. 357.

25. *Ibid.*

26. *Ibid.*, p. 365.

27. Bernard Lewis, *The Middle East and the West* (New York, 1964), p. 94.

28. The Sykes-Picot agreement was signed on May 16, 1916, by Sir Mark Sykes for the British Government and Georges Picot for the French. It provided for the partition of the Ottoman Empire after World War I. France was to obtain the whole of Syria, Lebanon, Cilicia, and Mosul, while Britain was to received Transjordan, Iraq, and northern Palestine. The remainder of Palestine was to be under an international regime. There would be what was to be called "an Arab State." The agreement violated the assurances given by T. E. Lawrence to the Arabs he had led in revolt against the Turks.

29. The Balfour Declaration was made in a note on November 2, 1917, by A. J. Balfour, British Foreign Secretary, to Lionel Walter Rothschild, a Zionist leader, declaring British support for the establishment of a Jewish national home in Palestine with the proviso that safeguards would be reached for the rights of "existing non-Jewish communities" in Palestine.

30. Rowland Evans and Robert Novak, in the New York *Post*, July 2, 1982.

31. See Marvin Howe, in the *New York Times*, July 24, 1977.

Chapter 9
Zionism as Macro-Nationalism

1. The *Diaspora*, at the root of revived Jewish nationalism, refers to Jewish communities living in exile outside of Palestine. The Hebrew word *galut* ("exile") refers to the *Diaspora*, but *tefuzot* ("dispersion") better describes the scattering of Jews throughout the world. The first Jewish *Diaspora* came after the Babylonian Exile of 586 B.C.

2. The *Diaspora* carried special religious and political implications for those who had the messianic hope for the eventual return of exiles to the Home of Zion. This urge was less emphatic in democratic countries, where Jews had found emancipation and assimilation.

3. On the history of Zionism, see Nahum Sokolow, *History of Zionism, 1800-1918* (2 vols., London, 1919); Israel Cohen, *The Zionist Movement* (New York, 1946); Elihu Katz, *Source Book of Zionism and Israel* (New York, 1948); Martin Buber, *Israel and Palestine: The History of an Idea*, trans. by Stanley Goodman (New York, 1952); Oscar I. Janowsky, *The Foundations of Israel* (Princeton, N.J., 1959); Ben Halpern, *The Idea of the Jewish State*, (Cambridge, Mass., 1961); Arthur Hertzberg (ed.), *The Zionist Idea: A Historical Analysis and Reader* (Cleveland, 1964); Bernard A. Rosenblatt, *Two Generations of Zionism* (New York, 1967); and Shlomo Avineri, *The Making of Modern Zionism* (New York, 1981).

4. Janowsky, *Foundations of Israel, op.cit.*, p. 10.

5. Salo W. Baron, *Nationalism and Religion* (New York, 1947), p. 227.

6. See H. R. Trevor-Roper, "Jewish and Other Nationalisms," *Commentary*, vol. XXXV (January 1963), p. 21.

7. Hans Kohn, "Zionism," in *Encyclopedia of the Social Sciences* (New York, 1937), vol. 8, p. 530.

8. The policy of pogroms was associated closely with Russification in Imperial Russia. See Bernard Pares, *A History of Russia* (New York, 1953); Michael T. Florinsky, *Russia: A History and Interpretation* (2 vols., New York, 1953); George Vernadsky, *A History of Russia* (New Haven, Conn., 1954); and Hugh Seton-Watson, *The Decline of Imperial Russia, 1853-1914* (New York, 1956).

9. On the Dreyfus Case, see Louis L. Snyder (ed.), *The Dreyfus Case: A Documentary History* (New Brunswick, N.J., 1973).

10. Quoted in Parker T. Moon, *The Social Catholic Movement in France* (New York, 1921), p. 207.

11. On German anti-Semitism, see Constantin Brunner, *Der Judenhass und die Juden* (Berlin, 1919); and Kurt Wawrzinek, *Die Entstehung der deutschen antisemitenparteien, 1837-1890* (Berlin, 1927).

12. On Friedrich Max Müller, see Louis L. Snyder, *Race: A History of Modern Ethnic Theories* (New York, 1939), pp. 67-71.

13. On *The Protocols of the Elders of Zion,* see John S. Curtiss, *An Appraisal of the Protocols of Zion* (New York, 1942).

14. The slanderous forgery was proved by the journalist P. Graves in *The Times* (London), August 16, 17, 18, 1921, in "The Truth About the Protocols." Graves demonstrated that, not only were they a hoax and forgery, but also a literary plagiarism. Most of the text was shown to have been taken from a political tract published in 1865 and 1868 by a French republican, and aimed at Napoleon III. The anonymous forger, believed to have been a member of the Russian secret police, merely added a Jewish and Marxian content.

15. On Moses Hess, see Edmund Silberner, *The Works of Moses Hess* (Leiden, 1958); Isaiah Berlin, *Life and Opinions of Moses Hess* (London, 1959); Edmund Silberner, *Moses Hess: Geschichte seines Lebens* (Leiden, 1966); and Horst Lademacher, *Moses Hess in seiner Zeit* (Bonn, 1977).

16. On Pinsker, see Asher Ginzburg, *Pinsker and His Brochure,* trans. from Hebrew by H. Szold (Baltimore, Md., 1892); and Yochan Block, *Judentum in der Krise: Emanzipation, Socialismus und Zionismus* (Göttingen, 1966).

17. Trevor-Roper, "Jewish and Other Nationalisms," *op.cit.*, p. 15.

18. Hans Kohn, *Nationalism: Its Meaning and History* (Princeton, N.J., 1955), p. 7.

19. On Achad Ha'am, see Asher Ginzberg, *Nationalism and the Jewish Ethic: Basic Writings of Achad Ha'am* (New York, 1962).

20. On Herzl, see *The Congress Addresses of Theodor Herzl,* trans. by Bellie Straus (New York, 1917); Jacob de Haas, *Theodor Herzl: A Biographical Study* (Chicago, Ill., 1927); Joseph Fränkl, *Theodor Herzl: Des Schöpfers erstes Wollen* (Vienna, 1934); Oscar Benjamin Frankl, *Theodor Herzl: The Jew and the Man* (New York, 1949); Israel Cohen, *Theodor Herzl: Founder of Political Zionism* (New York, 1959); André Chouraqui, *Théodore Herzl* (Paris, 1960); Alex Bein, *Theodor Herzl: A Biography,* trans. by Maurice Samuel (New York, 1970); Amos Elon, *Herzl* (New York, 1975); and Ernst Pinchus Blumenthal, *Diener am Licht* (Cologne, 1977).

21. Theodor Herzl, *Der Judenstaat (The Jewish State)* (Leipzig, 1896). The first English edition was translated by S. d'Amgdor (London, 1896).

22. Theodor Herzl, *The Jewish State* (New York, 1943), p. 24.

23. *Ibid.*, p. 38.

24. From the Preamble of the Constitution proposed at the First Zionist Congress (1897).

25. After Herzl's death in 1904, the World Zionist Organization moved from Austria to Germany, where it remained until 1920, when it was transferred to London.

26. Halpern, *The Idea of the Jewish State, op.cit.*, pp. 22-23.

27. For a discussion of differences between religious and political Zionism, see George Lenczowski, *The Middle East in World Affairs* (New York, 1952), pp. 314-16.

28. In obtaining the Balfour Declaration from Britain, Weizmann was aided by Nathan Sokolow (1859-1932).

29. In 1982 the administration of Premier Menachem Begin was forced to grant many demands made by Orthodox rabbis, who held the political balance of power.

30. See full-page advertisement in *The New York Times*, June 21, 1982, by the *Neturei Karta* of Brooklyn, New York.

31. *Ibid.*

32. Masada, from the Hebrew term *Horvot Mezada*, meaning "ruins of Masada," refers to the ancient mountaintop fortress in southeast Israel, where Jews made their last stand in the revolt of 66-73 A.D. against the Romans. After the fall of Jerusalem and the destruction of the Temple (70 A.D.), a Roman army of 15,000 men attacked a defending force of 1,000 at Masada. Preferring death to enslavement, the Jews at Masada chose the way of mass suicide. Masada became a symbol of Jewish national heroism.

33. *The New York Times*, June 21, 1982.

34. From an advertisement by the American *Neturei Karta* in *The New York Times*, April 18, 1983.

35. Quoted in J.M.N. Jeffries, *Palestine: The Reality* (London, 1939), p. 147.

36. *Ibid.*, p. 153.

37. Anthony Lewis, in *The New York Times*, April 29, 1982.

Chapter 10
Pan-Africanism: The Black Man's Burden

1. It is an unfortunate fact that scholars of nationalism continue to confuse race with nationality. Disregarding scientific conclusions on the meaning of race, they tend to use race as a cultural rather than a biological term. It is a mistake to describe supranational Pan-Slavism as a "racial movement": the Slavs form a major sub-branch of the Indo-European family of languages, divided into West Slavic (Polish, Serbian, Czech, and Slovak); South Slavic (Old Church Slavonic, Bulgarian, Serbo-Croatian, and Slovene); East Slavic (Great Russian, Ukrainian, or Little Russian); and Byelorussian or White Russian. To label these peoples a distinct "Slavic race" is historically and semantically wrong. A similar error is made in assuming that the racial element is dominant in pan-Turanism, that the Turks form a common "race."

There is, however, a distinct racial element in Pan-Africanism, by which African and other black people seek unity in opposition to white oppression.

2. On imperialism in general, see Parker T. Moon, *Imperialism and World Politics* (New York, 1926); William L. Langer, *The Diplomacy of Imperialism, 1890-1902* (2 vols., New York, 1935); Grover Clark, *A Place in the Sun* (New York, 1936); Harry Rudin, *The Germans in the Cameroons, 1884-1914: A Case Study in Modern Imperialism* (New Haven, 1938); John A. Hobson, *Imperialism: A Study* (3rd ed., London, 1938); Mary Evelyn Townsend, *European Colonial Expansion Since 1871* (Philadelphia, Pa., 1941); Earle M. Winslow, *The Patterns of Imperialism: A Study of the Theories of Power* (New York, 1948); Joseph Schumpeter, *Imperialism and Social Classes* (Village Station, N.Y., 1951); Robert Straus-Hupé and Henry W. Hazard (eds.), *The Idea of Colonialism* (New York, 1958); and Louis L. Snyder, *The Imperialism Reader: Documents and Readings on Modern Expansionism* (Princeton, N.J., 1962).

3. On the meeting between Stanley and Livingstone, see Louis L. Snyder and Richard B. Morris, *A Treasury of Great Reporting* (New York, 1949), pp. 189-97.

4. See *ibid.*, pp. 189-90.

5. For a typical African blank treaty, see Edward Hertslet (ed.), *The Map of Africa by Treaty* (London, 1894), vol. 1, pp. 467 ff. Imperialist treaty-making in Africa followed a preconceived pattern. Agents bearing supplies of liquors and tinseled ornaments, together with blank treaty forms, set out on expeditions. A blank treaty of the Royal Niger Company in its drive for sovereign rights in the valley of the Tiger began:

We, the undersigned Chiefs of   , with a view of bettering the condition of our country and people, do this day cede to the Royal Niger Company (Chartered and Limited), forever, the whole of our territory extending from [   ].

We also give to the said Royal Niger Company (Chartered and Limited) full power to settle all native disputes arising from any cause whatever, and we pledge ourselves not to enter into any war with other tribes without the sanction of the said Royal Niger Company (Chartered and Limited).

We understand that the said Royal Niger Company (Chartered and Limited) have full power to mine, farm, and build in any portion of our country. . . .

6. Moscow supported a weak Cuban economy with a huge outlay of funds, but at the same time expected Fidel Castro's *quid pro quo* by such assistance as sending thousands of Cuban troops to help the guerrillas in Angola.

7. W. E. Burkhardt Du Bois, "The Pan-African Movement," in George Padmore (ed.), *History of the Pan-American Congress: Colonial and Colored Unity* (London, 1947, 1963), p. 11.

8. From *African Repository*, vol. LIII (April 1929), p. 75, quoted in John H. Bracey, August Meier, and Elliott Rudwick, *Black Nationalism in America* (Indianapolis, Ind., 1970), pp. 170-77.

9. Henry M. Turner, "The Negro Has Not Sense Enough," in *Voice of Missions*, July 1, 1900.

10. Henry M. Turner, "Emigration," *Voice of Missions*, April 1, 1900.

11. J. D. Fage, *A History of Africa* (London, 1978), p. 472.

12. Garvey's middle name was sometimes given as Moziah.

13. For biographies of Garvey, see Roi Ottley, *New World A-Coming* (Boston, 1943); and E. Davis Cronon, *Black Moses: The Story of Marcus Garvey and the Universal Negro Improvement Association* (New York, 1955).

14. Frederick Douglass (1817-1895) was an escaped slave whose oratorical and literary brilliance thrust him into the van of the Abolition movement. The first black citizen to hold high rank in the U.S. Government, he became a hero among American blacks.

15. See Ottley, *New World A-Coming, op.cit.*, pp. 66-81.

16. The Liberian Government came to the conclusion that Garvey was interested not in a moderate settlement of his followers but that he had more ambitious plans possibly for influence in Liberian affairs. It confiscated property in Liberia acquired by the Universal Negro Improvement Association.

17. Fage, *History of Africa, op.cit.*, p. 472.

18. Donald L. Wiedner, *History of Africa South of the Sahara* (New York, 1964), p. 319.

19. Quoted in Ottley, *New World A Coming, op.cit.*, pp. 66-81.

20. For the life of Du Bois, see Julius Lester (ed.), *The Seventh Son: The Thoughts and Writings of W.E.B. Du Bois* (2 vols., New York, 1921); Dorothy Sterling, *Lift Every Voice* (New York, 1965); Elliot Rudwick, *W.E.B. Du Bois* (New York, 1968); Rayford Logan (ed.), *W.E.B. Du Bois* (New York, 1971); Shirley Graham, *His Day is Marching On* (Philadelphia, Pa., 1971); and William L. Tuttle, *W.E.B. Du Bois* (Englewood Cliffs, N.J., 1973).

21. Du Bois's dissertation, *The Suppression of the Slave Trade to the United States, 1638-1870,* was the initial publication of the Harvard Historical Series.

22. Among Du Bois's prolific works, some reprinted after his death, were: *The Conservation of Races* (Washington, D.C., 1897); *Souls of Black Folk* (Chicago, Ill. 1903); *The Negro Church* (Atlanta, Ga., 1903); *The Negro* (New York, 1915); *The Gift of Black Folk* (Boston, 1924); *Dusk of Dawn: An Essay Toward an Autobiography of a Race Concept* (New York, 1940); *Color and Democracy* (New York, 1945); *Autobiography* (New York, 1960); *ABC of Color* (Berlin, 1964); *Voices from Within the Veil* (New York, 1969); *The Correspondence of W.E.B. Du Bois*, ed. by Herbert Aptheker (Amherst, Mass., 1973-1978); *Black Reconstruction* (Millwood, N.Y., 1976); and *Africa: Its Geography, People and Products* (Millwood, N.Y., 1977).

23. Du Bois, *Dusk of Dawn, op.cit.*, p. 2.

24. Du Bois expressed these themes in his *Conservation of Races, op.cit.*

25. Journalist George Creel was head of the Committee on Public Information, set up by President Woodrow Wilson on April 14, 1917, to unite American public opinion behind the war effort.

26. Quoted in a dispatch from Paris in the Chicago *Tribune*, January 19, 1919.

27. *Ibid.*

28. Du Bois, "The Pan African Movement," *op.cit.*, pp. 11-27.

29. Some African scholars say that the first Pan-African Congress was convened in London in 1900. Most, however, stay with the 1919 date.

30. Du Bois, "The Pan-African Movement," *op.cit.*, pp. 16-17.

31. *Ibid.*

32. Brussels *Neptune*, June 14, 1921.

33. Du Bois, "Manifesto of the Second Pan-African Congress," in *The Crisis*, vol. XXIII (November 1921), p. 10.

34. *Ibid.*

35. Quoted in Du Bois, "The Pan-African Movement," *op.cit., pp. 22-23.*

36. *Ibid.*, pp. 23-24.

37. *Ibid.*, pp. 24-26.

38. A. T. Grove, *Africa* (London, 1978), p. 315.

39. Paul Johnson, "Gadafi in Action," *Spectator* (August 29, 1981), p. 14.

40. Alan Cowell, in *The New York Times*, August 4, 1982.

Chapter 11
Pan-Asianism: Racial Xenophobia

1. Sun Yat-sen, "The Principles of Nationalism," in *San Min Chui I* (*The Three Principles of the Peoples*) (Shanghai, 1929), p. 100.

2. *The New York Times*, January 7, 1938. Fearing the effects of such statements on foreign opinion, the Japanese Foreign Office issued a statement holding that Admiral Suetsugu's views did not represent those of the Japanese Government. Moreover, it was added, his assertion was made before he became Home Minister.

3. On Genghis Khan, see Boris I. Vladimirisov, *The Life of Chingis-Khan*, trans. by D. S. Mirsky (London, 1930); René Grousset, *L'empire mongol* (Paris, 1941); and George Vernadsky, *The Mongols and Russia* (New Haven, Conn., 1953).

4. On Attila, see E. A. Thompson, *The History of Attila and the Huns* (Oxford, Eng., 1948); and H. Homeyer, *Attila: Der Huhhenkönig von seinen Zeitgenossen dargestellt* (Berlin, 1951).

5. The Manchus, with the help of General "Chinese" Gordon, managed to suppress the Tai-pings, who had set up a state in South China. Charles George Gordon (1833-1885) became a British national hero for his exploits in China and his ill-fated defense of Khartoum against Sudanese rebels. He personally directed the burning of the Emperor's Summer Palace in Peking in October, 1860. His engineers strengthened the European trading center at Shanghai, which had been threatened by the Tai-pings. (See Godfrey Elton, *General Gordon* [London, 1954].)

6. American merchants, too, took part in the illegal opium trade, operating in both Turkey and China. The American opium traffic was, in fact, an early and primitive example of multinational enterprise. (See James C. Thomson, Jr., Peter W. Stanley, and John Curtis Perry, *Sentimental Imperialisms: The American Experience in East Asia* [New York, 1981], pp. 35 ff.

7. *Ibid.*, p. 59.

8. On the Boxer Rebellion, see George N. Steiger, *China and the Occident: The Origin and Development of the Boxer Movement* (New Haven, Conn., 1927); Chester C. Tan, *The Boxer Catastrophe* (New York, 1955); and V. P. Purcell, *The Boxer Uprising, 1900* (New York, 1963).

9. The indemnity amounted to $330 million. Of this, the United States received $24 million, but cancelled the balance due in 1924. Most of the American indemnity was used to provide scholarships for Chinese students.

10. Willard Price, "Japan's Divine Mission," in *New Republic*, November 17, 1937.

11. The Japanese scholar Okakura held that "every family in Japan claims descent from the grandson of the Sun Goddess in his descent on earth by the light-rayed pathway of the clouds". (See S. Washnio, "Japanese Origins," in *Trans-Pacific*, November 17, 1928.)

12. *Ibid.*

13. C. K. Parker, "The Origins of the Japanese," in *Trans-Pacific*, May 16, 1929.

14. *Ibid.*

15. Hideo Nishioka and E. E. Schenck, "An Outline of Theories concerning Prehistoric Peoples of Japan," *American Anthropologist*, vol. XXXIX, pp. 22-23.

16. Suyeo Nakano, "Japan's Turkish Blood," *Trans-Pacific*, July 18, 1925.

17. See P. Starr, "The Ainu of Japan," *Asia* (April 1919), pp. 381-87.

18. See A. E. Hindemarsh, *The Basis of Japanese Foreign Policy* (Cambridge, Mass., 1936), pp. 4-6.

19. Thomson and Perry, *Sentimental Imperialisms, op.cit.*, p. 61.

20. On Commodore Matthew Calbraith Perry, see Arthur Walworth, *Black Ships Off Japan: The Story of Commodore Perry's Expedition* (New York, 1946).

21. See Townsend Harris, *Complete Journal* (Garden City, N.Y., 1930).

22. J. Kennedy, *Asian Nationalism in the Twentieth Century* (London, 1968), p. 18.

23. On the British in India, see M. Edwards, *The Last Years of British India* (London, 1963); and P. Spear, *The Oxford History of Modern India* (Oxford, 1965).

24. Dadabhai Naoroji, "The Moral Poverty of India and Native Thoughts on the Present British-Indian Policy," in *Conditions of India: Correspondence with the Secretary of State for India* (Bombay, 1881), p. 69.

25. On Burma, see U Nu, *Burma Under the Japanese* (London, 1954); and D. Woodman, *The Making of Burma* (London, 1962).

26. On the French in South-East Asia, see D. Lancaster, *The Emancipation of French Indo-China* (Oxford, 1961); and M. E. Gettleman (ed.), *Vietnam* (1965).

27. Kennedy, *Asian Nationalism, op.cit.*, p. 15.

28. On the Dutch in South-East Asia, see D. Woodman, *The Republic of Indonesia* (London, 1950); and B. Grant, *Indonesia* (New York, 1964).

29. See Chapter 6.

30. Edwin O. Reischauer, *The Japanese* (Cambridge, Mass., 1977), pp. 414-15.

31. The text of the Tanaka Memorial held that "for her self-protection as well as for the protection of others, Japan cannot remove the difficulties in Eastern Asia unless she adopts a policy of blood-and-iron." Japanese officials vehemently denied the memorial and its implications. For the complete text, see *The China Critic* (Shanghai, 1931), pp. 923-24.

32. The delegates to the Bandung Conference included the Colombo Powers (Burma, Ceylon, India, Indonesia, and Pakistan), together with representatives from Afghanistan, Cambodia, People's Republic of China, Egypt, Ethiopia, Gold Coast, Iran, Iraq, Japan, Jordan, Sudan, Syria, Thailand, Turkey, Democratic Republic of (North) Vietnam, State of Vietnam, Yemen, and several small states.

33. From the complete text in George M. Kahin, *The Asian-African Conference, Bandung, Indonesia* (Ithaca, N.Y., 1956), pp. 71-85.

34. *Ibid.*

35. See Carlos P. Romulus, *The Meaning of Bandung* (New York, 1956).

Chapter 12
Pan-Americanism: Drive for Hemispheric Solidarity

1. See Arthur P. Whitaker, *Nationalism in Latin America: Past and Present* (Gainesville, Fla., 1962), pp. 55-57 for an excellent discussion of "Continental Nationalism and the United States."

2. "It appears that Pan-Americanism and Pan-Latin-Americanism are not necessarily competitors, and may even be co-workers, as long as the respective relationships connoted by them remain international. It will be otherwise, however, when either of them takes on the character of extended nationalism." (Whitaker, *Nationalism in Latin America, op.cit.*, p. 66.)

3. *Time*, June 21, 1982.

4. On the Monroe Doctrine, see Alejandro Alvarez, *The Monroe Doctrine: Its Importance in the International Life of the States of the New World* (New York and London, 1924); and Dexter Perkins, *A History of the Monroe Doctrine* (Boston, 1955).

5. In fact, the original Monroe Doctrine had no standing in international law until the U.S. Senate ratified the Act of Havana in 1940 by defining the role of the United States in international relations.

6. On Simón Bolivar, see Harold A. Bierck, *Selected Writings of Bolivar (2 vols., New York, 1951);* Víctor A. Belaúnde, *Bolivar and the Political Thought of the Spanish American Revolution* (Baltimore, Md., 1938); Gerhard Masur, *Simón Bolívar* (Albuquerque, N.M., 1948); Vincente Lacuna, *Colección de cartas del Liberatador,* trans. by Lewis Bertrand (2 vols., New York, 1951); John B. Trend, *Bolívar and the Independence of Spanish America* (London, 1951); and Harold Osborne, *Bolivia: A Land Divided* (London, 1954).

7. John Edwin Fagg, *Pan Americanism* (Malabar, Fla., 1982), p. 12.

8. For a discussion of the 1826 Panama Congress, see L. B. Lockey, *Pan-Americanism: Its Beginnings* (New York, 1920), pp. 432 ff.

9. *The New York Tribune*, April 21, 1890.

10. Quoted in Fagg, *Pan Americanism, op.çit.*, p. 133.

11. *Ibid.*, p. 26.

12. Theodore Roosevelt, in his annual message to Congress, December 6, 1904.

13. Report of the Delegates of the United States to the Third International Conference of American States; (Washington, D.C., 1907).

14. Quoted in *The Literary Digest*, June 18, 1928.

15. *Ibid.*, February 4, 1928.

16. *Ibid.*, March 10, 1928.

17. From Franklin D. Roosevelt's inaugural address, March 4, 1933.

18. See *The Public Papers and Addresses of Franklin D. Roosevelt*, vol. 2. *The Year of Crisis, 1933* (New York, 1938).

19. *Ibid.*

20. Preamble of the Charter of the Organization of American States (1948).

21. "Now that after infinite victories we have succeeded in annihilating the Spanish hosts, the Court of Madrid in desperation has vainly endeavored to impose upon the mind of the magnanimous sovereigns who have just destroyed usurpation and tyranny in Europe, and must be the protectors of the legality and justice of the American cause. Being incapable of attaining our submission by force of arms, Spain

has recourse to her insidious policy: being unable to conquer us she has brought into play her devious artfulness." (From Simón Bolívar's Address at the Congress, Angostura, February 15, 1819 [Washington, D.C., 1819], pp. 17-21.)

22. Fagg, *Pan Americanism op.cit.*, pp. 34-35.

23. José Figueres, in *Hearings before the Subcommittee on Inter-American Affairs of the Committee on Foreign Relations,* 2nd Session (Washington, D.C. 1958), extracted from pp. 73-93. Courtesty of U.S. Government Printing Office.

24. *Title I. Objectives of the Alliance for Progress,* Department of State Publication 7276, Inter-American Series 73, October 1961.

25. Fagg, *Pan Americanism, op.cit.,* p. 98.

26. Richard E. Feinberg, "Rethinking Policy in Central America," in *The New York Times,* November 16, 1982.

27. *Newsweek,* November 8, 1982, p. 48.

28. *Ibid.*

29. Lawrence E. Harrison, "Waking from the Pan-American Dream," *Foreign Policy,* no. 5 (Winter, 1971-1972), p. 163. Courtesy of the Carnegie Endowment for International Peace.

Chapter 13
Retrospect and Prospect

1. Lewis Namier, *Vanquished Supremacies: Essays on European History* (London, 1958).

2. Isaiah Berlin, 'The Bent Twig: A Note on Nationalism," *Foreign Affairs,* vol. 51, no. 1, (October 1972), p. 15.

3. Hans Kohn, *Nationalism: Its Meaning and History* (Princeton, N.J., 1955), p. 90.

4. From *The Einstein Papers* (Princeton, N.J., 1972), quoted in *The New York Times,* March 29, 1972.

5. *Ibid.* Thus ended the passage that Einstein agreed to delete. However, he concluded his essay by saying, "But why so many words, when I can say everything in one sentence, and also in a sentence that suits my being a Jew: Honor your master, Jesus Christ, not only with words and hymns, but above all through your deeds."

BIBLIOGRAPHY _____

Abrahams, Willie E. *The Mind of Africa.* Chicago, 1962.
Adams, Charles C. *Islam and Modernism in Egypt.* London, 1933.
Adera, Teshome. *Nationalist Leaders and African Unity.* Addis Ababa, 1963.
Afifi, M. El-Hadi. *The Arabs and the United Nations.* London, 1964.
Aflaq, Michel. *For the Resurrection.* Beirut, 1959.
African Society of African Culture. *Pan-Africanism Reconsidered.* Berkeley, Calif., 1962.
Aguilar, Alonso. *Pan-Americanism from Monroe to the Present.* New York and London, 1968.
Alba, Victor. *Nationalities Without Nations.* New York, 1968.
Alvarez, Alejandro. *The Monroe Doctrine: Its Importance in the International Life of the States of the New World.* New York and London, 1924.
Ameer, Ali Syed. *The Spirit of Islam.* London, 1922.
Andler, Charles Philippe. *Pan-Germanism.* Paris, 1915.
Antonius, George. *The Arab Awakening: The Story of the Arab National Movement.* Philadelphia, Pa., 1939.
Arabism in the Balance of Nationalism. Beirut, 1950.
Arberry, A. J. *The Koran Interpreted.* New York, 1955.
Arendt, Hannah. *The Origins of Totalitarianism.* New York, 1951, 1966.
Armand, Louis, and Michael Drancourt. *The European Challenge.* London, 1970.
Armstrong, Harold C. *Grey Wolf: Mustafa Kemal.* London, 1932.
Arnold, T. W. *The Preaching of Islam.* London, 1935.
Assaf, Michael. *The Pan-Islamic Movement.* New York, 1937.
Avineri, Shlomo. *The Meaning of Modern Zionism.* New York, 1981.
Banse, Ewald. *Germany Prepares for War: A Nazi Theory of "National Defense."* Trans. by Alan Harris. London and New York, 1934.
Barbes, Leonard. *Africa in Eclipse.* London, 1971.
Barnes, Harry Elmer. *The Genesis of the War.* New York, 1926.
Baron, Salo W. *Nationalism and Religion.* New York, 1947.

Bauer, Otto. *Die Nationalitätenfrage und die oesterreichische Sozialdemokratie.* Vienna, 1907.

Baum, Warren. *The French Economy and the State.* Princeton, N.J., 1958.

Bein, Alex. *Theodor Herzl. A Biography.* Trans. by Maurice Samuel. New York, 1970.

Belaúnde, Victor A. *Bolívar and the Political Thought of the Spanish American Revolution.* Baltimore, Md., 1938.

Beneš, Edvard. *Uvahy o slovanstí hlavni problemy slovanské politiky (Reflections on the Slavs: The Main Problems of Slav Policy).* Prague, 1947.

Ben Gurion, David. *The Jews in Their Land.* London, 1964.

Bentwich, N. *Israel Resurgent.* London, 1960.

Berendt, Richard F. W. *Inter-American Economic Relations: Problems and Prospects.* New York, 1948.

Berger, Morroe. *The Arab World Today.* London, 1962.

Berkenkopf, Galina. *Welterlösung ein geschichtliche Traums Russlands.* Munich, 1962.

Berlin, Isaiah. *Life and Opinions of Moses Hess.* London, 1959.

Bernhard, Otto. *Geschichte des All-deutschen Verbandes.* Leipzig and Berlin, 1920.

Bernstein, Harry. *Making the Inter-American Mind.* Gainesville, Fla., 1961.

Bibl, Viktor. *Georg von Schoenerer: Ein Vorkämpfer des Grossdeutschen Reiches.* Leipzig, 1942.

Block, Yochan. *Judenthum in der Krise: Emanzipation, Sozialismus und Zionismus.* Göttingen, 1966.

Bracey, John H., August Meier, and Elliott Rudwick. *Black Nationalism in America.* Indianapolis, Ind., 1970.

Brochade, José I. F. de Costa. *Infante d. Henrique.* Lisbon, 1942.

Brockelman, C. *History of the Islamic People.* Trans. by J. Carmichael *et al.* New York, 1947.

Brugmans, Hendrik. *L'idée européen.* Bruges, 1970.

Brunner, Constantin. *Der Judenthum und die Juden.* Berlin, 1919.

Buber, Martin. *Israel and Palestine: The History of an Idea.* Trans. by Stanley Goodman. New York, 1952.

Buchan, Alistair (ed.). *Europe's Futures, Europe's Choices.* London, 1969.

Burt, Robert N., and Roland D. Hussey. *Documents on Inter-American Cooperation.* 2 vols. Philadelphia, 1955.

Bury, George Wyman. *Pan-Islam.* London, 1919.

Caicedo, Castilla José Joaquin. *El panamericanisme.* Buenos Aires, 1961.

Carlyle, Thomas. *Past and Present.* New York, 1918.

Carr, E. H. *Michael Bakunin.* London, 1937.

Carr, William. *A History of Germany.* London, 1969.

Carter, Gwendolen M. (ed.). *National Unity and Regionalism in African States.* Ithaca, N.Y., 1966.

Chamberlain, Houston Stewart. *Die Grundlagen des 19. Jahrhunderts.* Munich, 1899.

Cheradamé, André. *The Pan-German Plot Unmasked.* London, 1917.

Chouraqui, André. *Theodor Herzl.* Paris, 1960.

Chui, San Min. *The Principles of the People.* Shanghai, 1929.

Ciller, Alois. *Die Vorläufer des Nationalsozialismus.* Vienna, 1932.

Clark, Colin. *British Trade in the Common Market.* London, 1962.

Clark, Grover. *A Place in the Sun.* New York, 1938.

Clark, W. *The Politics of the Common Market.* Englewood Cliffs, N.J., 1967.

Cocks, Barnett. *The European Parliament: Structure, Procedure, and Practice.* London, 1973.

Cohen, Israel. *The Zionist Movement.* New York, 1946.

_____. *Theodor Herzl: Founder of Political Zionism.* New York, 1959.

Colendrander, Herman T. *Koloniale Geschiedenis.* 3 vols. The Hague, 1925.

Connell-Smith, Gordon. *The Inter-American System.* London, 1966.

Copeland, Miles. *The Game of Nations.* New York, 1969.

Cosgrove, C. A., and K. J. Twitchett. *The New International Actors: The United Nations and the European Economic Community.* London, 1970.

Coudenhove-Kalergi, Richard N., *Europa Erwacht.* Paris, 1934.

_____. *Europe Must Unite.* Glarus, Switzerland, 1939.

_____. *Crusade for Pan-Europe.* New York, 1943.

_____. *Kampf um Pan-Europa.* Zurich, 1949.

_____. *Die europäische Nation.* Stuttgart, 1953.

_____. *Eine Idee erobert Europa.* Munich, 1958.

_____. *Pan-Europa.* Munich, 1966.

_____. *Ein Leben für Europa.* Cologne, 1966.

Cowan, Laing Gray. *The Dilemma of African Independence.* New York, 1964.

Cowen, George F. *History and Historians of the Nineteenth Century.* London and New York, 1913.

Cox, Richard Hubert Francis. *Pan-Africanism in Practice.* New York, 1964.

Cramb, John Adams. *Germany and England.* New York, 1915.

Cronon, E. Davis. *Black Moses: The Story of Marcus Garvey and the Universal Negro Improvement Association.* New York, 1955.

Curtiss, John S. *An Appraisal of the Protocols of Zion.* New York, 1942.

Daim, Wilfried. *Der Mann der Hitler die Ideen gab.* Munich, 1958.

Davidson, Basil. *Which Way Africa? The Search for a New Society.* London, 1964.

Davies, Reginald Trevor. *The Golden Age of Spain, 1501-1621.* London, 1964.

Decraine, P. *Le panafrikanisme.* London, 1965.

Diebold, William, Jr. *The Schuman Plan: A Study in Economic Cooperation in 1950-1959.* New York, 1959.

Dilke, Charles Wentworth. *Greater Britain.* London, 1868.

Directorate-General for Research and Documentation. *Elections to the European Parliament by Direct Universal Suffrage.* Luxembourg, 1977.

Dorpalen, Andreas. *The World of General Haushofer: Geopolitics in Action.* New York, 1942.

Dostoevsky, Feodor Mikhailovich. *The Diary of a Writer.* New York, 1949.

Douglas, William O. *The Holocaust or Hemispheric Co-operation.* New York, 1971.

Dozer, Donald Marquand (ed.). *The Monroe Doctrine.* New York, 1965.

Du Bois, W. E. Burghardt. *The Conservation of Races.* Washington, D.C., 1897.

_____. *Souls of Black Folk.* Chicago, 1903.

_____. *The Negro Church.* Atlanta, Ga., 1903.

_____. *The Negro.* New York, 1915.

_____. *The Gift of Black Folk.* Boston, 1924.

_____. *Color and Democracy.* New York, 1940.

_____. *Autobiography.* New York, 1960.

_____. *ABC of Color*. Berlin, 1964.

_____. *The World and Africa*. New York, 1965.

_____. *Darkwater Voices from Within the Veil*. New York, 1920.

_____. *The Correspondence of W.E.B. Du Bois and Herbert Aptheker*. Amherst, Mass., 1973-1978.

_____. *Black Reconstruction*. Millwood, N.Y., 1976.

Dugdale, B.E.C. *Arthur James Balfour*. New York, 1937.

Duggan, Laurence. *The Americas: The Search for Hemispheric Security*. New York, 1949.

Edwards, M. *The Last Years of British India*. London, 1963.

Efrat, Edgar Shlomo. *The Application of Federalism to Emergent States in Central Africa*. Austin, Tex., c. 1963.

Ehrmann, Henry W. *Organized Business in France*. Princeton, N.J., 1957.

Elon, Amos. *Herzl*. New York, 1975.

Elton, Godfrey. *General Gordon*. London, 1954.

Emerson, Rupert. *From Empire to Nation*. Boston, 1962.

Ergang, Robert R. *Herder and the Foundations of German Nationalism*. New York, 1931.

Essien-Udom, E. U. *Black Nationalism: The Search for Identity in America*. Chicago, 1962.

Fage, J. D. *A History of Africa*. London, 1978.

Fagg, John Edwin. Pan Americanism. Malabar, Fla. 1982.

Farr, Walter (ed.). *Guide to the Common Market*. London, 1972.

Fay, Sidney B. *The Origins of the World War*. 2 vols. New York, 1930.

Fischel, Alfred. *Der Panslawismus bis zum Weltkrieg, ein geschichtlicher Ueberblick*. Stuttgart, 1919.

Fischer, Fritz. *Germany's Aims in the First World War*. New York, 1967.

Florinsky, Michael T. *Russia: A History and Interpretation*. 2 vols. New York, 1953.

Forsyth, M. *The Parliament of the European Communities*. London, 1964.

Franck, Thomas M. (ed.). *Why Federations Fail: An Inquiry into the Requisites for Successful Federation*. New York, 1968.

Fränkl, Joseph Theodor. *Theodor Herzl*. Vienna, 1934.

Frankl, Oscar Benjamin. *Theodor Herzl: The Jew and the Man*. New York, 1949.

Gabrieli, Francesco. *Gil Arabi*. Florence 1957.

_____. *The Arab Revival*. New York, 1961.

Garvey, Amy J. *Garvey and Garveyism*. Kingston, Jamaica, 1963.

Garvey, Marcus. *Philosophical Opinions*. 2 vols. New York, 1923-1926.

Gaulle, Charles de. *War Memoirs: Salvation, 1944-1946*. Trans. by Richard Howard. New York, 1960.

Geiss, Imanuel. *Pan-Afrikanismus: Zur Geschichte der Dekolonisation*. Frankfurt-am-Main, 1968.

Gettlemen, M. E. (ed.). *Vietnam*. New York, 1965.

Gibbons, Herbert A. *The Foundations of the Ottoman Empire*. London, 1916.

Gil, Frederico. *Latin-American-United States Relations*. New York, 1971.

Ginzberg, Asher. *Nationalism and the Jewish Ethic*. New York, 1962.

Gobineau, Arthur. *Nationalism and the Jewish Ethic*. New York, 1962.

    Collins. New York, 1915.

Gökalp, Ziyā. *Turkish Nationalism and Western Civilization*. Trans. and ed. by N. Berkes. London and New York, 1959.

Graham, Shirley. *His Day Is Marching On*. Philadelphia, Pa., 1971.

Grant, B. *Indonesia*. New York, 1964.

Grant, Madison. *The Passing of the Great Race*. New York, 1918.

Green, Reginald Herbold, and Ann Seidman. *Unity or Poverty? The Economics of Pan-Africanism*. London, 1968.

Gross, Felix (ed.). *European Ideologies*. New York, 1948.

Gross, Vladimir. *The Pan-German Web*. New York, 1944.

Grousset, René. *L'empire mongol*. Paris, 1941.

Grove, A.T. *Africa*. London, 1978.

Hass, Ernest B. *Beyond the Nation-State: Functionalism and International Organization*. Stanford, Calif., 1964.

Haas, Jacob de. *Theodor Herzl: A Biographical Study*. Chicago, Ill., 1927.

Haim, S. G. *Arab Nationalism*. Berkeley and Los Angeles, Calif., 1962.

Halpern, Ben. *The Idea of the Jewish State*. Cambridge, Mass., 1961.

Hanke, Lewis (ed.). *Do the Americas Have a Common History?* New York, 1964.

Harrison, Austin. *The Pan-Germanic Doctrine*. New York and London, 1904.

Harrison, Marguerite Elston (Baker). *Asia Reborn*. New York and London, 1928.

Hatch, John. *Africa Emergent*. Chicago, 1974.

Haushofer, Karl. *Geopolitik der Pan-Ideen*. Berlin, 1931.

Hay, Stephen N. *Asian Ideas of East and West*. Cambridge, Mass., 1970.

Hayes, Carlton J. H. *Essays on Nationalism*. New York, 1926.

_____. *The Historical Evolution of Modern Nationalism*. New York, 1931.

_____. *Nationalism: A Religion*. New York, 1960.

Heiden, Konrad. *Geschichte des Nationalsozialismus*. Berlin, 1932.

Heller, Joseph. *Zionist Idea*. New York, 1949.

Hepner, Benoit. *Bakounine et le panslavisme révolutionnaire*. Paris, 1950.

Herr, Richard, and Harold T. Parker (eds.) *Ideas in History*. Durham, N.C., 1965.

Hertslet, Edward (ed.). *The Map of Africa by Treaty*. 3 vols. London, 1894.

Hertzberg, Arthur R. (ed.). *The Zionist Idea: A Historical Analysis and Reader*. Cleveland, Ohio, 1959, 1964.

Herzl, Theodor. *Der Judenstaat*. Leipzig, 1896.

_____. *The Congress Address*. Trans. by B. Straus. New York, 1917.

_____. *Theodor Herzl: A Portrait for This Age*. Cleveland, Ohio, 1955.

Hgita, Ionescu. *The New Politics of European Integration*. London, 1972.

Hilton, Ronald (ed.). *The Movement Toward Latin-American Unity*. New York, 1969.

Hindemarsh, A. E. *The Basis of Japanese Foreign Policy*. Cambridge, Mass., 1936.

Hitler, Adolf. *Mein Kampf*. Munich, 1943.

Hitti, Philip K. *The Near East in History*. Princeton, 1961.

_____. *History of the Arabs*. New York, 1964.

_____. *Islam and the West*. Princeton, N.J., 1962.

_____. *Lebanon in History*. London, 1967.

Hobson, John A. *Imperialism: A Study*. 3d. rev. ed. London, 1938.

Hoch, Karl. *Pangermanismus*. Prague, 1946.

Hoetsch, Otto. *The Evolution of Russia*. London, 1966.

Homeyer, H. *Attila: Der Hunenkönig von seinen Zeitgenossen dargestellt*. Berlin, 1951.

Hovde, Brynjolf J. *The Scandinavian Countries, 1720-1863*. 2 vols. Boston, 1943.

Hume, Martin A. S. *Spain: Its Greatness and Decay, 1479-1788*. Cambridge, England, 1913, 1940.

Humphrey, John T. *The Inter-American System: A Canadian View*. Toronto, 1942.

Ingenieros, José. *Por la unión latino americana*. Buenos Aires, 1922.

Inman, Samuel Guy. *Inter-American Conferences, 1826-1954*. Washington, D.C., 1965.

Jackson, Robert, and John Fitzmaurice. *The European Parliament*. London, 1979.

Janowsky, Oscar I. *The Foundations of Israel*. Princeton, N.J., 1959.

Jäschke, Gotthard. *Der Turanismus der Jungtürken*. Leipzig, 1941.

Jeffries, J.M.N. *Palestine: The Reality*. London, 1939.

Jung, Eugene. *La révolte Arabe*. 2 vols. Paris, 1924-1925.

Kahin, George M. *The Asian-African Conference, Bandung, Indonesia*. Ithaca, N.Y., 1956.

Kann, Robert A. *The Multinational Empire: Nationalism and Reform in the Habsburg Monarchy*. 2 vols. New York, 1950.

_____. *The Habsburg Monarchy: A Study in Integration and Disintegration*. New York, 1957.

_____*Das Nationalitätenproblem der Habsburger Monarchie*. 2d. ed. 2 vols. Graz and Cologne, 1964.

Karnes, Thomas L. *Readings in the Latin American Policy of the United States*. Tucson, Ariz., 1972.

Katz, Elihu. *Source Book of Zionism and Israel*. New York, 1948.

Keddie, Nikka R. *An Islam Response to Imperialism*. London, 1968.

Kedourie, Elie (ed.). *Nationalism in Asia and Africa*. New York and Cleveland, Ohio, 1970.

Kennedy, J. *Asian Nationalism in the Twentieth Century*. London and New York, 1968.

Keohane, Robert, and Joseph S. Nye, Jr. (eds.). *Transnational Relations and World Politics*. Cambridge, Mass., 1972.

Khalili, Muhammad. *The Arab States and the Arab League*. Beirut, 1962.

Kindleberger, Charles. *The International Corporation*. Cambridge, Mass., 1970.

Kingsley, Donald. *The Undiscovered Dostoevski*. London, 1962.

Kirschbaum, Jos. M. *Pan-Slavism in Literature*. Winnipeg, Canada, 1966.

Kitzinger, Uwe. *The Politics and Economics of European Economic Integration*. New York, 1963.

Klaveren, J. J. van. *The Dutch Colonial System*. Rotterdam, 1953.

Knapp, W. *Unity and Nationalism in Europe Since 1945*. London, 1969.

Knoll, Kurt. *Geschichte der deutschnationalen Bewegung*. Jena, Germany, 1926.

Kohl, Hans. *Dreissig Jahre preussische-deutsche Geschichte*. Giessen, Germany, 1888.

Kohl, Horst. *Die politischen Reden des Fürsten Bismarcks: historisch-Kritische Gesammtausgabe*. Stuttgart, 1892-1904.

Kohn, Hans. *Nationalism and Imperialism in the Hither East*. London, 1932.

_____. *The Idea of Nationalism*. New York, 1944.

_____. *Pan-Slavism: Its History and Ideology*. Notre Dame, Ind. 1953.

_____. *Nationalism: Its Meaning and History*. Princeton, N.J. 1955.

_____. *The Mind of Germany.* New York, 1960.

Kohnstamm, Max, and Wolfgang Hager (eds.). *A Nation Writ Large? The Policy Problems of the European Community.* London, 1973.

Köprülü, Mehmed F. *Les origines de l'Empire Ottoman.* Paris, 1935.

Kraus, Michael. *A History of American History.* New York, 1937.

Kryck, Alfred. *Geschichte des Alldeutschen Verbandes.* Wiesbaden, 1954.

Lacuna, Vincente. *Colleción de cartas del Liberatador.* Trans. by Lewis Bertrand. 2 vols. New York, 1951.

Lademacher, Horst. *Moses Hess in seiner Zeit.* Bonn, 1977.

Lambert, John. *Britain in a Federated Europe.* London, 1968.

Lancaster, D. *The Emancipation of French Indo-China.* London, 1961.

Langer, William L. *The Diplomacy of Imperialism, 1890-1902.* 2 vols. New York, 1935.

Laqueur, Walter Z. *Communism and Nationalism in the Middle East.* New York, 1956.

_____. *Europe Since Hitler.* London, 1970.

Léger, Louis. *Souvenirs d'un slavophile, 1863-1897.* Paris, 1905.

_____. *Le Panslavisme et l'intérêt français.* Paris, 1917.

Legum, Colin. *Pan-Africanism: A Short History.* London, 1962.

Leiva, Vivas Rafáel. *El sistema interamericana.* Tegucigalpa, Honduras, 1962.

Lenczowski, George. *The Middle East in World Affairs.* New York, 1952.

Lester, Julius (ed.). *The Seventh Son: The Thought and Writings of W.E.B. Du Bois.* 2 vols. New York, 1921.

Lewis, Bernard. *The Origins of Ismailism.* Cambridge, England, 1945.

_____. *The Arabs in History.* London, 1958.

_____. *The Middle East and the West.* New York, 1964.

Lewis, Geoffrey. *Modern Turkey.* London, 1974.

Lewis, W. R. *Rome or Brussels?* London, 1971.

Lieber, R. J. *British Politics and European Unity.* Berkeley, Calif., 1970.

Lincoln, C. Eric. *The Black Muslims in America.* Boston, Mass., 1961.

Lindeiner-Wildau, K. von. *Le supernationalité en tant que principle de droit.* Leiden, 1970.

Lister, L. *Europe's Coal and Steel Community.* New York, 1960.

Livermore, Harold V. *A History of Portugal.* Cambridge, England, 1947.

Lobo, Helio. *O Pan-Américanismo e o Brasil.* Saõ Paolo, 1939.

Lockey, Joseph B. *Pan-Americanism: Its Beginning.* New York, 1920.

_____. *Essays on Pan-Americanism:* Berkeley, Calif., 1939.

Logan, Rayford W. (ed.). *W.E.B. Du Bois.* New York, 1971.

London, K. (ed.). *New Nations in a Divided World: The International Relations of the Afro-Asian States.* New York, 1965.

Lutz, Ralph Haswell. *Fall of the German Empire, 1914-1918.* Stanford, Calif., 1932.

Lützow, Count. *Lectures on the Historians of Bohemia.* London, 1905.

MacDonald, H. W. *The League of Arab States.* Princeton, N.J. 1965.

McGann, Thomas F. *Argentina, the U.S. and the Inter-American System, 1880-1904.* Cambridge, Mass., 1957.

MacKenzie, David. *The Serbs and Russian Pan-Slavism.* Ithaca, N.Y., 1967.

Malcolm X. *Autobiography of Malcolm X.* New York, 1965.

Malik, H. *Moslem Nationalism in India and Pakistan.* London, 1963.

Manger, William. *Pan-America in Crisis: The Future of the OAS.* Washington, D.C., 1961.

Mansergh, Philip Nicholas. *The Coming of the First World War, 1878-1914*. London, 1947.

Margoliouth, D. S. *Mohammed and the Rise of Islam*. New York, 1927.

Martínez, Ricardo A. *El panamericanisme*. Buenos Aires, 1957.

Masur, Werner. *Hitler's Letters and Notes*. New York, 1973.

Mathijsen, R.S.R.F. *A Guide to the European Community Law*. London, 1974.

Mayne, Richard. *The Community of Europe*. New York, 1963.

Mazro, Ali Al'Amin. *Towards a Pax Africana: A Study of Ideology and Ambition*. London, 1967.

Mboya, Tom. *The Challenge of Nationhood*. London, 1970.

Meecham, J. Lloyd. *The United States and Inter-American Security, 1889-1960*. Austin, Tex., 1961.

Meier, August. *The Emergence of Negro Nationalism*. New York, 1949.

Merriman, Roger B. *The Rise of the Spanish Empire in the Old World and the New*. 4 vols. New York, 1918.

Metnitz, Gustaf Adolf von. *Hundert Millionen Deutsche schaffen Raum*. Graz, Austria, 1942.

Meyer, Henry Cord. *Mitteleuropa in German Thought and Action, 1815-1945*. The Hague, 1955.

Mezu, Sebastian Okechukwu (ed.). *The Philosophy of Pan-Africanism*. Washington, D.C., 1965.

Mikusch, Dagobert von. *Mustapha Kemal*. New York, 1931.

Montagu, Ashley. *Man's Most Dangerous Myth: The Fallacy of Race*. New York, 1942.

Moon, Parker T. *The Social Catholic Movement in France*. New York, 1921.

———. *Imperialism and World Politics*. New York, 1926.

Morgan, K. W. (ed.). *Islam*. New York, 1958.

Motley, John Lothrop. *The Rise of the Dutch Republic*. 3 vols. New York, 1856.

———. *History of the United Netherlands, 1584-1600*. 4 vols. The Hague, 1860-1863.

Mousset, Albert. *The World of the Slavs*. London, 1950.

Mowat, R. C. *Creating the European Community*. London, 1973.

Muir, William. *The Caliphate: Its Rise, Decline and Fall*. Edinburgh, 1915.

Nadolny, Rudolf August H. *Germanisierung oder Slavisierung*. Berlin, 1928.

Namier, Lewis. *Vanquished Supremacies: Essays on European History*. London, 1958.

Nasser, Gamal Abdel. *Egypt Liberated: The Philosophy of the Revolution*. Washington, D.C., 1956.

Neal, Larry. *Black Fire: An Anthology of Afro-American Writing*. New York, 1968.

Nikitin, Sergeo Aleksandrovich. *Slavianskie Momitety V, 1858-1870*. Moscow, 1960.

Nkrumah, Kwame. *Africa Must Unite*. London, 1963.

Nowell, Charles A. *A History of Portugal*. New York, 1952.

Nu, U. *Burma Under the Japanese*. London, 1954.

Nussibeh, Hazim Zaki. *The Idea of Arab Nationalism*. Ithaca, N.Y., 1956.

Nutting, Anthony. *Europe Will Not Wait*. London, 1960.

Nye, Joseph S. *Pan-Africanism and East African Integration*. Cambridge, Mass., 1965.

Osborn, Harold. *Bolivia: A Land Divided*. London, 1954.

Osborn, Henry Fairfield. *Man Rises to Parnassus*. New York, 1927.

Ottley, Roi. *New World A-Coming*. Boston, 1943.

Padelford, N. J., and M. Goodrich (eds.). *The United Nations in the Balance: Accomplishments and Prospects*. New York, 1965.

Padmore, George. *Pan-Africanism and Communism*. New York, 1956.

_____. *History of the Pan-African Congress: Colonial and Colored Unity*. Manchester, n.d.

Palumbo, Michael, and William O. Shanahan (eds.). *Nationalism: Essays in Honor of Louis L. Snyder*. Westport, Conn., 1981.

Pan-German Program. Trans. with an introduction by E. Beven. London, 1918.

Pares, Bernard. *A History of Russia*. New York, 1953.

Parkhurst, Frederick S. (ed.). *Africa in the Seventies and Eighties*. New York, 1970.

Pasley, Malcolm (ed.). *Germany*. London, 1972.

Patney, Richard. *The Community of Europe*. New York, 1963.

Perkins, Dexter. *A History of the Monroe Doctrine*. Boston, 1955.

Pichl, Eduard [Herwig]. *Georg Schönerer und die Entwickelung des Deutschtums in der Ostmark*. 6 vols. Oldenberg and Berlin, 1938.

_____. *Georg Ritter von Schönerer*. Vienna, 1940.

Picht, Ulrich. *M. P. Pogodin und die Slavische Frage*. Stuttgart, 1969.

Pickthal, M. M. *The Meaning of the Glorious Koran*. New York, 1956.

Pike, Frederick B. *Hispanism*. Notre Dame, Ind., 1971.

Pinder, John (ed.). *The Economics of Europe*. London, 1971.

Pinson, Koppel. *Modern Germany: Its History and Civilization*. New York, 1954.

Poliakov, Leon. *The History of Anti-Semitism*. 4 vols. New York, 1965.

Pope-Hennesey, Una. *Canon Charles Kingsley*. London, 1848.

Poschinger, H. von. *Fürst Bismarck als Volkswirt*. Berlin, 1889.

Purcell, V. P. *The Boxer Uprising, 1900*. New York, 1963.

Rado, P. R. *Who Are the Slavs?* Boston, 1919.

Raymond, E. T. *Disraeli: Alien Patriot*. New York, 1925.

Reischauer, Edwin O. *The Japanese*. Cambridge, Mass., 1971.

Riasanovsky, Nicholas V. *A History of Russia*. New York, 1977.

Robertson, W. S. *Hispanic-American Relations with the United States*. New York, 1923.

Rohrbach, Paul. *Die alldeutsche Gefahr*. Berlin, 1918.

Romulu, Carlos P. *The Meaning of Bandung*. New York, 1956.

Ronaldshay, Earl of. *The Life of Lord Curzon*. London, 1928.

Roosevelt, Franklin D. *The Public Papers and Addresses*. Vol. 2, *The Year of Crisis, 1933*. New York, 1938.

Rosenblatt, Bernard A. *Two Generations of Zionism*. New York, 1967.

Royal Institute of International Affairs. *The Scandinavian States and Finland: A Political and Economic Survey*. London, 1951.

Rubin, Leslie, and Brian Weinstein. *Introduction to African Politics*. New York, 1974.

Rudin, Harry. *The Germans in the Cameroons, 1884-1914: A Case Study in Modern Imperialism*. New Haven, Conn., 1938.

Rudwick, Elliot. *W.E.B. Du Bois*. New York, 1968.

Sampson, Anthony. *The New Europeans*. London, 1968.

Sayegh, F. A. *Arab Unity: Hope and Fulfillment*. New York, 1958.

Schmitt, Bernadotte. *The Coming of the War, 1914.* 2 vols. New York, 1930.

Schott, George (ed.). *Houston Stewart Chamberlain: Der Seher des Dritten Reiches.* Munich, 1934, 1941.

Schumpeter, Joseph. *Imperialism and the Social Classes.* Village Station, N.Y., 1951.

Seton-Watson, Hugh. *The Decline of Imperial Russia, 1853-1914.* New York, 1956.

Shafer, Boyd C. *Nationalism: Myth and Reality.* New York, 1955.

_____. *Faces of Nationalism: New Realities and Old Myths.* New York, 1972.

_____. *Nationalism and Internationalism: Belonging in Human Experience.* Malabar, Fla., 1982.

Shao chì, Liu. *Nationalism and Internationalism.* Peiping, 1954.

Shapiro, Samuel (ed.). *Cultural Factors in Inter-American Relations.* Notre Dame, Ind., 1968.

Sharabi, Hisham B. *Nationalism and Revolution in the Arab World.* Princeton, N.J., 1966.

Shepherd, George W. *The Politics of African Nationalism.* New York, 1962.

Silberner, Edmund. *The World of Moses Hess.* Leiden, 1958.

Sithole, Ndabaningi. *African Nationalism.* London, 1959.

Snyder, Louis L. *Race: A History of Modern Ethnic Theories.* New York and Toronto, 1939.

_____. *The Meaning of Nationalism.* New Brunswick, N.J., 1964.

_____. *The New Nationalism.* Ithaca, N.Y., 1968.

_____. *The Imperialism Reader: Documents and Readings on Modern Expansionism* Princeton, N.J., 1962. Reprint. Port Washington, N.Y., 1972.

_____. *The Dreyfus Case: A Documentary History.* New Brunswick, N.J., 1973.

_____. *Global Mini-Nationalisms: Autonomy or Independence.* Westport, Conn., 1982.

Snyder, Louis L., and Richard B. Morris (eds.). *A Treasury of Great Reporting.* New York, 1949.

Sokolow, Nahum. *History of Zionism, 1800-1918.* 2 vols. London, 1919.

Spanier, David. *Europe, Our Europe.* London, 1972.

Spear, P. *The Oxford History of Modern India.* London, 1965.

Spinelli, Altiero. *The Eurocrats.* Baltimore, Md., 1966.

Steiger, George N. *China and the Occident: The Origin and Development of the Boxer Movement.* New Haven, Conn., 1927.

Stein, Leonard J. *The Balfour Declaration.* New York, 1961.

Stephens, W.R.W. *The Life and Letters of E. A. Freeman.* London, 1895.

Stephenson, Hugh. *The Coming Clash.* London, 1972.

Sterling, Dorothy. *Lift Every Voice.* New York, 1965.

Stern, Fritz. *The Politics of Cultural Despair: A Study of the Rise of the Germanic Ideology.* New York, 1965.

Stocks, J. L. *Politics and the Super-State.* London and New York, 1920.

Stoddard, Lothrop. *Panturanisme.* New York, 1917.

_____. *The Rising Tide of Color against White Supremacy.* New York, 1920.

_____. *The New World of Islam.* New York, 1921.

Stoezer, O. Carlos. *The Organization of American States.* Dallas, Tex., 1963.

Strausz-Hupé, Robert, and Henry W. Hazard (eds.). *The Idea of Colonialism.* New York, 1958.

Strong, Josiah. *Our Country: Its Possible Future and Its Present Crisis*. New York, 1891.

Stubbs, C. W. *Charles Kingsley*. New York, 1899.

Stuermer, Henry. *The War Years in Constantinople*. Trans. by E. Allen and the author. New York, 1917.

Sun Yat-sen. *The Three Principles of the People*. Shanghai, 1929.

Suval, I. *The Anschluss Question in the Weimar Era: A Study of Nationalism in Germany and Austria, 1918-1936*. Baltimore, Md., 1951.

Svineri, Shlomo. *The Making of Modern Zionism*. New York, 1981.

Swann, Donald. *The Economics of the Common Market*. London, 1970.

Tan, Chester C. *The Boxer Catastrophe*. New York, 1955.

Tevoedjre, Albert. *Pan-Africanism in Action*. Cambridge, Mass., 1965.

Thayer, P. E. (ed.). *Nationalism and Progress in Free Asia*. Baltimore, Md., 1956.

Thomas, Hugh. *Europe: The Radical Challenge*. London, 1973.

Thompson, E. A. *History of Attila and the Huns*. Oxford, 1948.

Thompson, Vincent. *African Unity: The Evolution of Pan-Africanism*. New York, 1970.

Townsend, Mary Evelyn. *European Colonial Expansion Since 1871*. Philadelphia, 1941.

Trend, John B. *Bolívar and the Independence of Spanish America*. London, 1951.

Trevelyan, George Otto. *The Life and Letters of Macaulay*. London and New York, 1876, 1908, 1959.

Turner, Louis. *Invisible Empire*. New York, 1971.

Tuttle, William L. *W.E.B. Du Bois*. Englewood Cliffs, N.J., 1973.

Usher, Roland. *Pan-Germanism: From Its Inception to the Outbreak of the War: A Critical Study*. New York, 1914.

Uya, Okon Edet (ed.). *Black Brotherhood: Afro-American and African*. Lexington, Mass., 1971.

Vagts, Alfred. *Deutschland und die Vereinigten Staaten in der Weltpolitik*. 2 vols. New York, 1935.

Valentine, Herman, and Juliet Lodge. *The European Parliament and the European Community*. London, 1978.

Van Ahen, Mark I. *Pan-Hispanism: Its Origin and Development in 1866*. Berkeley, Calif., 1959.

Vernadsky, George. *The Mongols and Russia*. New Haven, Conn., 1954.

Vernon, Raymond. *Sovereignty at Bay: The Multinational Spread of the U.S. Enterprises*. London, 1971.

Viereck, Peter. *Metapolitics from the Romantics to Hitler*. New York, 1941.

Vladimirisov, Boris I. *Chinghis-Khan*. Trans. by D. S. Mirsky. London, 1930.

Vlahović, Vlahos. *Two Hundred and Fifty Million and One Slavs*. New York, 1945.

Vlavianos, Basil J., and Feliks Gross (eds.). *Struggle for Tomorrow: Modern Political Ideologies and the Jewish People*. New York, 1952.

Walworth, Arthur. *Black Ships Off Japan: The History of Commodore Perry's Expedition*. New York, 1946.

Wawrzinek, Kurt. *Die Entstehung der deutschen antisemitenparteien, 1837-1890*. Berlin, 1927.

Weigert, Hans Werner. *German Geopolitics*. New York, 1941.

Weingart, Miloš (ed.). *Slované, Kulturni obraz slovanského suĕta (The Slavs,*

A Culture Picture of the Slav World). 3 vols. Prague, 1927-1929.

Weizmann, Chaim. *Trial and Error: The Autobiography of Chaim Weizmann.* New York, 1929.

Welch, Claude E., Jr. *Dream of Unity: Pan-Africanism and Political Unification in West Africa.* Ithaca, N.Y., 1966.

Wenck, Martin. *Alldeutsche Taktik.* Jena, Germany, 1917.

Wensinck, A. J. *The Muslim Creed.* Cambridge, England, 1932.

Wertheimer, Mildred S. *The Pan-German League, 1890-1914.* New York, 1924.

Wessely, Kurt. *Pangermanismus.* Linz-an-den-Donau, Austria, 1938.

Whitaker, Arthur P. *The Western Hemisphere Idea: Its Rise and Decline.* Ithaca, N.Y., 1954.

_____. *Nationalism in Latin America: Past and Present.* Gainesville, Fla., 1962.

Whitaker, Arthur P., and David C. Jordan. *Nationalism in Contemporary Latin America.* New York, 1966.

Whiteside, Andrew C. *The Socialism of Fools: George Ritter von Schöenerer and Austrian Pan-Germanism.* Berkeley, Calif., 1975.

Winkler, Paul. *The Thousand Year Conspiracy.* New York, 1943.

Winslow, Earle M. *The Patterns of Imperialism: A Study of the Theories of Power.* New York, 1948.

Winter, Eduard. *Der Panslawismus nach den Berichten der österreichen-ungarischen Botschafter in St. Petersburg.* Prague, 1944.

Wollman, Frank. *Slavismy a antislavismy.* Prague, 1968.

Woodman, D. *The Republic of Indonesia.* London, 1950.

_____. *The Making of Burma.* London, 1962.

Woronoff, Jon. *Organizing African Unity.* Metuchen, N.J., 1970.

Wynn, Wilton. *Nasser of Egypt: The Search for Dignity.* New York, 1959.

Yepes, Jesus M. *Philosophie du Panamericanisme et organisation de la paix.* Neuchâtel, 1945.

Zenkowsky, Serge A. *Pan-Turkism and Islam in Russia.* Cambridge, Mass., 1960.

Zurcher, Arnold J. *The Struggle to Unite Europe, 1940-1958.* New York, 1958.

Zwanzig Jahre alldeutscher Arbeit und Kämpfe. Leipzig, 1910.

Articles

Abensour, Léon. "Les origines der pangermanisme." *Grand Revue,* LXXXIX (1916), 77-84.

Ajami, Fouad. "The End of Arabism." *Foreign Affairs* (Winter, 1978-1979), 354-73.

Arendt, H. "Imperialism, Nationalism, Chauvinism." *Review of Politics,* VII (1945), 441-63.

Asmussen, P. "Der Panslavismus." *Gelbe Hefte,* II, no. 1 (1925), 408-14.

Barbour, N. "Variations of Arab National Feeling in French North Africa." *Middle East Journal,* VIII (1954), 308-30.

Baron, Salo. "The Jewish Question in the 19th Century." *Journal of Modern History,* XIX (March 1938), 56-75.

Barrett, John. "What the War Has Done to the Monroe Doctrine." *Current Opinion,* LXV (1918), 291-93.

Berlin, Isaiah. "The Bent Twig: A Note on Nationalism." *Foreign Affairs,* LI, no. 1 (October 1972), 11-30.

Broszat, Martin. "Von der Kulturnation zur Volksgruppe." *Historische Zeitschrift,* no. 200 (1965), 572-605.

Carrillo Dlores, Antonia. "El nacionalismo de los paises latino-americanos en la postguerra." *Jornadas,* no. 28 (1945).

Castro, Rodolfo Baron. "Españolismo y antiespañolismo en la América Hispana." *Tierra Firme,* no. 4 (1935), 41-54.

Cline, Howard F. "Mexico—A Mature Latin-American Revolution." *Annals of the American Academy of Political and Social Science* (March 1961), 84-94.

Dehio, Ludwig. "Gedanke über die deutsche Sendung, 1900-1918." *Historische Zeitschrift,* CLXXIV, no. 2 (October 1952).

Diffie, Bailey W. "The Ideology of Hispanidad." *Hispanic-American Historical Review,* XXIII (1943), 457-82.

Dorneth, J. von. "Die Herrschaft des Panslawismus." *Preussische Jahrbücher* LXXV (1898), 136-52.

Drescher, Wahrhold. "Der panamerikanismus." *Preussische Jahrbücher,* CCVI (1926), 288-315.

Duggan, Stephen. "The Western Hemisphere as a Haven of Peace?" *Foreign Affairs,* XVIII (1940), 614-31.

Edwards, Albert. "The Menace of Pan-Islamism." *North American Review,* CXLVII (1913), 645-57.

Erickson, John. "Panslavism." London Historical Association pamphlet, series G55 (1964).

Ferber, Walter. "Georg Ritter von Schoenerer: Zur Revision der Vorgeschichte des Nationalsozialismus." *Neues Abendland,* X (1955), 139-48.

Gil Torre, R. "Panislamismo, panarabismo y acción ibérica." *Nuestro tiempo,* XXV (1925), 257-72.

Giusti, Roberto F. "La restauración nacionalista." *Nosotros,* IV, no. 26 (1910), 139-54.

Goodman, Edward J. "Spanish Nationalism in the Struggle Against Napoleon." *Review of Politics,* XX (1958), 330-40.

Grabowsky, A. "Das Problem Paneuropa." *Zeitschrift für Politik,* XVII (1927-1928), 673-704.

Guidi, Michelangelo. "Islam e Arabisme." *Reale Academia d'Italia,* I (1941), 7-28.

Haas, A. "Das pan-hispanische Gedanke in America." *Zeitschrift für Politik,* XVI (1926-1927), 1-31.

Halil, Halid Bey. "Panislamische Gefahr." *Neue Rundschau,* XXVII, no. 1 (1916), 289-309.

Haushofer, Karl. "Das erwachende Asien." *Süddeutsche Monatshefte,* XXIV (1926-1927), pt. 1, 97-122.

Heyck, Edward. "Die geschichtliche Berechtigung des deutschen Nationalbewusstseins." *Alldeutscher Verband Flugschriften* (Munich, 1897). Heft 1.

Hoffmann, Karl. "Die rechtliche Stellung der Nationalitäten in Oesterreich." *Oesterreichische Zeitschrift für Verwaltung,* X (1911), 192-201.

Hymer, S. "Is the Multinational Corporation Doomed?" *Innovation,* no. 28 (1972), 10-18.

Jäschke, Gotthard. "Der Turanismus der Jungtürken." *Welt des Islams,* XXIII, nos. 1, 2 (1941), 1-34.

Jessen, J. "Die ökonomische Grundlage der panamerikanischen Idee." *Schmollers Jahrbuch,* LII (1928), 840-41.

Karbach, Oscar. "The Founder of Modern Political Anti-Semitism, Georg von Schönerer." *Jewish Social Studies*, IV (1945), 3-30.

Kegan, Arthur G. "Germany and the Germans of the Hapsburg Monarchy on the Eve of the Armistice in 1918: Genesis of the Anschluss Problem." *Journal of Central European Affairs*, XX (1960), no. 1, 24-50.

Khalili, Walid. "Toward the Unthinkable: A Sovereign Palestine State." *Foreign Affairs* (July 1978), 695-713.

Kilson, M. L., Jr. "The Analysis of African Nationalism." *World Politics*, X (1957-1958), 484-97.

Kohn, Hans. "Twilight of Nationalism." *American Scholar*, VI (1937), 259-70.

_____. "Romanticism and Realism among the Czechs and Slovaks." *Review of Politics*, XIV, no. 1 (January 1957), 25-46.

Labonne, Roger. "La crise orientale et le nationalisme en Asie." *Correspondent*, CCLXXXVII (1922), 385-406.

"Le mouvement pantouranien." *"L'Asie Française*, XVII (1917), 174-82.

Langer, William L., and E. R. Blake. "The Rise of the Ottoman Turks and Its Historical Background." *American Historical Review* (April 1932), 468-505.

Lee, Dwight E. "A Turkish Mission to Afghanistan." *Journal of Modern History*, XIII (1941), 335-56.

Leger, Abel Nicolas. "La doctrine de Monroe est-elle à la base du Panaméricanisme?" *France-Amérique Latine*, XXVIII (1937), 197-201.

Leger, Louis. "L'organisation du panslavisme et l'intérêt européen." *Revue des Sciences Politiques*, XXXVIII (1917), 341-52.

Marshall, R. "Rudyard Kipling and Racial Instinct." *Century Illustrated Monthly*, LVIII (July, 1899), 375-77.

Martin, Percy F. "The Pan-American Phantom." *Fortnightly Review*, XCVIII (1915), 514-28.

Masaryk, Thomas G. "Pangermanism and the Eastern Question." *New Europe*, I (1916), 2-19.

Melin, Nelly. "Le Pangermanisme et la Scandinavie." *Grand Revue*, XIX (1917), 682-710.

Mexico, Secretaría de Relaciones Exteriores. "El Congreso de Panama y algunos otros proyectos de unión hispano-americana." *Archivo Histórico Diplomático Mexicana*, no. 10 (Mexico City, 1926), iii-xxviii.

Milyukov, Paul. "World War and Slavonic Policy." *Slavonic Review*, VI (1927-1928), 268-90.

Montemayor, Mariano. "Les corrientes politicos en Hispano-américa." *Dinámica Social*, II, no. 13-14 (1951), 18-19.

Munro, Dana Gardner. "Our New Relation to Latin-America." *Unpopular Review*, X (1918), 307-18.

Nasanov, N., and A. Garrcyism. "Reactionary Utopia." *Anti-Imperialism Review*, I (1932), 323-40.

Niceforo, Alfredo. "Mito germanico e mito mediterraneo." *Rivista d'Italia*, XIX (1916), 4811-50.

Nittner, Ludwig. "Georg Schönerer, der Vorkämpfer Grossdeutschlands." *Historische Zeitschrift*, CLIX (1942), 56-67.

Nye, Joseph S. "Multinational Enterprises and Prospects for Regional and Social Integration." *Annals of the American Academy of Political and Social Science*, CCCCIII (September 1972), 116-26.

Rippy, J. Fred. "Pan-Hispanic Propaganda in Hispanic America." *Political Science Quarterly*, XXXVII (1922), 389-414.

Rome, Roman. "The Origins of the Second World War and the A.J.P. Taylor Controversy." *Intellect*, CIV (September-October 1975), 126-29.

Roucek, J. S. (ed.). "Nationalistic Ideology and Goals." *Annals of the American Academy of Political and Social Science*, CCXXXII (1944), 25-115.

Schnee, Heinrich. "Bismarck und der deutscher Nationalismus in Oesterreich." *Historisches Jahrbuch*, LXXXI (1962), 123-51.

Seton-Watson, Hugh. "Soviet Nationalist Ideology." *The Russian Review*, XV (1956), 3-13.

Seton-Watson, R. W. "Pan-Slavism." *Contemporary Review*, CX (1916) 419-29.

Silvert, K. H. "Nationalism in Latin America." *Annals of the American Academy of Political and Social Science*, CCCXXXIV (March 1961), 10-19.

Snyder, Louis L. "The Role of Herbert Bismarck in the Angra Pequena Negotiations between Germany and Britain, 1880-1885." *Journal of Negro History*, XXXV (1950), 435-52.

Sosnosky, Theodore von. "The New Pan-Germanism." *Quarterly Review*, CCXXXIX (1923), 308-22.

Starr, P. "The Ainu of Japan." *Asia* (April 1919), 381-87.

Stoddard, Lothrop. "Pan-Turanism." *American Political Science Review*, II, (1917), 12-23.

Syroczynski, Léon. "Le panslavisme." *Revue de Belgique*, II (1869), 181-201.

Tanenbaum, Frank. "Agarisme, Indianismo, Nationalismo." *Hispanic-American Historical Review*, XXIII (1943), 394-423.

Thomson, S. Harrison. "A Century of a Phantom, Pan-Slavism and Western Slavs." *Journal of Central European Affairs*, XI, no. 1 (1951), 55-57.

Usher, Roland G. "Pan-Germanism Once More." *University of Toronto Quarterly*, IX (1940), 125-37.

Walters, Robert S. "International Organization and Multinational Corporations: An Overview and Observations." *Annals of the American Academy of Political and Social Science*, CCCCIII (1972), 127-52.

Wirth, Albrecht. "Panslawismus." *Deutsche Rundschau*, CLXIII (1915), 429-40.

"X." "Le panislamisme et le panturcquisme." *Revue du Monde Musulman*, XXII (1913), 170 ff.

INDEX